Investments

Volume 2

Investments

Volume 2:
Securities Prices and
Performance

Edwin J. Elton
Martin Gruber

The MIT Press
Cambridge, Massachusetts
London, England

This book was set in Palatino by Asco Typesetters, Hong Kong.
Printed and bound in the United States of America.

Library of Congress Cataloging-in-Publication Data

Elton, Edwin J.
Investments / Edwin J. Elton, Martin Gruber.
p. cm.
Includes bibliographical references and index.
Contents: v. 1. Portfolio theory and asset pricing —
v. 2. Securities prices and performance.
ISBN 978-0-262-51531-3 (v. 1, pb. : alk. paper)
ISBN 978-0-262-51530-6 (v. 2, pb. : alk. paper)
1. Portfolio management. 2. Investment analysis. I. Gruber, Martin Jay, 1937– . II. Title.
HG4529.5.E468 1999
332.6—dc21 98-51526
CIP

To our wives Diane Elton and Ellie Gruber,
To our children:

Annette Elton Bietel

Ned Elton

Kathryn Elton

John Elton

and

Jonathan Gruber

Stacey Gruber

Joelle Gruber

and to our grandchildren, the next generation of our readers:

Eric Bietel

Samuel Gruber

Jack Gruber

Contents

Foreword

Harry Markowitz

I recall viewing Mount Fuji from the bullet train on a cloudless day. It was an impressive sight: a single snowcapped volcanic cone towering above its surroundings. An impressive sight of a different sort is the view of the Andes from Santiago, Chile. That presents the viewer with an unending wall of huge mountains—any one of which would be magnificent on its own—with even taller mountains visible here and there behind the front row of giants.

Contemplating the works of Elton and Gruber is like viewing the Andes. There are so many towering works that one has difficulty keeping track of them all, or knowing what percent one has seen. The present two-volume set helps the reader in this matter by assembling in one place what the authors refer to as their "favorite articles." This is not their entire work; indeed, just beyond the cutoff for these two volumes are articles that the authors refer to as "almost our favorites"—like tall mountains not visible because of other mountains.

The two volumes are divided into seven parts with introductions summarizing their contents, plus an eighth, one-article part that needs no introduction. Taken together, the eight introductions constitute a definitive survey of Elton and Gruber's favorite works. I will not try to provide an alternate survey. Rather, I will focus on two related topics—namely, models of covariance and properties of mean-variance efficient sets—that occupy several of their papers. I will discuss the state of the art prior to the Elton and Gruber (and the Elton, Gruber, Padberg [EGP]) discoveries, and the impact of these discoveries.

I begin by reviewing what was known about mean-variance efficient sets prior to publication of the revolutionary EGP (1976). Markowitz (1952) defined mean-variance efficiency and illustrated the nature of mean-variance efficient sets in terms of 3- and 4-security diagrams (requiring 2-

and 3-dimensional drawings). The only constraint set considered is what I now refer to as the "standard" constraint set

$$\sum_{i=1}^{n} X_i = 1 \qquad (1a)$$

$$X_i \geqslant 0 \qquad i = 1, \ldots, n, \qquad (1b)$$

where X_i is the fraction of the portfolio invested in the i-th of n securities. It was assumed that the covariance matrix is nonsingular. The 3-security examples illustrated that the set of efficient portfolios is piecewise linear —the successive pieces meeting at points called "corner portfolios." The nature of the lines connecting the successive corner portfolios is better seen in the 4-security case. Given any nonempty subset I of the numbers 1 through 4, that is, $I \subset \{1, 2, 3, 4\}$, we define a subspace s_I and a critical line ℓ_I. The subspace s_I consists of all points (X_1, X_2, X_3, X_4) in which $X_j = 0$ for j *not* in I. The other X_i are only required to satisfy $\sum X_i = 1$. The critical line ℓ_I is the locus of all points (portfolios) that minimize V for some given E among points in the subspace s_I. Under the given assumptions, the set of efficient portfolios

> may be traced out by starting at the point of minimum available variance, moving continuously along various $\ell_{a1,\ldots,a\alpha}$ according to definite rules, ending in a point which gives maximum E. Typically we proceed along a given critical line until either this line intersects one of a larger subspace or meets a boundary (and simultaneously the critical line of a lower dimensional subspace). In either of these cases the efficient [set] turns and continues along the new line. The efficient [set] terminates when a point with maximum E is reached. (Markowitz [1952], note 8)

The efficient sets can similarly be traced out starting with the efficient portfolio with maximum E and ending with the one with minimum V. This is the more frequent practice now.

While the preceding quote is correct qualitatively, Markowitz (1952) did not supply the formulas for the critical lines. These were supplied in Markowitz (1956), which presented the "critical line algorithm" for tracing out the set of efficient portfolios, under more general assumptions concerning the constraint set than the standard set (1) assumed in Markowitz (1952). Specifically, Markowitz (1956) permitted securities that might or might not be required to be nonnegative; might be subject to linear equality constraints in addition to, or instead of, (1a); and/or might be subject to linear inequality constraints (with weak inequalities $\leqslant$ or $\geqslant$ rather than strong ones, $>$ or $<$). These various cases cluttered the exposition. Markowitz (1959) notes that all these cases are handled if one simply treats the case in which the constraints are linear equalities in nonnegative variables. In matrix notation

$$\mathbf{AX} = \mathbf{b} \tag{2a}$$

$$\mathbf{X} \geqslant 0 \tag{2b}$$

where $\mathbf{A}$ is an m by n matrix, $\mathbf{b}$ an m component column vector, and $\mathbf{X}$ an n component portfolio vector. For example, a variable X_i that is allowed to be either positive or negative in the 1956 exposition is treated as the difference between two nonnegative variables, the positive and negative parts of X_i. Inequalities are transformed into equalities by the introduction of "slack" variables as in linear programming.

Another difference between Markowitz (1956) and Markowitz (1959) is that, while the former does not require the covariance matrix $\mathbf{C}$ to be nonsingular, it does require variance, $V = \mathbf{X'CX}$, to be a strictly convex function over the set of feasible $\mathbf{X}$; Markowitz (1959) dispenses with this assumption and allows any possible covariance matrix, that is, any positive semidefinite $\mathbf{C}$. In this case more than one feasible portfolio may have the same efficient mean and variance. But (provided the model is feasible and has efficient portfolios) there is always a set of efficient portfolios that meets the qualitative description quoted above. This then was the state of knowledge about the shapes and properties of efficient sets, and how to compute them, in 1959. It is approximately the state at present if efficient portfolios for all efficient EV combinations is sought (see Perold [1984]). In particular, the critical line algorithm in Markowitz (1987) differs from that in Markowitz (1959) only in the handling of some "funny cases," like unbounded E or more than one portfolio with maximum E.

Consider the case with the standard constraint set (1) and with a universe of securities consisting of n risky securities with nonsingular covariance matrix, plus one risk-free asset ("cash"). Tobin (1958) showed that the piecewise linear set of efficient portfolios consists of zero, one, or more pieces containing risky securities only, plus a final (lowest variance) piece consisting of mixtures of cash and one particular portfolio $\hat{\mathbf{X}}$ of risky securities. Thus all efficient portfolios that hold cash and risky assets hold the latter in the proportions $\hat{\mathbf{X}}$. Sharpe (1964) showed that if, in addition, the investor could borrow any desired amount at the risk-free rate r_f (equal to the rate paid by cash) then any efficient portfolio would consist of either cash only, or a mixture of $\hat{\mathbf{X}}$ and cash, or of $\hat{\mathbf{X}}$ and borrowing.

Thus (except for the cash-only portfolio) all efficient portfolios would contain risky securities in the proportions $\hat{X}$.

EGP (1976) solves for $\hat{X}$ when one of two models of covariance is assumed. One model for which they find $\hat{X}$ is the one-factor model. Markowitz (1959) thought means and variances would be estimated by security analysts, but noted that there are too many covariances to expect an analyst team to estimate them individually. I suggested that a model of covariance is needed, and I proposed a model in which the return on the i-th security is

$$r_i = \alpha_i + \beta_i F + u_i, \tag{3}$$

where α_i and β_i are constants (which may vary between securities), F is a common random factor and the u_i are idiosyncratic random terms. The u_i are assumed to be uncorrelated with each other and with F. The one-factor model (3) is also referred to as the market model or the single index model, since F is usually interpreted as "the market," and the αs and βs usually estimated by regressions against some market index. It is also referred to as the "diagonal" model for reasons given below.

Sharpe (1963) backtested the one-factor model, as compared to using historical covariances as estimates, and cautiously concluded that the results were "too fragmentary to be considered conclusive but they do suggest that the diagonal model may be able to represent the relationships among securities rather well and thus that the value of portfolio analyses based on the model will exceed their rather nominal cost. For these reasons it appears to be an excellent choice for the initial practical applications of the Markowitz technique." Elton and Gruber (1973) backtested several methods of estimating covariance including the one-factor model and the "constant correlation" model, which assumes that all correlation coefficients (ρ_{ij} $i \neq j$) are the same. They concluded that "in particular, we have found that in the case of five-year estimates three average techniques [including the constant correlation model] outperformed all other techniques. The fact that these models consistently outperformed the SSI [i.e., one-factor] and Historical models, which have been the two most commonly used ways to generate input to portfolio analysis, has major implications for future empirical research."

By 1963 Bill Sharpe and I had observed that when the one-factor model is assumed, the critical line computation can be much simplified by use of a certain "gimmick." From equation (3) deduce that the return on the portfolio may be written as

$$R = \left(\sum \alpha_i X_i\right) + \left(\sum \beta_i X_i\right) F + \sum X_i u_i \tag{4}$$

Since F and all the u_i are uncorrelated

$$V(R) = \left(\sum \beta_i X_i\right)^2 V(F) + \sum X_i^2 V(u_i) \tag{5}$$

If we add an $(n + 1)$st variable and a new constraint thus

$$X_{n+1} = \sum_{i=1}^{n} X_i \beta_i \tag{6a}$$

then

$$V = \sum_{i=1}^{n} V(u_i) X_i^2 + V(F) X_{n+1}^2 \tag{6b}$$

Thus V becomes a sum of squares. Only the diagonal elements of the covariance matrix are nonzero, whence the name "diagonal" model. The equations which describe a critical line, obtained by setting to zero the partial derivatives of a certain Lagrangian expression, are much simplified and easily solved.

A similar gimmick can be applied to the constant correlation model provided that ρ, the common correlation coefficient, is nonnegative. In general

$$V = \sum \sum X_i X_j \sigma_{ij} \tag{7}$$

From

$$\sigma_{ij} = \rho \sigma_i \sigma_j \qquad \text{for } i \neq j$$

$$\sigma_{ij} = \sigma_i^2 \qquad \text{for } i = j$$

$$= (1 - \rho)\sigma_i^2 + \rho \sigma_i^2$$

we derive

$$V = (1 - \rho) \sum X_i^2 \sigma_i^2 + \rho \left(\sum X_i \sigma_i\right)^2 \tag{8}$$

If we add a variable and constraint thus

$$X_{n+1} = \sum_{i=1}^{n} X_i \sigma_i \tag{9a}$$

then

$$V = \sum_{i=1}^{n} X_i^2((1-\rho)\sigma_i^2) + \rho X_{n+1}^2 \tag{9b}$$

Once again the model is diagonalized. In fact, the constant correlation model with $\rho \geqslant 0$ is equivalent to the one-factor model with the added condition that $\beta_i/\sigma(u_i)$ is the same for all i.[1]

Since the one-factor model is a special case of an arbitrary covariance matrix **C**, and the constant correlation model with nonnegative ρ is a special case of the one-factor model, if heaven supplied us true parameters there would never be an advantage to assuming the constant correlation model with nonnegative ρ rather than the one-factor model, or the one-factor model rather than an arbitrary **C**. But estimates have sampling error, and **C** probably varies over time. Therefore it is possible that estimates of the parameters of more complex models provide more noise than news, and that it is better in practice to use a simpler, more restrictive model. Sharpe concluded that this seemed to be the case for the one-factor model as compared to an arbitrary **C**; Elton and Gruber concluded the same for the constant correlation model as compared to the more general one-factor model.

The EGP (1976) discovery is not a faster way to trace out the whole efficient frontier; rather, it supplies a simple rule for finding the portfolio $\hat{\mathbf{X}}$. One benefit of this discovery was computational speed. The critical line algorithm traces out the frontier starting with the portfolio with maximum expected return as determined by the simplex algorithm of linear programming.[2] It determines in turn all the corner portfolios of the efficient frontier ending with $\hat{\mathbf{X}}$ next to the last, and finally the all-cash portfolio. Thus, if it is given that $\hat{\mathbf{X}}$, or a mixture of $\hat{\mathbf{X}}$ and cash, is the desired efficient portfolio then the critical line algorithm will generate a (possibly long) sequence of portfolios of which only the next to last one is of interest. This contrasts with the EGP procedure that directly computes $\hat{\mathbf{X}}$. (See also Christofi and Theodossiou [1995].)

But speed of computation is only part of the value of the EGP discovery. The other part is the insight it provides concerning the nature of $\hat{\mathbf{X}}$. For example, a basic lesson of portfolio theory is that one should think in terms of the portfolio as a whole. A portfolio which maximizes some criteria may or may not consist only of securities which have high or highest value of that criteria. For example, on the one hand (for the standard constraint set) the efficient portfolio that maximizes expected return E is a portfolio consisting of that security (or those securities) with maximum expected return; on the other hand the same is *not* true for geometric mean. (See Markowitz [1959], chapter 6.) But what can be said about the Sharpe ratio, $(E - r_f)/\sigma$? Does the portfolio that maximizes the latter necessarily consist of securities whose Sharpe ratios are greatest? What may we say to an investment manager who tries to maximize the Sharpe ratio of his or her portfolio by holding securities with maximum Sharpe ratio? Are there plausible assumptions that would make this optimum?

The efficient $\hat{X}$ which mixes with cash is the one which maximizes the Sharpe ratio. EGP (1976) tells us that, when the constant correlation model holds, $\hat{X}$ may be computed by ranking securities according to their Sharpe ratio, selecting all those above a certain cutoff point, then weighting them in the portfolio according to a formula that depends on more than the Sharpe ratio. Thus the manager who seeks a high Sharpe ratio for the portfolio by selecting securities with highest Sharpe ratio may be told that, implicitly at least, he or she is assuming the constant correlation model of covariance. He or she can also be advised to see EGP (1976) concerning where in the list of securities, ranked by Sharpe ratio, one should cut off, and how one should weight the securities selected.

But EGP (1976) also shows that it is not always true that the portfolio with highest Sharpe ratio contains securities with highest such. If the one-factor model is true then the EGP (1976) procedure starts by ranking securities according to $(E_i - r_f)/\beta_i$. In general this is not the same as ranking according to $(E_i - r_f)/\sigma_i$ unless β_i is proportional to σ_i.

EGP (1976) finds $\hat{X}$ for a given r_f, and other parameters, for the one-factor and constant correlation models. EGP (1978) presents a procedure that traces out the entire efficient frontier by varying r_f and updating the EGP (1976) solution for that r_f. Personally, I am not convinced that the EGP (1978) procedure will compute the efficient frontier faster than the critical line algorithm taking full advantage of the diagonalized versions of the one-factor or constant correlation models.[3] The relative merits of the two algorithms on this problem remain to be determined.

Among the works in these two volumes, other than those cited above, my favorite is Elton, Gruber, and Rentzler (1989). Depending on tastes and interests, the reader will have her or his own favorites. The authors are to be thanked for assembling this collection so that we all can have our old favorites readily at hand, and have the opportunity to pursue new favorites. Also, the authors are to be much congratulated for a lifetime (more precisely, two lifetimes) of monumental contributions.

Notes

1. For, on the one hand, given any positive $\rho, \sigma_1, \sigma_2, \ldots \sigma_N$, equations (6) and (9) show that the one-factor model with $\sigma(u_i) = \sqrt{1-\rho}\sigma_i$, $V_F = \rho$ and $\beta_i = \sigma_i$ has the same relationship between the portfolio and its variance as does the constant correlation model with these parameters; and, conversely, if a one-factor model has

$\beta_i = k\sigma(u_i)$ for every i

then $\text{cov}(r_i, r_j) = \beta_i\beta_j V_F$ for $i \neq j$, which is known for the one-factor model, and $\rho_{ij} = \text{cov}(r_i, r_j)/\sigma_i\sigma_j$, which is the definition of correlation, implies that all correlations are the same. We may always arrange for k to be nonnegative, by defining a new underlying factor $F^N = -F$, if necessary.

2. Special procedures must be instituted for starting the critical line algorithm if the simplex algorithm finds that feasible E is not bounded above, or that many portfolios maximize E. (See chapter 9 of Markowitz [1987]). Once thus started it proceeds as in the case of a unique E maximizing portfolio.

3. The diagonalized critical line calculation solves two linear equations in two unknowns to determine two Lagrangian multipliers. Given the latter, the formula for the critical line follows from a few arithmetic operations per "*IN*" variable. The coefficients of the two by two include sums such as $\sum_{i \in IN} \beta_i / Vu_i$. Note that the sum is over the i, which are "*IN*" on the particular critical line. Since only one i goes into or comes out of the *IN* set at each corner portfolio, these sums should be updated by adding or subtracting a term, rather than being added up from scratch, at each iteration. Since there is not too much else to do per iteration, this detail will materially affect the time required to compute the frontier for a large problem.

References

Christofi, A., and Theodossiou, P. (1995). "Simple Criteria for Optimal Portfolio Selection Revisited." *Advances in Mathematical Programming and Financial Planning* 4: 45–59.

Elton, E. J., Gruber, M. J. (1973). "Estimating the Dependence Structure of Share Prices—Implications for Portfolio Selection." *Journal of Finance* 28, no. 5 (December): 1203–1232.

Elton, E. J., Gruber, M. J., and Padberg, M. W. (1976). "Simple Criteria for Optimal Portfolio Selection." *Journal of Finance* 31, no. 5 (December): 1341–1357.

Elton, E. J., Gruber, M. J., and Padberg, M. W. (1978). "Simple Criteria for Optimal Portfolio Selection: Tracing Out the Efficient Frontier." *Journal of Finance* 33, no. 1 (March): 296–302.

Elton, E. J., Gruber, M. J., and Rentzler, J. (1989). "New Public Offerings, Information, and Investor Rationality: The Case of Publicly Offered Commodity Funds." *Journal of Business*, 62, no. 1: 1–16.

Markowitz, H. M. (1952). "Portfolio Selection." *Journal of Finance* 7, no. 1 (March): 77–91.

Markowitz, H. M. (1956). "The Optimization of a Quadratic Function Subject to Linear Constraints." *Naval Research Logistics Quarterly* 3: 111–133.

Markowitz, H. M. (1959). *Portfolio Selection: Efficient Diversification of Investments.* New Haven: Yale University Press, 1970.

Markowitz, H. M. (1987). *Mean-Variance Analysis in Portfolio Choice and Capital Markets.* New York: Basil Blackwell.

Perold, A. F. (1984). "Large-Scale Portfolio Optimization." *Management Science* 30, no. 10 (October): 1143–1160.

Sharpe, W. F. (1963). "A Simplified Model for Portfolio Analysis." *Management Science,* January.

Tobin, J. (1958). "Liquidity Preference as Behavior Towards Risk." *Review of Economic Studies,* February, 65–86.

Preface

We were very pleased when MIT Press approached us to put together a set of our favorite articles in the area of portfolio analysis and investments for this two-volume publication. We have written an introduction to each section of these volumes but decided to write a more personal overall introduction.

Many people have asked us about a collaboration that has lasted almost thirty-five years. We started working together in 1965, the year in which we both arrived at NYU, Marty from Columbia and Ned from Carnegie Mellon. NYU classes were primarily in the evening in those days, and a group of young faculty used to go to a local bar after teaching on Wednesday nights. Soon after we arrived the two of us had a major disagreement in the bar about the benefits of share repurchase. We each went home to write up our argument and this turned into our first article. By the way, in putting together these works we reread our first article and each of us still thinks he was right. This pattern has continued through our thirty-five years of working together. The partnership has remained productive because we approach problems differently and argue them through until both of us are convinced that we have the best answer. We discuss where we are going, work out theoretical problems, look at empirical results, and then divide up the writing of individual sections. We then attempt to rip each other's ideas apart. In a field where truth does not yet exist and there are only better answers and worse answers, we find that a collaboration of individuals with different attitudes and backgrounds who can remain friends through (at times) severe disagreements has been, and will continue to be, highly fruitful. Over the years we have published with several authors, many of them our Ph.D. students, who have enriched our research and made great contributions to our work. These include Vijay Bawa, Chris Blake, Jeff Busse, David Cho, Sanjiv Das, Seth Grossman, Mustafa Gultekin, Matt Hlavka, Paul Kleindorfer, Zvi

Lieber, John Lightstone, Roni Michaely, Suk Mo Koo, Prafulla Nabar, Manfred Padberg, Joel Rentzler, and Tom Urich.

We have also benefited from discussions with our doctoral students, with whom we did not directly collaborate. These include Dong-Hyun Ahn, George Allayannis, Andy Benartzy, Finbar Bradley, Lance Brofman, Lewis Chakrin, Tom Conine, Charles Ellis, Cheol Eun, Jim Farrell, Bob Ferguson, Jim Greenleaf, Allan Greenspan, George Handjinicolaou, Gabriel Hawawini, Jeff Heisler, Jingzhi Huang, Sung Wng Hwang, Alex Kane, Richard Kolodny, Mario Lavalee, Gerald Levin, Eric Lindenberg, Joshua Livnat, Massoud Mussavian, Jerry Pinto, William Remaley, Tavy Ronen, Meir Schneller, Jim Stanard, Olivier Tabutoni, Nick Travlos, and Irwin Vanderhoof.

We would like to thank Sue Cubberly for her excellent assistance in compiling the material for this book, Victoria Richardson at the MIT Press for her encouragement, and Depak Agrawal, George Comer, Chris Mann, and Barbara Remmers for help in preparation of the manuscript.

This book contains our favorite articles in the field of investments and portfolio management. We have not included the many articles that we wrote on corporate finance and regulation in the early days of our collaboration. We both started out teaching and doing research in corporate finance; over the years we switched to teaching investments. In the interest of space we have also had to exclude many articles on investments and portfolio analysis. In rereading our research we find that we still like almost all of the work we have published. In fact, each of us had forgotten some articles we wrote years ago; it was a pleasure to rediscover them.

We would like to thank some people who had a major impact on our work. Ned and Marty would like to thank our respective mentors, Kal Cohen and Rodger Murray, who first showed each of us the joys of financial research. Larry Ritter, chairman when we arrived at NYU, was a guide and major influence in shaping our professional careers. Finally, we would like to thank Harry Markowitz for discovering portfolio analysis, a field in which we have had so much fun.

We have divided our work into two volumes. Volume I contains papers on portfolio theory and management and asset pricing. Volume 2 contains papers on pricing of individual securities and performance evaluation.

Sources

1. "Improved Forecasting through the Design of Homogeneous Groups." Reprinted with permission from the *Journal of Business* 44, no. 4 (1971): 432–450.

2. "Professional Expectations: Accuracy and Diagnosis of Errors." Reprinted with permission from the *Journal of Financial and Quantitative Analysis* 19, no. 4 (1984): 351–363.

3. "Expectations and Share Prices." Reprinted with permission from *Management Science* 27, no. 9 (1981): 975–987.

4. "Expectational Data and Japanese Stock Prices." Reprinted with permission from *Japan and the World Economy* 1 (1989): 391–401.

5. "Discreet Expectational Data and Portfolio Performance." Reprinted with permission from the *Journal of Finance* 41, no. 3 (1986): 699–714.

6. "Differential Information and Timing Ability." Reprinted with permission from the *Journal of Banking and Finance* 15 (1991): 117–131.

7. "Professionally Managed Publicly Traded Commodity Funds." Reprinted with permission from the *Journal of Business* 60, no. 2 (1987): 175–199.

8. "New Public Offerings, Information and Investor Rationality: The Case of Publicly Offered Commodity Funds." Reprinted with permission from the *Journal of Business* 62, no. 2 (1989): 1–15.

9. "The Performance of Publicly Offered Commodity Funds." Reprinted with permission from the *Financial Analysts Journal*, July/August 1990, 23–30.

10. "Efficiency with Costly Information: A Reinterpretation of Evidence from Managed Portfolios." Reprinted with permission from the *Review of Financial Studies* 6, no. 1 (1993): 1–22.

11. "Survivorship Bias and Mutual Fund Performance." Reprinted with permission from the *Review of Financial Studies* 9, no. 4 (1996): 1097–1120.

12. "The Persistence of Risk-Adjusted Mutual Fund Performance." Reprinted with permission from the *Journal of Business* 69, no. 2 (1996): 133–157.

13. "The Performance of Bond Mutual Funds." Reprinted with permission from the *Journal of Business* 66, no. 3 (1993): 371–403.

14. "Fundamental Economic Variables, Expected Returns, and Bond Fund Performance." Reprinted with permission from the *Journal of Finance* 50, no. 4 (1995): 1229–1256.

15. "Intra-Day Tests of the Efficiency of the Treasury Bill Futures Market." Reprinted with permission from the *Review of Economics and Statistics* 66, no. 1 (1984): 129–137.

16. "Employing Financial Futures to Increase the Return on Near Cash (Treasury Bill) Investments." Reprinted with permission from *Management Science* 31, no. 3 (1985): 293–300.

17. "Bond Returns, Immunization and the Return-Generating Process." Reprinted with permission from *Studies in Banking and Finance* 5 (1988): 125–154.

18. "The Structure of Spot Rates and Immunization." Reprinted with permission from the *Journal of Finance* 45, no. 2 (1990): 629–642.

I Expectations and Performance

In volume 1 we included papers that deal with portfolio theory and asset pricing. While the mathematics of portfolio optimization are well developed, the success of applying these techniques depends on the quality of the input data. Some of the articles in volume 1 deal with estimating the variance covariance matrix between returns. Another key input to the portfolio management problem is estimates of future mean returns and/or the ranking of securities. The management process designed to estimate future mean returns almost always starts with estimates of future earnings. The first four chapters in this section deal with earnings estimates and their impact on share price. The final chapter deals with the accuracy of rankings of securities produced by security analysts.

The first chapter in this section is one of our favorites because of the techniques it employs. It is one of the first to discuss an application of factor analysis, principal component analysis, and cluster analysis to financial data. These are tools that later gained widespread use as part of the literature on arbitrage pricing theory. We summarize, and then apply, the techniques we previously published for forming homogeneous groups of firms or pseudo-industries.[1] Forecasts are developed using cross-sectional regressions on economic variables within a group. We show that grouping firms into pseudo industries provides a better basis for forecasting than using SIC (standard industrial classification) codes to define industries. Finally, we explore the accuracy of forecasts based on pseudo industries with both mechanical extrapolation methods and the forecasts of security analysts.

The next three chapters discuss earnings expectations and their role in security pricing. The second and third chapters were the first to use the IBES (Institutional Brokers Estimate System) database, which has become so important in finance. Chapter two deals with the accuracy of the forecasts of security analysts. Using 242 forecasts of security analysts, we examine the size of the errors and then develop and apply several techniques that decompose the errors into components which have economic significance.

The third chapter in this section is one of the most important in the earnings-expectation literature. Having discussed the accuracy of analysts' forecasts, we proceed to examine the role this expectational data plays in the price-formation process. We illustrate that consensus (average) forecasts are incorporated in prices so that buying stocks for which high growth is forecast does not produce excess returns. We also show that knowledge about future earnings growth that differs from consensus growth can lead to excess returns but knowledge about future consensus forecasts leads to large excess returns. This article was the first to demonstrate the key role of analysts' forecasts in setting prices. It also demonstrated that forecasts, even correct forecasts which do not differ from consensus forecasts, cannot lead to excess returns. At the IBES twentieth anniversary celebration, this article was voted the most important of all that had been written on the subject.

The fourth chapter in this section reexamines the impact of consensus forecasts on stock prices in Japan, a capital market which is very different from the U.S. market. We found that the incorporation of forecast data into stock prices in Japan occurs much more slowly than it does in the United States. The relationship between forecast data and earnings realizations are similar to the U.S. but the speed of adjustment allows for investment strategies that earn an excess return.

In the final chapter in this section we explore a very different database to examine the impact of analysts' forecasts on stock returns. In 1981, Bankers Trust began collecting buy/sell/hold recommendation (on a five-point scale) from thirty-three brokerage firms with which they did business. This data is very useful because unlike, for example, the value-line studies, there is no ex-post selection bias. It therefore provides an unbiased test of whether analysts have forecasting ability. Unlike earnings forecasts from which a market action must be inferred, these data are a direct recommendation for a portfolio decision. The accuracy of the data was important to the firms that supplied them because Bankers Trust used the accuracy of the forecasts in allocating brokerage business. We find that while analysts' recommendations contain useful information on an overall basis, there is no evidence that particular analysts are superior forecasters.

Note

1. See Edwin J. Elton and Martin J. Gruber, "Homogeneous Groups and the Testing of Economic Hypotheses, *Journal of Financial and Quantitative Analysis*, January 1970, 581–602.

1 Improved Forecasting through the Design of Homogeneous Groups

Edwin J. Elton and
Martin J. Gruber

The purpose of this paper is both to discuss the need to disaggregate economic data into meaningful groups in order to better understand and forecast the future course of economic phenomena, and to illustrate with a specific example that such disaggregation can lead to improved results.

The reasons for placing observations into homogeneous groups has already been documented by the authors but will be reviewed briefly in the first section of this paper.[1] The next section will be concerned with the general procedure for grouping observations. The remainder of the paper will discuss in some detail the improvement in forecasting ability that comes from a specific application of grouping procedures to the problem of forecasting earnings per share for a large group of manufacturing concerns. Forecasts prepared on the basis of statistically grouped data will be compared with forecasts made on data grouped on traditional industrial criteria as well as with forecasts prepared by mechanical extrapolation techniques.

The Heterogeneity of Homogeneous Groups

In this section we will discuss the reasons for grouping observations and will show that the grouping of observations is not unique but rather is determined by the general objective in grouping and the specific problem under study.

The reasons for grouping observations fall into two categories: (*a*) to isolate homogeneous units that should act alike, and (*b*) to isolate units which should have the same structural relationship between two or more variables.

Although, as the discussion below will make clear, these reasons are not mutually exclusive, nevertheless this dichotomy serves a useful purpose in understanding why we group.

The Need for Homogeneous Groups

One often tries to form groups of homogeneous units that have had or will continue to have the same value for one or more variables. For example, the SIC industrial codes can be viewed as forming groups of firms which are homogeneous with respect to end product.

The SIC codes have also been used to group firms for purposes of security and portfolio analysis. Security analysts typically evaluate a stock by comparing its performance against other stocks in the same industry. For example, a company may be judged to be a good buy when its price-earnings ratio is low compared with the average price-earnings ratio for its industry. The assumption being made is that the price-earnings ratio for an industry is a good predictor of the price-earnings ratio of each stock in the industry. Similarly, the typical portfolio manager who attempts to obtain risk diversification by buying stocks from different industries is acting as if he believed that the SIC industrial classifications were homogeneous with respect to market risk.

The second reason for forming homogeneous groups is to find a sample of observations (firms) within which the same structural relationship between two or more variables exists. There are two related conditions under which the failure to properly select a sample can result in the misspecification of the relationships between two or more variables.

The first is where an omitted variable is correlated with both the dependent variable and one or more independent variables.[2] The failure to hold the effects of an omitted variable constant will result in biased regression coefficients, biased correlation coefficients, and both regression and correlation coefficients which are extremely sample sensitive.[3]

The problem of omitted variables has been recognized by several authors, and the solution accepted has often been to accept SIC industrial classification as a suitable metric for homogeneity (regardless of the variable with respect to which homogeneity was being sought). For example, Modigliani and Miller restricted their study of the effect of financial risk on the cost of capital to one industry in an attempt to hold business risk constant.[4] Similarly, many of the early studies of dividend policy on cost of capital or stock price felt that they could eliminate omitted variable bias by restricting their study to a single industry.[5]

The second case where homogeneous groups are needed is where the magnitude or sign of a relationship between two variables can be affected by the value a third variable takes on. For example, suppose we were examining a sample of firms which finance their investments solely from internally generated funds. Then, one would expect a positive relationship between stock price and payout for firms which earned a low return on their marginal investment and a negative relationship for firms which earned a high return. Pooling the data could result in a multiple regression which found no relationship between payout and price, although in fact two very different relationships were present.

Once again, the way to avoid the problem of nonhomogeneous relationships has typically been to accept SIC industrial classification as a suitable metric for homogeneity and so to confine regression analysis to data within one industry. This has been the practice in almost all stock-pricing and cost-of-capital models.

These three reasons for grouping overlap to a considerable extent. For example, one may try to find a group of firms which are homogeneous with respect to risk so that security analysts can ignore risk in their analysis and so that portfolio managers can treat the group as one firm in determining appropriate diversification. Second, if risk is difficult to measure, then one may try to find a grouping that allows the relationship between the two other variables to be studied (e.g., stock price and growth) without having to worry about the effect of risk. On the other hand, if a measure of risk can be found, one might consider entering it into the regression equation as a second independent variable (rather than confining the study to a homogeneous risk group) unless the relationship between stock price and growth changes for different levels of risk. If it does change, we should group for the third reason outlined above.

Homogeneity and Traditional Industry Groupings

Both the practice of security and portfolio analysis and the empirical testing of theory in finance has been based on either implicit or occasionally explicit groupings of firms. The groupings employed by almost all authors have been the same—SIC industrial classification. In other words, the assumption has been made that classification by end product is a suitable technique for grouping in almost all studies in finance.[6] But we have a host of evidence that grouping by industries is not particularly suitable for most of the purposes for which it is employed. Let us review some of the evidence.

As mentioned earlier, industry groupings are often used as a basis for comparative analysis by the security analyst. For example, the analyst will typically compare price-earnings (P/E) ratios for a stock with the typical P/E ratio for the industry. Breen has tested the profitability of buying high-growth low-P/E-ratio stocks.[7] His study defined low P/E ratios both in absolute terms and relative to the industry average P/E ratio.[8] Buying stocks with low P/E ratios relative to the industry means yielded a lower rate of return than buying stocks with a low P/E ratio relative to the overall means. This indicates that using traditional industries as a homogeneous group did not aid in formulating a strategy to produce high rates of return. This does not indicate that a proper grouping did not exist, but it does indicate that the SIC industrial classifications were not appropriate.

Similar conclusions can be drawn with respect to portfolio analysis. Cohen and Pogue attempted to see if introducing industry effects into the Sharpe model could improve portfolio performance.[9] Sharpe assumed that the interrelationships between the price movements of stocks could be expressed in terms of their movement with an index of general stock-price movement. Cohen and Pogue added a second influence—the movement of stocks with their respective industrial average.[10] Cohen and Pogue's model did not outperform Sharpe's simple market model, indicating that no new information was gained by viewing stocks as members of traditional industries.[11]

We can also question the use of industrial classification as a method of holding certain variables constant. In finance, the most common variable researchers desire to hold constant is business risk. Wippern has used an analysis of variance to test differences in the stability of net operating income (his measure of business risk) within and between industries.[12] He found that there was virtually no difference and concluded that his testing "provides clear evidence that industry groups do not provide an adequate basis on which to insure homogeneity of basic business uncertainty." If, in fact, an industry was a homogeneous risk class, then the relationships, as hypothesized by Modigliani and Miller, between cost of capital and financial risk should be reasonably stable across samples of firms from the same industry. Keenan has demonstrated the extreme sample sensitivity of the Modigliani and Miller models with small random changes in a one-industry sample, indicating clearly that the industries he tested are not homogeneous risk classes.[13] A different homogeneous group must be found in order to hold business risk constant.[14]

The normal solution to the problem of holding the effect of omitted variables constant has been to introduce additional variables (as proxies of the previously omitted variable) into the regression equation. Problems can still arise because some variable correlated with both the dependent and one or more independent variables has been omitted or because the nature of the relationship between some of the variables changes as the magnitude of an included variable changes. Such problems would be evidenced by extreme sensitivity of the regression parameters to changes in the sample.

Keenan has used analysis of covariance in examining the models presented by Barges, Benishay, Gordon, and Modigliani and Miller.[15] In this study, Keenan has shown that the parameters of all the models which he tested are so extremely sample sensitive that the removal of one or two firms from the sample can change the sign of the regression parameter even when all firms in the sample are drawn from the same universe. A similar result is contained in Durand when he demonstrates that a stock-pricing model can yield statistically significant differences in parameters when it is estimated across geographical subsectors of an industry.[16]

The purpose of this section has been both to show the necessity of finding homogeneous groups of observations and to demonstrate that one particular grouping (specifically that based on SIC industrial classification) is not an appropriate grouping for all purposes. The grouping of observations that is appropriate for any study depends on the objective of the study and the nature of the process under investigation. One must first decide on why one wants homogeneous groups and then, with that objective in mind, select a variable or group of variables with respect to which homogeneity is desired. For example, in seeking a group of firms which are homogeneous with respect to business risk, one might well be content to find firms which have had the same amount of variation in past operating earnings.[17] This, rather than industrial classification, should be the basis of grouping.

In the next section of this paper, we will discuss the way homogeneous groups of observations can be formed once a set of variables with which homogeneity is desired has been selected. We will then present a case study that illustrates the improvement in forecasting ability which can be obtained through the use of grouping techniques.

An Alternative Method of Forming Homogeneous Groups

An alternative to grouping on the basis of traditional industries is to group on the basis of a variable or set of variables which are deemed relevant for the problem under study. If N variables are chosen as relevant for grouping, each firm can be viewed as a point in N-dimensional space. The distance between firms can be measured by simple Euclidean distance and firms grouped according to their distance from other points.[18] This grouping can be accomplished by using cluster analysis, which, in its present state of development, consists of a group of heuristics for partitioning points in N-dimensional space into groups. The clustering algorithm used in this study combines points which are close together, in order to minimize the sum of the squared distance between each point and its group centroid.[19]

In order for this process to yield reasonable groupings, the method of measuring interpoint distances in the N-dimensional space must be meaningful.

If we locate all firms in N-dimensional space and clustered on the basis of the Euclidean distance between firms, then the groups that would result would depend on the scale of the original variables and the extent of their orthogonality. For example, the squared distance between two points is:

$$D_{jk}^2 = \sum_{i=1}^{N} (P_{ji} - P_{ki})^2, \tag{1}$$

where (1) D_{jk} = the Euclidean distance firms j and k, and (2) P_{ji} = the value of variable i for firm j. If two variables P_1 and P_2 are perfectly correlated, then it is obvious from (1) that their influence is counted first as $P_{j1} - P_{k1}$ and then as $P_{j2} - P_{k2}$, or double counted. The greater the correlation of P_1 with other variables, the greater the effect of the common influence.

Further, from (1) it is obvious that the scale of the data influences the distance measure. If each P_{j1} is in units of thousands rather than millions, then the influence of P_{j1} is 1,000-fold higher.

Unfortunately, in most economic problems, the variables are multicollinear and the scaling of the variables is arbitrary. It would be very undesirable if multi-collinearity and the scaling of variables affected final groupings.

Fortunately, a technique exists for decomposing a set of variables (axes) into a new set of variables that are both orthogonal and insensitive to the unit of original measurement. The first step is to perform a principal components analysis of the correlation matrix of the raw data. This produces a new set of variables (axes) which are a linear transformation of the original variables and which are uncorrelated with each other. The new variables (axes) are ordered by their ability to account for the original joint variation in the data. That is, the first principal component explains the greatest amount of variation of the original data. These new variables now define an N-dimensional space in terms of orthogonal directions.[20]

The value of any new variable for any firm can be found by simply multiplying the relevant factor loadings by the normalized value of the original variables for the firm.[21] By repeating this procedure for each new variable, we can locate any firm in an orthogonal *N*-dimensional space.

However, the distances defined in the principal components space will still be determined by the amount of correlation in the original data, despite the fact that the space is defined in terms of orthogonal dimensions. The variance of the values of any new variable will be a function of the ability of that component to account for the original joint variation in the data. The more highly correlated the original variables, the better a particular component can account for original variance, and so the larger the interpoint distances will be in that dimension. This again would result in the double counting of correlated variables and is likely to lead to the overpowering of important firm differences. To overcome this problem, one need only divide each new variable by its standard deviation (eigen value) across all firms.[22] This will produce a set of firm measurements and differences which are both insensitive to the correlation and scale of the original variables and so can be used to group firms.[23]

Forecasting Earnings—An Application

This section illustrates the application of grouping techniques to a particular problem and shows that these techniques can improve forecasting ability. The particular problem we chose to study was the forecasting of earnings per share for industrial corporations.

This problem was selected for several reasons:

1. Almost every valuation and cost of capital model reported in the literature employs an earnings or earnings-growth variable.[24] Furthermore, the results of these models have proven to be extremely sensitive to the way the earnings or growth variable was defined.
2. We had already explored a series of more naïve techniques for forecasting earnings per share, and so a bench mark existed against which to judge the results of this study.[25]
3. We felt that the determinants (forecasts) of earnings per share were not homogeneous across all companies and that improvement in forecasts would result from the substitution of statistical grouping techniques for groupings based on final product.

The first steps which had to be taken in the study were the selection of criteria with respect to which we wished our groups to be homogeneous and the selection of a set of variables which could be used to forecast earnings per share within each group.

These are not really independent problems. We felt that earnings per share could be forecast by relating the change in earnings per share to corporate variables. The definition of the variables used to predict earnings per share are included in Appendix B. In general, this list includes measures of the type and size of sources of funds (e.g., 1, 2, 3, 4), measures of uses of funds (e.g., 11, 12), measures of profitability (e.g., 14, 20), measures of historical growth rates (e.g., 15, 16, 17), and measures of liquidity (e.g., 6, 7, 18).[26] While these variables should, in general, be good predictors of earnings per share, the way in which different firms responded to change in any variable might differ. For example, a decrease in profitability for a firm with a cyclical earnings pattern may mean a very different thing from a decrease in profitability for a firm which has demonstrated a steady growth in earnings.

We wanted to place firms into groups which had had the same earnings-growth pattern over time. This was done because we felt that, if firms have demonstrated the same patterns of growth over time (management reacted the same way to changes in economic condition), then differences in such things as profitability or liquidity would be likely to trigger the same reaction on management's part and so have the same effect on future earnings.

Having decided on the variables to use in forming homogeneous groups for the purpose of forecasting, the next step was to design our basic sample.

The sample could have been formed by randomly selecting a predetermined number of firms.[27] However, it was desirable to have a large sample of firms from each of several traditional industries so that (*a*) the dispersion of firms from traditional industries across our homogeneous groups could be studied, and (*b*) we could compare forecasts based on assuming that each traditional industry is a homogeneous group with forecasts based on our pseudoindustries (statistically homogeneous groups). To accomplish this, stratified sampling was employed.[28] We selected nine large four-digit-industry classifications at random from among those included on the compustat tape and included all firms with a suitable history from each of these traditional industries.[29] Sixty-one additional firms were then selected at random from the compustat tape. These firms were included so that we could examine whether they would cluster with traditional industries or segments of traditional industries or whether they would remain as outliers. Our final sample consisted of 180 firms representing forty-four industries. Our sample classified by both traditional and pseudoindustry is presented in Appendix A.

The next step in the study was to find homogeneous groups of firms. Annual growth rates in earnings per share were computed using earnings-per-share data for the years 1948–63.[30] This gave us fifteen growth rates for each of our 180 companies. Principal components analysis was then performed on the correlation matrix of the raw data. The results of the principal components analysis (both eigen vectors and eigen values) are reproduced in Appendix C. As can be seen from the eigen values in Appendix C, the first eleven principal components accounted for 88 percent of the variation of the raw data, while the next four only accounted for 16 percent. The decision was made to cluster the data in terms of eleven orthogonal axes (principal components).[31] As discussed earlier, if principal component scores for each company were computed simply by multiplying the eigen vector (principal component loadings) for each component by the standardized growth rates for each company, the resultant scores would still be a function of the amount of correlation in the raw data. To correct this, each of the first eleven principal components was standardized by dividing its eigen vector by the square root of its eigen value (which is the same as the standard deviation of the principal component scores on that component). The resultant standardized principal component loadings are displayed in Appendix D. The principal component scores were calculated for each firm in terms of these standardized principal component loadings. We now had a score for each firm on each of eleven standardized principal components.[32] We viewed each of the 180 firms as a point in eleven dimensional orthogonal space and employed clustering techniques to group them in terms of Euclidean distance. Specifically, we grouped firms by sequentially combining a firm (or a previously formed group) with the firm or group to which it was closest in terms of Euclidean distance. This sequential process was continued until further aggregation involved a "large" change in within-group distances. At this point, there were ten groups. The composition of the groups we obtained are presented in Appendix A.

The Forecast Procedure

Having obtained pseudoindustries, we are now ready to examine the usefulness of these groupings for forecasting purposes and to answer the specific question, "Do these grouping techniques yield better forecasts than aggregation along traditional industry lines?"

The first step in the experimental design was to select the method for forecasting earnings per share within each group. The specific procedure adopted involved running a cross-sectional, stepwise regression within each group and using the regression equations to estimate future earnings. In running the regression, the dependent variable was defined as the change in earnings between the end of 1960 and 1961; while the independent variables were those presented in Appendix B, calculated as of the end of 1960. Independent variables were added to the regression until no excluded variables were statistically significant at the 1 percent level.[33]

The regression equations which meet the above criteria differed both across pseudoindustries and traditional industries. Most equations contained some measure of sources of funds (1, 2, 3, or 4), profitability (14 or 20), and/or past growth rates (15, 16, 17). Though the measure of each of these influences which entered the forecasting equation differed from one industry to the next, each entered with a plus sign. This is what one would expect since the higher the profitability, the higher the historic growth rate; or the more funds raised by a firm, the higher one would expect future growth to be. All of the regressions had statistically significant coefficients of determination. However, the performance of the models should be determined by their forecasting ability (which we discuss below) rather than by their R^2.

After establishing the parameters of the regression equation, we forecast the value of earnings for 1964. This forecast was prepared by calculating the value of the independent variables as of 1963, substituting in the regression equations discussed above and adding the estimated change in earnings to the actual earnings for 1963.[34]

The next step was to select a procedure for comparing forecast techniques. It was desirable both to select an external criterion against which our forecasts could be compared and to set up a procedure for analyzing the statistical significance of results.

In an earlier study we compared nine techniques for forecasting earnings, using mechanical extrapolation techniques against each other and against analysts' estimates.[35] The results of this study showed that one technique dominated the other mechanical techniques at a statistically significant level. Furthermore, the performance of this technique, an exponentially weighted moving average with an arithmetic trend, could not be differentiated from the performance of the security analysts at the three large financial institutions studied (see Appendix E).[36] Forecasts using this technique should be a useful bench mark against which to judge the performance of our within-group regression.

In order to measure differences in the performance of our three forecasting techniques (the exponentially weighted moving average with an arithmetic trend, regressions within traditional industries, and regressions within pseudoindustries), we examined the frequency functions of the differences in the squared error between various pairs of forecasts. As an example, consider the determination of the frequency function used to compare the exponential with the regression within traditional industries. One observation determining this frequency function would be the squared error in the exponentially weighted forecast for company A minus the squared error for the regression forecast for company A. When we repeated this for all possible companies, we have one frequency function from which we can judge the comparative performance of the two forecasting techniques. If the frequency function had all positive or all negative values then this would indicate that one technique always had a lower squared error than a second technique and that dominance existed. Given the size of our sample, this would be unlikely to occur. What could and did happen was that some frequency functions had mostly positive or negative values and had a mean significantly different from zero. When the mean is significantly different from zero, we can state that it is highly unlikely that the techniques being compared forecasted equally well, and we will say that one technique is dominated by a second.[37]

The first comparisons we made were over all firms for which we had either type of within-industry forecast. Since neither the classifications by SIC industrial code nor by pseudoindustries included all firms in our sample (nor did the two classifications include the same firms), we could not directly compare pseudoindustry forecasts with forecasts using SIC industrial classifications. Instead, we compare forecasts based on regressions within traditional industry groupings against mechanical forecasts for the same firms and forecasts based on regressions within our pseudoindustries against mechanical forecasts for these firms.[38] The results are shown in table 1.1. The forecast prepared using regression analysis within pseudoindustries outperforms the mechanical forecast at the 5 percent level of significance. On the other hand, the forecast prepared using regression analysis within traditional industries is outperformed by the mechanical technique at the 0.1 percent level. The results indicate the dominance of pseudoindustry forecasts over both mechanical forecasts and forecasts prepared on the basis of traditional industries.

Table 1.1
Forecast comparison—all firms

Forecasting techniques compared	Mean difference in squared error $(a - b)$*	Standard error of mean	Significance level of the mean difference (%)
a) Forecasts based on traditional industry groupings b) Mechanical forecasts	0.8366	.2360	0.1
a) Forecasts based on pseudoindustries b) Mechanical forecasts	−0.0907	.0445	5

* If the number is negative, technique *a* dominates technique *b*.

Table 1.2
Forecast comparison—common firms

Forecasting techniques compared	Mean difference in squared error	Standard error of mean	Significance level of the mean difference (%)
a) Forecasts based on traditional industry groupings b) Mechanical forecasts	0.8862	.2546	0.1
a) Forecasts based on pseudoindustries b) Mechanical forecasts	−0.1185	.0692	10
a) Forecasts based on pseudoindustries b) Forecasts based on traditional industry groupings	−1.0047	.2549	0.1

There is some possibility that these results arose because of differences in the pattern of earnings between firms which were selected as members of pseudoindustries and firms which were members of traditional industries. For example, mechanical techniques might just work better for those firms that are members of traditional industries than they do for those firms that are not members of traditional industries but are members of pseudoindustries. To avoid this possibility, tests were repeated on only those firms which had been grouped as members of both traditional industries and pseudoindustries.[39] The results (reported in table 1.2) once again support the dominance of forecasts based on pseudoindustries. Forecasts based on pseudoindustries were statistically better than forecasts based on traditional industries at the 0.1 percent level and forecasts based on the mechanical model at the 10 percent level. Once again, the mechanical technique dominates forecasts based on traditional industries at the 0.1 percent level.

When the data were decomposed and forecasts prepared by each of the three methods examined for each traditional industry, the forecasts based on pseudoindustries outperformed the forecasts based on traditional industries for eight out of the nine traditional industries with the one reversal not being statistically significant.[40]

The results in this study have been based on an intensive analysis of forecasts for one year (1964). Although forecasts based on pseudoindustries outperform those based on traditional industries, mechanical methods, and subjective analysts' estimates at a statistically significant level for this year, it is possible that the results could differ for other years. However, there is no a priori reason to believe that this will happen. Furthermore, previous tests have shown that the ranking of alternative mechanical techniques against each other and against different analysts' estimates are reasonably stable over time.

Conclusion

In this paper we have (1) discussed the need to disaggregate economic data into meaningful groups in order to both better understand and predict economic phenomena; (2) presented a technique which can be used to partition observations into groups which are homogeneous with respect to a predetermined set of criteria; and (3) demonstrated that this technique can lead to better estimates of earnings per share that a grouping based on SIC industrial classifications. In addition, the forecasts based on our statistical groupings were shown to outperform mechanical extrapolation techniques, which we had previously shown to perform about as well as security analysts.[41]

Appendix A

Standard industrial classification code	Pseudoindustry	Name of company
Chemicals:		
2800 006900	P6	Air Reduction Co.
2800 013000	P2	Allied Chemical Corp.
2800 021900	P6	American Cyanamid Co.
2800 053841		Atlas Chemical Industries, Inc.
2800 131500	P5	Celanese Corp.
2800 144244		Chemetron Corp.
2800 171700	P7	Commercial Solvents Corp.
2800 215701	P2	Diamond Shamrock Corp.
2800 225000	P4	Dow Chemical
2800 229300	P3	E. I. Dupont de Nemours & Co.
2800 236400	P3	Eastman Kodak Co.
2800 281740	P4	FMC Corp.
2800 351700	P4	Hercules, Inc.
2800 359900	P4	Hooker Chemical Co.
2800 381200	P3	Interchemical
2800 413600	P8	Koppers Co.
2800 443000	P4	MacAndrews & Forbes
2800 482800	P3	Minnesota Mining & Manufacturing Co.
2800 491010	P4	Monsanto Co.
2800 512900	P5	National Lead Co.
2800 588500	P1	Pittsburgh Plate Glass Co.
2800 627900	P3	Rohm & Haas Co.
2800 734100	P6	Union Carbide Corp.
Drugs:		
2830 026000	P3	American Home Products Corp.
2830 091000	P4	Bristol-Myers Co.
2830 313600	P3	Gillette Co.
2830 397700	P4	Johnson & Johnson
2830 406300	P4	Kendall Co.
2830 471000	P4	Merck & Co.
2830 479000	P3	Miles Laboratories, Inc.

Appendix A (continued)

Standard industrial classification code	Pseudoindustry	Name of company
2830 543200	P3	Norwich Pharmacal Co.
2830 565800	P4	Parke, Davis & Co.
2830 579000	P4	Pfizer Uchasco & Coct Inc.
2830 591800	P3	Plough, Inc.
2830 619550	P3	Richardson-Merrell, Inc.
2830 648000	P3	G. D. Searle Co.
2830 665500	P3	Smith Kline & French Laboratories, Inc.
2830 693600	P4	Sterling Drug, Inc.
Machinery specialty:		
3550 028100		American Machine & Foundry Co.
3550 079300	P2	Black & Decker Manufacturing Co.
3550 089200	P1	Briggs & Stratton
3550 195800		Crompton Knowles Corp.
3550 252200	P1	Ex-Cell-O Corp.
3550 399200		Joy Manufacturing Co.
3550 477470	P6	Midland Ross Corp.
3550 555300	P4	Otis Elevator Co.
3550 555700	P1	Outboard Marine Corp.
3550 746200	P4	United Shoe Machinery Corp.
Machinery industrial:		
3560 021000	P6	American Chain & Cable Co., Inc.
3560 081700	P2	Blaw-Knox Co.
3560 147700	P2	Chicago Pneumatic Tool Co.
3560 294800	P2	Gardner-Denver Co.
3560 378400	P2	Ingersoll-Rand Co.
3560 471900	P4	Mesta Machine Co.
Automobile suppliers:		
3714 085100	P10	Borg-Warner Corp.
3714 159700	P6	Clevite Corp.
3714 203800	P6	Dana Corp.
3714 237236	P10	Eaton Yale & Towne, Inc.
3714 259600	P4	Federal Mogul Corp.
3714 406000	P10	Kelsey Hayes Co.
3714 718900	P9	Timken Roller Bearing Co.

Appendix A (continued)

Standard industrial classification code	Pseudoindustry	Name of company
Oils:		
2912 053377	P8	Atlantic Richfield Co.
2912 152800	P2	Cities Service Co.
2912 187700	P4	Continental Oil Co.
2912 373250	P5	Imperial Oil Ltd.
2912 407900		Kerr McGee Corp.
2912 452180	P2	Marathon Oil
2912 583700	P4	Phillips Petroleum Co.
2912 606500	P6	Quaker State Oil Refining
2912 656500	P2	Shell Oil Co.
2912 659300	P2	Signal Oil Gas Co.
2912 662800	P2	Sinclair Oil Corp.
2912 686300	P2	Standard Oil Co. of Indiana
2912 686700	P7	Standard Oil Co. of Ohio
2912 699600	P2	Sun Oil Co.
2912 701220	P2	Sunray DX Oil Co.
2912 736700	P2	Union Oil Co. of California
Tire and rubber:		
3000 047430	P4	Armstrong Rubber
3000 266300	P2	Firestone Tire & Rubber Co.
3000 317900	P4	B. F. Goodrich Co.
3000 318100	P5	Goodyear Tire & Rubber Co.
3000 738651	P2	Uniroyal, Inc.
Steels:		
3310 011600	P9	Allegheny Ludlum Steel Corp.
3310 046800	P7	Armco Steel Corp.
3310 076700	P7	Bethlehem Steel Corp.
3310 127400	P1	Carpenter Steel Co.
3310 187900	P4	Continental Steel Corp.
3310 189500	P10	Copperweld Steel
3310 214000		Detroit Steel Corp.
3310 322500	P9	Granite City Steel Co.
3310 378800	P7	Inland Steel Co.
3310 381710	P10	Interlake Steel Co.

Appendix A (continued)

Standard industrial classification code	Pseudoindustry	Name of company
3310 409600		Keystone Steel Wire Co. of Delaware
3310 441200	P6	Lukens Steel Co.
3310 464750	P9	McLouth Steel Corp.
3310 616800	P7	Republic Steel Corp.
3310 655400		Sharon Steel Corp.
3310 692700	P2	Steel Company of Canada
3310 752200	P7	U.S. Steel Corp.
3310 801700	P9	Youngstown Sheet & Tube Co.
Machinery fabricating:		
3400 073200	P10	Belden Corp.
3400 252000		Eversharp, Inc.
3400 298300	P2	General Cable Corp.
3400 516300	P6	National Standard Co.
3400 659900	P4	Signode Corp.
Other firms:		
1042 358930	P1	Homestake Mining
1311 016400	P2	Amerada Petroleum Corp.
1311 663600	P2	Skelly Oil Co.
1311 702300	P2	Superior Oil Co.
2000 405900	P3	Kellogg Co.
2052 349910	P4	Helme Products
2063 016100	P4	Amalgamated Sugar Co.
2121 298700	P2	General Cigar Co., Inc.
2200 164400		Collins Aikman Corp.
2510 226200	P4	Drexel Enterprises
2600 644600	P3	Scott Paper Co.
2700 462200	P5	McCall Corporation
2844 057610	P3	Avon Products
2899 188091	P4	Conwood Corp.
2899 232728		Eagle Picher Industries
2899 263000	P4	Ferro Corp.
2899 503230	P3	Nalco Chemical Co.
2912 048900	P2	Ashland Oil Refinery
2950 279100	P6	Flintkote Co.

Appendix A (continued)

Standard industrial classification code	Pseudoindustry	Name of company
3241 466600	P3	Medusa Portland Cement Co.
3321 133800	P7	Central Foundry Co.
3430 195000		Crane Company
3511 059000	P5	Babcock & Wilcox Co.
3511 169700	P4	Combustion Engineering, Inc.
3522 014600	P6	Allis-Chalmers Manufacturing Co.
3522 383300	P6	International Harvester Co.
3522 788800	P3	Wickes Corp.
3531 131000	P5	Caterpillar Tractor Co.
3531 156800	P10	Clark Equipment Co.
3531 617760	P6	Rex Chainbelt
3533 225900	P2	Dresser Industries, Inc.
3533 336700	P5	Halliburton Co.
3540 151600		Cincinnati Milling Machine Co.
3540 488200		Monarch Machine Tool Co.
3540 504400	P1	National Acme Co.
3540 663900	P4	Skil Corp.
3540 701100		Sundstrand Corp.
3540 768800		Warner & Swasey
3569 694600	P6	Stewart-Warner Corp.
3569 704900		Symington Wayne Corp.
3570 004000	P4	Addressograph-Multigraph
3570 382700	P3	International Business Machines Corp.
3570 507600	P4	National Cash Register Co.
3570 587000	P3	Pitney-Bowes, Inc.
3570 798830		Xerox Corp.
3600 299800	P4	General Electric Co.
3600 359025	P3	Honeywell, Inc.
3600 386100	P4	International Telephone & Telegraph
3600 608100	P6	Radio Corp. of America
3600 784700		Westinghouse Electric Corp.
3610 244900	P8	Emerson Electric Co.
3610 316200	P6	Globe Union Inc.
3610 463600	P1	McGraw-Edison Co.

Appendix A (continued)

Standard industrial classification code	Pseudoindustry	Name of company
3610 545800	P2	Ohio Brass Co.
3610 614500	P2	Reliance Electrical Engineering
3622 202300	P2	Cutler-Hammer, Inc.
3622 624500	P4	Robertshaw Controls
3622 683500	P2	Square D Company
3630 461000	P4	Maytag Co.
3630 563100		Packard Bell Electronics
3630 662900	P2	Singer Co.
3670 253900		Fairchild Camera & Instrument Corp.
3670 305610	P2	General Signal Co.
3679 369705		IRC Inc.
3679 447500	P6	P. R. Mallory Co.
3679 682600	P1	Sprague Electric Co.
3711 303010	P1	General Motors Corp.
3713 199900	P6	Cummins Engine
3713 291100		Fruehauf Corp.
3713 787000	P9	White Motors Co.
3725 586900		Piper Aircraft Corp.
3811 039080	P2	Ametex Inc.
3811 131900	P8	Cenco Instruments
3811 627000	P6	Rockwell Manufacturing Co.
3999 338600	P5	Hammond Corp.
3999 386000		International Silver Co.
3999 628700		Ronson Corp.
3999 724300	P8	M. E. Torrington Co.

Appendix B: Definition of Variables*

1. $\dfrac{\text{Debt }(t) - \text{Debt }(t-1)}{\text{Total assets }(t-1)}$

2. $\dfrac{\text{Equity }(t) - \text{Equity }(t-1) - \text{Retained earnings }(t)}{\text{Total assets }(t-1)}$

3. $\dfrac{\text{Retained earnings }(t)}{\text{Total assets }(t-1)}$

4. $\dfrac{\text{Preferred stock }(t) - \text{Preferred stock }(t-1)}{\text{Total assets }(t-1)}$

5. $\dfrac{\text{Depreciation }(t)}{\text{Total assets }(t-1)}$

6. $\dfrac{\text{Cash }(t)}{\text{Current liabilities }(t)}$

7. $\dfrac{\dfrac{\text{Receivables }(t) + \text{Receivables }(t-1)}{2}}{\text{Sales }(t)}$

8. $\dfrac{\text{Long-term debt }(t)}{\text{Market-value stock }(t)}$

9. $\dfrac{\text{Long-term debt }(t) - \text{Long-term debt }(t-1)}{\text{Market-value stock }(t) - \text{Market-value stock }(t-1)}$

10. $\dfrac{\text{Preferred }(t)}{\text{Market-value common }(t)}$

11. $\dfrac{\text{Total dividends }(t)}{\text{Earnings available }(t) + \text{Depreciation }(t)}$

12. $\dfrac{\text{Capital expenditure }(t)}{\text{Change in total assets }(t) - (t-1)}$

13. Total assets (t)

14. $\dfrac{\text{Operating income }(t)}{\text{Long-term debt }(t) + \text{Preferred }(t) + \text{Book common }(t)}$

15. Five-year average growth in earnings per share†

*All variables except 15, 16, 17, 19, and 21 are defined as three-year averages of the definition given above. The values of t in establishing the regression equation for 1961 were 1958, 1959, and 1960. The values for t when preparing the forecast for 1964 were 1961, 1962, and 1963.

†These variables were calculated using per-share data. All data were adjusted for stock dividends and stock splits.

16. Five-year average growth in sales per share†

17. Five-year average of the product of retention rate and the rate of return on common equity†

18. $\dfrac{\text{Cash }(t)}{\text{Total assets }(t)}$

19. STD deviation of growth in earnings over five years†

20. $\dfrac{\text{Operating income }(t)}{\text{Net sales }(t)}$

21. Growth in market price, five years†

22. $\dfrac{\text{Current liabilities }(t) - \text{Current liabilities }(t-1)}{\text{Total assets }(t-1)}$

23. $\dfrac{\text{Total assets }(t) - \text{Total assets }(t-1)}{\text{Total assets }(t-1)}$

Appendix C

Eigen vectors

Growth rate for year	Principal component number 1	2	3	4	5	6	7	8
1949	.4633	−.0436	−.2144	−.1485	−.0709	−.0302	−.0366	−.0155
1950	.3634	−.0304	.3992	−.0433	.4006	.2838	.0897	.0790
1951	−.0414	−.2524	.2505	−.1678	−.3140	−.3051	.4988	.1307
1952	.0118	−.4894	−.2154	−.1430	−.1694	.0265	.3115	.2461
1953	−.0848	−.1153	−.5094	.0884	.2906	−.0448	.3093	−.3192
1954	.1464	−.2096	−.4371	.3293	.0897	.3173	.0591	.3851
1955	−.0070	.2023	−.3570	.0475	.1765	−.3711	−.1162	−.0552
1956	−.0848	−.4968	−.0176	−.1938	.1042	−.2214	−.4511	−.1564
1957	.0998	−.0462	−.0727	.0060	−.4359	.5088	.0380	−.6521
1958	.2926	.1507	−.0107	.4506	−.2768	−.0617	−.2166	.2138
1959	−.1399	.1542	−.0719	−.4476	.3707	.3721	.0588	.1343
1960	.0710	−.5154	.1550	.1362	.1960	.0223	−.3401	−.1209
1961	−.4236	−.1602	.1245	.3296	−.0387	.3233	−.0398	.1995
1962	−.3452	.0921	−.2133	−.3363	−.3196	.1267	−.3659	.2516
1963	−.4436	.0239	.1074	.3574	.1629	−.1142	.1602	−.1772
Eigen values	2.006	1.774	1.604	1.409	1.115	1.043	.985	.956

Appendix C (continued)

Growth rate for year	Principal component number						
	9	10	11	12	13	14	15
1949	−.0445	−.4846	−.3921	−.4698	−.1873	−.1751	−.1732
1950	−.1266	.1368	−.1630	−.1394	.3372	−.1759	.4789
1951	−.4215	−.2753	.0805	.1132	.3238	−.0302	−.0891
1952	.0874	.3906	.1055	−.2752	−.3997	.0327	.3142
1953	.1595	−.3859	.0685	.2603	.1033	−.1038	.4012
1954	−.0622	.1199	−.0470	.0258	.4395	.1575	−.3714
1955	−.6790	.3540	−.1135	−.0264	−.0612	−.1803	.0826
1956	.1440	.0674	.2849	−.1627	.3224	−.4085	−.1362
1957	−.2533	.1584	.0824	−.0709	.0966	−.0309	−.0167
1958	−.0987	−.2281	.5815	−.1232	−.0254	−.0671	.3065
1959	−.2737	−.2078	.5024	−.1422	−.1651	.0352	−.1748
1960	−.3301	−.2111	−.0758	.1824	−.2446	.5113	.0741
1961	−.1584	−.1757	−.2097	.0999	−.2582	−.5804	−.0092
1962	−.0526	−.1582	−.2313	−.0768	.3005	.1955	.4235
1963	−.0026	−.0649	−.0078	−.6973	.1453	.2414	.0019
Eigen values	.867	.779	.664	.571	.452	.402	.375

Appendix D

Normalized eigen vectors

Growth rate	Principal component number										
for year	1	2	3	4	5	6	7	8	9	10	11
1949	.3271	−.0327	−.1693	−.1251	−.0672	−.0296	−.0369	−.0159	−.0478	−.5492	−.4813
1950	.2566	−.0228	.3152	−.0365	.3794	.2780	.0904	.0808	−.1360	.1550	−.2001
1951	−.0292	−.1895	.1978	−.1414	−.2974	−.2988	.5027	.1337	−.4526	−.3120	.0988
1952	.0083	−.3675	−.1701	−.1205	−.1604	.0260	.3139	.2517	.0939	.4427	.1295
1953	−.0599	−.0866	−.4023	.0745	.2752	−.0439	.3117	−.3264	.1713	−.4373	.0841
1954	.1034	−.1574	−.3452	.2774	.0550	.3108	.0596	.3938	−.0668	.1359	−.0577
1955	−.0049	.1519	−.2819	.0400	.1672	−.3635	−.1171	−.0564	−.7292	.4012	−.1393
1956	−.0599	−.3730	−.0139	−.1633	.0987	−.2168	−.4546	−.1599	.1546	.0764	.3497
1957	.0705	−.0347	−.0574	.0051	−.4129	.4983	.0383	−.6668	−.2720	.1795	.1012
1958	.2066	.1132	−.0084	.3796	−.2622	−.0604	−.2183	.2186	−.1060	−.2585	.7138
1959	−.0988	.1158	−.0568	.3771	.3511	.3644	.0593	.1373	−.2939	−.2355	.6167
1960	.0501	−.3870	.1224	.1147	.1856	.0218	−.3428	−.1236	−.3545	−.2392	−.0931
1961	−.2991	−.1203	.0983	.2777	−.0367	.3167	−.0401	.2040	−.1662	−.1991	−.2575
1962	−.2437	.0692	−.1684	.2833	−.3027	.1241	−.3688	.2573	−.0565	−.1793	−.2839
1963	−.3132	.0179	.0848	.3011	.1543	.1119	.1615	−.1812	−.0028	−.0735	−.0096

Appendix E

Relative performance of security analysts and additive exponential model (based on squared error)*

	Investment advisory service	Brokerage house	Pension fund
Sample size	213	177	84
Security analysts	.0231	.0342	.0310
Additive exponential	.0221	.0352	.0441
t-value	+0.12	−0.34	−1.23

* A positive value indicates that the mechanical technique outperformed the analysts' estimates.

Notes

The research for this paper was supported by grants from the Institute for Quantitative Research in Finance and by TIAA–CREF. We would like to thank Steve Replen for computational assistance.

1. Edwin J. Elton and Martin J. Gruber, "Homogeneous Groups and the Testing of Economic Hypotheses," *Journal of Financial and Quantitative Analysis* 4 (January 1970): 581–602.

2. Often the omitted variable cannot be included in the regression equation because it cannot be specified exactly.

3. For a full explanation of the source of bias, see Elton and Gruber (n. 1 above).

4. F. Modigliani and M. Miller, "The Cost of Capital, Corporation Finance, and the Theory of Investment," *American Economic Review* 48 (June 1958): 261–97.

5. See, e.g., Myron Gordon, *The Investment, Financing, and Valuation of the Corporation* (Homewood, Ill.: Richard D. Irwin, Inc., 1962).

6. See, e.g., ibid.; Ronald Wippern, "Financial Structure and the Value of the Firm," *Journal of Finance* 21 (December 1966): 615–33; F. D. Arditti, "Risk and the Required Return on Equity," *Journal of Finance* 22 (March 1967): 19–36; and Martin J. Gruber, *The Determinants of Common Stock Prices* (College Park: Pennsylvania State University, 1971).

7. William Breen, "Low Price-Earnings Ratios and Industry Relatives," *Financial Analyst Journal* 24, no. 4 (July/August 1968): 125–27.

8. Since differences in growth rates were adjusted for in the Breen study, we can consider differences in P/E ratios as due to risk plus market imperfections. Adjustment by the industry-average P/E can be viewed as an attempt to correct for risk differentials between industries.

9. See K. Cohen and J. Pogue, "An Empirical Evaluation of Alternative Portfolio Selection Models," *Journal of Business* 40, no. 1 (January 1967): 163–93; and William Sharpe, "A Simplified Model for Portfolio Analysis," *Management Science* 9, no. 2 (January 1963): 277–93.

10. Cohen and Pogue actually tested two models. In the first model, the industrial averages were assumed to be uncorrelated except for their common movement with the overall mar-

ket. In the second, the industrial averages were assumed to have covariance above that due to movements with the general market.

11. Benjamin King ("Market and Industry Factors in Stock Price Behavior," *Journal of Business* 39 [January 1966]: 139–90) provides evidence that traditional industrial groupings explain part of the historical variability in the firms' rate of return. The results of his study suggest that some traditional industrial grouping might be appropriate for portfolio selection.

12. See Wippern (n. 6 above).

13. M. Keenan, "Toward a Positive Theory of Equity Valuation" (Ph.D. diss., Carnegie Institute of Technology, 1967).

14. I. Friend and M. Puckett, "Dividends and Stock Prices," *American Economic Review* 54 (September 1964): 656–82.

15. See Keenan (n. 15 above); Alexander Barges, *The Effect of Capital Structure on the Cost of Capital* (Englewood Cliffs, N.J.: Prentice-Hall, Inc., 1963); H. Benishay, "Determinants of Variability in Earnings Price Ratios of Corporate Equities" (Ph.D. diss., University of Chicago, 1960); Gordon (n. 5 above); and Modigliani and Miller (n. 4 above).

16. David Durand, *Bank Stock Prices and the Bank Capital Problem*, National Bureau of Economic Research, Occasional Paper no. 54 (New York: National Bureau of Economic Research, 1957).

17. Assuming such variation is a proxy for the basic uncertainty associated with earnings.

18. We will take up the problem of using Euclidean distance in the unadjusted N-dimensional space shortly.

19. Other objective function assumed and maximization of the squared distance between group centroids and the minimization of average squared distance between all points within a group. These are equivalent to the one in the test. See Elton and Gruber (n. 1 above) for proofs of the equivalence as well as for a discussion of clustering techniques which assume different objective functions.

20. One may use the information produced by the principal components analysis to decrease the dimensionality of the space in which firms are examined. The first P components where $P < N$ may explain so much of the original variation (e.g., 99 percent or more) that one is willing to assume that these P dimensions capture the relevant differences between firms.

21. There is one set of factor loadings for each new variable. The values of each original variable are normalized across all firms to a mean of zero and a standard deviation of one.

22. This procedure can be simplified by dividing the eigen vectors by the eigen values before computing factor scores. For more rigorous proof of the analysis in this section, see Donald Farrar, "Multivariate Measures of Profile Similarity for the Objective Stratification of Economic Data" (working paper, Alfred P. Sloan School of Management, M.I.T., 1968).

23. If all adjusted principal components are used to group firms, one can pick up and misinterpret large amounts of random noise from the last few components (which usually explain very little of the variance in the original data). To overcome this problem, one will usually use a number of principal components which is smaller than the number of variables included in the analysis. There is no optimum way to decide on the number of components to use and the ultimate justification for our choice must rest with the usefulness of our results.

24. Benishay (n. 15 above); Gordon (n. 5 above); Gruber (n. 6 above); Modigliani and Miller (n. 4 above); Wippern (n. 6 above).

25. See Edwin J. Elton and Martin J. Gruber, "Earnings Forecasters and Expectational Data," *Management Science* (in press).

26. The particular definition of an influence (such as profitability) that we use is, of course, somewhat arbitrary. The actual list of definitions was obtained from standard definitions reported in the literature and from the suggestions made by officers of thirty large financial institutions. These suggestions were made after hearing the research proposal on which this study was based.

27. Our universe is biased in favor or large firms, since we restrict it to firms included on the compustat tape.

28. All firms for which the compustat service did not record earnings in one or more years from 1953 to 1966 or which reported negative earnings from 1953 to 1962 were eliminated from the sample. This was done so that the final results could be compared with the outcome from mechanical techniques reported in Elton and Gruber (n. 25 above). This also biases our sample in favor of large, stable firms.

29. This meant that the probability of a firm being selected in the first part of our sample was a function of the number of firms in the industry to which it belonged.

30. Data for the years 1964, 1965, 1966 are not used in the analysis, for the clustering patterns obtained are to be used to test forecast accuracy for these years.

31. The decision as to how many of the principal components to preserve must, to some extent, be arbitrary. Preserving all components standardized to unit variance would pick up and magnify the large amount of random fluctuations contained in the last few principal components. Using too few principal components would ignore important dimensions of the original data.

32. We can express this analytically as follows. Let G_i stand for the vector of standardized growth rates for firm i over time; F_j stand for the vector of principal component loadings for component j (the eigen vector for component j); and λ_j, the eigen value for component j. Then the standardized principal components loadings in Appendix D are derived from the raw principal component loadings in Appendix C by calculating F_j/λ_j. Furthermore, the principal component score of firm i on component j (or the location of firm i in the jth dimension) is equal to G_iF_j/λ_j.

33. Alternative procedures might be used for establishing the best forecasting equations. However, since our emphasis is on establishing the usefulness of pseudoindustries and since a large number of forecasting equations had to be established for pseudoindustries (ten) and for traditional industries (nine), we felt such a procedure was justified.

34. The question may arise as to why we estimated earnings for 1964 rather than for 1962. Most of the independent variables used in our regressions were constructed in terms of three-year averages of data (in order to damp out random fluctuations). If we had recalculated the independent variables as of 1961 in order to forecast for 1962, two out of three of the observations used in constructing the independent variables would be the same as those used in running the regression. To avoid this problem, the period ending in 1963 was used in defining the independent variables. If this gap in time introduces a bias, it should increase the inaccuracy of our regression results rather than work in favor of our results.

35. The sample for this earlier study was identical with the sample used in this study. The nine forecasts were prepared in the following manner: (1) the previous year's earnings plus the previous year's change in earnings; (2) a four-year moving average; (3) a moving average of optimum length; (4) a linear regression on time; (5) a log linear regression on time; (6) an exponentially weighted moving average with an arithmetic growth trend; (7) an exponen-

tially weighted moving average with a geometric growth trend; (8) the same as (6) except an arithmetic growth in the trend was added; (9) the same as (7) except a geometric growth in the trend was added. See Elton and Gruber (n. 25 above) for a fuller description of the results and a detailed description of the procedure used to determine optimum weights for the exponential weighting.

36. The results of the comparison of the mechanical extrapolation technique with the forecasts of security analysts are contained in Appendix E. The test used to analyze possible statistical differences in the forecasts is discussed in the next several paragraphs of the text. None of the differences between analysts' forecasts and the mechanical forecasts were statistically significant. Several comments are in order concerning the analysts' estimates. The analysts' estimates come from three financial institutions. These institutions were not selected at random; rather, we would expect them to be among those institutions that had produced the best earnings projections. The investment-advisory service was selected after analysts in a number of financial institutions indicated that this was the service in whose projections they placed the greatest faith. Furthermore, the other two institutions represented the only ones among those contracted which were willing to expose their forecasts to rigorous testing. Since this had potential repercussions within their own firms, this indicated some confidence in their projections.

37. From the central limit theorem, we can state that the distribution of the mean of our frequency functions is normally distributed with mean equal to the mean of the frequency function and standard deviation equal to the standard deviation of the frequency function divided by the square root of the number of observations. That the frequency functions under question were derived from differencing two variables should not bother the reader. The central limit theorem states that, as the number of observations increases, the distribution of the mean is normally distributed, no matter what the original frequency function.

38. Only SIC industries and pseudoindustries with five or more firms were included in preparing forecasts. Extremely small industries would not allow enough degrees of freedom for the regression analysis.

39. The sample of firms that are included in both groups consists of ninety-eight firms, as seen from Appendix A.

40. It is interesting to note the extent to which traditional industries are rearranged among pseudoindustries. We have noted the SIC number of the traditional industry, the number of firms in our sample from that industry, and the number of pseudoindustries into which the traditional industries split (see table below).

Traditional industry no.	No. firms in each industry	No. pseudoindustries among which the traditional industry is split
2800	21	7
2830	15	2
2912	16	5
3000	5	3
3310	15	7
3400	4	4
3550	7	4
3560	8	3
3714	7	4

41. See Elton and Gruber (n. 25 above).

2 Professional Expectations: Accuracy and Diagnosis of Errors

Edwin J. Elton, Martin J. Gruber, and Mustafa N. Gultekin

I Introduction

Expectations play an important role in the theoretical literature of financial economics as well as in the day-to-day world of the investment community. Expectations as to the future dividend-paying capacity of the firm are often held to be a key variable in the determination of share price. Almost every model of share valuation that has been proposed, whether part of a theoretical system or invented by a practicing analyst, requires estimates of earnings or cash flow. The perceived importance of forecasts of next year's earnings to the valuation process can be seen from the fact that almost without exception, analysts at major brokerage firms and financial institutions produce estimates of next year's earnings. Firms often (and, in fact, should) forecast earnings into the future as well as a myriad of other variables. The potpourri of other forecasted variables differs from firm to firm, but forecasts of the next fiscal year's earnings per share are almost always produced.

The purpose of this chapter is to analyze the errors made by professional forecasters (analysts) in estimating earnings per share for a large number of firms over a number of years.[1] We have demonstrated in a previous paper that consensus (average) estimates of earnings per share play a key role in share price determination. In this paper, we examine consensus estimates with respect to the following questions: 1. What is the size and pattern of analysts' errors? 2. What is the source of errors? 3. Are some firms more difficult to predict than others? 4. Is there an association between errors in forecasts and divergence of analysts' estimates?

The first of these topics involves an examination of the average size and the time pattern of analysts' errors. The second topic involves an examination of the type of errors that analysts make. For example, what percent of the error in forecasting is due to an inability to forecast correctly the average growth rate in earnings in the economy; what percent is due to the inability to forecast how well individual industries will perform; and what percent is due to an inability to forecast how well individual companies will do? The second topic also examines other forecast characteristics. The third topic involves an examination of the persistence of errors over time. Are there particular industries or companies for which it is particularly hard or easy to forecast earnings?[2] The final topic involves an examination of disagreement among analysts concerning forecasts and the relationship of this disagreement to the error in the consensus forecast.

II Sample

Our data source was the I/B/E/S database put together by Lynch, Jones and Ryan, a New York brokerage firm. Lynch, Jones and Ryan collect, on a monthly basis, earnings estimates from all major brokerage firms on over 2,000 corporations. The earnings estimates are for each of the next two years. Lynch, Jones and Ryan publish a number of characteristics of these earnings estimates for each corporation followed. These include among others the arithmetic mean, median, range, and standard deviation of the estimates of earnings per share for each corporation.

For part of this study, we wanted to have earnings estimates prepared a given number of months before the end of the fiscal year to be at a common calendar time. This restriction means that all analysts would have access to the same macroeconomic information at the time these forecasts were prepared (*N* months before the end of the fiscal year). Because the majority of firms have fiscal years ending in December, only these firms were selected.

Our second restriction was to include only firms followed by three or more analysts. We studied properties of consensus estimates of earnings. Requiring three analysts was a trade-off between a desire for a large sample and a desire to have the forecasts reflective of a consensus rather than of the idiosyncrasies of one or two analysts. Our final sample consisted of 414 firms for each of the years 1976, 1977, and 1978.[3]

III Size of Analysts' Errors and Their Time Series Properties

Our first set of tests involved looking at the accuracy of analysts' estimates of earnings (and growth in earnings) and the change in the error with successive forecasts over the fiscal year. We used several different measures of analysts' errors. The first measure was the dollar error, defined as the absolute value of the difference between actual earnings and forecasted earnings. If F_t is the earnings forecast made t months before the end of the fiscal year and A is the actual earnings, then dollar error is

$$|A - F_t|. \tag{1}$$

The second measure of analysts' accuracy was the error in estimated growth. This is the metric that will be emphasized in the latter section of this paper. There is ambiguity in this metric if actual earnings were negative or zero. In addition, if firms with extremely small earnings were included in the sample, the average results would be dominated by these few observations. To avoid these problems, we excluded firms with earnings less than 20¢.[4] Eliminating firms with negative earnings resulted in deletion of 21 observations and eliminating firms with very small earnings resulted in deletion of an additional nine observations out of a total of 1,242 observations. With last year's actual earnings denoted by A_L, the second error measure can be expressed as the difference between the actual growth and forecasted growth, or

$$|(A/A_L) - (F_t/A_L)| \quad \text{for} \quad A, A_L > 0. \tag{2}$$

Our final measure was Theil's [10] inequality coefficient. Define the subscript i as referring to firm i and define[5]

	For Change in Earnings	For Growth in Earnings
Realized change	$R_i = A_i - A_{iL}$	$R_i = (A_i - A_{iL})/A_{iL}$
Predicted change	$P_i = F_{it} - A_{iL}$	$P_i = (F_{it} - A_{iL})/A_{iL}$

Theil's inequality coefficient is

$$U = \sum_{i=1}^{N}(R_i - P_i)^2 \Big/ \sum_{i=1}^{N} R_i^2. \tag{3}$$

One advantage of this measure is that it is scaled. A value of zero is associated with a perfect forecast. A value of one is associated with a forecast that on average has the same error as a "naive" no change forecast.

All the analysis in this article was done for alternative measures of error. Alternative formulations were employed because without knowledge of a potential user's loss function, one measure could not be singled out as best. Because the results of the analysis were sufficiently similar

Table 2.1
Regressions of mean consensus error on time

	$P = a + bT + \varepsilon$											
	Dollar error			Error in growth			Theil's U in change			Theil's U in growth		
	a	b	R^2	a	b	R^2	a	b	R^2	a	b	R^2
Overall	.146	.036	.997	.043	.013	.998	.083	.054	.990	−.061	.061	.947
1976	.144	.035	.996	.048	.015	.998	.038	.045	.988	−.049	.048	.944
1977	.159	.036	.991	.045	.013	.991	.164	.079	.985	−.077	.081	.891
1978	.136	.037	.994	.036	.013	.993	.062	.042	.949	−.068	.064	.980

under alternative measures, in most cases the analysis is reported in terms of error in growth, and differences that arise from other measures are briefly noted.

To analyze the time-series properties of errors in forecasts, we regressed each of our measures on time. The results are presented in Table 2.1. Month 1 is the month in which analysts prepared their last forecast of earnings per share for a fiscal year and month 12 is 12 months earlier. Thus, the positive regression slope indicates a decrease in errors in forecasts over time. The most striking feature of Table 2.1 is the regularity of the decline in errors over successive forecasts. The reader might well anticipate a decline in error size over time, given that additional information is made available throughout the year. The high degree of association between error and time (over 99 percent in some cases) shows that the decline in error is about the same size from month to month over the year.

The second striking feature of Table 2.1 is the similarity between years for most of our error measures. For example, the change in the error for different years between months was 3.5 cents, 3.6 cents, and 3.7 cents for dollar error. Using the Chow test, we cannot reject the hypothesis that the equations are the same at the 5 percent level of significance. Thus, one cannot reject the appropriateness of pooling the observations across years.

For error in growth, the decline per month was .015, .013, and .013 in the three years. Once again, one could not reject the hypothesis that the regressions were the same in each year.[6] Similar results held for other measures.

Before leaving this section, some comments on the Theil inequality coefficient are in order. Theil's measure for growth ranged from .801 in month 12 down to .055 in month 1. This pattern implied that analysts forecasted better than the naive model of no change and that their forecasts became more accurate as the fiscal year progressed.

IV Error Diagnosis

While the size and time pattern of analysts' error is interesting in itself, more can be learned about analysts' performance by diagnosing the source of analysts' errors. In this section, we examine two sets of error partitions:

1. Level of aggregation—how significant are errors that are unique to each company in comparison with a more general level of aggregation?
2. Forecast characteristics—are there recognizable patterns in errors?

The partition results are for the mean squared error of analysts' estimates of the growth in earnings per share. The analysis also was performed in terms of the dollar change in earnings; when differences or similarities in the alternative metrics are sufficiently interesting, we comment upon them.

The formula for the average mean squared forecast error in growth is

$$\text{MSFE} = 1/N \sum_{i=1}^{N} (P_i - R_i)^2 \tag{4}$$

where

P_i is the consensus prediction of growth for firm i

R_i is the actual of growth for firm i

N is the number of observations.

Note that MSFE can be calculated for each month in which forecasts are prepared. Thus, we have twelve values of MSFE for each year. We now examine the partitioning of the MSFE.

A Partitioning by Level of Aggregation

Institutions differ in the way their analysts prepare forecasts for individual firms. Some institutions start with forecasts for the economy as a whole, then prepare industry studies, and finally prepare forecasts for individual firms (top-down approach). Other institutions start with the forecasts for individual firms and only after such forecasts are prepared, check with the economists' forecasts for macroeconomic consistency (bottom-up approach). Thus, it is useful to examine the level of aggregation at which serious errors are being made: are they made at the economy level, the industry level, or the individual firm level?

The mean squared error of the forecasts can be partitioned as follows

$$\text{MSFE} = 1/N\sum_{i=1}^{N}(P_i - R_i)^2 = (\bar{P} - \bar{R})^2 + 1/N\sum_{j=1}^{J} N_j[(\bar{P}_j - \bar{P}) - (\bar{R}_j - \bar{R})]^2$$

$$+ 1/N\sum_{j=1}^{J}\sum_{i=1}^{Nj}[(P_i - \bar{P}_j) - (R_i - \bar{R}_j)]^2 \qquad (5)$$

where

$\bar{P}$ is the mean value for P across all companies

$\bar{R}$ is the mean value for R across all companies

$\bar{P}_j$ is the mean value for P across all companies in industry j

$\bar{R}_j$ is the mean value for R across all companies in industry j

J is the number of industries in our sample

N_j is the number of firms in industry j.

The first term measures how much of the forecast error is due to the inability of analysts to predict what earnings per share will be for the economy (actually for the total of firms in our sample). The second term is a measure of how much of the total error is due to the analysts' mis-estimating the differential performance of individual industries. The final term measures how much of the error is due to the inability to predict how each firm will differ from its industry average.

By dividing both sides of equation (5) by MSFE and multiplying by 100, we express each source of error as a percentage of the total mean squared forecasting error. To perform this analysis, modification of our sample was necessary. In our earlier analysis, several industries were represented by very few firms. Because we are interested in errors in forecasting for industries as well as firms, for this part of our study we limited the sample to all industries containing seven or more firms. This restriction reduced our sample size to 225 firms.

B *Partitioning by Forecast Characteristics*

The decomposition discussed above was designed to aid management in finding the level of aggregation at which mistakes were made. This section presents a partitioning that looks for systematic errors in analysts' forecasts to improve (either mechanically or through discussions with analysts) their forecasts. Error is partitioned into bias, inefficiency, and a random component. The partition is given by[7]

$$\text{MSFE} = (\bar{P} - \bar{R})^2 + (1 - \beta)^2 S_P^2 + (1 - \rho^2) S_R^2 \tag{6}$$

where

β is the slope coefficient of the regression of R on P.

ρ is the correlation of P and R.

S_p is the standard deviation of P.

S_R is the standard deviation of R.

The first term represents bias, the tendency of the average forecast to overestimate or underestimate the true average. The second term represents inefficiency or the tendency for forecasts to be underestimated at high values of P and overestimated at low values, or vice versa. If the beta of actual growth regressed on forecasted growth is greater than one, forecasts are underestimates at high values and overestimates at low values. If beta is less than one, the forecasts are overestimates at high values and underestimates at low values. The final component is the random disturbance term, a measure of error not related to the value of the prediction P or the realization R.

C *Results*

The results of both decompositions are presented in Table 2.2.

1 Partition by Level of Aggregation

Table 2.2 presents the partition of MSFE, in percentage terms, by level of aggregation. Note that the error in forecasting the average level of growth in earnings per share for the economy is quite small and is below 3 percent of the total error. Analysts on average make very little error in estimating the average growth rate in earnings per share for the economy.

The vast majority of error in forecasting arises from misestimates of industry performance and company performance. The percentage of error due to industry misestimates starts as 37.3 percent in January and declines over time to 15.5 percent. Similarly, the percentage of error due to misestimating individual companies starts at 60.7 percent in January and increases to 83.7 percent by December.[8] We already know (from Section

Table 2.2
Partitioning of percentage error in growth

	Economy	Industry	Company	Bias	Inefficiency	Random error
January	2.0	37.3	60.7	1.0	27.4	71.6
February	2.2	36.8	61.0	1.1	26.3	72.6
March	2.4	36.2	61.5	1.7	14.2	84.1
April	2.1	33.1	64.8	1.8	8.6	89.6
May	2.5	32.6	64.9	2.2	7.8	90.0
June	2.7	29.4	67.9	2.5	9.5	88.0
July	2.8	30.2	67.0	2.6	6.7	90.7
August	2.7	30.6	66.8	2.4	7.7	89.9
September	2.7	26.5	70.8	2.4	8.5	89.1
October	2.3	26.3	71.5	2.2	6.4	91.4
November	1.3	23.0	75.7	1.6	3.4	95.0
December	0.8	15.5	83.7	0.9	3.0	96.1

III) that analysts become more accurate as the fiscal year progresses. Now we see that while analysts become more accurate in forecasting both industry performance and company performance, their ability to forecast industry performance grows relative to their ability to forecast company performance over the year.

2 Partitioning by Forecast Characteristics

Table 2.2 also presents the results of partitioning analysts' mean square error by forecast characteristics. It is apparent that bias is an extremely small source of error and in all months is below 3 percent.[9] Note that inefficiency starts as a fairly important component of the error but its importance diminishes as successive forecasts are made. The percentage of error accounted for by inefficiency begins at about 27 percent for early forecasts and shrinks to 3 percent as successive forecasts are made during the year. The percent of error due to random error grows from 71.6 percent to 96. 1 percent over the year. This initial importance of inefficiency is due primarily to the tendency of analysts to systematically overestimate the growth for high growth companies and to overestimate shrinkage in earnings for very low growth companies. This can be seen from the fact that the beta from equation (6) was below one for all three years examined.[10] This indicates that a linear correction applied to analysts' forecasts of growth could improve these forecasts.

V Relationship of Errors in Adjacent Periods

Are the firms for which analysts make large errors in forecasting in one year the same as those for which they make large errors in the adjacent year? The answer to this question is clearly *yes*. For both errors in change and errors in growth, we divided firms into five equal groups by size of error in each month for each year. We then examined whether a firm that fell into one quintile in a particular month in one year ended up in the same or adjacent quintiles that month in the next year.

The tendency for firms to remain in the same quintile is statistically significant in all cases (by a chi-squared test) at the 1 percent level. This is true whether the analysis is performed in terms of change in earnings or growth rates in earnings. These results support the proposition that firms for which analysts prepare poor forecasts in any year tend to be the same firms for which they prepare poor forecasts in the subsequent year.

VI Dispersion of Analysts' Estimates

Up to this point, we have examined properties of estimates by consensus. The forecasts by consensus are an average of the forecasts produced by all analysts following that company. In this section, we examine some characteristics of the differences of opinion among analysts about a company's growth rate in earnings per share. We use the standard deviations computed across different analysts' estimates of the same company's growth rate at a point in time as our measure of difference of opinion. We examine three topics in this section. First, does the standard deviation of analysts' estimates decrease over time? Second, do the analysts consistently make more diverse forecasts for companies in some industries than they do for others? Finally, is the divergence of opinion between analysts associated with the size of forecast error in the average (consensus) forecast? When analysts disagree about the level of future earnings for any firm, a plausible reason is that earnings for that firm are difficult to forecast. If this is true, then a high standard deviation of forecasts by different analysts should be associated with a high error in the forecast by consensus.

We now examine the first of these issues, the time pattern of the divergence of analysts' estimates. Table 2.3 presents the average standard deviation of analysts' estimates of growth for each month from January to December. Note that, although there is some decline in the average dispersion as the estimates get closer to the end of the year, the dispersion

Table 2.3
Average standard deviation of analysts' estimates of growth

Number of months before December	Overall	1976	1977	1978
11	.104	.134	.096	.081
10	.102	.126	.099	.080
9	.093	.105	.098	.077
8	.086	.100	.083	.074
7	.080	.092	.081	.067
6	.080	.096	.077	.066
5	.079	.094	.079	.065
4	.080	.094	.079	.068
3	.076	.087	.074	.068
2	.073	.082	.071	.066
1	.074	.086	.072	.065
0	.067	.073	.065	.062

is not uniform. Most of the decrease in dispersion across analysts occurs in the first four months of the year. From May on, there is only a slight decline and this decline does not occur in every month in either the combined three year analysis or in any individual year.[11] The only other month of major decline occurs from November to December. Note that, while the standard deviation of the analysts' estimates is fairly stable over the last eight months of the year, the accuracy of the analysts' estimate by consensus is markedly improving. Analysts are producing more accurate forecasts, but the disagreement between analysts is not shrinking.

The second question we examined was whether the disagreement among analysts differed across industries. To test this effect, we first calculated the average standard deviation in analysts' estimates of growth for firms in each industry. This result gave us a measure of divergence of opinion of analysts' forecasts for each industry. We then calculated the Spearman rank correlation between the dispersion (standard deviation) of analysts' estimates for each industry in one year with the same measures in other years. When we compared the standard deviations for June estimates across the 17 industries for 1976 and 1977, the rank correlation was .63 and for 1977 and 1978 it was .79. The rank correlation between forecasts' dispersions for other months was similar. In all cases, the results were statistically significant at the 1 percent level. The industries we

Table 2.4

SIC	Industry name
451	Air transportation
331	Steel
401	Railroads
260	Paper and paper containers
280	Chemical
371	Automobile, automobile parts, and trucks
291	Integrated oil
208	Beverages
353	Machinery construction and oil well
602	Banks
492	Pipelines and natural gas distribution
491	Electric companies
271	Newspaper and magazines
284	Soaps and cosmetics
631	Life insurance
357	Office and business equipment
283	Drug

Three digit industries ranked from (top) those industries for which analysts had most disagreement about future earnings to those for which they had least (bottom).

examined are listed in Table 2.4 in order (from top to bottom) of those with the greatest disagreement on average over the three years to those with the least.

The final question we examined was whether the error in the forecast by consensus of earnings growth was related to analysts' uncertainty about earnings growth. To study this, we used the absolute error in the forecast of growth for each company as our measure of error. We used the standard deviation of analysts' estimates in growth rates as our measure of analysts' uncertainty. For each month, we regressed the absolute error in the forecasts of growth against our measure of uncertainty of analysts' forecasts. This gave us a total of 36 regressions.[12]

The results of those regressions for every other month in each year are displayed in Table 2.5. From the full results, we see that the *t* value associated with the regression coefficient was statistically significant in each of the 36 regressions. There is a strong and significant relationship between

Table 2.5
Absolute error in growth = $a + b$ (divergence of analysts' opinion) + ε

	January			March			May			July			September			November		
	76	77	78	76	77	78	76	77	78	76	77	78	76	77	78	76	77	78
a	.134	.015	.068	.051	.007	.097	.060	.023	.068	.061	.047	.053	.051	.015	.048	.014	.021	.046
b	.769	2.030	1.585	1.565	1.891	1.107	1.401	1.701	1.296	.972	1.195	1.233	1.295	1.334	.772	1.051	.853	.402
R^2	.42	.72	.28	.34	.69	.19	.25	.65	.25	.24	.50	.29	.44	.42	.30	.50	.46	.16

Median *R*-square .40
Range of *R*-square .13–.77

error and uncertainty. The median R-square was .40 with a range from .13 to .77. Although there was no clear time pattern to the parameters of the regression relationship, the coefficient on analysts' uncertainty appeared to be smaller in the last two months of the year.

VII Summary

In this paper, we have explored the characteristics of analysts' estimates of the growth rate in earnings per share. We have shown that, on average, over a wide variety of error measures, analysts' errors decline monotonically as the end of the fiscal year approaches. When we partitioned analysts' error we found that analysts were accurate in estimating the average level of growth in earnings for all stocks in our sample. The error in estimating company growth (with industry error removed) was larger (and in some months much larger) than the size of the error due to misestimating the level of industry earnings. When partitioning by source of error we saw that early in the forecasted year, analysts had a marked tendency to overestimate the growth rates of securities they believed would perform well and to underestimate the growth rate of companies they believed would perform poorly. We next showed that there is persistent difficulty in forecasting growth rates for some companies. If analysts on average have large errors when forecasting the growth of a company in one year, they are likely to have difficulty in the next year.

Finally, we examined some characteristics of the divergence across analysts in their estimates of growth rates in earnings per share. Analysts tend to have greater divergence of opinion for the first four months of a year. However, there is no systematic decrease in divergence of opinion over the rest of the year. Analysts have greater disagreement about the growth of certain industries. They tend to disagree more about the earnings of the same industries in different years. Finally, disagreement is related to analysts' errors.

Notes

This paper won a prize from the Institute of Quantitative Research in Finance competitive paper competition for the year 1982.

1. See [2], [3], [5], and [8]. Crichfield, Dyckman, and Lakonishok [4] use data on a larger number of forecasts over a long period of time for a relatively small (46) sample of firms. This last article comes closest to the analysis in this paper. See [1] for additional discussion of related work.

2. Crichfield, Dyckman, and Lakonishok [4] examine the size and convergent rate of errors as well as present one partitioning of sources of errors. Our study differs from theirs in several ways. Our sample of firms is much larger (over 400 versus 46). We present more analysis of pattern of errors within years and the partitioning of errors. We analyze predictability of errors for individual firms and the relationship of difficulty of prediction to error size. Their sample of years was larger than ours and they placed more emphasis on pattern of errors between succeeding years.

3. A large amount of data checking was performed. We ran all the normal screens. We crosschecked all stock splits and stock dividends with CRSP and COMPUSTAT. As a further check on splits and dividends we used Moody's. In almost all cases, we were able to resolve inconsistencies. Lynch, Jones and Ryan were very helpful in this process and we thank them. In total, we deleted 11 firms in which an inconsistency existed, but we were unable to check its accuracy. An example would be the appearance of a $16 forecast when all other analysts were forecasting about 16¢. We eliminated only firms with this type of extreme divergence in estimates. In practice, we either found this type of extreme estimate or an estimate such as 36¢ that could be legitimate and, hence, was retained.

4. At several points in the analysis, the impact of including firms with earnings of less than 20¢ is discussed. The large impact of deleting firms with earnings of less than 20¢ can be seen by the fact that while only 30 out of 1242 observations were deleted, the mean square error in the analysts' estimates of growth was cut by more than one-half when these few observations were excluded.

5. See [9] and [10]. Once again, firms with earnings less than 20¢ were deleted when growth was examined.

6. Before eliminating firms with earnings less than 20¢, we did not observe this consistency from year to year in measures using growth, although the error declined from month to month. This inconsistency was caused primarily by a firm with earnings of 1¢ in one year causing an error in the thousands. For such a skewed sample, it is worthwhile examining the median as a measure of central tendency. We did so, and the results similar to those shown in Table 2.1 were obtained.

7. This method of partitioning was derived by Mincer and Zarnovitz [7]. It is the same method of partitioning used by Crichfield, Dyckman, and Lakonishok [4]. Our results differ from theirs in that they examine the log of growth and used a much smaller sample size.

8. This analysis was repeated for the entire industry sample, including firms with earnings less than 20¢. This increased the sample size from 216 to 225 in 1976 but resulted in an entirely different breakdown of error in growth. These firms had gigantic analysts' errors in terms of growth rate and because they were not concentrated in one industry, the importance of industry error dropped markedly. The analysis also was repeated in terms of error in earnings change per share. The partitioning is indistinguishable from that presented in Table 2.2.

9. Note that the measure of bias used here is the same as the first term in the partitioning by level of aggregation. The numerical value is different because the sample is different. The analysis by level of aggregation used a subsample with heavy representation from a few industries. In this section, we use the full sample. However, note that with either sample the misestimate of average earnings is very small.

10. When the error in forecasting earnings change was examined, beta was much closer to one and the percentage error due to inefficiency was much smaller.

11. Crichfield, Dyckman, and Lakonishok [4] found no significant pattern when they examined the same question. They found some tendency for a decrease but not in all years. The number of analysts following the firm is fairly constant over the year.

12. Regressions were also run between the absolute dollar error in forecast and the standard deviation of analysts' dollar forecasts. In addition, squared errors were examined. The results were consistent with the results described in the text and reported in Table 2.5. The relationships were not quite so strong though still statistically significant and were more unstable. For example, when the relationship was formulated in dollar values rather than growth, the median R-square was .29 instead of .40.

References

[1] Armstrong, J. "Relative Accuracy of Methods Used to Forecast Annual Earnings." Working Paper, Wharton School, University of Pennsylvania (1982).

[2] Brown, L., and M. Rozeff. "The Superiority of Analysts Forecasts as a Measure of Expectations: Evidence From Earnings." *The Journal of Finance*, Vol. 33 (March 1978), pp. 1–16.

[3] Cragg, J., and B. Malkiel. "The Consensus and Accuracy of Some Predictions of the Growth of Corporate Earnings." *The Journal of Finance* Vol. 23 (March 1968), pp. 67–84.

[4] Crichfield, T.; T. Dyckman; and J. Lakonishok, "An Evaluation of Security Analysts' Forecasts." *The Accounting Review*, Vol. 53 (July 1978), pp. 651–668.

[5] Elton, Edwin J., and Martin J. Gruber. "Earnings Estimate and The Accuracy of Expectational Data." *Management Science*, Vol. 19 (April 1972), pp. 409–424.

[6] Elton, Edwin J.; Martin J. Gruber; and Mustafa Gultekin. "Earnings Expectation and Share Prices." *Management Science*, Vol. 27 (September 1981), pp. 975–987.

[7] Elton, Edwin J.; Martin J. Gruber; and Suk Mo Koo. "Expectational Data: The Effect of Quarterly Reports." Working Paper, New York University.

[8] Mincer, J., and V. Zarnovitz. "The Valuation of Economic Forecasts." In *Economic Forecasts and Expectations*, Jacob Mincer, ed., National Bureau of Economic Research (1969).

[9] Richard, R. "Analysts' Performance and the Accuracy of Corporate Earnings Forecasts." *The Journal of Business*, Vol. 49 (July 1976), pp. 350–357.

[10] Theil, H. *Applied Economic Forecasting*. North-Holland Publishing Company (1966).

[11] ———. *Economic Forecasts and Policy*. North-Holland Publishing Company (1958).

3 Expectations and Share Prices

Edwin J. Elton, Martin J. Gruber,
and Mustafa Gultekin

I Introduction

A central theme of modern investment theory is that expectations about firm characteristics are incorporated into security prices. This theme can be found in most investment texts and is utilized in much of the current research in finance. Not only does this belief pervade academia it is commonly held by the financial community.

Surprisingly, in light of the strength of this belief, there is very little empirical evidence to support it. Almost all research which attempts to measure the impact of expectations utilizes not expectational data but historical extrapolations of past data that the authors hope will serve as a proxy for expectational data. This is true for most tests of valuation models as well as almost all tests in the efficient markets literature.

The purpose of this article is to examine the importance of expectations concerning one variable, earnings per share, in the determination of share price. Earnings per share is considered a key variable in determining share price and has been studied extensively in the efficient markets literature. In almost all studies, expectations of future earnings per share are formulated as an extrapolation of past earnings.[1] Justification for using historical extrapolation is sometimes found in tests of the accuracy of extrapolated data in forecasting future earnings.

While tests such as those found in [3], [4], and [5] provide some evidence of the relative accuracy of historical extrapolation versus expectational data as forecasts of the future, they do not address the question of the role of expectations in share price formation. The purpose of this paper is to directly address this question. More specifically, we will address the question of the role of actual future changes in earnings on stock returns, the role of expected changes in earnings, and finally the role of changes in expectations.

In addition to examining the importance of expectations and earnings, we briefly explore the issue of the scale of returns that can be earned by being "more accurate" than average forecasts. If market prices reflect average expectations, then superior forecasting ability should be rewarded with excess returns. We will explore both the size of these returns and the timing of their occurrence.

II Overview: Variables Examined and Sample Design

The testing of the impact of earnings expectations has awaited the development of a broad consistent data base. Lynch, Jones and Ryan have constructed a data base which contains one and two-year consensus earnings estimates on all corporations followed by one or more analysts at most major brokerage firms.[2] Lynch, Jones, and Ryan define the consensus earnings estimate for any stock as a simple arithmetic average of the estimates prepared by all of the analysts following that stock. Given this data base, a study can be made of the role of average expectations in price formation and in particular the importance of earnings expectations in determining share price.

In order to study the role of expectations, we need some measure of the excess returns that can be earned from knowledge concerning future earnings. To examine this, we analyzed the actual growth rate in earnings. The actual growth rate was defined as actual earnings for the forecast year minus actual earnings in the previous fiscal year, divided by actual earnings in the previous fiscal year. This variable is computed only for those firms for which the denominator is positive. This does not bias the results of our tests as the denominator is known at the time this variable is formulated. However, the population of stocks to which our tests apply is restricted. Letting G_t stand for the growth rate in earnings,

$$G_t = \frac{E_t - E_{t-1}}{E_{t-1}} \quad \text{for } E_{t-1} > 0 \qquad (1)$$

where E_t is reported earnings per share at time t.

Anticipating our results for a moment, we will find that knowledge of actual growth will allow a significant risk adjusted excess return to be earned. This indicates that growth in earnings is an important variable affecting share price, and that expectations concerning this variable are worth studying.

If expectations determine share price, then knowledge of the average value of these expectations should already be incorporated in the share price, and buying on the basis of average expectations should not lead to excess returns. Thus, the second variable we examined was the consensus forecast of the growth rate in per share earnings. We call this the forecasted growth rate. It is formulated as the consensus forecast of fiscal year earnings minus the actual earnings in the previous fiscal year divided by the actual earnings that occurred in the previous fiscal year. Since this measure cannot be interpreted for a negative denominator, it is computed only for those companies for which the denominator is positive. To be more explicit, let

$$FG_t = \frac{C_t - E_{t-1}}{E_{t-1}} \quad \text{for } E_{t-1} > 0, \tag{2}$$

where C_t is the consensus forecasts of the earnings per share that will occur at time t, and FG_t is the consensus forecast of the growth rate in earnings per share.

If expectations are important and are incorporated in present prices, then one should observe larger excess returns by having knowledge concerning the error in the growth estimate, than by knowing actual growth itself. Investment in a firm with high actual growth should not necessarily lead to excess returns unless investors were forecasting low growth. Thus, if expectations are important, knowledge concerning differences between actual growth and forecasted growth should lead to higher excess returns than knowledge concerning growth itself. Thus, the third variable we examine is actual growth minus forecasted growth. This differential growth can be expressed as

$$DG_t = G_t - FG_t. \tag{3}$$

Since the effect of differences between expectations and realizations is the key phenomena that we wish to study, we have measured this phenomena in two additional ways. The first is the error in the earnings forecast defined at the actual earnings in the forecast year minus the forecast earnings. If we denote this variable by M_t for misestimate in consensus forecast of earnings, then

$$M_t = E_t - C_t. \tag{4}$$

The second is the percentage forecast error, which is measured as the actual earnings in the forecast year minus the forecast earnings divided by the absolute value of the actual earnings. If we use $\%M_t$ to stand for the percentage, then

$$\%M_t = \frac{E_t - C_t}{|E_t|}. \tag{5}$$

While most of our analysis consists of an examination of one year forecasts, we decided to take a brief look at the excess returns associated with errors in two year forecasts. We duplicated the one-year measures and examined the error in earnings forecast for two years and the percentage error in earnings forecast for two years.

If consensus forecasts are more important than the actual level of future earnings in determining prices, then one should be able to do a better job of selecting stocks by knowing the change in consensus forecasts than by knowing actual earnings. To test this hypothesis, a variable measuring the percentage adjustment in forecasts over time was used. This variable is formulated as negative of the following quantity: the forecast of earnings prepared for the next (as opposed to this) fiscal year minus the forecast of earnings for the same fiscal year made one year later divided by this latter number. To better understand this variable, let ${}_{t-a}C_t$ stand for the consensus forecast for earnings at time t which are produced at time $t - a$, and ${}_{(t-a+12)}C_t$ stands for the forecast for time t which is produced 12 months later. Then the forecast revision denoted by FR_r can be represented as

$$FR_t = -\frac{{}_{(t-a)}C_t - {}_{(t-a+12)}C_t}{{}_{(t-a+12)}C_t}. \tag{6}$$

III The Sample

The raw data consisted of a monthly file of one and two-year earnings forecasts prepared in the years 1973, 1974, and 1975. We limited our sample of data in several ways. First, the sample was restricted to firms having fiscal years ending on December 31. By confining our sample to firms with fiscal years ending on the same date, forecasts prepared a certain number of months (e.g., nine) in advance of the end of the fiscal year, fall on the same calendar date. This procedure assures that the same general economic influences (e.g., the economy, the market, etc.) were available to all forecasters at the time forecasts were prepared. The date of December 31 was selected because more companies had fiscal years ending on that date than on any other.

Second, forecasts are restricted to two forecast dates, March and September. March was selected because it is the earliest date on which financial data for the previous fiscal year would be reported by most companies. September was selected as a month that is far enough from the first forecast and far enough into the fiscal year that significant evidence on companies' performance during the year should be available. Yet it is not so far into the year that earnings are known with certainty. Both dates are used for all variables involving one-year forecasts. However, so few two-year forecasts were available in March that only the September date could be used when examining two-year forecasts.

Finally, because we are interested in the impact of consensus forecasts, the sample was restricted to companies which were followed by three or more analysts. The consensus prepared from less than three forecasts could be idiosyncratic and not typical of broad feelings about the stock.

The final sample consisted of a total of 919 one-year forecasts of the fiscal years 1973, 1974, and 1975 and a total of 710 two-year forecasts of fiscal years 1974, 1975, and 1976. Because of negative earnings, some firms had to be eliminated over several measures. This caused the sample size to fall to as low as 913 and 696 for one and two-year forecasts, respectively. As discussed earlier Lynch, Jones and Ryan survey most large brokerage firms. Since we have included all stocks followed by three or more analysts, the group of stocks in our sample can be considered a universe of all stocks with important analyst interest. Since brokerage firms are interested in providing information to their customers, our sample should include most stocks of major institutional interest.

IV Methodology

The first step in our procedure was for each time period studied (March and September) and for each year to rank all stocks on each variable and to divide the stocks into deciles by each variable. For example, we formed deciles for the forecasted growth rates made in September 1973 with the first decile containing the 10% of the stocks with the highest forecasted growth rate. For each decile, we calculated the average value of the variable being studied (in this case, forecasted growth).

In order to determine whether certain types of information lead to excess returns, it is necessary to have a measure of what return is expected. If we have a measure of expected return, then excess return is the difference between actual return and expected return. In order to measure expected return, we use the market model. The market model is a relationship between the return on a security and the return on a market index.

Let

1. r_{it} be the return on portfolio i in period t.
2. r_{mt} be the return on the market in period t.
3. α_i and β_i be parameters for portfolio i.
4. e_{it} be deviations from the model.

The market model is:

$$r_{it} = \alpha_i + \beta_i r_{mt} + e_{it}$$

Using the market model leads to expected returns being determined by the security's normal relationship with the market (β_i), the market return in the period (r_m) and the security's average nonmarket return (α_i). Using the market model excess return is

$$r_{it} - (\alpha_i + \beta_i r_{mt}).$$

Although the market model is frequently used in finance, there are some problems with its use that can lead to biased tests. First there is measurement error in the coefficients and if this varies systematically with the test statistic, it can lead to an appearance of a relationship when none exists. This was guarded against in several ways.

First we calculated the market model for the deciles discussed earlier. Using grouped data is one way of reducing the measurement error. The one variable where measurement error can be especially bothersome is beta. As Blume [1] has shown the error in measuring beta varies systematically with its difference from one. The use of grouped data helps. In addition, we examined the individual betas on the groups. There was no systematic pattern, nor did any group beta differ very much from one (the range was 0.93 to 1.09). Given this result, we judged that any further adjustment in beta was unnecessary. In the original CAPM tests grouping data was common. Litzenberger and Ramaswamy [7] and Ross and Roll [9] have criticized this on the grounds that the CAPM is a theory of the pricing of single assets and as such has to be shown to explain differences in asset returns. Our purpose here is not to test CAPM but rather to examine the effect of expectations on share price. Hence grouping is a reasonable procedure for dealing with measurement error.

The second problem in the use of the market model is its difference from a capital asset pricing model. There are numerous general equilibrium models that have been derived. If one of these ultimately is shown to be correct, then better estimates of returns should be obtained by using that model rather than the market model. Brennan [2] has shown that the use of alternative models can make some difference. However, in this study the magnitude of the results, the grouping techniques, and the spread in the β_i's should mean that there is minimal chance of this source of potential bias explaining the results.[3] For example, assuming that the beta for each group was equal to one would not change any of our conclusions.

The market model was estimated by treating each decile as an equally weighted portfolio of the stocks which composed it and estimating the market model parameters for each decile. The market index we used was the Standard and Poor's index adjusted for dividends. The parameters of the model were estimated in each case using 60 monthly observations on returns up to and including the forecast month. The data dissemination procedure followed by Lynch Jones and Ryan means that forecasts are in the hands of the subscriber by the end of the month. The estimated parameters of the market model were then used in conjunction with actual market returns to forecast normal risk adjusted returns for each of the deciles during each of the 24 months after the forecast month. The risk adjusted returns in each month were close to but not exactly equal to zero. This should not be surprising to the reader. The sum of the residuals in any one month should equal zero only if they are weighted in market proportions and include all stocks in the index. Our sample meets neither of these conditions. We adjusted our residuals to have a mean (across all deciles) of zero for ease of presentation. Our primary statistical test is a *rank* correlation test, subtracting a constant from each entry can not effect the rank. Thus our adjustment had very little effect on the numbers reported and had no effect on their statistical significance or on our conclusions.

As discussed earlier, we calculated risk adjusted excess returns for each of the deciles for each of the variables for the 24 months after the forecast month. In the case of the March data we calculated risk adjusted excess returns from April on and in the case of September from October on. This was done for each of the three years for which we had data. We combined these years and have reported the average risk adjusted return across the three years for each decile.

To aid in understanding the results, we report the sum of the risk adjusted excess returns from the month after the forecast month to the month under consideration, rather than reporting the risk adjusted excess returns in any one month.[4] Thus, for March forecasts, the entry in month 3 is the sum of the risk adjusted excess returns earned in April, May, and

June. This allows the reader to more easily determine the cumulative effect of any influence.

After examining the data we determined that there were no further effects after month 15 for March data and month 9 for September data. Thus, we have not reported results beyond these dates.

In reporting results we have combined the deciles in two ways. First, we report the cumulative risk adjusted excess returns in the upper 30%, middle 40%, and lowest 30% of firms ranked on each variable. Second, we report the cumulative risk adjusted excess returns in the upper 50%. Since the risk adjusted excess returns add to zero, across all deciles the risk adjusted excess return in the upper 50% is the negative of the lowest 50%. We chose to present the data in this way since using the ungrouped deciles increases the size of the tables substantially without providing additional insights.

The reader can judge the economic significance of the results by examining the cumulative residuals in Tables 3.1 through 3.4. These excess returns are reported before transaction costs. While estimates of round trip transaction costs differ, a reasonable estimate is in the range of two to four percent. Thus, cumulative residuals in excess of 4% can be accepted as of economic significance.

It is also logical to examine whether the relationship between any of the variables under study and excess return is statistically significant. This was examined by computing Spearman rank order correlation coefficient between the decile and the rank order of the cumulative excess return for each decile. A statistically significant rank order correlation coefficient would indicate that there was a significant relationship between the variable under study and cumulative excess returns. Furthermore, by using a nonparametric test this statement is free of any distributional assumptions (across deciles) about the pattern of excess returns and/or the variables under study. Note that when we compute, the statistical significance of the cumulated residuals in successive periods these tests are not independent.

Table 3.5 presents the average values for each variable studied in this paper.

V Results

The first question to analyze is: Can an investor earn excess returns by selecting stocks on the basis of the consensus growth rate forecasted by security analysts (Equation (2))? The answer is no. There is no discernable pattern in the cumulative excess returns. In some months the stocks for

Table 3.1
Time series of cumulative excess returns ranked by error in the forecast of the growth rate (equation (3)) for March data

Month	1	2	3	4	5	6	7	8
Upper 30%	0.0166	0.0221	0.0221	0.0321	0.0630	0.0698	0.0767	0.0782
Middle 40%	−0.0069	−0.0037	+0.0037	−0.0001	−0.0139	−0.0170	−0.0038	−0.0041
Bottom 30%	−0.0075	−0.0169	−0.0173	−0.0320	−0.0444	−0.0470	−0.0719	−0.0726
Rank correlation[a]	0.71**	0.73**	0.76**	0.83*	0.83*	0.76**	0.84*	0.87*
Month	**9**	**10**	**11**	**12**	**13**	**14**	**15**	
Upper 30%	0.0855	0.0664	0.0729	0.0775	0.0909	0.0801	0.0897	
Middle 40%	−0.0063	−0.0162	−0.0107	−0.0120	−0.0144	−0.0209	−0.0126	
Bottom 30%	−0.0773	−0.0448	−0.0588	−0.0731	−0.0717	−0.0523	−0.0729	
Rank correlation[a]	0.89*	0.90*	0.85*	0.87*	0.93*	0.92*	0.89*	

a. Rank correlation coefficients
* Indicates significance at the 1% level.
** Indicates significance at the 5% level.

Table 3.2
Time series of cumulative excess returns for the error in the forecast of growth rate using September data (equation (3))

	1	2	3	4	5	6	7	8	9
Upper 30%	0.0187	0.0272	0.0421	0.0429	0.0466	0.0506	0.0618	0.0638	0.0680
Middle 40%	0.0100	0.0092	0.0014	−0.0035	−0.0036	−0.0045	−0.0069	−0.0065	−0.0034
Lower 30%	−0.0318	−0.0394	−0.0441	−0.0384	−0.0421	−0.0445	−0.0526	−0.0550	−0.0635
Rank correlation[a]	0.77*	0.88*	0.84*	0.88*	0.99*	0.92*	0.95*	0.94*	0.85*

a. Rank correlation coefficients are computed across deciles.
* Indicates significance at 1% level.
** Indicates significance at 5% level.

Table 3.3
Excess returns for months 7 and 13 March data

Time of analysis		Forecasted growth equation (2)	Actual growth equation (1)	Error in growth equation (3)	Error in forecast (one year) equation (4)	Percentage error in forecast equation (5)
MONTH 7	Upper 30%	−0.0064	+0.0591	+0.0767	0.0633	+0.0711
	Middle 40%	0.0068	0.0006	−0.0033	0.0092	−0.0033
	Lower 30%	−0.0028	−0.0597	−0.0719	−0.0754	−0.0719
	Upper 50%	−0.0080	0.0463	0.0426	0.0426	0.0426
	Rank correlation[a]	−0.35	0.90*	0.84*	0.98*	0.90*
MONTH 13	Upper 30%	+0.0006	+0.0748	+0.0908	+0.0715	+0.0861
	Middle 40%	−0.0093	−0.0191	−0.0144	+0.0022	−0.0156
	Lower 30%	+0.0019	−0.0493	−0.0717	−0.0743	−0.0651
	Upper 50%	−0.0139	0.0411	0.0577	0.0571	0.0554
	Rank correlation[a]	−0.30	0.88*	0.93*	0.96*	0.85*

a. Rank Correlation coefficients are computed across deciles.
* Indicates significance at the 1% level.
** Indicates significance at the 5% level.

Table 3.4
Excess returns for month 7 from September data

	Forecasted growth equation (1)	Actual growth equation (2)	Error in growth equation (3)	Error in forecast (one year) equation (4)	Error in forecast (one year) equation (5)	Error in forecast (two years) equation (4)	Error in forecast (two years) equation (5)	Forecast revision equation (6)
Upper 30%	0.0135	0.0399	0.0618	0.0567	0.0652	0.0773	0.0792	0.0889
Middle 40%	−0.0079	−0.0161	−0.0069	−0.0053	−0.0084	−0.0023	−0.0062	−0.0141
Lower 30%	−0.0029	−0.0186	−0.0526	−0.0497	−0.0541	−0.0741	−0.0711	−0.0701
Upper 50%	0.0073	0.0245	0.0405	0.0402	0.0409	0.0496	0.0498	0.0512
Rank correlation[a]	0.37	0.53	0.95*	0.95*	0.89*	0.96*	0.98*	0.83*

a. Rank correlation coefficients are computed across deciles.
* Indicates significance at the 1% level.
** Indicates significance at the 10% level.

Table 3.5
Mean values for each variable

	Equat. (1) forecasted growth	Equat. (2) actual growth	Equat. (3) error in growth	Equat. (4) forecast error (1 yr)	Equat. (5) percentage forecast error (1 yr)	Equat. (4) percentage forecast error (2 yrs)	Equat. (5) percentage forecast error (2 yrs)	Equat. (6) forecast revision
March data								
Upper 30%	56.61%	107.45%	63.62%	1.08%	26.24%			
Middle 40%	6.9	8.27	1.35	0.01	−0.32			
Lower 30%	−9.16	−34.95	−38.88	1.05	−159.24			
Sept. data								
Upper 30%	81%	98.83%	26.36%	0.53%	14.72%	0.13%	26.74%	43.76%
Middle 40%	9.34	8.32	−0.17	−0.07	−0.23	−0.09	−3.75	1.19
Lower 30%	−15.75	−32.95	−27.02	−0.67	−94.01	−1.64	−155.29	−27.34

which high growth was forecasted had positive risk adjusted cumulative excess returns; in other months they had negative ones. As a further check we performed a rank order correlation test on the deciles in each month. The rank order correlation between forecasted growth and risk adjusted cumulative excess return was never significantly different from zero at the 1% level and only significantly different from zero from the 5% level in two months. In the months it was significant it was negative, which is opposite to what one would expect if growth estimates contained information which was not incorporated in stock prices. The lack of a pattern was even more evident in the September data. In no month was the cumulative excess return significantly different from zero at even the 5% level and the average cumulative excess return varied frequently from positive to negative. The results for each individual month is not reported in the paper but the results for selected months can be seen by examining Tables 3.3 and 3.4.

This lack of risk adjusted excess returns occurs even though the analysts were projecting some very large growth rates. In September the analysts were projecting that the average growth rate for the top decile would be over 100% and the growth rate in the second decile would be 33%. In contrast the earnings of stocks in the last decile were expected to decline by 34%.

A number of financial institutions purchase growth stocks as an investment strategy. In the three years we examined, pursuing such a strategy based on consensus estimates would not have led to superior returns, growth forecasts were already incorporated in the security prices. This is what one would expect if expectations are incorporated into security price.

On the other hand, our results show that growth is an important determinant of security returns. Investors with perfect forecasting ability could make risk adjusted excess returns. The results for individual months are not reported. However, the results for selected months, can be seen by examining Tables 3.3 and 3.4. From month 4 on, the rank order of excess returns for the deciles is significant at the 1% level. The excess return builds up to 7.23% for the upper 30% of all stocks by month 9. It then declines and builds up again to over 7%. A similar but less distinct pattern can be seen by examining the lowest 30%.

The risk adjusted excess returns from possessing perfect forecasting ability in September are much lower than they were from possessing perfect forecasting ability in March. Furthermore in most months the rank order of the deciles is insignificant at the 1% level (although it's still sometimes significant at the 5% level). This is what one would expect. By September investors have a much better idea of actual growth than they do in March.

If prices reflect consensus forecasts, then knowing the error in the consensus estimate of growth should lead to larger profits than just knowing actual growth. How large is the mis-estimate of actual growth by the analysts? In March, the average error for the 30% of the companies for which earnings growth was most underestimated was 63.6%, while the average error for the 30% of the companies for which growth was most overestimated was 38.9%. The corresponding numbers for September forecasts are 26.4% and 20.3%. It is apparent that while there are still large size errors in the September forecasts, the size of the error has decreased markedly between March and September. Analysts can improve the accuracy of their forecasts as interim earnings reports or as other information comes out and more information is available on company performance.

Tables 3.1 and 3.2 show the time series of cumulative risk adjusted excess return for the errors in the March and September estimates (Equation (3)). The rank order of the deciles is significant from the first month for both the September and March estimates. The risk adjusted excess returns build up very quickly in both cases. For the March forecasts, the risk adjusted excess returns are close to 7% by month 6 (September), the major increase occurring in month 5. Once again, the risk adjusted excess returns have a temporary peak in month 9 and then increase to a global peak in month 13. This rapid build-up is consistent with information about true earnings growth being disseminated over time and the market correctly incorporating the information.

Even in September investors with a better estimate of growth than the consensus had an opportunity for excess profits. Notice that while knowledge of the forecast error as of September allows an excess profit to be earned, perfect forecast ability did not allow an excess profit to be earned. This suggests that on average forecasts are accurate enough in September that excess profits can be earned only by isolating those cases where forecasted growth is very much different than actual.

The time pattern for all variables is very similar with March forecasts producing excess returns which level out after month 13 and September forecasts producing excess returns which level out after month 7. Consequently, we shall only report results for these months. The cumulated excess returns in these months are reported in Table 3.3 and Table 3.4. In addition, in Table 3.3 we show the risk adjusted cumulative excess returns

7 months after the March forecasts for comparison with the effect 7 months after the September forecast.

Note that among the variables discussed so far for both March and September forecasts, the risk adjusted excess return was highest for the error in the growth rate, next highest for actual growth and close to zero for the forecasted growth. What an investor desirous of making excess profits should be most concerned with is finding securities where his forecasts are not only good in the sense of being right but where they are both accurate and different from the consensus.

The same conclusion can be reached by examining errors in the earnings estimates. Tables 3.3 and 3.4 present the analysis of excess returns for the error in forecast earnings and the percentage error in earnings forecasts for one year forecasts as of March and September and two-year forecasts as of September. In each case the excess returns appear to be sufficient to cover transaction costs and the rank order correlation coefficient is significant at the 1% level.

Furthermore, the amount of excess returns that can be earned vary with the magnitude of the forecast error. The two-year estimates made in September and the one-year estimates made in March were considerably less accurate than the one-year forecast made in September. They also produced higher risk adjusted excess returns. However, even in September there is a considerable forecast error in year-end earnings. In September, the percentage forecast error was 26% for the top decile, 11.6% in the next decile, and 6.3% in the next. These errors, while lower, were still significant enough to lead to an excess risk adjusted return.

We have now examined evidence that consensus forecasts are incorporated into price. Further, we have seen that the ability to forecast with more accuracy than the consensus forecast can lead to an excess risk adjusted return. If consensus forecasts play a major role in price determination, then the ability to forecast consensus forecasts themselves should lead to a superior return. Since we have estimates of the earnings for each company made 15 months in advance (the two-year forecast as of September) and estimates of the same earnings made 12 months later (one-year forecast made in September of the following year), we can measure the impact of being able to forecast the change in the estimate (Equation (6)). As shown in Table 3.4, the returns from being able to estimate forecast revision are substantial. In fact, the return from forecasting future forecasts themselves is higher than the return from being able to forecast actual earnings. This is consistent with our other evidence that it is consensus forecasts which determine security prices.

Table 3.6
Error in growth* (forecast-actual)

Percentage of firms eliminated	Excess return if completely accurate	Excess return if 50% error	Excess return if 90% error
0%	0	0	0
10%	1.56	0.78	0.16
20%	2.88	1.44	0.29
30%	3.07	1.53	0.31
40%	4.32	2.16	0.43
50%	5.77	2.88	0.58
60%	7.35	3.67	0.74
70%	9.08	4.54	0.91
80%	9.90	4.95	0.99
90%	10.42	5.21	1.04

* Forecasts of one year growth rates prepared in March. Cumulative returns calculated as of April of the following year.

All of the results presented in this section could be used to analyze the amount of accuracy necessary to earn excess returns. Assume the analysts can identify firms that are in various deciles with respect to the error in estimated earnings. For example, suppose he could identify the 10% of the firms with the largest forecast error. Column 2 of Table 3.6 shows the cumulative excess return he would earn. Columns 3 and 4 assumes that he identifies the members of a decile with error. Column 3 assumes that 50% of the time he identifies a firm as a member of a decile he is randomly selecting from among all firms and 50% of the time he is accurate. Column 4 assumes that 90% of the time he is randomly selecting from all firms.

For example, if an analyst is attempting to select from among the 30% of the firms for which the consensus forecast most underestimate true earnings, and he is right 50% of the time, he will earn an excess risk adjusted return of 4.54%.

As can be seen from an examination of the table, a little bit of information leads to substantial cumulative excess returns. These kinds of excess returns provide some justification for the effort undertaken by many organizations to forecast earnings.

VI Conclusions

In this study we present evidence in support of the hypothesis that expectations are incorporated into security prices. In addition, we have analyzed the timing and size of returns from forecasts which are more accurate than the consensus. Since prices reflect consensus forecasts, the payoff from being accurate in forecasting is increased markedly as the consensus forecast becomes inaccurate. Finally, we have demonstrated that the payoff from being able to forecast the consensus estimate is higher than the payoff from being able to forecast earnings. The market reacts to expectational data. But despite this, or rather because of it Lord Keynes [6] appears to have been right when he likened professional investing to participating in a newspaper contest on a beauty contest, where "... each competitor has to pick, not those faces which he himself finds prettiest, but those which he thinks likeliest to catch the fancy of other competitors, all of whom are looking at the contest from the same point of view."

Notes

1. Malkiel and Cragg [8] used expectational data on earnings growth in a valuation model. However, their sample of expectational data was very limited.

2. Lynch, Jones and Ryan, a New York-based brokerage firm, have available in computer readable form consensus (average) earnings estimates updated monthly for the current and next fiscal year as well as forecasts of each individual analyst following each stock. They designate this as the I/B/E/S service. During the time period studied Lynch, Jones and Ryan surveyed brokerage firms. Our sample consisted of all stocks listed on the New York Stock Exchange which were followed by three or more analysts. The average number of analysts following each of these firms was slightly above seven. Furthermore, slightly less than 70 stocks were followed by ten or more analysts. The maximum number of analysts following any stock was 18.

3. We could have used differences from R_m, rather than the market model in reporting our results. However the reader might then question to what extent our conclusions were due to differences in market risk. Alternatively we could have followed Watts [10] methodology to force the Beta on each Portfolio to be exactly one. However since the differences in Beta from one were neither large nor systematically related to any criteria across our deciles we did not take this additional step.

4. Many authors accumulate residuals by calculating the product of one plus the residuals. The justification for this is that return over N periods is the product of the N one period returns. There is a difficulty with this procedure. The null hypothesis is that the residuals average zero. If this hypothesis is true, it is easy to show that the product of one plus the one period residuals minus one becomes negative and significantly so as N gets large. The sum of the residuals is zero under the null hypothesis and deviations from zero are indications of real effects.

References

1. Blume, Marshall, "Betas and their Regression Tendencies," *J. Finance* (June, 1975).

2. Brennan, M., "The Sensitivity of the Efficient Market Hypothesis to Alternative Specifications of the Market Model," *J. Finance*, Vol. 34 (1979), pp. 53–69.

3. Brown, B. and Rozeff, M., "The Superiority of Analyst Forecasts as Measures of Expectations: Evidence from Earnings." *J. Finance*, Vol. 33 (1978), pp. 1–16.

4. Cragg, L. and Malkiel, B., "The Consensus and Accuracy of Some Predictions of the Growth of Corporate Earnings," *J. Finance*, Vol. 23 (1968), pp. 67–84.

5. Elton, B. J. and Gruber, M. J., "Earnings Estimate and the Accuracy of Expectations Data," *Management Sci.*, Vol. 18 (1972), pp. 409–424.

6. Keynes, M., *The General Theory of Employment, Interest, and Money*, Harcourt, Brace and World, New York, 1964, p. 156.

7. Litzenberger, Robert and Ramaswamy, K., "The Effects of Personal Taxes and Dividends on Capital Asset Prices: Theory and Empirical Evidence," *J. Financial Econom.* (June 1979).

8. Malkiel, B. and Cragg, J., "Expectations and the Structure of Share Prices," *Amer. Econom. Rev.*, Vol. 60 (1970), pp. 601–617.

9. Roll, Richard and Ross, Steve, "An Empirical Investigation of Arbitrage Pricing Theory," *J. Finance* (December, 1980), pp. 1073–1105.

10. Watts, R. L., "Systematic 'Abnormal' Returns After Quarterly Savings Announcements," *J. Financial Econom.* (1978), pp. 127–150.

4

Expectational Data and Japanese Stock Prices

Edwin J. Elton and
Martin J. Gruber

I Introduction

A number of articles have appeared which analyze the impact of (earnings and) earnings estimates on security returns.[1] These articles contribute to our understanding of what variables affect security prices, the role of expectations in security price formation and the speed with which information is incorporated into share price. The majority of this literature has been concerned with the relationship between consensus of estimates of earnings and security returns. While the results of this literature are occasionally ambiguous the major conclusions are that:

(1) Actual earnings impact stock returns.

(2) The consensus forecast of growth in earnings is already incorporated in stock price and hence does not impact returns.

(3) Knowing the change in consensus forecast of growth in earnings ahead of time leads to a excess returns.

(4) Changes in consensus ranking of stocks may have an impact on returns after they are made public. The evidence here is more ambiguous than the evidence supporting the first three conditions.

While the results for consensus earnings forecasts and general performance forecasts are reasonably clear, the results for individual forecasters are much more ambiguous. For example, Elton, Gruber and Grossman (1986) found that past forecast accuracy could not be used to select individual forecasters who would subsequently perform well although consensus data was useful. In contrast, studies of the investment advice of Value Line show superior forecasting ability.[2]

The bulk of the research on analysts' predictions and performance has been done on U.S. markets. The purpose of this paper is to examine the impact of forecasts of earnings and sales in the Japanese economy, a topic that has not been examined before. The study is interesting because of the similarity and differences between the Japanese and U.S. markets. The aggregate value of shares listed on the Tokyo Stock Exchange is larger than the value of shares listed on the New York Stock Exchange. Given the volume of shares traded it should be as competitive as the New York Stock Exchange. On the other hand, the number of suppliers (brokerage firms and institutions) of information and in particular forecast data to the market is much smaller in Japan than in the U.S. The average number of analyses supplying forecasts of earnings per share for the 400 largest NYSE stocks according to IBES is 22. While for the 400 largest firms on the Tokyo Stock Exchange IBES reports six estimates.[3] Given the difference in number and the fact that for many Japanese stocks only one forecast exists, the impact of any forecaster can potentially be much more important in Japan than in the United States. The Japanese market may be more informationally inefficient than the U.S. markets.

In this chapter we examine the forecasts of earnings and sales prepared by Nomura Research Institute for Japanese stocks. We selected a single forecasting source rather than the consensus forecast since there is only a short history for consensus forecasts and for many stocks Nomura is the only forecaster in the consensus. Nomura was selected because it is the largest financial institution in Japan and prepares forecasts for more stocks than any other Japanese or non-Japanese participant in the market.

In section 2 we examine the impact of four types of variables on returns: actual growth, forecasted growth, errors in forecasted growth and changes in forecasted growth. The results indicate that earnings and sales impact share price and that estimates of these variables contain information. To study the impact of forecasts, returns had to be examined as excess returns. Section 2 closes with some evidence that information on changes in analysts' forecasts is not rapidly incorporated in share price. If information is incorporated slowly in share price then a potential for excess returns exists. This is examined in Section 3.

Section 3 examines the utilization of changes in analysts' estimates to construct a portfolio, highly correlated with an index, that capitalizes on analysts' forecasts while controlling risk. Using information that is clearly available to a decision maker, a portfolio is constructed that closely resembles the market and yet earns a consistently higher rate of return. Tests of the performance of this portfolio involve the incorporation of realistic transaction costs.

II The Importance of Growth in Sales and Earnings

The purpose of this section is to analyze the impact of estimates of growth in sales and earnings on share prices. In order to do so we need to employ a model of return expectations.

2.1 Estimating Expected Returns

In most studies of earnings surprises in the U.S. market, excess returns from following any strategy are measured relative to expectations formed from a single-index (market) model. While a single-index model may do an adequate job of describing risk in the U.S. market (debate continues as to whether it does or does not) empirical evidence strongly suggest one index is not a sufficient description of the risk structure of the Tokyo Stock Exchange. For example, the empirical work of Elton and Gruber (1988) and Hamao (1988) indicates that four indexes are necessary to describe risk. Some of the problems involved with the single-index model are shown in Elton and Gruber (1988) who find that using the single-index model:

(a) Return is inversely related to Beta in the Japanese market.

(b) Explanatory power decreases dramatically as the size (market capitalization) of companies decreases. One index accounts for less than 25% of the return on the smallest 20% of the stocks included in the Nomura Research Institute 400 security stock index. The four-index model accounts for better than 70% of the return on these same stocks.

These problems have motivated us to use the four-index model rather than the market model to adjust for risk in all the research which follows.

The four-index model we employ is derived using factor analysis on historical data. The detailed description of the methodology behind the four-index model is beyond the scope of this paper. The reader interested in a detailed description of how these indexes are developed is referred to Elton and Gruber (1988). However, in the last section of this paper the validity of the four-index model will be demonstrated by its usefulness in constructing an index fund.

2.2 Tests

Having constructed a model of return expectations we now turn to the impact of earnings and sales as well as earnings estimates and sales estimates on price.

The tests in this section are based on all companies listed on the Tokyo Stock Exchange which had a March fiscal year and for which Nomura Research Institute prepared earnings and sales forecasts for the fiscal years 1985 and 1986. We chose March since more firms had a March fiscal year than any other. Thus the choice of March gave us the largest number of firms in our sample. We chose a common fiscal year because for some of our tests we wanted all firms to be subject to the same economic influences. Our sample consisted of 941 firms for fiscal year 1984 and 864 firms for fiscal year 1985.

To examine the importance of sales and earnings growth as variables affecting price we ranked all stocks from highest to lowest value on the variable being examined. The stocks were then divided into three groups equal in number of stocks. The return on each portfolio was calculated by taking an equally weighted average of the return on each stock in a group.

We then calculated an excess return for each group relative to the excess return for the whole sample. As discussed earlier expected return was calculated using the four-factor model. In each case the four-factor model was fit by regressing the actual return of the three ranked portfolios on the return on the four factors for the five-year period prior to the period being analyzed. Expected return was calculated using actual return on the factors during the sample period and the coefficients estimated in the prior five-year period. Excess return is the difference between actual return of the three ranked groups and the expected return estimated from the four-factor model. The excess return was adjusted by subtracting out the average percentage excess return for the whole sample. This last adjustment has the effect of making the excess return net to zero across the three subsamples and adjusts for abnormal performance for the stocks for which earnings and sales are forecasted.

We will now discuss the definition of each of our variables in more detail. The first variable we analyzed was actual growth. If actual growth does not impact share prices then estimated growth, even if the estimate is correct, should not impact share prices. If growth in earnings and sales impact share price, then knowledge about the future value of these variables should lead to excess returns. Actual growth in earnings and sales were calculated as follows:[4]

$$G_E^A = \frac{E_{t+1}^A}{E_t^A} - 1, \tag{1}$$

$$G_S^A = \frac{S_{t+1}^A}{S_t^A} - 1, \tag{2}$$

where

G_E^A = actual growth in earnings,

G_S^A = actual growth in sales,

E_t^A = actual earnings in t,

S_t = actual sales in t.

For example, for the 1984 sample period actual sales for the fiscal year ending March, 1985 was divided by actual sales for the fiscal year ending March, 1984.

Table 4.1 shows the results for actual earnings growth and sales growth. The results are the cumulative excess return for 13 months, starting two months after the end of the earlier fiscal year (t). For example, for the year titled 1984 the results are the cumulative returns for the 13 months beginning June, 1984 and ending June, 1985. An investor would not know actual growth over this period so that if growth in earnings or

Table 4.1
Cumulative excess return

	1985			1984		
	Top	Middle	Low	Top	Middle	Low
Earnings						
1. Actual growth	8.96	0.63	−9.59	2.49	3.47	−5.96
2. Forecasted growth	−3.62	3.74	−0.12	−3.74	−1.85	5.59
3. Error in forecast	11.54	−0.10	−11.44	9.65	−1.20	−8.45
4. Change in forecast	12.41	−0.04	−12.37	5.26	−0.58	−4.68
5. Forecast revision	4.00	−0.34	−3.65	1.88	−0.38	−1.50
Sales						
1. Actual growth	4.06	−0.42	−3.64	1.89	2.99	−4.89
2. Forecasted growth	−7.52	4.35	3.18	−7.48	5.69	1.79
3. Error in forecast	8.27	−0.30	−7.95	3.90	1.87	−5.77
4. Change in forecast	4.67	4.91	−9.59	−0.54	1.63	−1.09

sales affects security prices, knowledge about the future value of these variables should lead to excess return. The period during which we cumulated excess returns was selected for the following reason. First, we start cumulating returns in June because the fiscal year ends in March and by June data on prior year earnings and sales is public. We present results ending in June of the subsequent year because analyzing monthly returns for 24 months after the start of the sample period showed that in all cases any impact was fully captured by the end of June.

Table 4.1 shows that knowledge concerning actual earnings leads to excess returns being earned. The one third of the stocks with the highest actual growth in earnings had excess returns which exceeded those of the lowest one third by over eight percent in 1984 and over eighteen percent in 1985. This is evidence that earnings growth is an important factor in determining share price. If we had performed the same analysis with a variable that did not affect share price, excess returns would not have been earned. While the results are consistent for both years they are much weaker in the 1984 sample period.

We also earn excess returns with knowledge concerning sales growth. What is surprising, and the same result consistently shows up in our other tests, is that the importance of sales growth is less than earnings growth. This is consistent with U.S. results but is inconsistent with popular beliefs about the Japanese markets. The popular belief is that Japanese share prices are driven by sales, while U.S. prices are driven by earnings. Here we find evidence that in Japan earnings is the more important variable effecting share prices. This is consistent with results using U.S. data.

The second variable we examined is expectations about earnings growth. The variables we examined were:

$$G_E^F = \frac{E_{t+1,\text{June}}^F}{E_t^A} - 1, \tag{3}$$

$$G_S^F = \frac{S_{t+1,\text{June}}^F}{S_t^A} - 1, \tag{4}$$

where

G_E^F = the forecasted earnings growth,
G_S^F = the forecasted sales growth,
$E_{t+1,\text{June}}^F$ = the forecast of earnings reported in June for period $t + 1$,
$S_{t+1,\text{June}}^F$ = the forecast of sales reported in June for period $t + 1$, and
other symbols are as before.

We used the June forecast since we believe by June the prior year's actual figures are known. To clarify the dates the 1984 figures are calculated by taking the June, 1984 forecast of earnings for the fiscal year ending March of 1985 and dividing by actual earnings for the fiscal year 1984. We would expect that forecasts were fully incorporated into share price so that no excess return could be earned. When consensus data is used for an analysis of U.S. security markets we find no excess return. However, here we are examining the forecasts prepared by a single firm in the Japanese market. The results could be different.

Examining table 4.1 shows that while excess returns are earned it is the low forecasted growth firms which have positive excess returns. This is evidence that investors have overreacted to the forecast. However, not much importance should be placed on these results since the month-by-month pattern is very unstable. For all other variables we analyzed the month-by-month pattern is very consistent. The results for sales are even more ambiguous than the results for earnings.

The third variable we examined was errors in the forecast. If expectations are important then knowledge that forecasts are in error should lead to excess return. We computed percentage error. The measures were:

$$\varepsilon_E = \frac{E^A_{t+1} - E^F_{t+1,\text{June}}}{E_t},$$

$$\varepsilon_S = \frac{S^A_{t+1} - S^F_{t+1,\text{June}}}{S^A_t},$$

where

ε_E = error in the forecast of earnings,

ε_S = error in the forecast of sales, and

other symbols are as before.

For example, the number shown for 1984 uses the forecast of earnings prepared in June of 1984 for earnings reported in March of 1985 and compares this forecast with the actual earnings reported for March, 1985.

Knowledge that forecasts were in error produced larger positive excess returns than knowledge of the actual values of the variables themselves. The excess return differential between the top and bottom portfolio was over 18 percent in 1984 and 22 percent in 1985. This is evidence of the importance of the variables (earnings and sales) and that expectations drive security prices. Note that the use of sales forecasts rather than earnings forecasts once again produces positive but smaller differentials between portfolios.

The fourth variable we analyzed is change in the forecast. If we are analyzing variables that affect share price, and if expectations are important in determining share price then knowledge concerning changes in expectations should be more important than knowledge about the actual values of the variable itself. The variables we examined were:

$$\Delta E^F_{t+1} = \frac{E^F_{t+1,\text{Dec.}} - E^F_{t+1,\text{June}}}{E^F_{t+1,\text{June}}},$$

$$\Delta S^F_{t+1} = \frac{S^F_{t+1,\text{Dec.}} - E^F_{t+1,\text{June}}}{S^F_{t+1,\text{June}}},$$

where

ΔE^F_{t+1} = change in the earnings forecast,

ΔS^F_{t+1} = the change in the sales forecast,

$E^F_{t+1,\text{Dec.}}$ = the earnings forecast for $t+1$ made in December,

$S^F_{t+1,\text{Dec.}}$ = the sales forecast for $t+1$ made in December, and

other symbols are as before.

For example the number shown under 1984 utilizes the difference between the December, 1984 forecasts and the June, 1984 forecasts. Both forecasts are of earnings reported March, 1985. In this case excess returns are examined from June, 1984 to June, 1985.

Table 4.1 shows the results. Knowing how earnings forecasts will change leads to greater excess returns than knowledge of actual growth. This is strong evidence that expectations affect share price and that in particular Nomura's forecasts impact share price. Once again knowledge concerning earnings is more important than knowledge concerning sales.

The effects of these four variables in the Japanese market are remarkably similar to their effects in United States markets. In both markets the pattern across variables is the same. Thus, in both markets knowledge about expectations is more important than knowledge about the variables themselves. This is evidence that expectations drive security prices. The results analyzed here are for forecasts prepared by one firm rather than consensus forecasts used in U.S. studies but these results show that this firm has an important influence on share price. The surprising result given general beliefs is that earnings growth is more important than sales growth. This is the result shown in U.S. studies but popular belief is that it differs in Japan. Here we see it does not.

Before leaving this section we will re-examine the change in forecasted earnings to see if some of the impact of the change is captured in market price after it becomes public. This is a topic that will be examined in great detail in later sections of the paper where we examine month-by-month changes. To get a rough idea of the phenomenon let us return to the change in forecast variables. Let us look at the excess returns which would accrue to an investor who bought after the change in estimates was realized (in 1985.1 or 1986.1) and held for three months.

Examining the row labeled Forecast revision in table 4.1 indicates that a considerable amount of the excess returns associated with a revision of analysts' estimates is realized after the date of the revision. In fact, approximately one third of the excess returns accrued after the revision is made. We now turn to a further exploration of this phenomenon.

III An Indexed Earnings Estimate Change Model

The analysis in section 2 indicated that market prices do not instantly reflect the informational content of a change in analysts' estimates. If the market is not efficient with respect to a change in analysts' beliefs buying and selling on these beliefs might lead to excess returns. Even if this is true the question remains as to whether these excess returns are sufficient to cover transaction costs.

We wished to investigate buy and sell rules based on changes in analysts' forecasts within a framework which would be relevant for institutional portfolio managers. We selected as our goal investigating a portfolio which closely resembled the first tier of the Tokyo Stock Exchange, where appropriate for institutional ownership stocks, and capitalized on any information in the change in analysts' forecasts of growth rates.[5]

The procedure we used involved the following steps. Since we were interested in institutional ownership we desired to consider buying and selling only very liquid stocks. We selected as of December, 1982, 600 highly liquid stocks from among the 1100 stocks making up the first tier of the Tokyo Stock Exchange. The 600 stocks selected were divided into 13 industry sectors. In each month for each stock the rate of change in analysts' estimates of earnings was computed. For each industry sector the one-third of the stocks for which analysts had the largest percentage increase in estimates were considered candidates for the index fund. Using these 200 stocks a quadratic programming problem was solved which

Table 4.2
Earnings surprise index fund

	Percent per month				
	Portfolio return	Excess return	Excess return after transaction cost	Periods better than index	Percent turnover
1983	2.685	0.689	0.356	10/12	31.6
1984	2.791	0.551	0.263	8/12	28.3
1985	1.920	0.512	0.272	8/12	25.7
1986	4.350	0.606	0.343	8/12	33.8
1987	2.069	0.949	0.775	9/12	24.6
Average	2.763	0.661	0.405	43/60	28.9
Beta = 1.0495					
$R^2 = 0.927$					

a. Excess return is defined as the return on the portfolio minus the return on the first section of the Tokyo Stock Exchange.

formed a portfolio which minimized residual risk from the four-factor model (described in section 2) while matching the TSE index in its sensitivities to each of the four factors and involved holding no more than 100 securities. The portfolio was held for one month, the sample reformed and the quadratic programming problem resolved to develop a new portfolio. The output was the monthly composition and return on a series of portfolios formed from January, 1983 through December, 1987. Each portfolio was formed using only data that was available at the time of its construction and returns recorded for the month subsequent to its formation.

The results of following this portfolio strategy are presented in table 4.2. Note that we have been fairly successful in matching the index for the first tier of the Tokyo Stock Exchange. Our beta of 1.05 is close to one and the coefficient of determination of 0.927 indicates a close fit. In order to match the index while attempting to capitalize on earnings surprises the amount of turnover incurred in the portfolio is fairly substantial. Over 28% of the portfolio is sold each month and replaced with different stocks. If we examine the return on the portfolio before transaction costs it is obvious that earnings surprises contain information. The average monthly return on the index fund for the period 1983–1987 was 2.76% per month while during the same period of time the monthly return on the first tier of the Tokyo Stock Exchange was only 2.10% per month. The average monthly excess return of more than 0.66% per month is surely of economic significance. The real tests of the trading model and the relevant test of informational efficiency is whether excess returns remain after transaction costs are paid. In table 4.2 we examine returns after transaction costs. Transaction costs were calculated using the Tokyo Stock Exchange table of transaction costs. The transaction costs differed over time depending on the price and volume of stock traded.[6] Examining table 4.2 we see that transaction costs accounted for over one third of the pre-cost excess return. However, even when transaction costs were taken into consideration excess returns were still larger than 40 basis points per month. Furthermore, the earnings surprise index fund outperformed the first tier of the Tokyo Stock Exchange in over two thirds of the 60 months examined and outperformed it in each calendar year. The minimum average monthly differential over a year holding period is 26 basis points and the maximum is 78 basis points.[7]

In summary, using only data that is available to an investor we have constructed a portfolio which contains 100 stocks, closely resembles an index fund on the first tier of the Tokyo Stock Exchange, and outperforms such an index fund by over 40 basis points per month on a post-transaction cost basis.

IV Conclusion

In this paper we have examined the impact of one firm's estimates of earnings and sales on stock prices in the Japanese market. We have shown that, contrary to popular belief, earnings, not sales, drive stock prices in Japan. Analysts' estimates are incorporated in stock prices but changes in analysts' estimates are incorporated with a lag. Because of this lag extra returns can be earned by buying stocks immediately after an upward revision in analysts earning estimates. Furthermore, using changes in forecasts, a fund which mirrors the first tier of the Tokyo Stock Exchange but which offers a greater return can be created.

Notes

This paper owes much to our collaboration with the quantitative analysis team of the Nomura Securities group (MERRIT 21). In particular, our research would have been almost impossible without the efforts by two individuals, Mr. Y. Akeda and Mr. Y. Kato of the Nomura Research Institute.

1. See for example Brown et al. (1985) and Dimson and Marsh (1984) for an extensive bibliography.

2. See for example Black (1973). The Value Line studies as well as many others in this area are suspect because of selection bias. After the fact a forecaster or firm such as Value Line is identified as doing well and then back testing shows that the forecaster did in fact do well.

3. IBES is a collection of analysts' forecasts prepared by Lynch, Jones and Ryan.

4. In all cases we deleted firms with negative earnings or such small earnings that growth in excess of 100% was found. This is consistent throughout.

5. The first tier or section of the Tokyo Stock Exchange consists of the 1100 largest stocks (by capitalization) listed on the Tokyo Stock Exchange.

6. We use the retail commissions on the Tokyo Stock Exchange. Assuming a portfolio size of 10 billion yen a year. For retail orders the Tokyo Stock Exchange has a table of fixed commissions similar to those which existed on the New York Stock Exchange prior to the introduction of negotiated commissions.

7. Subsequent to examining this simple rule for selection more complex rules were examined with different revision intervals and different populations of stocks. While turnover changed the result of superior returns (positive alpha) with high R^2 was robust across a wide range of model parameters and samples.

References

Black, Fisher, 1973, Yes Virginia there is hope: Tests of the value line ranking system, *Financial Analysts Journal* 29, no. 5.

Brown, Philip, George Foster and Noreen Eric, 1985, *Security analysts multi-year earnings forecasts and the capital market*, Studies in Accounting Research, no. 21 (American Accounting Association, Sarasota, FL).

Dimson, Elroy and Paul Marsh, 1984, An analysis of brokers' and analysts' unpublished forecasts of UK stock returns, *Journal of Finance*, Dec., 1257–1292.

Elton, Edwin J., Martin J. Gruber and Mustafa Gultekin, 1981, Expectations and share prices, *Management Science*, Sep., 975–987.

Elton, Edwin J., Martin J. Gruber and Mustafa Gultekin, 1984, Professional expectations: Accuracy and diagnosis of errors, *Journal of Financial and Quantitative Analysis*, Dec., 351–363.

Elton, Edwin J., Martin J. Gruber and Seth Grossman, 1986, Discrete expectational data and portfolio performance, *Journal of Finance*, July, 699–712.

Elton, Edwin J. and Martin J. Gruber, 1988, A multi-index model of the Japanese stock market, *Japan and the World Economy* 1, no. 1, 21–44.

Givoly, D. and J. Lakonishok, 1979, The informational content of financial analysts' forecasts, *Journal of Accounting and Economics*, Winter, 165–185.

Hamao, Yasushi, 1988, An empirical examination of the arbitrage pricing theory: Using Japanese data, *Japan and the World Economy* 1, no. 1, 45–61.

Hawkins, E. H., S. C. Chamberlin and W. E. Daniel, n.d., Earnings expectations and security prices, *Financial Analysts Journal*, forthcoming.

5 Discrete Expectational Data and Portfolio Performance

Edwin J. Elton, Martin J. Gruber, and Seth Grossman

In this chapter we examine the information contained in analysts' buy, hold and sell recommendations. There are a number of reasons why such a study is important. As we discuss in more detail below, this study provides an evaluation of forecast ability and a test of strong form efficiency. In addition, this study provides some insight into whether information is lost in the investment process. What makes this study unusual is that it is one of the few cases in evaluating informational content where the forecaster is recommending a clear and unequivocal course of action rather than producing an estimate of a number, the interpretation of which is up to the user. In addition, the large number of forecasts collected and the manner in which they were collected (with no ex post bias) differentiates this study from most others.

While expectations play an important role in most economic theories, studies evaluating expectational data are not common. In addition, studies which do evaluate forecasts generally assume an arbitrary payoff (penalty) function for forecast errors. The squared forecast error is the most commonly used criteria for judging the accuracy of forecasts. The value of analysts' recommendations is conceptually easy to measure. A more natural metric exists (risk-adjusted excess returns) for measuring the value of a recommendation and whether the recommendations are useful or not.

Our study also has implications for the efficient market literature. Strong form tests of efficient markets are perhaps the most important and least frequently performed tests. All other efficiency tests require a theory of what type of information (e.g., earnings increases) should affect stock prices and then a test of whether the information hypothesized as affecting stock prices does in fact affect stock prices. For example, in previous papers [2, 3] it was found that although analysts' forecasts of earnings per share are quite accurate relative to naïve models, the market is efficient with respect to these forecasts. In this paper, we examine whether analysts' recommendations can lead to superior returns. No knowledge is needed or hypothesized about how the analysts would or do use any type of information. The question examined is whether analysts, using any method and information they deem effective, can form forecasts which can be used to produce an excess return.

Studies evaluating mutual fund performance have generally found that mutual fund performance does not dominate random selection. This study will help us to understand whether this performance has been due to poor forecasts of returns on securities or a poor ability to utilize these forecasts.

This clearly is not the first study on the value of analysts' recommendations. Dimson and Marsh [1] provide an excellent review of previous studies and we will not repeat the review here. Our study is different from past studies in that we employ a larger and more carefully constructed data base than those used by most past researchers and we use a more robust methodology to adjust for risk. Most previous studies of recommendations use Value Line data. There is nothing wrong with this per se. Most psychological studies analyze sophomore college students. One wonders whether these studies generalize to the "normal population". The same is true with Value Line studies. There is another problem with Value Line studies. Value Line has the reputation of producing good forecasts. Researchers who have studied this have found it to be true. Thus, studies of Value Line involve an ex post selection bias (Gregory, [4]). This same selection bias is present in many of the other studies reviewed by Dimson and Marsh. Namely, for many of the studies the data was requested and provided long after the forecasts were made. One would expect that data would more likely be provided if analysts' recommendations were good. The current study analyzes by far the most extensive data base of analysts' recommendation ever assembled and does not have the ex post selection bias of many previous studies. For this study a large number of brokerage firms were asked to submit rankings. Once a brokerage firm started submitting rankings, it continued for the entire time period of the study with only one exception. In the next section we will present the details of the data base, but to give an idea of its size, it contains data from 720 analysts at 33 brokerage firms, producing over 10,000 forecasts per month. The data base is three times larger than the total of the data used in all prior studies.

In addition, this study has the advantage that the timing of availability of the data is fairly precise. The collection procedure and the dissemination of data followed a consistent procedure over time.

Our methodology differs from that used in previous studies in that we do not assume that a particular capital asset pricing model holds. We make the more robust assumption that beta is either in general a sufficient metric for risk or the only metric that systematically differs across recommendations. Thus, we develop comparison portfolios based on differing recommendations but having the same beta.

The chapter is divided into three sections. In the first section we discuss the data in more detail. In the second section we analyze the effect of a change in an analyst's recommendation. In the final section we look at the value of a firm's recommendation list.

We place major emphasis on analyzing changes in analysts' recommenations because a change in recommendation should be the direct signal that analysts expect a discontinuity in a stock's performance. Analysts' recommendations at any moment in time represent an accumulation of past changes. If information is quickly incorporated into share price and analysts revise recommendations more slowly (recommendations are sticky) then a change in recommendation on a stock should contain more information than a continuation of a past recommendation.

I Data

The data we utilized was compiled by the investment group at Banker's Trust Company and was marketed under the name IBOS. Starting in March, 1981, forecast data was collected from 33 brokerage firms. One brokerage firm was changed over the period so that we have data from 34 firms. Although data is still being collected, we end our study in November, 1983 because of the need for data on returns after the forecast is made. Thus we have 33 months of data.

The data collected consisted of the rank of each stock on a five-point scale. A rating of 3 was a neutral rating. A rating of 1 or 2 was a buy recommendation with a 1 the more desirable. A rating of 4 or 5 was a sell recommendation with a 5 the least desirable. The average number of analysts utilized by the 33 brokerage firms was 659 in 1981, 734 in 1982 and 766 in 1983. The data was collected over the last week of every month. However, the recommendation could have been made at any time over the month. This data base was constructed by an institution the business of which was valued by the brokerage firms. Thus, the brokerage firms had an incentive to supply good forecasts and the forecasts are likely to be more accurate than those employed in normal academic surveys.

Table 5.1
Number of firms in each rating category

Rating	1981*	1982	1983**	Averaged over 33 months
1	1475	1592	1654	1577
2	3185	3135	3420	3245
3	2785	3920	4575	3794
4	895	1144	1307	1122
5	127	264	313	239
Total	8467	10655	11269	9977

* 10 months
** 11 months

Table 5.2
Number of changes to each rating category

New rating	1981*	1982	1983**	Averaged over 33 months
1	168	150	178	165
2	278	385	386	353
3	338	485	401	412
4	116	228	189	181
5	127	58	46	45
Total	927	1306	1200	1156

* 10 months
** 11 months

As should come as no surprise to anyone who has observed brokerage firms, there were many more buy recommendations than there were sell recommendations. Table 5.1 shows the breakdown by rating for our three sample years and the overall period. Forty-eight percent of the recommendations were buys (1's or 2's) and only two percent were rated 5's (a grading distribution that would warm the heart of most students). Table 5.2 shows the distribution of changes in classifications. On average, about 11% of the classifications are changed in a month.

We deleted some stocks from our data base. As we will discuss later, we were concerned about holding constant other influences. One influence we would like to control is any small firm effect. To control for this, we effectively eliminated small firms. We eliminated all firms that were not followed by three or more analysts.[1] We found that this rule led to a sample of large capitalization stocks. This eliminated 12% of the forecasts on average over the three years.

We also utilized the CRSP data base to calculate monthly returns and betas.

II The Value of a Change in Recommendation

In this section we analyze whether there is information in changes in analysts' recommendations. We analyze this in two ways, first by polling the data from all brokerage firms, and second by using the data for each brokerage firm separately. In all cases we analyze the information content by calculating the return on a portfolio of stocks that were upgraded or downgraded in ranking and comparing it to a neutral portfolio with the same beta. Each of these analyses will now be discussed.

A *Aggregate Comparison*

The analysis is easiest to understand in the context of a specific example. Consider securities which were upgraded to 1's and 2's. For all 33 brokerage firms for each month we collect newly upgraded 1's and 2's. We also collect downgrades to 4's and 5's as a benchmark portfolio. For each month, we then construct a portfolio of upgraded 1's and 2's that has the same beta as a portfolio of downgraded 4's and 5's. This was accomplished as follows. First we calculated a beta on each security using the market model for the five years prior to the month in question. The market index was a value-weighted index of all stocks on the NYSE. Then the two groups of upgraded 1's and 2's and downgraded 4's and 5's were each ranked from highest to lowest beta. The beta on an equally-weighted portfolio was calculated for each group. For the group with the largest number of firms, firms were deleted at the extreme (e.g., if its beta was higher than the other groups, the biggest beta stocks were deleted) until the betas on the two groups were within .01 of each other.[2]

Having formed two portfolios with the same beta, one with a change to a more positive and one with a change to a more negative recommendation, we then computed the differential return on the two groups to see if changes in analysts' recommendations contain information.

This procedure differs from the procedure used in past studies of analyst performance. We believe that our procedure is superior for two reasons. First, our procedure only assumes that beta is a reasonable measure of risk and thus it is robust across many alternative definitions of the "correct" equilibrium process. The last decade has produced a large number of alternative general equilibrium models. Not only are there a dozen alternative CAPM models, but arbitrage pricing theory has been put forward as a competing paradigm. Since arbitrage pricing theory does not require any particular set of factors influencing expected returns, each test of APT can be viewed as producing a unique model. Additional research in evaluating expectational data requires either a delay until equilibrium theory has been sorted out or the use of a research design that is likely to be robust across a number of alternative theories. We believe our design is robust. The beta adjustments we make would be appropriate if either the zero-beta or the standard CAPM is a reasonable model and avoids specifying a specific intercept. If an alternative CAPM is the correct equilibrium model, then the adjustment is still appropriate if rcommendations are not based on sensitivity to other influences. For example, if the post-tax CAPM were appropriate, then our adjustment would hold constant the market influence but not the effect of dividend yield. Not adjusting for dividend yield just adds random noise unless rankings correspond to dividend yield. Furthermore, the first index in most APT models is very closely related to a market portfolio. Once again, as long as brokerage selection is not based on sensitivity to other factors, this adjustment is appropriate.

Second, our results are not affected if brokerage firms as a whole follow only a homogenous subsection of the market. Brokerage firms tend to concentrate on certain types of stocks. At the very least, they concentrate on large capitalization companies. In addition they may well concentrate on certain sectors. Insofar as these sectors outperform or under-perform the market as a whole, then comparison of new 1's to the average securities in the market is in part an examination of how the sample of stocks followed by the brokerage firms performed as a whole. By comparing a broker's 1's and 2's to the broker's 4's and 5's, we alleviate this problem.

Before examining the results, one other issue needs to be examined. A stock which is upgraded to a 1 by one broker may be rated a new 5 by a second. Thus, the same firms may be in both groups. We did do a second analysis where we eliminated all firms that were in both portfolios. This did not change the results so we only report results where the overlaps were not eliminated. In addition, a single firm may be upgraded to a 1 by more than one brokerage firm. Our procedure weights the firm by the number of times it has been upgraded to a 1. For example, a firm that is upgraded to a 1 by four different brokerage firms receives four times the weight of a firm that has been upgraded once. There are an enormous number of alternative weighting schemes that could be tried. We are making no claims that the two weighing schemes we tried are the only possible ones or even the best. However, insofar as they are imperfect, it biases the results against finding information. Thus if we find no information a justifiable comment is that a superior weighing scheme might have disclosed real information. To search for the optimal weighing scheme, while interesting, is well beyond the purpose of the paper.

In Table 5.3 we present results of the performance of a portfolio of newly recommended 1's compared to a portfolio of new 3's. Similarly results on newly downgraded 4's are compared to new 3's. This pattern is similar for all comparisons we make and therefore this is the only table in which we present an extensive time series of results. Let's examine the results. Before time zero the differential return is insignificant.[3] In the

Table 5.3
Return in percent

Month	up to 1 compared to 3	down to 4 compared to 3
−6	0.07	−0.33
−5	0.55	−0.24
−4	0.19	−0.08
−3	−0.07	−0.10
−2	0.17	0.06
−1	−0.27	−0.02
0	1.91	−0.56
1	1.24	−0.74
2	0.28	−0.08
3	−0.11	0.04
4	0.37	0.17
5	0.06	0.00
6	0.28	−0.14
7	0.04	−0.07
8	−0.04	0.22
9	−0.05	0.13
10	−0.11	0.13
11	−0.34	−0.33
12	−0.34	0.53
13	0.18	−0.04

month of the recommendation, time zero, the differential return is large and positive. The large positive return persists in the month after the change in recommendation, and persists but is somewhat smaller in the second month after the change in recommendation. For downgraded stocks a negative return occurs in the month of the change in recommendation. A negative return of a larger size occurs in the month after the recommendation. While there are additional negative returns in later months none of these are statistically significant. In subsequent tables we will present results only for the month of the recommendation and the subsequent two months, since these are the only months with significant returns.

Table 5.4 presents results for all possible changes in recommendations as well as a comparison of new 1's and 2's to new 4's and 5's. Except for securities that were upgraded to 4s, the results for upgrades are uniformly of the correct sign and highly significant.[4] For upgrades there is a large differential return in the month of the announcement. An additional increment in return occurs in the month after the announcement and a smaller, generally insignificant return two months after. For downgrades the negative returns generally are insignificant in the month of the announcement. However, there is a substantial negative return in the month after the announcement. Once again, two months after the announcement there are insignificant returns. Also, note the monotonicity across changes. Upgraded 1's result in greater returns than upgraded 2's and upgraded 2's give higher returns than upgrades to 4's. Rank monotonicity is observed with downgrades as well. The magnitude of these numbers is substantial. For example, for new 1's, the total excess return was almost 3.43% over the three months. This is clearly in excess of transaction costs.[5]

Another way to examine the effect of upgrades is to look at the sign of the differential return on upgraded stocks for each of the 33 months (cases) in which forecasts were made. This is a different test since the return numbers shown in Table IV are the average over all 33 months. For upgrades, negative returns occurred in only 5 of 33 months (cases) for the announcement month, 3 of 33 for the month after and 11 of 33 for two months after. In only 2 of 33 cases was the total return negative over the three-month period.

Finally, comparing a portfolio of upgrades with a portfolio of downgrades gives the greatest excess return of all. It is large and significant in each of the periods although only at a 5% level for two months after the forecast was made.

Table 5.4
Excess portfolio return comparisons—combined

		Month of recommendation			1 month after			2 months after		
Change in class	Comparison	Mean	t value	Number negative	Mean	t value	Number negative	Mean	t value	Number negative
up to 1 or 2	down to 4 & 5	2.43	6.04	3	1.86	6.83	4	0.37	1.68	9
up to 1	3	1.91	7.25	5	1.24	5.17	6	0.28	1.51	13
up to 2	3	1.65	8.64	4	0.84	5.53	6	0.20	1.03	13
up to 4	3	0.68	0.93	11	0.09	0.14	18	−0.80	−1.12	19
down to 2	3	0.29	1.30	13	−0.37	−1.77	23	−0.09	−0.38	20
down to 4	3	−0.56	−1.78	22	−0.74	−3.19	26	−0.08	−0.39	17
down to 5	3	−0.38	−0.60	17	−1.48	−4.05	26	−0.40	−1.17	19

It is hard to attribute these results to anything but information in analysts' rankings. Brokerage firms concentrate on large capitalization stocks. As discussed earlier our sampling rule eliminated all low capitalization stocks. Thus, excess returns on small firms is not an explanation.[6] As an example of other possible omitted influences, consider dividend policy. Some researchers find that high dividend stocks give higher risk-adjusted return. One possible explanation of our results is that upgrades are high dividend stocks and downgrades are low dividend stocks. Not only is this implausible but it cannot explain the consistency of our results from month to month. Even the most ardent advocates of excess returns on high dividend stocks have not argued that this occurs in every month. In fact, no one has found a non-beta influence that could account for the consistency of these results.

B Broker by Broker Comparison

Table 5.5 disaggregates the results to the brokerage firm level. The major difference in disaggregating at the brokerage firm level is that each brokerage firm is examined separately and matching portfolios are formed for each broker as opposed to across all brokers. There are several changes in the research design when the results are disaggregated to the brokerage firm level. First, at the brokerage firm level we do not have as many firms with changes in recommendations. Thus, for upgrades, we combine upgrades to 1's and 2's. Likewise for downgrades, we combine downgrades to 4's and 5's. The comparison group is also changed. There are not enough new 3's. Thus we use a comparison group, 3's whose rating had not changed from the prior month. The second change is in the way we construct our portfolios. Consider upgrades. For each brokerage firm we match the beta on the upgrades with the beta on the unchanged 3's. Matching at the brokerage firm level has the disadvantage that we had to combine 1's and 2's and also 4's and 5's. It has an advantage in controlling for other factors. Insofar as a brokerage firm specializes in a sector, this design eliminates the effect of abnormal performance in that sector on our results.

Once again the same pattern emerges for the upgrades. A large return in the month of an announcement is followed by a substantial return in the month after and a smaller return two months after the announcement. Similarly, for downgrades there is a substantial negative return in the month of the announcement (more so than the prior table) and a still substantial return the month after. Note that these results are the average

Table 5.5
Excess portfolio return comparisons—broker

Change in class	Number of brokers	Month of recommendation			1 month after			2 months after		
		Mean	*t* value	Number negative	Mean	*t* value	Number negative	Mean	*t* value	Number negative
up to 1 or 2	all	1.05	5.50	5	0.87	4.73	5	0.54	4.44	5
up to 1 or 2	Best 5	1.50			2.08			0.67		
down to 4 or 5	all	−1.74	−3.88	29	−1.30	−4.19	28	−0.06	−0.22	15
down to 4 or 5	Best 5	−2.08			−1.64			1.38		

results across the 33 brokerage firms. In Table 5.4 all data was combined. Thus the portfolios used to produce the results in Tables 5.4 and 5.5 were not constructed in the same manner. Table 5.5 also shows two results that do not have a parallel in Table 5.4. First, for upgrades the total return was negative over the 33 periods for only 5 of the 34 brokerage firms in the month of the announcement, 5 in the month after and 5 two months after. These are not the same five firms in all cases. Only three of the brokerage firms had negative returns over the full three-month period. Correspondingly for downgrades, 29 of 34 brokerage firms had negative differential returns in the month of the announcement and 28 of 34 in the month after the announcement while only 7 of 34 firms had the wrong sign over the 3 months.

All of these results are statistically significant so that we can state that analysts' recommenations have value at a brokerage firm level. We made several comparisons to see if the ranking across brokerage firms was consistent over time. We ranked brokerage firms by the size of the differential excess return earned on their upgraded 1's and 2's versus unchanged 3's in each month. We then computed the Spearman rank correlation coefficient between this ranking across all pairs of adjacent months. The average correlation coefficient was .10. Likewise, the rank correlation of the excess return on firms downgraded to 4 or 5 in adjacent months was on average .06. These are not very high and are insignificant. We tried one other way to see if superior brokerage firms could be selected. In each month we examined the differential return for the five firms ranked highest in the prior month. This did lead to some improvement in return (see Table 5.5) compared to the sample as a whole. However, we can not claim statistical differences in the return. Furthermore, the results in the month of the announcement, while indicative of information, are not amenable to a trading rule since the best five firms cannot be determined until the end of the month.

In this section we have shown that there is substantial information in the change in analysts's forecasts, both in the aggregate and at the individual brokerage firm level. In the next section we will examine performance of the recommended list as a whole.

III Brokers' Buy and Sell Lists

In the previous section of the article we examined the size of differential returns which could be earned if an investor took appropriate action (bought or sold stocks) when analysts changed their recommendations.

However, there is a second question worth examining. How much information is conveyed by looking at the list of analysts' recommendations put out by brokers at a point in time?

This question is of interest because this is the way in which the brokerage firms are suggesting that customers use their data. In the previous section we showed that when an analyst changes his or her recommendation about a stock (reacts to new information), positive returns can be earned and that the information is absorbed into stock prices within three months. On the other hand, only 11.6% of recommendations are changed by analysts every month. This suggests that, on average, a stock stays in a particular recommended grouping for more than eight months. Thus, at any point in time, a recommendation category is going to contain a mixture of stocks that were placed there recently (and thus about which one has real information) and stocks which have been in the group a number of months. According to results of Section II, the latter should have no differentially positive return. Given the nature of the recommended groups, does it pay to act on the recommendations of brokerage firms at a point in time? This is the question to which we now turn. More specifically, in this section we shall examine whether excess returns can be made by following brokerage firm recommendations. In particular we shall examine whether holding the buy list versus holding the sell list, with risk adjusted appropriately, leads to excess return. We shall do this in two different ways. First we construct portfolios of buys and sells, holding beta and industry composition constant. This will enable us to comment on the impact of industry selection. Finally, we shall examine whether brokers who do well in recommendations one period have a tendency to do well in subsequent periods.

A *Performance of Recommended List*

In this part we examine whether an investor could earn a differential return by selecting a brokerage firm at random and purchasing the stocks that are ranked 1 while selling those ranked 4's and 5's. To compare 1's with 4's and 5's, it was necessary to hold beta constant between the two groups, or else what appeared to be excess returns could be due simply to risk differentials. Following this we will examine what happens when we constrain the industry composition as well as the beta to be the same for both groups.

For each broker and for each quarter starting March, 1981, all stocks identified as 1's of the date under study were placed in one equally-

Table 5.6
Overall performance of a randomly selected broker*

	Average in the 3 months before listing	Month of listing	One month after listing	Two months after listing
A. Nonindustry matched samples				
Return	0.87	0.80	0.57	−0.32
t-value	3.07	2.90	2.40	−1.07
Number plus	25/34	28/34	27/34	17/34
B. Industry matched sample				
Return	0.53	0.52	0.10	0.11
t-value	3.80	3.87	0.87	0.77
Number plus	25/34	25/34	18/34	21/34

* Differential performance from selecting one broker and following its advice over the sample period—1's minus 4's and 5's.

weighted portfolio while all stocks labelled 4's and 5's were placed in a second portfolio. All 1's were compared with 4's and 5's rather than just 5's because of the small number of 5's identified by most brokers.

If the beta on these two portfolios for any broker differed by more than .01, then stocks were deleted from the appropriate extreme for the larger of the two portfolios until the betas differed by less than .01.

Table 5.6 presents information about the differential return on 1's versus the return on 4's and 5's. The number can be considered the return from buying 1's rather than 4's and 5's with the beta on the overall portfolio remaining the same. All numbers in this table are expressed in terms of monthly differential returns. We see that the differential returns from buying 1's and selling 4's and 5's was .8% per month in the month the recommended list is completed and .57% per month in the following month. Both of these numbers are significantly different from zero at the 1% significance level. Standard deviations were computed across brokerage firms. The question we are examining is this: if an investor picked a brokerage firm at random and followed its recommendation, what are the odds of positive differential returns? Perhaps this is easier to see by noting that, in the month of the recommendation, 28 out of 34 brokerage firms had positive differential returns on average while in the following month it was 27 out of 34. One month after the recommendation 27 firms would produce positive differential returns for their customers while only 7 would produce returns below random selection. This is reasonably impressive performance.

Returning to the table, we see that stocks did not perform very differently in the month prior to the publication of a recommendation list than they did in the publication month. Remember that 78% of the stocks on the recommended list had the same classification two months earlier. From the earlier section we know that the extra return occurs in the month of change and in the subsequent months. At any point in time a recommendation list is a combination of changes that occurred in the prior month, two months ago, three months ago, etc. Thus, given the results discussed in an earlier section, we would expect positive differential returns in the months before we examine the recommended list. Any benefit that can be gained from buying a recommended list disappears within two months of compilation of the list.

Before examining the case where industry membership was held constant, it is worthwhile to compare the results of using the recommended list with results presented in Tables 5.4 and 5.5 of analyzing the excess returns from a change in recommendation. While Table 5.5 did not compare upgrades to 1's and downgrades to 4's and 5's, it did show upgrades to 1's and 2's compared to downgrades to 4's and 5's. The differential returns were 2.43% in the recommendation month and 1.86% in the next month. Looking at changes gives us returns that are 279% and 230% of the returns to be attained by acting on the recommended list. Clearly it pays to buy and sell a portfolio of securities based on changes in recommendation. However, enough of this information is captured by the contents of a firm's recommended list at any point in time that it conveys useful information.

B Recommended List Performance with Industry Constraints

In this section we repeat the procedure of the last section except that we match high-rated stocks with low-rated stocks by industry classification as well as by beta.[7] Because we are selecting stocks within an industry and thus from a smaller sample, we often had to take a 2 rather than a 1 (i.e., no stock in the industry was rated a 1) or a 4 rather than a 5. It is logical to ask whether performance increases or decreases as we hold industry composition constant. This, in essence, eliminates industry betas from stock selection. There are two reasons for this further refinement. First, insofar as there are industry factors in an equilibrium model, holding industry classification constant accounts for this influence. Second, analysts generally follow an industry. Insofar as analysts have different ranking methods, this corrects the problem. Comparing the two parts of Table 5.6

clearly shows that holding industry composition constant eliminates most of the payoff from following the recommended list. While there is a statistically differential return earned in the month of the recommendation, it is smaller than in the non-industry-matched sample. In the month following the compilation of the recommended list, any differential return has all but disappeared. Most of the payoff from recommendation seems to come from differentiating between industries rather than from selecting individual issues.

C *Performance of Individual Firms*

The purpose of this section is to see whether an investor would be better off by following the recommended list of those brokers which did best in the past rather than selecting brokerage firms at random. Two types of tests were conducted. In the first test, the correlation between differential returns for brokerage firms in successive periods was calculated. In the second part the differential returns earned by following the recommendations of the top five brokers were compared with the return from the average brokerage firm. We review each test in turn.

In the first set of tests all brokerage firms were ranked by the size of the three month differential return (after the recommended list is determined). They were then ranked by the three month differential return after their next list was determined (one quarter later). Spearman rank correlations were calculated between all adjacent quarters. The average rank correlation when an industry constraint was not imposed was .10 while when an industry constraint was imposed it was .05. There does not seem to be very much correlation between performance in successive quarters.

It is still possible that some increase in return could be earned by selecting the very best brokerage firm even though the performance across all brokers show very little correlation from period to period. To examine this we computed the incremental return that would have been earned by following the advice of the five brokerage firms that performed best over the previous quarter rather than by selecting a brokerage firm at random. The added return for the non-industry constrained sample is .32% one month after the forecast and −.37% two months after the forecast. The differences are even smaller in the case of industry constraints. Not only are these differences statistically insignificant, but they were also of a very small order of magnitude. It does not appear that looking for the best brokerage firm list has any payoff.

IV Conclusions

In this paper we have shown that there is information in brokerage firm recommendations, in that excess returns are found in the month during which there is a change in the brokerage firm recommendations, as well as during the next two months. There is a consistency across changes and across time that suggests that the results cannot be due to an extraneous factor. Buying the brokerage firm list leads to excess returns, but excess returns not as large as those to be earned by acting on changes. We can find no evidence that a superior brokerage firm can be identified or that one brokerage firm is consistently better than a second.

Discussion

Dennis E. Logue

This chapter explores the value of brokerage firm stock recommendations. It first asks whether significant changes of opinion regarding a stock have some information content. In other words, when analysts boost their evaluation of a stock, does the price rise? It then asks whether there is persistence to the recommendations. For instance, can an investor who buys the stocks presently rated "best" do better than by buying some other portfolios of stocks? Finally, it addresses the persistence of the forecasting ability of any brokerage firm. Can a specific broker continually pick those stocks that subsequently rise relative to other stocks?

The paper shows first that changes of opinion by analysts are correlated with subsequent stock price movements. Stocks elevated to the highest categories have superior risk-adjusted excess returns relative to those either not elevated or downgraded. What was not shown is whether the analysts had true forecasting ability or whether the strength of the marketing effort associated with upgrades led to the price rise. That is, are analysts really identifying positively altered company situations or are the salesmen simply convincing enough investors that company prospects have improved because the experts said so? I do not think we will ever get to untangle this question with the kind of data available, but it is worth pondering.

The authors also evaluate "buy lists." These contain securities that were recently upgraded, but preponderantly have securities that have been labelled "buy" for a while. The findings here are surprising. Buy lists relative to sell lists do very well on a risk adjusted basis. However, we do not know how well they would do if upgrades and downgrades were excluded. The high returns might result from the impact of the upgrades.

Finally, the authors ask whether there is a "best" broker or group of brokers. Specifically, they choose the five best from a prior period, then see if their ability to pick stocks continues into the future. The answer is no: last month's "hot" brokers are not likely to be this month's.

As it stands, the paper is pretty straightforward, and meets the authors' objectives. However, there are some interesting questions that could be addressed with the same data base.

One question is whether there really are "star" researchers. Every year the *Institutional Investor* compiles an "All American" list of analysts. Are these analysts any better at forecasting than others, or are they merely better marketers of their own status or their firm's commission generating activity?

Another question is how much disagreement there is among research analysts. In the analysis, when a stock's rating was simultaneously altered by more than one broker, it was weighted accordingly in the portfolio. However, when a stock is moved up by one broker and down by another it is included in both the upgrade and downgrade portfolio. Might a portfolio of stocks with changed opinions that excluded those stocks that were simultaneously raised and lowered produce even better results than those shown?

Another question that might also be explored with the data base is the degree of "me-tooism." When an analyst upgrades a stock and it moves up, how quickly, if at all, do other analysts follow with a changed recommendation? This sort of me-tooism could account for the stock gains in the months following a first change of opinion. Analyst 1 upgrades a stock in January and Analyst 2 upgrades the same stock in February. In Table 3, that stock is shown (weighted twice) in time 0, but also occurs in time 1 simultaneously with the second recommendation. It could cause sufficient observation period overlaps to make interpretation of Tables 3, 4, and 5 tenuous regarding persistence of excess returns.

Professors Elton, Gruber, and Grossman have begun an interesting research program. How experts collectively operate and how well they forecast (or move the market as a result of their forecasts) are subjects worthy of investigation. Indeed, recent rulings by the Federal Energy Regulatory Commission wherein it indicated a willingness to use analysts' growth forecasts in computing allowable equity costs, make learning more about the accuracy of experts' predictions and the ways they reach them all the more important.

Notes

We would like to thank Banker's Trust Company for supplying the data.

1. A brokerage firm may follow a small stock because of a special underwriting relationship. However, firms followed by multiple brokerage firms are large capitalization stocks. We could have used size directly. However, examining several samples showed this procedure served the same function and was much easier to implement.

2. Whether it was high or low betas that were deleted varied randomly over time.

3. In this particular case the return is primarily positive for upgrades and negative for downgrades. This pattern varies with different upgrades and downgrades and is never significant.

4. For each of our 33 months we have a differential return. The mean is the average return over the 33 months and the standard deviation used in the *t*-test is the standard deviation of the 33 differential returns divided by the square root of 33.

5. We can not be certain that the return in month zero is after the announcement so the 3.43% may be an overestimate. However, we do not see any excess return in the month before the announcement. If there were returns before the announcement we should see an effect in month—1 for firms with announcements at the beginning of the month. We do not see such an effect. Thus the data suggests the effect is after the announcement.

6. If small firms was an explanation the effect would be concentrated in January and we do not observe such a pattern. Furthermore, small firm effect can not explain the persistent month-to-month pattern.

7. The algorithm for forming these groups was more complex than the previous algorithm. Industries were defined by 2 digit SEC code. An industry was selected at random. The stock with a beta closest to one was selected from the smallest group (high or low classified stock). Then the stock with the closest beta was selected from the larger group. This was repeated. When a stock was selected from the larger group an attempt was made to eliminate prior differences. After all industries were examined replacements were made if the differences in betas on an equally weighted portfolio was greater than .05.

References

1. Elroy Dimson and Paul Marsh. "An Analysis of Broker's and Analysts' Unpublished Forecasts of U.K. Stock Returns." *Journal of Finance* 39 (December 1984), 1257–1293.

2. Edwin Elton, Martin Gruber, and Mustafa Gultekin. "Professional Expectations: Accuracy and Diagnosis of Errors." *Journal of Financial and Quantitative Analysis* 19 (December 1984), 351–63.

3. Edwin Elton, Martin Gruber and Mustafa Gultekin. "Expectations and Share Prices." *Management Science* 27 (September, 1981), 975–87.

4. N. A. Gregory. "Testing an Aggressive Investment Strategy Using Value Line Ranks: A Comment." *Journal of Finance* 38 (March 1983), 257.

II The Performance of Managed Portfolios

One of the most interesting and intensely studied academic areas in finance is performance measurement. The profession has been concerned with performance measurement at least since Alfred Cowles's famous article, "Can Stock Market Forecasters Forecast?" published in *Econometrica* in July 1933. While the correct measures of performance are of interest to academics and investment professionals, how well managers do is of interest to everyone. Performance measurement is an area where authors can attempt to implement and apply the latest theories in finance to data that represents the best efforts of investment professionals. The results have strong implications for the efficiency of capital markets.

This section of the book starts with a theoretical chapter on timing measures. The remainder of the section consists of three parts dealing with the performance of commodity funds, stock mutual funds, and bond funds. While the chapters in these parts represent an examination of managed portfolios, the sequence also explores alternative methods of performance measurement.

Theoretical

In the chapter in this part we examine potential weaknesses in standard measures of performance. We reexamine the problem first pointed out by Dybvig and Ross. If management possesses private information, then correct timing decisions can result in a misestimate of management selection ability. We were the first researchers to develop measures that can correct for this and correctly differentiate between timing ability and selectivity.

Empirical

In this section, we begin our examination of manager performance by studying the performance of publicly offered commodity funds. At the time of this study, publicly offered commodity funds had undergone a tremendous growth from 12 to 685 funds in a five-year period. These funds had wide public appeal because they allowed investors to place funds in a managed pool of futures contracts on which both high returns and inflation hedging was promised. These studies have added importance because these funds represent a type of investment vehicle, private partnerships, offered by prospectus to large numbers of investors using managers whose experience is largely in managing individual accounts. The type of vehicle studied has been used for real estate partnerships, oil and gas partnerships, venture capital partnerships, and the other types of private partnerships that have become public in recent years.

In the first chapter on commodity funds, we examined the performance of all funds which existed at any time over the June 1979 to June 1985 time period. We were careful to adjust for the fact that the databases on commodity funds suffer from survivorship bias and that often the data on a fund that has developed problems is not reported in databases for the month or months before it disappears. In this chapter we show that commodity funds have poor returns and very high risk, that they do not provide a hedge against inflation, and that they are not efficient investments to add to a portfolio of stocks and bonds. Furthermore, we find no consistency or predictability among fund managers. There is no way, based on past performance, to select a manager who will do well in the future.

If the performance of these funds is so dismal, why do people buy them and how can they continue to exist? This is the question we examine in the next chapter in this section. Commodity funds are limited partnerships offered by prospectus. The principal sources of information on these funds are the description of the fund and the past return of the fund manager reported in the prospectus and the coverage of fund performance by the financial press. We find that the returns reported in the prospectuses are so much higher than the subsequent returns earned by the funds after they are sold as to be totally misleading. The reason for this is a prime example of self-selection bias. We can also show that the financial press almost exclusively reports good information about funds (such as a spectacular success story) since the source of the stories is often the funds themselves. We show that even if a large subset of investors realize the true performance of these funds, since there is no way to trade against this performance (make an arbitrage profit), all that is necessary for growth in this industry is for some investors to believe the biased information that reaches the marketplace. This chapter is the first to document a case where a class of assets can sell at a price above their value even if the average investor is rational. The analysis and conclusions have major implications for capital market efficiency for limited partnerships in general, and for the legal framework governing security sales.

The final chapter in this section re-examines several of the attributes of funds examined in the previous two papers. Several questions were raised by the industry concerning the validity of the initial studies. In the third chapter we reexamine our original conclusions using new data and find that they are unchanged. We also look at higher moments of the return distribution and more sophisticated techniques for selecting winning funds. The original conclusions continue to hold. This article won the Graham Dodd Award from the Financial Analysts Federation.

Mutual Funds—Stock Investments

This section contains three studies on mutual fund performance. In the first, we reexamine a recent article published in the *Quarterly Journal of Economics* that showed that mutual funds outperformed index funds, that mutual funds with higher fees outperformed funds with lower fees (net of fees), and that mutual funds that charged a load did no worse, even after paying the load, then funds with no loads. These results were dramatically opposite to previous results in the literature. We develop a new model for evaluating mutual funds in the first chapter of this section. We believe that to measure excess returns on mutual funds a model must contain enough indexes to span the type of securities held by the funds under study. The use of the capital asset pricing model can be defended from notions of general equilibrium or from the simpler notion of comparing a manager to a combination of the S&P index and Treasury bills that has the same risk (beta) as the portfolio under consideration. If a manager holds securities not in the S&P Index, then one defensible strategy for evaluation is to employ a multi-index model and notions of arbitrage pricing theory. Another way to think of this is to define a passive portfolio by finding a set of index funds with the same risk as the fund under study and comparing the fund against this composite passive portfolio. In this article we use two additional indexes (to the S&P Index), a small stock index and a bond index. These indexes are appropriate because funds in our sample hold a large portion of their portfolio in stocks that are smaller than those in the S&P Index, and many of the funds also hold bonds. When the three-index model is used, the results obtained are more consistent with theory. Active managed mutual funds tend to underperform a combination of index funds with the same risk, funds with high fees tend to do worse than funds with low fees, and load funds tend to be inferior investments when compared to no-load funds. In addition, we show that using a multi-index model to measure fund performance also allows us to infer style. The use of multi-index models to diagnose style has recently gained attention and is known as return-based style analysis.

In working with mutual fund data, one of the major problems is that the commonly available databases suffer from survivorship bias. Most databases contain historical data on funds that exist today. They answer questions such as "How well could I have done if ten years ago I had bought a random mutual fund that exists today?" It doesn't answer the question "How well would I have done if I selected a mutual fund at random ten years ago?" To answer this question, and to correct for survivorship bias, one must track the performance of all funds that existed at some point in the past. In the second article on stock fund performance we show how to correct for and estimate the size of this bias for stock mutual funds. We provide one of the first estimates of survivorship bias in the literature, and the first based on multi-index measures of performance. In addition, we provide the first study of the characteristics of funds that did not survive and the characteristics of funds which absorb these funds which did not survive.

One of the major questions in mutual fund analysis is the persistence of performance. After all, if measuring post-performance tells you nothing about the future, why bother? In the last chapter in this section we examine whether the past performance of mutual funds tells us anything about future performance. The answer is yes. Bad performing funds tend to remain bad performing funds. To a lesser, but still significant extent, good performing funds tend to remain good performing funds. Persistence is statistically and economically significant, but the extent of persistence depends on the method used for measuring performance.

Mutual Funds—Bond Investments

In this section of the book we review the performance of bond mutual funds. Approximately 25 percent of the assets under management in all mutual funds (including money market funds) are held by bond funds. At the time we wrote these articles, bond mutual funds had more assets under management than stock mutual funds. Given their size and continued growth, and given the large number of articles that have been published on stock mutual funds, it is surprising that so little research had been devoted to bond mutual funds. In the two articles in this section we examine the performance and style analysis of bond mutual funds.

In the first chapter we examine bond mutual funds employing many of the tools and types of analysis we discussed in the chapters included in the section on stock mutual funds. This is the first to study survivorship bias among bond mutual funds and to build a database that is free of survivorship bias. The results show that survivorship bias is an important influence on measured bond mutual fund performance but, as we would suspect, it is smaller in magnitude than it is for stock funds since bond funds are not as risky. In this study we construct and test multi-index models of performance where the indexes are constructed to span the types of bonds held by bond mutual funds. While the use of a multi-index model compared to a single index model does not have as much of an impact on general results for bond mutual funds as it does for stock funds, the use of a multi-index model is important for evaluating bond funds which invest in more than one type of bonds. The high yield (junk bond) index and mortgage indexes are particularly important, in addition to a general bond index, for many funds. We also demonstrate the use of multi-indexes to infer management style employing both regression methods and constrained regression (quadratic programming algorithms) to infer style. We show how these techniques may lead to a better diagnosis of management style than simply looking at the securities management holds. Finally, we examine the impact of management expenses and the predictability of performance.

In the second chapter of this section we continue to explore the use of multi-index models to explain bond and bond fund returns. We examine the time series of returns (the return-generating process) and the cross section of expected returns (APT models). We use the return on portfolio of securities (as in the previous chapter) and changes in the expectations of fundamental economic variables to explain return. It is the first to employ expectational variables to explain bond returns and to measure unexpected changes as the change in the forecasts of professionals over time. This ties back to the first part of this volume where we studied the role of expectations in price formation.

We find that while the return on portfolios of securities does a good job of explaining the time series of returns, over time the use of unexpected changes in fundamental economic variables is important in explaining cross-sectional differences in returns. The use of models using fundamental variables is shown to do a good job of explaining bond mutual fund performance.

Theoretical

6 Differential Information and Timing Ability

Edwin J. Elton and
Martin J. Gruber

I Introduction

Recently, a number of papers have appeared which call into question many of the standard methods of performance measurement. Questions have been raised about the use of standard methods to measure the timing ability of managers, to identify selection ability, and to differentiate between the two.[1] By building on a framework developed by Dybvig and Ross (1985), we are able to develop a set of performance measures which both correctly identify the accurate use of information and can be computed in terms of observable variables.

The principal reason that these measures overcome the Dybvig and Ross problem is that we assume the existence of additional information available to the outside observer. Dybvig and Ross assume that the outsider observer is furnished only information on the time series of returns. Most of the literature on portfolio evaluation such as Sharpe (1966), Friend, Blume and Crockett (1970), Jensen (1969), Admati and Ross (1985), and Admati et al. (1986) develop measures based on only observed returns.[2] We assume the observer knows the portfolio proportions at frequent intervals over time (e.g., daily) as well as a time series of returns for each asset. The information on portfolio composition clearly exists in master trust accounts and custodian accounts. In fact, it is the master trustee or custodian who normally provides the information to the pension fund trustees or mutual fund for the purpose of evaluating fund managers. Pension funds are important consumers of portfolio evaluation services and they are clearly in a position to obtain the type of information needed to use our proposed measures.[3] In addition, any mutual fund or trust account is in a position to compute these measures should they be requested by customers.

This paper is divided into three sections. In section 2, we deal directly with one problem initially studied by Dybvig and Ross (1985): can we discern superior timing ability by management in the absence of selection ability? In this section, we show that security market line (SML) analysis can be employed to measure timing, if the proper information is available, and the problems raised by Dybvig and Ross can be overcome. In addition, this section serves as a review of the Dybvig and Ross methodology which will be used throughout the rest of this paper. In section 3, we propose one solution to measuring timing and selectivity when a decision maker receives both market-wide signals and signals on the performance of individual securities. This section defines market timing and selection using traditional ideas of what these measures are. In section 4, we develop measures of timing and selectivity under a more stylized description of the decision-making firm. If the signal on any stock can be viewed as either a signal about the stock market in general or a signal which is unique to the security, then the payoff from each type of signal can be clearly differentiated by an investor observing the transactions of management.

II The Detection of Timing Ability

In a very important article, Dybvig and Ross (1985) have shown that an informed manager making correct timing decisions between a risky portfolio and a riskless asset can appear to have inferior performance in terms of SML analysis. That is, a manager who acts correctly on the basis of true information can have a negative abnormal return on his portfolio.

The analysis is particularly important because it implies that all prior analysis of portfolio performance using SML analysis is suspect. Since almost all commercial and academic studies use SML analysis, this implies that most prior studies of portfolio performance, and in particular, of the performance of mutual funds must be discarded. Even studies that did not use SML analysis but use betas to categorize comparable funds such as Friend, Blume and Crocket (1970) must be discarded. This follows since, as shown later, managers' timing leads to a misestimation of the average beta by the observer.

The Dybvig and Ross analysis is both correct and insightful when betas are computed using traditional simple regression on portfolio returns. The purpose of this section is to develop a measure that can separate managers who have superior timing ability from those who do not. We shall first briefly review the major results of Dybvig and Ross and then derive our measure of performance due to timing.

2.1 *The Dybvig and Ross Model*

Dybvig and Ross (D–R) assume that the manager can allocate funds between a risky portfolio and a riskless asset and that returns on the risky portfolio are generated by the following process:

$$x = r + \pi + s + e,$$

where r is the riskless rate of interest; π is the risk premium; s is a signal observed by the manager with s_t a particular value for the signal; and e is an unobservable noise term with e_t a particular value of e; s and e are assumed to be uncorrelated with each other and each have a mean of zero. The variance of e is σ_e^2.

Dybvig and Ross make the assumption that r is zero since this assumption simplifies the analysis without affecting the results. We shall make the same assumption throughout the remainder of the paper. Assuming the manager tries to maximize the expected utility from an exponential utility function of the form $-\exp(Ax)$, D–R show that the fraction of funds which the manager places in the risky portfolio $[\gamma(s)]$ is given by

$$\gamma(s_t) = (\pi + s_t)/\sigma_e^2 A.$$

Dybvig and Ross show that the abnormal returns to any portfolio using security market line (SML) analysis is

$$\delta = E[\gamma(s)x] - \frac{\text{Cov}(x, \gamma(s)x)}{\text{Var}(x)} E(\pi + s + e)$$

or

$$\delta = E[\gamma(s)x] - \beta_\gamma E(\pi + s + e).$$

They proceed to show that this can be negative even if the manager possesses and acts correctly on real information as long as $\pi^2 > \sigma_e^2 + \sigma_s^2$. Similarly, a manager can have perverse information (act on $-s$ rather than s) and still show positive performance. In fact, the only case in which abnormal return analysis can be guaranteed to lead to correct answers is where the manager has no information ($s = 0$). The driving force behind the D–R proof is that the investor does not have the same information set as the manager and performs the analysis without being able to observe s_t or $\gamma(s_t)$.

The problems pointed out by D–R carry over logically to ex post performance evaluation.[4] Assume that returns follow an i.i.d. distribution and that investors can only observe the returns on a managed portfolio over time. Then all the D–R analysis discussed above holds exactly with realizations substituted for expectations.

However, as we shall show, the problem raised by D–R can be eliminated by assuming the investor gains access to additional data beyond that assumed by D–R. This is data which, while not costless, can be obtained by at least some investors. A manager makes decision on $\gamma(s_t)$ at some interval (a day, week, or month) and changes his portfolio accordingly. The frequency of the interval is unimportant though obviously it must be considered in doing empirical work. If the investor has access to the portfolio composition of the manager's portfolio, then both $\gamma(s_t)$ and β_γ can be observed by the investor at any point in time. With this information we can reformulate the D–R analysis to find an appropriate metric for timing ability. This is the subject to which we now turn.[5]

2.2 A Market Timing Measure

In this section, we will propose a metric to measure market timing ability and will show that the metric produces a correct indication of whether the manager does or does not have timing ability. We will retain unless otherwise stated the assumptions and terminology of D–R.[6] The proposed metric is

$$d = E[R_p] - E[R_{\beta=\bar{\beta}}], \tag{1}$$

where R_p is the return on the managed portfolio; and $R_{\beta=\bar{\beta}}$ is the return that would have been obtained if the manager operated at the average level of beta at all points in time.

It is convenient to assume that the market portfolio is an all equity portfolio.[7] This assumption does not effect the results of the proof but makes it easier to follow. D–R have an ex ante perspective or an infinitely long ex post perspective. In the ex post perspective $E(R_p)$ is the average return on the portfolio. $E(R_{\beta=\bar{\beta}})$ is the average beta on the portfolio times the average return on the market.

The beta on the stock portfolio is one since the market is assumed to be the stock portfolio.[8] The beta in any period on the manager's portfolio which is a combination of the stock portfolio and T-bills is simply the proportion in the stock portfolio or in D–R terms $\gamma(s_t)$. Thus, the average beta is the average $\gamma(s)$. From the definition of $\gamma(s)$, $\bar{\beta} = E[\gamma(s)] = \pi/\sigma_e^2 A$. If x is the random return of the market, then the expected return on the manager's portfolio is

$$E[R_p] = E[\gamma(s)x]. \tag{2}$$

Likewise,

$$E(R_{\beta=\bar{\beta}}) = \bar{\beta}E(x) = E(\gamma(s))E(x). \tag{3}$$

With these two substitutions our measure becomes[9]

$$d = E(\gamma(s)x) - E(\gamma(s))E(x) = \mathrm{Cov}(\gamma(s), x). \tag{4}$$

As shown in D–R, if the manager acts on the signal s_t. Then $\gamma(s_t)$ is

$$(\pi + s_t)/\sigma_e^2 A. \tag{5}$$

Substituting this expression into (4),

$$d = E\{[(\pi + s)/\sigma_e^2 A - \pi/\sigma_e^2 A](\pi + s + e - \pi)\} \tag{6}$$

$$= (1/\sigma_e^2 A)(\sigma_s^2) > 0. \tag{7}$$

Since, from the form of the utility function, A must be positive for any risk averse investor, and since σ_e^2 and σ_s^2 must be positive, d is positive for any manager who receives and correctly acts on the signal (s_t).[10] If the manager uses the signal perversely, then the proportion placed in the stock portfolio is $(\pi - s_t)/\sigma_e^2 A$. In this case, eq. (7) becomes

$$d = (1/\sigma_e^2 A)(-\sigma_s^2). \tag{8}$$

For the reasons given above d must be negative in this case. If, on the other hand, the signal contains no information (is random), then $\mathrm{Cov}(\gamma(s), x) = 0$. Thus, the proposed measure correctly identifies timing information. In order to obtain our measure one needs to know the composition of the portfolio at each point in time. While this information is not generally available to all observers, it is available to at least some subset of market participants. For example, all pension trustees can obtain it from master trust accounts.

One further issue should be discussed. Is our measure affected by a noisy signal? The situation we have in mind is where there are multiple signals and the manager only picks up one of them or alternatively the manager misjudges the signal (interprets it with error). Consider the following situation. At a point in time the manager believes the expected return on the stock portfolio is

$$\bar{x} = \pi + s_t, \tag{9}$$

and the true mean is

$$\bar{x} = \pi + s_t + k. \tag{10}$$

The process generating return is

$$x = \pi + s_t + k + \varepsilon.$$

k can either be considered as a signal the manager does not see or s_t can be viewed as a misinterpretation of the true signal $s_t + k$. Further assume that k is independent of s_t and e. The manager's perception of the return process is $x = \pi + s_t + \varepsilon'$, where ε' will in fact be equal to $k + \varepsilon$. Employing the methodology of D–R yields

$$\gamma(s_t) = (\pi + s_t)/[(\sigma_\varepsilon^2 + \sigma_k^2)A]. \tag{11}$$

Continuing with an ex ante perspective, we have

$$d = E\left[\left(\frac{\pi + s}{(\sigma_\varepsilon^2 + \sigma_k^2)A} - \frac{\pi}{(\sigma_\varepsilon^2 + \sigma_k^2)A}\right)(\pi + s + k + \varepsilon - \pi)\right]$$

$$= \frac{1}{(\sigma_\varepsilon^2 + \sigma_k^2)A}(\sigma_s^2) > 0. \tag{12}$$

Proofs analogous to those presented above hold when the manager acts perversely or has no information. Thus, our measure to detect manager's timing ability is unaffected by the manager reacting to the signal with error.

III Timing and Selectivity

In the previous section, we examined the measurement of timing when there was a single risky asset and a riskless asset. In this section, we explore timing and selectivity. To do this we introduce two risky assets. The generalization to N risky assets is straightforward. We assume two types of signals, a market-wide signal and individual security signals. In this section we will derive timing and selectivity measure within their traditional meanings. In a later section, we will develop measures that isolate the value of the signals directly. Continuing with the simplification of zero return on the riskless asset, the returns on the two assets are given by x_1 and x_2, where

$$x_1 = \pi_1 + \beta_1 s_0 + s_1 + \varepsilon_1, \qquad x_2 = \pi_2 + \beta_2 s_0 + s_2 + \varepsilon_2, \tag{13}$$

where π_1 is the expected risk premium of asset 1; π_2 is the expected risk premium of asset 2; s_0 is the market-wide signal with s_{0t} a particular value of s_0; s_i is the individual signal unique to security i with s_{it} a particular value of s_i; ε_i is the residual return (ε_i has an expected return of zero and a variance of $\sigma^2_{\varepsilon i}$); and β_i is the sensitivity of the return on security i to a market signal.

It is assumed that the signals have a mean of zero and are uncorrelated. Thus, the market-wide signal is independent of the unique security signal. Furthermore, we will assume that the residuals are uncorrelated with the signal and with each other.[11] Once again we will follow D–R and assume that the investors have the exponential utility function described in section 2.

Letting γ_1 and γ_2 be the proportions in the risky securities and continuing the assumption of a zero return on the riskless asset, the return on the total portfolio is

$$\gamma_1(\pi_1 + \beta_1 s_{0t} + s_{1t} + \varepsilon_1) + \gamma_2(\pi_2 + \beta_2 s_{0t} + s_{2t} + \varepsilon_2).$$

Making this substitution, using moment generating functions, and taking logs, the utility of wealth at the end of the period $U(W_i)$ is

$$U(W_i) = A\gamma_1(\pi_1 + \beta_1 s_{0t} + s_{1t}) + A\gamma_2(\pi_2 + \beta_2 s_{0t} + s_{2t})$$
$$- A^2 \operatorname{Var}(\gamma_1\varepsilon_1 + \gamma_2\varepsilon_2).$$

Taking the derivative with respect to γ_1 and γ_2, respectively, setting the resulting expression equal to zero, and solving for γ_1 and γ_2 yields

$$\gamma_1 = \frac{\pi_1 + \beta_1 s_{0t} + s_{1t}}{A\sigma^2_{\varepsilon_1}}, \qquad \gamma_2 = \frac{\pi_2 + \beta_2 s_{0t} + s_{2t}}{A\sigma^2_{\varepsilon_2}}.$$

Before analyzing market timing and selectivity a couple of comments are in order. First, note that the proportion of wealth invested in any security (γ_i) depends on the market signal (s_{0t}) as well as the security signal (s_{it}). A positive s_{0t} will in general change the ratio of γ_1 and γ_2. Thus, market-wide signals can change the relative proportion invested in the two securities. Likewise, security signals can affect the aggregate amount invested in all risky assets. For example, a positive s_{1t} causes the amount invested in security one to increase without affecting security two. However, it also causes the aggregate amount invested in all risky securities to increase. Thus, security specific information leads to changes in the aggregate amount invested in risky assets. This was recognized by D–R and Mayers and Rice (1979). Both authors assumed away these effects. In this section, we will follow their procedures and define timing in terms of the allocation between risky and riskless assets. In the next section, we will make a complete break with traditional meanings of timing and selectivity, and present an evaluation scheme that separates general effects from the effect of security-specific signals.

The aggregate return is a function of the proportion invested in securities one and two. Letting R be the return as a function of the proportion in each security, we can formulate three return measures. The first, shown in eq. (14), is the actual return earned:

$$R(\gamma_1, \gamma_2) = E[\gamma_1 x_1 + \gamma_2 x_2]. \tag{14}$$

The second, shown in eq. (15), is the return that would have been earned if the total proportion of funds invested in stocks was held constant (at the average level) but the proportion invested in each individual stock was allowed to vary. Since $\gamma_1 + \gamma_2$ varies over time, we maintain constant proportions in stocks by multiplying the actual proportions by the average proportions $\bar{\gamma}_1 + \bar{\gamma}_2$:

$$\begin{aligned} R&\left[\frac{\gamma_1}{\gamma_1 + \gamma_2}(\bar{\gamma}_1 + \bar{\gamma}_2), \frac{\gamma_2}{\gamma_1 + \gamma_2}(\bar{\gamma}_1 + \bar{\gamma}_2)\right] \\ &= (\bar{\gamma}_1 + \bar{\gamma}_2)E\left[\frac{\gamma_1}{\gamma_1 + \gamma_2}x_1 + \frac{\gamma_2}{\gamma_1 + \gamma_2}x_2\right]. \end{aligned} \tag{15}$$

The third, shown in eq. (16), is the return that would have been earned if the amount invested in each stock was held at the average level:

$$R(\bar{\gamma}_1, \bar{\gamma}_2) = E(\gamma_1)E(x_1) + E(\gamma_2)E(x_2). \tag{16}$$

As we will show, timing is measured by eq. (14) minus eq. (15) and selectivity is measured by eq. (15) minus eq. (16). Let us examine each in turn. First consider what happens if a manager has no timing ability. We will use the conventional meaning of no timing, namely, that the aggregate amount invested in risky securities is independent of the return on the securities. In other words, greater return on securities is not associated with greater investment in risky assets.[12] This definition of no timing ability in equation form is:

$$\mathrm{Cov}\left(\gamma_1 + \gamma_2, \frac{\gamma_1}{\gamma_1 + \gamma_2}x_1 + \frac{\gamma_2}{\gamma_1 + \gamma_2}x_2\right) = 0.$$

The left-hand side of this equation is analogous to eq. (4) which was our timing measure when we considered timing alone. We know that

$$\mathrm{Cov}(A, B) = E(AB) - E(A)E(B).$$

Thus, the definition of no timing ability becomes

$$E\left[(\gamma_1 + \gamma_2)\left\{\frac{\gamma_1}{\gamma_1 + \gamma_2}x_1 + \frac{\gamma_2}{\gamma_1 + \gamma_2}x_2\right\}\right]$$

$$- E(\gamma_1 + \gamma_2)E\left[\frac{\gamma_1}{\gamma_1 + \gamma_2}x_1 + \frac{\gamma_2}{\gamma_1 + \gamma_2}x_2\right] = 0,$$

or, after rearranging,

$$E[\gamma_1 x_1 + \gamma_2 x_2] = E(\gamma_1 + \gamma_2)E\left[\frac{\gamma_1}{\gamma_1 + \gamma_2}x_1 + \frac{\gamma_2}{\gamma_1 + \gamma_2}x_2\right].$$

Thus, with no timing ability in the conventional meaning of timing, our proposed measure of timing ability, eq. (14) minus eq. (15), is identically zero. The selectivity measure is positive, negative, or zero depending on whether the signals are correctly utilized in decision making. With no timing, eqs. (14) and (15) are identical. Thus, the difference between eq. (15) and eq. (16) is identical to the difference between (14) and (16). If the signals are used correctly, this difference is

$$\frac{\sigma_{s_1}^2 + \beta_1^2\sigma_{s_0}^2}{A\sigma_{\varepsilon_1}^2} + \frac{\sigma_{s_2}^2 + \beta_2^2\sigma_{s_0}^2}{A\sigma_{\varepsilon_2}^2}.$$

Therefore, the selectivity measure has the correct sign if the information is used correctly.[13]

Our proposed measure also leads to correct conclusions if there is zero selectivity but timing exists. One case of zero selectivity is that the proportion of investment in all risky assets which is held in any particular asset is a constant.[14] Employing this traditional meaning for selectivity $\gamma_1 = K\gamma_2$ where K is some constant. With this substitution eqs. (15) and (16) are identical and equal to

$$(K\pi_1\pi_2 + \pi_2^2)/A\sigma_{\varepsilon_2}^2.$$

Thus, the proposed selectivity measure is zero when there is no selectivity. Since eqs. (15) and (16) are identical, we can examine the difference between eqs. (14) and (16) to analyze the timing measuring. As before, this difference if the signal is correctly used is

$$\frac{\sigma_{s_1}^2 + \beta_1^2\sigma_{s_0}^2}{A\sigma_{\varepsilon_1}^2} + \frac{\sigma_{s_2}^2 + \beta_2^2\sigma_{s_0}^2}{A\sigma_{\varepsilon_2}^2}.$$

If the signal is ignored, then this measure is zero, and finally if the signal is used perversely, this measure is negative. So, the timing measure has the correct sign. Note that employing eqs. (14), (15), and (16) the timing and selectivity measures proposed in this section can be computed for any manager as long as the composition of the investment portfolio can be observed. The generalization to N securities is straightfoward.

IV An Alternative Approach to Timing and Selectivity

In the last section of this paper, we developed measures of timing and selectivity under a particular and widely used definition of selectivity and timing. In particular, we assumed that timing involved the allocation between risky and riskless assets. Selectivity was what was left to performance after timing. In fact, as pointed out earlier, part of what this analysis attributes to timing is really the response to signals on individual securities rather than signals about securities in general. In this section of the paper, we shall develop a new and less conventional set of measures. Now timing will be defined as a response to the economy-wide signal s_{0t} and selectivity the response to signals on individual securities. Our framework and measures are completely different from those used in previous research [e.g. Dybvig and Ross (1985), Grinblatt and Titman (1985), Mayers and Rice (1979)] where individual security signals can affect timing measures.

To aid in developing the new measures we will define a highly stylized model of a firm whose performance we wish to analyze. We will initially assume that the firm is only concerned with two risky assets but shortly will generalize to the case of N risky assets. We will continue with the return models developed in the last section of this paper. We will change the way signals are produced and hence our definition of timing. Assume the analytical functions of our stylized firm can be divided into two separate groups. One group (we could call them 'economists') produces forecasts of the economy and the market (signals s_0 in our world). The second group (we could call them 'security analysisists') received the signal s_{0t} and produces forecasts about individual stocks s_{1t} or s_{2t} given knowledge of s_0.[15]

We then define timing as decisions reached on the basis of s_{0t} and selectivity as decisions reached on the basis of s_{1t} and s_{2t}. All reaction and only reaction to s_{0t} is called timing. Recall that from our last section a signal s_{0t} also caused us to change the proportions invested in stocks on and two. This second-order effect was designed as part of selectivity. Here we identify any change in return resulting from s_{0t} as timing. Similarity, any change resulting from a signal s_{1t} or s_{2t} is called selectivity.

The advantage of this procedure is that it results in a completely unambiguous division of returns into two components. If the reader objects to us referring to these as timing and selectivity, he can think of them as payoff from processing economy-wide data and payoff from processing data unique to each firm.

Let us examine the payoff from the combination of timing and selectivity. This is simply

$$E[\gamma_1 x_1 + \gamma_2 x_2] - [E(\gamma_1)E(x_1) + E(\gamma_2)E(x_2)],$$

where γ_1, γ_2, x_1, and x_2 are defined earlier.

Substituting in the values for γ_1, γ_2, x_1, and x_2 developed earlier, the overall manager's payoff becomes

$$d_0 = \frac{\beta_1^2 \sigma_{s_0}^2}{A\sigma_{\varepsilon_1}^2} + \frac{\sigma_{s_1}^2}{A\sigma_{\varepsilon_1}^2} + \frac{\beta_2^2 \sigma_{s_0}^2}{A\sigma_{\varepsilon_2}^2} + \frac{\sigma_{s_2}^2}{A\sigma_{\varepsilon_2}^2}. \tag{17}$$

The measure we propose for timing should relate the change in proportions of any stock solely to the market signal and its impact on that stock. Timing can be thought of as:

$$E[\gamma_1(x_1 - s_1) + \gamma_2(x_2 - s_2)] - [E(\gamma_1)E(x_1 - s_1) + E(\gamma_2)E(x_2 - s_2)]. \tag{18}$$

The individual stock signal has been removed from earnings so that only timing remains. While, as one will shortly show, the above measure is correct, the form of eq. (18) is not observable. To implement this measure we have to recast (18) in terms of a set of observable variables. The above expression can be written as

$$\mathrm{Cov}\{\gamma_1, (x_1 - s_1)\} + \mathrm{Cov}\{\gamma_2, (x_2 - s_2)\}.$$

This is mathematically equivalent to[16]

$$\mathrm{Cov}(\gamma_1, (\beta_1/\beta_2)x_2) + \mathrm{Cov}(\gamma_2, (\beta_1/\beta_2)x_1).$$

This form of the measure is not only observable, but it has intuitive appeal. It points out that the only reason the fraction of wealth invested in any stock should change with the return on a second stock is because they are both affected by a common timing signal. Adjustment by the ratios of the betas is necessary to correctly incorporate the differential sensitivity (of the two stocks) to the market signal. Substituting the values for γ_1 and γ_2, and x_1 and x_2 in this expression yields

$$d_T = \frac{\beta_1^2\sigma_{s_0}^2}{A\sigma_{\varepsilon_1}^2} + \frac{\beta_2^2\sigma_{s_0}^2}{A\sigma_{\varepsilon_2}^2} \tag{19}$$

for the manager who perceives a signal s_{0_t} and correctly acts on it. If there is no perceived signal, this equals zero. If the manager acts perversely on any timing signal s_{0_t}, this becomes

$$d_T = -\frac{\beta_1^2\sigma_{s_0}^2}{A\sigma_{\varepsilon_1}^2} - \frac{\beta_2^2\sigma_{s_0}^2}{A\sigma_{\varepsilon_2}^2}.$$

So, our timing measure correctly identifies the manager's ability to act on s_{0_t}. Note that, unlike conventional measures, the sign of the timing measure only depends on the response to market-wide signals. With conventional measures the response to unique security signals can be picked up in the timing measure.

The measure of selectivity is simply the overall payoff to management, eq. (17), minus the reward to timing, eq. (19), or

$$d_s = \sigma_{s_1}^2/A\sigma_{\varepsilon_1}^2 + \sigma_{s_2}^2/A\sigma_{\varepsilon_2}^2. \tag{20}$$

Once again this measure has the properties we desire. It is independent of s_0. If the manager fails to act on individual signals, it equals zero. If the manager acts correctly for both stocks, it is positive. If the manager acts perversely for both stocks, it is negative. Finally, if the actions are correct for one and perverse for the other, it can be positive or negative depending on the impact of the actions on the portfolio return. Thus, these measures separate market signals and security signals. Furthermore, they are easily calculated by an outside party who has access to portfolio composition but not to the information signals on which managers act.

While these measures have been developed for the two-security case, they can easily be generalized to an N-security case:

$$d_T = \frac{1}{N-1}\sum_{i=1}^{N}\sum_{\substack{j=1\\ j\neq i}}^{N} \mathrm{Cov}(\gamma_i, (\beta_i/\beta_j)x_j). \tag{21}$$

The overall return due to timing and selectivity is simply

$$d_0 = E\left(\sum_{i=1}^{N}\gamma_i x_i\right) - \sum_{i=1}^{N}E(\gamma_i)E(x_i). \tag{22}$$

The selectivity measure is simply the overall return minus the timing measure. Substituting in for y_i and x_i timing is equal to

$$d_T = \sum_{i=1}^{N} \beta_i^2 \sigma_{s_0}^2 / A\sigma_{\varepsilon_i}^2, \tag{23}$$

and selectivity is equal to

$$d_s = \sum_{i=1}^{N} \sigma_{s_i}^2 / A\sigma_{\varepsilon_i}^2, \tag{24}$$

Eqs. (23) and (24) are interesting because they show that the selectivity and timing measures derived have the economic characteristics we desire. Eqs. (21) and (22) are important because institutions which have data on the composition of portfolios over time can measure the selection and timing ability of any manager.

V Conclusion

Recently, standard measures of performance evaluation have come under increased attack. Dybvig and Ross have shown that, if the manager possesses private information, then outsiders (parties not privy to that information) can reach an incorrect evaluation of management ability. We have shown that, under the assumptions of Dybvig and Ross, if an outsider has access to portfolio composition, portfolio evaluation can be done in a consistent and correct manner. We have argued that at least one important group of outsiders, pension-fund managers, are in a position to gain access to the transaction data necessary. We have been able to develop measures for identifying both selectivity and timing ability when a manager possesses both or neither. Two different sets of measures were developed because the meanings of timing and selectivity are ambiguous. In section 3, we follow common convention in identifying timing with a switch between stocks and T-bills. In section 4, we recognize that signals about individual stocks can affect this allocation and develop measures that separate out the impact of information about all stocks from information about individual stocks. The choice between the measures proposed in section 3 and those proposed in section 4 is largely a matter of taste. Both lead to the same conclusion about overall performance. They differ in allocating performance between selectivity and timing. All of the measures we propose can be computed by an outside who has access to transaction data. This data is available to an important group of outsiders.

It allows this group of outsiders to reach the same conclusions about management performance which they would reach, had they had access to all of the inside information which management employed.

Notes

1. See Amati et al. (1986), Dybvig and Ross (1985), Hendrickson and Merton (1981), Mayers and Rice (1979), Merton (1981) and Roll (1978).

2. The exceptions to this are Cornell (1979) and some of the measures employed by Grinblatt and Titman (1985) where the assumption is made that portfolio weights are available.

3. Hwang (1988) in a Ph.D. dissertation has obtained portfolio positions from a master trust account for several pension funds and has used the measures advocated in this paper to evaluate portfolio performance.

4. D–R results hold in the limit for a large sample. Since ex-post evaluation normally involves a sample, the D–R results should be modified because of possible dependence between random variables in the sample.

5. The ability to observe investment proportions reduces the *differential* information aspects of the problem because the investor can now in effect observe management's interpretation of the information it receives. The impact of this is made clear in the following analysis.

6. We are not the first one to propose this measure. This is equivalent to the Cornell measure if one assumes stationarity of returns, although in any application the results would be very different. Finally, Grinblatt and Titman (1985) reformulate Cornell's measure in a form that is identical to our eq. (1).

7. In D–R's terminology, α is the proportion of the market portfolio that is invested in risky assets. Thus we are assuming $\alpha = 1$.

8. The analysis throughout this paper is consistent with a one-factor model. For convenience in this section, we assume the beta on the pure stock portfolio which is mixed with the riskless asset is one. The extention of the model to a stock portfolio different from one is trivial. In later sections we recognize different betas on invidual assets.

9. Grinblatt and Titman (1985, Proposition 3) state that eq. (4) is equivalent to eq. (1). In utilizing these metrics for measures of portfolio performance, the covariance could be estimated from the sample period.

10. We have used the D–R assumption of exponential utility throughout this paper. The analysis is easiest to perform in this case, for portfolio proportions are linear functions of the signal (s). However, the conclusions hold under more complex definitions of the impact of a signal on returns or the forms of the utility function exhibited by the management. For example, d will have the correct sign as long as a utility function exhibiting non-increasing absolute risk aversion.

11. Since we allow for a market-wide signal, the assumption of independence in ε_i is analogous to the assumption of zero correlation in residuals from a single index model.

12. Recall that earlier we discussed how individual security signals could affect the aggregate amount invested in securities. Thus the conventional definition has ambiguity. We will deal with this in the next section.

13. By direct analogy, misinformation has the wrong sign.

14. The more general case with zero selectivity involves the proportion of risky assets invested in any one asset being independent of the return on that asset and the timing decision (the proportion in the aggregate of risky assets). The mathematics are more complex but the results are identical.

15. In the popular parlance of security analysis, this is known as top-down security analysis. An alternative model is bottom-up analysis. In this case security analysts make forecasts on individual stocks, and market forecasts are developed from the aggregate of these forecasts. In this latter case, after developing s_0 it could be removed from each individual forecast to produce the individual s_{it}.

16. This follows from the definition of x_1 and x_2, together with the assumption that s_0, s_1, s_2 are all uncorrelated.

References

Admati, A., S. Bhattachary, P. Pfleiderer and S. Ross, 1986, On timing and selectivity, *Journal of Finance* 41, 715–730.

Admati, A. and S. Ross, 1985, Measuring investment performance in a rational expectations equilibrium model, *Journal of Business* 58, no. 1, 1–26.

Cornell B., 1979, Asymmetric information and portfolio performance measurement, *Journal of Financial Economics* 7, 381–390.

Dybvig, P. and S. Ross, 1985, Differential information and performance measurement using a security market line, *Journal of Finance* 40, 383–399.

Friend, I., M. Blume and J. Crockett, 1970, *Mutual funds and other institutional investors: A new perspective* (McGraw-Hill, New York).

Grinblatt, M. and S. Titman, 1985, Portfolio performance evaluation: Old issues and new insights, Working paper (Graduate School of Management, UCLA).

Henricksson, R. and R. Merton, 1981, On market timing and investment performance. II. Statistical procedures for evaluating forecasting skills, *Journal of Business* 54, no. 4, 513–533.

Hwang, S.-W., 1988, Information quality and portfolio performance measures: The degree of robustness and empirical evidence, Ph.D. dissertation (New York University).

Jensen, M., 1969, Risk, the pricing of capital assets and the evaluation of investment portfolios, *Journal of Business* 42, no. 2, 167–247.

Mayers, D. and E. Rice, 1979, Measuring portfolio performance and the empirical content of asset pricing models, *Journal of Financial Economics* 7, 3–28.

Merton, R. C., 1981, On market timing and investment performance. Part I. An equilibrium theory of value for market forecasts, *Journal of Business* 54, no. 3, 363–406.

Roll, R., 1978, Ambiguity when performance is measured by the securities market line, *Journal of Finance* 33, 1051–1069.

Sharp, W. F., 1966, Mutual fund performance, *Journal of Business* 39, no. 1, part 2, 119–138.

Treynor, J. and M. Mazuy, Can mutual funds outguess the market, *Harvard Business Review* 44, no. 4, 131–136.

Empirical
Commodities Partnerships

7 Professionally Managed, Publicly Traded Commodity Funds

Edwin J. Elton, Martin J. Gruber,
and Joel C. Rentzler

The best laid schemes o' mice and men
Gang aft a-gley;
An lea's us nought but grief an pain,
for promis'd joy.

Robert Burns

The concept of a professionally managed investment portfolio composed of positions in commodity and financial futures is appealing to the investment community. One thinks of investment in commodities as a way to protect capital in times of high inflation. Perhaps this partially accounts for the tremendous growth of professionally managed public commodity funds. Prior to February 1979 there was only one fund for which monthly data existed, but by 1985 the number had grown to 94 funds, with over $600 million in assets under management.[1]

Most of the funds have the ability to trade in all available futures and commodities. These include financial instruments and futures on financial instruments, foreign currencies and futures and forward contracts on foreign currencies, and commodities and futures on commodities. Most funds do not restrict themselves to subsectors of the market but take positions across all sectors; funds can and do take both long and short positions in the futures market. A typical quote from a prospectus is as follows: "Diversification will be achieved by trading a variety of commodities...."[2]

Most commodity funds trade on the basis of technical systems. In particular, trend-following systems that assume that a trend in price will continue over time are typical. Here is a representative statement from a prospectus: "Trading decisions of the Advisor will be based primarily on technical analysis and trend-following trading strategies which seek to identify price changes and trends. The buy and sell decisions based on these strategies are not based on analysis of fundamental supply and demand factors, general economic factors or anticipated world events."[3]

Given the popularity of these funds and their probable continued growth, it seems worthwhile to examine their performance. Interest in their performance is increased because of the apparent handicaps that investors in these funds face. These handicaps are of two types. First, their management fees and transaction costs are very high compared with transaction costs and management fees for more traditional fixed-income or equity investments. Yearly management fees and transaction costs of commodity funds have been estimated to average over 19.2% of assets under management.[4] Second, most commodity fund managers appear to rely primarily on trend following and technical trading rules for decision making. These rules have been discredited in the common stock area. In fact, many of these rules were first tested (and found not to work) on commodity data (e.g., Mandelbrot 1966).

In this paper we will examine the performance of publicly traded commodity funds. One problem encountered in the analysis is that the data sample is small since these funds have not been in existence very long. There are only 6 years of performance figures. In addition, as we will see, the standard deviation of return on these funds is extremely large relative to other investments. This makes the problem of analysis from 6 years of data even more difficult.

This paper is divided into four sections. In Section I we discuss the data we analyze in the subsequent sections. In Section II we examine the performance of publicly traded commodity funds. In particular, we consider whether it is optimal either to hold such a fund in isolation or to add it to an existing portfolio of stocks and bonds. In Section III we examine whether we can differentiate between funds that will do well and funds that will do poorly in the future. If past performance data are indicative of future performance in either an absolute or a relative sense, then performance can be improved beyond that found in Section II. Section IV contains our conclusion.

I Data

The basic data set employed in this paper is the monthly total rate of return on each publicly traded commodity fund in existence from July 1979 to June 1985. Total return is defined as the cash distribution during any month plus the change in net asset value over the month divided by the value per unit at the beginning of the month.[5] When we performed

Table 7.1

		Average monthly return		
Year	No. of funds	For monthly holding period	For annual holding period	Average SD
1	12	.0182	.0027	.1577
2	16	.0219	.0090	.1211
3	34	.0149	.0112	.0824
4	49	−.0191	−.0267	.1167
5	70	−.0020	−.0054	.0793
6	85	.0097	.0048	.0943
Average	...	.0073	−.0007	.1130*

* Not simply an average of the six yearly numbers. Rather, it is an average arrived at using the technique discussed in the text.

this study, the latest data available were for the month of June 1985. Thus, we ended our last year in June 1985. We then had 6 years' worth of usable data. We could have started the data series 1 year earlier, but there were monthly data on only one fund in that year. Table 7.1 shows the number of funds in existence in June of each sample year that were publicly reporting monthly data.[6] When a fund dissolved midyear, we computed returns as if the proceeds were invested in the average commodity fund. However, dissolved funds were not included in standard deviation calculations.

In order to make some comparisons with alternative investments, we also employed indexes of monthly return performance on several other types of investments. Monthly returns on the Standard and Poor's 500 Stock Index, Treasury bills, long-term government bonds, long-term corporate bonds, and small stocks were taken from Ibbotson (1985). In addition, for our 6-year sample period the Shearson Bond Index was employed. Finally, to get some idea of how a long market position in commodities and futures might perform, monthly rates of return were calculated from the Dow Jones Spot Index and the Dow Jones Futures Index.

II The Performance of Publicly Traded Commodity Funds

In this section, we will look at the desirability of holding a randomly selected, publicly traded commodity fund. The appropriate way to analyze this question is to examine whether such a commodity fund should

Table 7.2

	June 1960–June 1985		Sample 6-year period	
	Average monthly returns (annual holding period)	SD monthly returns*	Average monthly returns (annual holding period)	SD monthly returns
Common stocks	.0074	.0414	.0131	.0399
Small stocks	.0123	.0639	.0168	.0465
Long-term corporate bonds	.0045	.0271	.0079	.0428
Long-term government bonds	.0041	.0279	.0075	.0435
Shearson Bond Index	N.A.	N.A.	.0097	.0293
Treasury bills	.0051	.0026	.0085	.0015

Source. Ibbotson (1984), except for Shearson Bond Index.
* 25 years ending December 1984.

be added to a bond or stock portfolio. However, before doing so, we will briefly examine whether a randomly selected commodity fund is a desirable stand-alone investment.

A Commodity Funds as an Alternative Investment Vehicle

Assume an investor, at the beginning of each year, selected a commodity fund at random. What would the performance look like? Table 7.1 gives a partial answer. Table 7.1 lists the average monthly returns (assuming both a 1-month and a 1-year holding period), the average standard deviation of returns, and the number of funds in our study at the beginning of each year. To provide points of comparison, table 7.2 shows some data for stocks and bonds. All of this data was also computed using a 1-year holding period.

The data shown for common stocks, small stocks, and the Shearson Bond Index can be considered typical of the performance of a widely diversified passive investment in each type of security. The common stock data are for the Standard and Poor's 500 Index and would be reflective of the results for most index funds before management fees. The small stock data are for the 20% of the stocks with the lowest capitalization on the NYSE. The amount invested in each stock is directly proportional to the stock's capitalization. Finally, the Shearson index is an index of all government and corporate bonds. Like the stock indexes described above, it is a capitalization-weighted index with the weights directly proportional to the bond's capitalization. Government bonds constitute about 75% of the Shearson Bond Index, and the index is dominated by bonds of intermediate maturity. The Shearson Bond Index is not used over the entire 25-year period because it has only been computed for recent years.

The Ibbotson and Sinquefield indexes (Ibbotson 1985) are indexes for single 20-year bonds. These indexes, which have become a standard for the industry, are employed here because, unlike the Shearson Bond Index, they exist over a long time period. The disadvantage of the Ibbotson and Sinquefield data for our purpose is that they may not be an accurate representation of a typical bond portfolio. The typical bond portfolio contains many bonds and has a shorter duration. The latter will surely cause differences in return. We would expect a bond portfolio to have less risk than the Ibbotson and Sinquefield data both because of the diversification effect of multiple bonds and because of shorter duration. This is reflected in our sample period. The standard deviation of the Shearson Bond Index is .0293 compared with .0435 for the Ibbotson and Sinquefield government bond index over the same time period.

Before examining commodity funds as an investment vehicle, one other issue needs to be discussed. We are using a mean-variance framework. On the surface it might seem that commodity funds could serve as a hedge against shifts in the prices of consumption goods or inflation. If this were true, then a more general framework such as Long's (1974) or Breeden's (1979) equilibrium model might be necessary to examine their relative value. However, a little reflection shows that this is an inaccurate perspective. As discussed before, commodity funds do not specialize in a commodity or group of commodities. They can hold commodities, commodity futures, financial instruments, financial futures, currencies, and currency futures long or short. Some months a fund can be long a commodity position, and the next period it may be short the same commodity position. Funds allow all these possibilities in their prospectuses. Thus an investor could not analyze a prospectus and determine that a particular commodity fund was a potential hedge against a price rise in any commodity or inflation in general. Further, as we discuss later, the actual return data does not allow an investor to determine which funds might serve as a hedge against inflation. The rank correlation between funds from one period to the next ranked on correlation with inflation is insignificant and sometimes positive and sometimes negative. The correlations of the average fund with inflation is close to zero. Thus an investor could not use an existing commodity fund as a potential inflation hedge, and therefore a general mean-variance framework is appropriate.

The most striking characteristic of commodity funds relative to bonds and stocks is their high standard deviation. The standard deviation of the typical commodity fund is more than three times as high as that of the bond index and more than twice as high as the stock index for most years.

There are two different monthly returns displayed in table 7.1. The monthly return labeled "monthly holding period" literally applies only if an investor has a 1-month holding period. The average monthly return with an annual holding period is the twelfth root of the annual return minus one. Why the difference in the two numbers? To get an annual return, one compounds the monthly returns. The average monthly return for the 1-year holding period is the twelfth root of this annual rate. This is, of course, a geometric average, while the figures shown in table 1 under the heading "monthly holding period return" are an arithmetic average. To see what a difference a change in holding period can make, let us examine one of the 12 firms in year 1. It had an arithmetic average return of 9.6% per month, or a 200% annualized return. The actual yearly return was 35%, or 2.53% per month. One reason for this difference was a decline in 1 month of 43% followed by a rise of 85%. The arithmetic mean of this is 21% while the geometric mean is 2.7%. We feel the assumption of an annual holding period is likely to be more relevant. Few, if any, investors have an investment horizon of only 1 month. In addition, the sales fees (for purchase of commodity funds) would virtually ensure a negative return on a 1-month holding period basis.

The same kind of considerations hold, of course, for bonds and stocks. We calculated these returns on the same annual holding period basis.[7]

How do publicly traded commodity funds compare as an investment alternative to bonds or stocks? As discussed earlier, the risk for commodity funds is two to three times larger than for stock or bond funds. While 6 years is a short period to generalize from, an examination of table 7.1 shows that returns on commodity funds were poor relative to actual performance on stocks and bonds over the sample period and relative to our expectations concerning stock and bond returns in the long run. The average return on commodity funds was negative in 2 of the 6 years and negative overall.[8] For the 266 fund years in our sample, 130 were negative and 136 were positive. These numbers assume that each fund year is equally likely to be picked. Since we have more funds in later years, it emphasizes performance in these years. If we assume that each year is equally likely to be picked and then randomly select a fund within that year, then the probability of picking a fund with a positive return is .56.

Commodity funds use Treasury bills as collateral for their futures contracts. With zero selection ability and no management fees or transaction costs we should observe a return equal to that on Treasury bills. We found that, of the 266 fund years in our sample, 162 funds had returns below this benchmark and 104 had returns above. The average probability over the 6 years of selecting a fund at random with a return above the riskless rate was .42. Over our sample period, the probability that the mean return on commodity funds was equal to or greater than the mean return of either the stock fund or the bond fund was about 5%.[9] Thus both risk and return considerations would suggest that commodity funds are not a useful stand-alone investment.

While commodity funds do not seem to be an attractive alternative to a portfolio of bonds or stocks, it is still possible that they are an appropriate *addition* to a portfolio of bonds and/or stocks. This depends not only on the expected value and standard deviation of fund returns but also on how these returns are correlated with bond and stock returns. It is to this issue that we now turn.

B Commodity Funds as Part of an Overall Portfolio

In this section we will examine whether a commodity fund selected at random should be added to a portfolio of stocks and bonds. In Appendix A, we show that a commodity fund should be added as long as[10]

$$\frac{\bar{R}_c - R_f}{\sigma_c} > \left(\frac{\bar{R}_p - R_f}{\sigma_p}\right)\rho_{cp}, \tag{1}$$

where $\bar{R}_c$ is the expected return of commodity fund c, R_f is the riskless rate, σ_c is the standard deviation of the commodity fund c, $\bar{R}_p$ is the expected return of portfolio p, σ_p is the standard deviation of portfolio p, and ρ_{cp} is the correlation between commodity fund c and portfolio p.

The left side of equation (1) should be familiar to most readers as the Sharpe ratio for evaluating mutual funds. Whether or not a commodity fund enters a portfolio depends on estimates of the expected return and standard deviation of return on commodity funds, the expected return and the standard deviation of the bond-stock portfolio, and the correlation between commodity funds and the portfolio.

We now examine each of these in turn. We will start with correlations and then examine standard deviations. We will save expected return for last since this is the most difficult quantity to estimate.

1 Correlation Coefficients

In this section of the paper, we examine the correlation of commodity funds with other investments. Our primary concern is how highly correlated these funds are with stock and bond indexes. However, some interesting insights can be gained into the performance of these funds by examining their correlation with some other indexes.

The arithmetic average of the funds' correlations with seven indexes are presented in table 7.3. A correlation coefficient for each year is reported along with two average correlation coefficients. The simple average is just the arithmetic average of the six yearly correlation coefficients, one for each year. The overall average is computed by finding the correlation coefficient of each fund with the relevant index using data over the full history of that fund and then averaging across funds.

In order to see if the typical commodity fund should be added to a portfolio of stocks and bonds, we need estimates of the correlation of funds with both stocks and bonds. Note that the correlation with both stocks and bonds is close to zero. The maximum association (coefficient of determination) between commodity funds and stocks is less than 5%. This correlation coefficient is positive in 2 years and negative in 4 years. The simple average of their correlation coefficients is −.036, while the overall average is −.121.

The correlation coefficients are on average close to and not statistically different from zero. We will use the overall average as our best estimate of the correlation coefficient in later sections. Since this is the smaller value, it gives the maximum chance for commodity funds to enter the portfolio.

When we turn to bonds, we find a parallel case. The largest value for the coefficient of determination is just over 5%. The two estimates of the average correlation are .007 and −.003. We will use −.003, the overall average, in later analysis.

The other numbers in table 7.3 are not directly related to the analysis in later sections, but they do shed some light on the characteristics of commodity funds. Commodity funds are often thought of as a hedge against inflation. Note that the correlation with the consumer price index is close to zero. Commodity funds do not exhibit the strong tendency to move with inflation usually attributed to them. Instead they show returns that are almost independent of inflation. The correlation of commodity funds with inflation is less than one-fifth of the correlation of Treasury bills with inflation. As a further test, we ranked funds by correlation with inflation in each of the 6 periods. A Spearman rank correlation was calculated

Table 7.3

Year	Stocks	Bonds	Treasury bills	Consumer price index	Commodity futures index	Commodity cash index	Average fund
1	.183	−.021	−.127	.180	.267	.236	.504
2	−.044	−.050	−.065	−.194	−.260	−.114	.541
3	−.003	.228	−.165	−.024	−.402	−.073	.705
4	.050	−.067	−.218	.067	.435	.365	.743
5	−.186	−.203	.194	−.024	.091	.119	.503
6	−.214	.114	.009	−.092	−.543	−.538	.676
Overall average*	−.121	−.003	.010	.009	−.021	−.018	.617
Simple average	−.036	.007	−.062	−.015	−.069	−.001	.612

* The overall average is not an average of the six yearly numbers but rather an average across funds of the correlation of each fund with the respective index for the entire time period over which we have data for the fund.

between adjacent periods. While this averaged .10, it was insignificant in each case and sometimes positive and sometimes negative. Thus commodity funds as a group or individually do not serve as a hedge against inflation.

Another interesting point to note from table 7.3 is that the return on commodity funds is not consistently correlated with the return on either a commodity cash index or a commodity futures index. The two correlations with each index are small, on average, and positive half the time. This indicates that the typical commodity fund does not consistently resemble either of those indexes. The major factor accounting for this probably is the tendency of the funds to sometimes sell and sometimes buy futures contracts, although the tendency of the funds to weight their long positions in futures differently from the indexes is also a contributing factor.

The last column in table 7.3 shows the average correlation of each fund with an equally weighted index of all funds. This is the only index with which the funds have consistently high correlation. However, if the same analysis were performed for mutual funds, the correlation would be much higher. For example, Sharpe (1966) reports an average correlation of close to .90 between mutual funds and a market index. Thus commodity fund managers do make decisions that lead to similar patterns of returns but not nearly to the extent of managers of common stock mutual funds.

2 Standard Deviation of Commodity Funds

Table 7.1 can be used to estimate the anticipated standard deviation for a randomly selected commodity fund. As noted above, the standard deviation of the typical commodity fund is two to three times the standard deviation of a bond or stock index.

Although there is year-to-year variability in the average standard deviation across funds, it is not so large as to suggest that the future will be much different from the past. What is our best estimate of the standard deviation of the average commodity fund? From the high correlation of returns on individual funds with the fund index, we see that fund returns exhibit strong cross-sectional dependence. If this dependence were reasonably stable and there were an equal number of funds each year, then an arithmetic average of the standard deviation across all funds and all years would be appropriate.

However, the number of funds varies dramatically over time from 12 in the first year to 85 in the sixth. To use a simple average of the variance on all funds does not take into account this change in the number of funds.

This would overemphasize the common element across funds in the sixth year relative to the first year. To adjust for this change in number, we regressed each fund's return against the return on an index of all funds. This divided the total variance into the systematic component and a component unique to each fund for each year. We then calculated an average unique variance by averaging across all funds and all years (266 fund-years). This variance was added to our best estimate of the systematic variance to produce an overall estimate. The details are discussed in Appendix B and the estimate is reported in table 7.1.

Although the estimate of the average standard deviation of monthly returns from the 6 years of data is likely to be a good estimate of the future standard deviation, it is hard to look at table 1 and feel very comfortable about any estimate of the mean return. It would be nice to have a longer history. Unfortunately, this does not exist. Instead of using table 1 to get an estimate of expected return, we will solve equation (1) for the break-even expected return and then use the data in table 1 to analyze whether or not commodity funds are likely to have returns higher than this break-even point.

3 Break-even Analysis

The other inputs we need in order to apply equation (1) are the expected return and standard deviation of the optimum bond-stock mix. What values might an investor expect for returns on stocks and bonds and for the covariance structure between them? We used two sets of data for stocks and bonds to estimate these: the last 6 years and the last 25 years of data. Both are shown in table 7.2. For the 25-year bond index we used an average of long-term government and corporate bonds. This gave us an expected return of .0043 and a standard deviation of .0275. For the 6-year bond index we used the numbers shown in table 7.2 for the Shearson Bond Index.

If one compares the return on bonds to the Treasury bill rate over the last 6 years and last 25 years, the Treasury bill rate is higher. Unless bond returns are negatively correlated with stock returns (and there is no evidence that they are), bonds will never enter the optimum portfolio. Thus the relevant question is, Should a commodity fund be added to a stock fund? For the 6-year data the inequality is

$$\frac{\bar{R}_c - .0085}{.1130} > \left(\frac{.0131 - .0085}{.0399}\right)(-.121).$$

Table 7.4

Scenario	% Stock	Excess return $(\bar{R}_p - R_F)^*$	SD $(\sigma)^*$	Correlation with portfolio $\rho(cp)$ † ‡	Break-even rate of return $(\bar{R}_c)$‡
6 year	100	.0046	.0399	−.121	.0069
25 year	100	.0023	.0414	−.121	.0077
6 year	63	.0033	.0309	−.099	.0073
25 year§	63	.0012	.0289	−.110	.0080

* Entries from table 2.

† The covariance of a commodity fund with a portfolio is the sum of the proportion in each asset in the portfolio times the correlation of the commodity fund with the asset times the product of the standard deviation of commodity funds times the standard deviation of the asset. For example, the covariance for the third entry is .63(−.121)(.1130)(.0399) + .37(−.003)(.1130)(.0293).

‡ Assumes standard deviation of commodity funds of .1130 (see table 1).

§ Assumes a correlation of .10 between stocks and bonds, which is the average correlation between corporate and government bonds and the stock index, as shown in Ibbotson (1985).

Solving for $\bar{R}_c$ gives the minimum expected return that a commodity fund must earn to enter the optimum portfolio. This result and a similar calculation for 25 years of data are shown in the first two rows of table 7.4.

We used a second set of stock and bond return forecasts to obtain break-even returns for commodity funds. The optimal bond-stock split using the full 1926–85 Ibbotson and Sinquefield data is 63% stock and 37% bonds.[11] We took these optimum proportions and applied these proportions to the 6-year and 25-year data shown in table 7.2. We again solved for the expected return on commodity funds that would just cause commodity funds to enter the optimum portfolio. These results are shown in the last two rows of table 7.4.

The expected return that would have commodity funds enter is very similar across the four sets of assumptions. It varies between .0069 and .0080 across the four scenarios examined with an average of .0075.

Examining tables 7.1 and 7.4 shows that, if a monthly holding period is used, and if we take the 6 years of actual return data as a reasonable estimate of expected returns, then the average return of .0073 is below the average number in table 7.4 and commodity funds should not enter. If an annual holding period is used and the 6-year average return of −.0007 is used as the expected return, the evidence is even stronger that commodity funds should not enter. As discussed earlier, we feel that an annual holding period is the more reasonable assumption. For our sample of 266 fund years, 163 had returns below and 103 had returns above .0075. The average probability of the return on a commodity fund being above .0075 over the 6 years is .42. The odds of the mean return on commodity funds being .0075 or better when the average return over the 6 years is −.0007 and the standard deviation of the mean return across the 6 years is .0052 are less than 6%.

An alternative way of examining expected returns for commodity funds is to utilize economic theory to examine what we might logically expect for returns. Commodity managers frequently go short as well as long in the futures contracts. Table 7.3 shows correlation coefficients of fund returns with futures and spot indexes of −.021 and −.018, respectively. Only 1% of the return of commodity funds can be explained by index movements. The average correlation is sometimes positive and sometimes negative. These results provide no evidence of a consistent pattern of long or short purchases. If managers were equally likely to be long or short, the expected return before transaction costs, management fees, and management forecasting ability would be zero. This is in contrast to stock and bond funds that have substantial positive expected returns before transaction costs and management fees, even with no management forecasting ability.

Transaction costs should not be taken lightly. Even though costs per transaction are low, transactions are frequent. Irwin and Brorsen (1985) find commissions averaging 10.7% for the 20 firms they sample. In addition, the management fee on commodity funds is substantially higher than the management fee on stock or bond funds. There are two types of management fees on commodity funds: a fee related to asset size and a fee related to performance. For the funds in our sample, asset fees ranged 3%–6% per year. This is in contrast to stock and bond funds where one-half of 1% is usual. In addition, there is an incentive fee. Examining table 7.1 might suggest that incentive fees are unimportant. However, given the tremendous variability of monthly returns and the basing of incentive fees on shorter-term performance, incentive fees can be high even with poor long-term performance. Irwin and Brorsen (1985) find that management and incentive fees average 8.5%. Thus total yearly fees of 19.2% can be expected. In contrast, Sharpe (1981) reports that total fees for mutual funds average about 1% per year.

Examining table 7.4 shows that commodity managers must earn a return of about 9% per year to be attractive investments. Adding this to transaction costs and management fees of above 19% and an expected return that is close to zero without forecasting ability suggests that a return to forecasting ability of over 28% is necessary for commodity funds to be attractive. Evidence from other security markets should lead to a healthy degree of skepticism.

Thus actual returns of commodity funds as well as the more general evidence of financial economics suggest that a randomly selected commodity fund should not be held. In the next section we will examine whether there are characteristics of commodity funds that allow funds that will have above-average performance to be selected.

III Prediction of Superior Performing Funds

Ex post, there is always a commodity fund that did best. Given the high variance in fund performance (both over time for any fund and cross sectionally among funds), it is not at all surprising that at any point of time or over any short period of time there always exists a fund that did well. The relevant question for an investor is, Can he or she identify, ex ante, the funds that will do well? In this section, we shall examine whether any of several attributes of fund performance is predictive of future performance. The degree of consistency and predictability of performance is interesting in its own right. It also has major implications for the inclusion of commodity funds in optimal portfolios.

This section is divided into two parts. In the first part, we discuss the tests of consistency and predictability we use as well as the performance series we look at. In the second part, we discuss empirical results.

A Consistency and Predictability

The majority of our analysis in this section is based on two types of tests. The first type is a test of consistency. That is, do funds that have high values on a measure in one period tend to have high values in the subsequent period? Two separate tests of consistency will be used. The first measures consistency across all funds, while the second examines consistency only for those funds that have done extremely well or extremely poorly. The second type is a test of predictability, namely, whether past values of a performance measure forecast better than a naive model.

1 Consistency

To test consistency we examined performance both across all funds and for the tails. In order to judge whether overall performance in one year was associated with performance in the next year, Spearman's rank correlation was computed between all adjacent years for all funds that were present in both of the paired years.[12] These results are contained in table 7.5.

For example, all funds that existed in the first year of our sample period were ranked by return from high to low in that year. The return of each of these funds was computed for the second year of our sample, and funds were again ranked from best to worst. The Spearman correlations were computed between the ranks for the first and second years. In the case of the first and second set of paired years, small sample tests of Spearman's coefficient were used.[13] For the third, fourth, and fifth paired sample years, Kendall's large sample test was used to compute the adjusted correlation coefficient, which is distributed as Student's t.[14]

A second set of tests were performed to examine consistency. That is, if we selected the funds that had unusually high (or low) values on a performance characteristic in one period, would we get unusually high or low values for that or another important characteristic in the next period? For example, the return from purchasing the three funds that had the highest return and holding them for 1 year was compared with the return from purchasing and holding the three funds with the lowest return. Similarly, the return from purchasing and holding the top third, middle third, and bottom third of funds in each period was computed and compared. Even if there is no consistency across the population of funds from period to period, it is possible that there is consistency in the very best and worst performing funds.

2 Predictability

While a measure of association is interesting in itself, perhaps the more important set of tests for our purposes is whether past values of a performance measure can be used to predict future performance. To test this, we examine whether past values of a performance measure are better predictors than the most naive possible prediction (see tables 7.6–7.9). In all cases (except for one noted in the next section), the naive prediction used is that the best estimate for all funds is zero. For example, in the case of predicting returns, we compare the prediction that next period's return equals this period's return with the prediction that next period's return equals zero. If past return is a better predictor than zero, then past return allows one to differentiate between funds.

For each fund present in a particular year, we predict performance in the subsequent year. We examined five pairs of adjacent years. For each fund, we computed the squared forecast error under each of our two forecasts. Since we have related samples (two forecasts for each fund), the

Table 7.5

	10 observations: year 1 vs. year 2		15 observations: year 2 vs. year 3		34 observations: year 3 vs. year 4		49 observations: year 4 vs. year 5		67 observations: year 5 vs. year 6	
	Correlation	*t*-value[a]	Correlation	*t*-value[a]	Correlation	*t*-value[b]	Correlation	*t*-value[b]	Correlation	*t*-value[b]
Sharpe ratio: year *t* vs. year *t* + 1[c]	.2242	...	.4393	**	.0591	.335	−.1008	−.695	.2886	2.43*
Returns: year *t* vs. year *t* + 1	.0667	...	.4679	**	.1499	.858*	.1023	.705	.3068	2.600*
SD: year *t* vs. year *t* + 1	.9152	*	.4464	**	.1704	.978	.6543	5.932*	.3357	2.873*
SD: year *t* vs. Sharpe ratio year *t* + 1	−.6485	**	−.4429	**	−.4460	−2.819*	−.0548	−.376	−.1923	−1.580

a. For small samples (under 30), the statistical significance of any correlation was arrived at using small sample tests based on the number of permutations possible. For a discussion of the tests, see Siegel (1956, pp. 210, 211); and for critical values, see Siegel (1956, table P, p. 284).
b. For large samples (over 30), *t*-values were computed using Kendall's procedure. See Siegel (1956, p. 212) for a discussion of the procedure.
c. These tests are conducted in terms of monthly returns assuming an annual holding period. The tests were also run on monthly returns assuming a monthly holding period. The results are very similar, and, in the interest of brevity, the second set of results have not been reported.
* Statistically significant at the 1% level.
** Statistically significant at the 5% level.

Table 7.6

	Period 2		Period 3		Period 4		Period 5		Period 6			
	Sharpe ratio	Rank	Sharpe ratio	Rank	Sharpe ratio	Rank	Sharpe ratio	Rank	Sharpe ratio	Rank	Avg. ratio	Avg. rank
Top 3	.3279	1	.1031	1	−.1834	2	−.0933	2	.3392	1	.0987	1.4
Bottom 3	.2898	2	−.1966	2	−.1032	1	.1262	1	.0770	2	.0386	1.6
Top $\frac{1}{3}$*	.3279	1	.0569	1	−.2427	1	−.1903	2	.0622	1	.0028	1.2
Middle $\frac{1}{3}$	−.1154	3	−.0567	2	−.4090	3	−.2308	3	−.0488	2	−.1495	2.6
Bottom $\frac{1}{3}$	.2898	2	−.1685	3	−.2691	2	−.1115	1	−.1613	3	−.0841	2.2

* In forming the three groups, if the total number of firms was not divisible by 3, the extra one or two firms were placed in the middle group.

Table 7.7

	Period 2		Period 3		Period 4		Period 5		Period 6			
	Return	Rank	Return	Rank	Return	Rank	Return	Rank	Return	Rank	Avg. return	Avg. rank
Top 3	.0167	1	.0170	1	−.0229	1	−.0109	2	−.0044	2	−.0009	1.4
Bottom 3	.0149	2	−.0054	2	−.0285	2	.0249	1	.0136	1	.0039	1.6
Top $\frac{1}{3}$*	.0167	1	.0127	1	−.0162	1	−.0009	2	.0152	1	.0059	1.2
Middle $\frac{1}{3}$	.0050	3	.0118	2	−.0351	3	.0035	1	.0003	3	−.0029	2.4
Bottom $\frac{1}{3}$	.0149	2	.0045	3	−.0275	2	−.0127	3	.0018	2	−.0038	2.4

* In forming the three groups, if the total number of firms was not divisible by 3, the extra one or two firms were placed in the middle group.

Table 7.8

	Period 2		Period 3		Period 4		Period 5		Period 6			
	SD	Rank	SD	Rank	SD	Rank	SD	Rank	SD	Rank	Avg. SD	Avg. rank
Top 3	.2300	1	.1131	1	.1795	2	.1599	1	.0364	2	.1438	1.4
Bottom 3	.0637	2	.0639	2	.1955	1	.0346	2	.0639	1	.0843	1.6
Top $\frac{1}{3}$*	.2300	1	.0934	1	.1244	1	.1077	1	.1326	1	.1376	1.0
Middle $\frac{1}{3}$	.1183	2	.0749	2	.1074	3	.0880	2	.0915	2	.0960	2.2
Bottom $\frac{1}{3}$	.0637	3	.0648	3	.1127	2	.0525	3	.0678	3	.0723	2.8

* In forming the three groups, if the total number of firms was not divisible by 3, the extra one or two firms were placed in the middle group.

Table 7.9

	Period 2		Period 3		Period 4		Period 5		Period 6			
	Sharpe ratio	Rank	Sharpe ratio	Rank	Sharpe ratio	Rank	Sharpe ratio	Rank	Sharpe ratio	Rank	Avg. ratio	Avg. rank
Top 3	−.1312	2	.0520	2	−.3518	2	−.0765	1	−.5559	2	−.2127	1.8
Bottom 3	.5380	1	.1335	1	−.1032	1	−.3483	2	.1481	1	.0736	1.2
Top $\frac{1}{3}$*	−.1312	3	−.0992	3	−.3722	3	−.2768	3	−.1229	2	−.2005	3.0
Middle $\frac{1}{3}$	.0420	2	−.0697	2	−.3637	2	−.0552	1	.0077	3	−.0878	1.6
Bottom $\frac{1}{3}$	.5380	1	.1160	1	−.1890	1	−.2116	2	−.0353	1	.0436	1.4

* In forming the three groups, if the total number of firms was not divisible by 3, the extra one or two firms were placed in the middle group.

Table 7.10

	10 observations: years 1 and 2	15 observations: years 2 and 3	34 observations: years 3 and 4	49 observations: years 4 and 5	67 observations: years 5 and 6
Sharpe ratio at t as forecaster of Sharpe ratio at $t+1$*	−.05	1.48	−1.72	.81	2.18
Returns at t as forecaster of return at $t+1$*	.49	2.04	4.94	2.36	2.57
SD at t as forecaster at SD at $t+1$†	−1.03	.89	1.02	−.60	.25

* These tests were conducted in terms of monthly returns assuming a yearly holding period. Similar results were obtained when monthly returns assuming a monthly holding period were used. The native model was zero for all funds.

† The naive model was the average (across all funds) SD for the previous year. The values used were .1577, .1211, .0824, .1167, and .0793, respectively.

properties of the mean difference in squared forecast error were examined. The average difference in squared forecast error and the standard deviation of the mean difference in squared forecast error was computed and the associated t-value of the difference is reported in table 7.10.

A positive value in this table indicates that the naive model led to lower forecast errors. For the later three pairs of years, the samples are large enough that, by the central limit theorem, the statistic should be normally distributed. A one-tailed test is used to see if past performance predicts better than the naive model. Statistical significance is indicated in table 7.10. For the first two pairs of years, the sample is too small to resort to the central limit theorem. Here, the Wilcoxon Matched Pairs Signed-Ranks Test was used to judge statistical significance.[15] In table 7.10, t-values are reported to show how many standard deviations away from zero the mean is, even though they are not used to test significance.

B *The Empirical Results*

Examining equation (1) shows that the condition for commodity funds to enter into an optimal portfolio is the Sharpe performance index. In this section, we first examine the Sharpe ratio itself to see if its value across funds is consistent and predictable over time. We then examine each of its components, return and standard deviation, in turn. If either of these shows predictability, we will then examine whether it can be used to better differentiate between funds with respect to their Sharpe ratios. In all cases we will use monthly returns based on an annual holding period. Results for a monthly holding period were very similar.

1 The Sharpe Ratio

The first question examined was, Do funds that have a high value for the Sharpe ratio in one period tend to have a high value for the Sharpe ratio in the subsequent period?

From table 7.5, the average of the five rank correlations for the Sharpe index for adjacent years is 0.182. While it is statistically different from zero at the 1% level in 1 out of 5 years, it is negative in 1 year and the average association is less than 4%.

When we examine the tails of the distribution (table 7.6), we find a slight amount of information in the Sharpe coefficients. On average, the top three funds (and the top third of funds) ranked by the Sharpe ratio have higher values for their Sharpe ratio than the bottom three funds (or bottom third of funds). Lest we place too much emphasis on these results, we should remark that, while the top three funds do better than the bottom three on average, they do worse in 2 of the 5 years. Furthermore, while the top third of funds does better than the bottom third on average, the bottom third does better than the middle third on average. Based on these results, it appears unlikely that using the Sharpe ratio to select funds will lead to improvement.

When we examine (table 7.10) whether this period's Sharpe ratio is a better predictor of next period's ratio than is zero, we get ambiguous results. Past Sharpe ratios forecast better in 1 year and worse in 4 years. They never forecast better at a statistically significant level, while the naive model performs best in 1 year at a statistically significant level.

We now turn to the components of the Sharpe ratio, return and standard deviation, to see if they show consistency and predictability over time.

2 Returns

From table 7.5 we see that the average of the five rank correlation coefficients in monthly returns assuming an annual holding period is 0.219. The correlation is positive in each sample case and is significantly different from zero at the 5% level in two of the five samples. While the association is always positive, the extent of association (less than 5%) is relatively small.

Table 7.7 shows that, if an investor bought the three funds that performed the worst and held them for 1 year, on average the investor would do very slightly *better* than buying the three funds that performed best. One would have done better in 2 years and worse in 3 years. If the sample is divided into three groups according to returns, the best performance, on average, would have been obtained by buying the third of the funds that performed best. The consistency of the return measure appears to be marginally better than the consistency of the Sharpe index. However, the change in ranking according to how the tails are defined warns us not to place undue reliance on this criterion. When we examine predictability of past returns (table 7.10), we find that the naive forecast of zero return for each fund is a better forecast of next year's average monthly return than assuming that next year's return equals last year's return. In fact, if a two-tailed test were used, the naive model would produce lower error at the 5% significant level in four out of five cases. Clearly, past returns of any fund provide no information for predicting future returns.

3 Risk

While past return might not tell the potential investor anything about the kind of returns he or she should expect to receive in the future, the past would still be useful if it could allow the investor to differentiate between funds in terms of riskiness. The measure of riskiness we examined was the standard deviation of fund returns.[16]

There does seem to be consistency in standard deviation. The average rank correlation (across the five sets of paired years) between standard deviation in one period and standard deviation in the next (table 7.5) was .0514. This is the highest value for any of our measures of performance. Furthermore, the average rank correlation across funds in each of the paired years is always positive, and it is statistically significantly different from zero on average and in 4 of the 5 paired years.

Turing now to an examination of the tails (table 7.8) of the distribution, we see evidence that past ordering by risk provides information about future ordering by risk. When we examine the top three and bottom three funds, the top three have the highest risk on average and in 3 out of 5 years. When we look at the three equally sized groups, the top third of the funds has the biggest risk on average and in each of the 5 years. There seems to be information about the future risk contained in past risk for firms with very high or low standard deviations.

In examining prediction for the other variables, we have used zero as the naive forecasting model. However, this seems inappropriate (too naive) in the case of standard deviation, since we know that all values have to be greater than or equal to zero. Instead of zero, we used as the naive forecast of next year's standard deviation for each fund the average standard deviation (across funds) for the prior year. Thus the naive model forecasts all standard deviations as identical and the naive model should perform better if differences in the standard deviation of funds from the mean in the past contain no information about future differences. The results do not allow us to conclude that past standard deviations are a useful predictive tool. However, past standard deviations do outperform the naive model in 3 of our 5 paired years. While past risk does not seem to be a good predictor of future risk, there is fairly strong evidence that past values of risk can be used to identify those funds that will be most (or least) risky in future periods.

4 Risk as a Predictor of Desirability

We have seen that, while there is at best weak evidence of return or the Sharpe ratio being able to rank funds according to future values of these measures, there is reasonably strong evidence of persistence in the relative riskiness of funds. The purpose of this section is to see whether selecting funds on the basis of standard deviation leads to improvements in the Sharpe ratio.

Table 7.5 shows the rank correlation of the standard deviation of funds in each year with the Sharpe ratio for funds in the next year. The relationship is negative in 5 of 5 paired years. It is statistically significantly different from zero (and negative) in 3 years. Thus, low standard deviation funds are associated with higher Sharpe ratios. The average rank correlation is −.357, which is considerably larger in absolute magnitude than the rank correlation between the Sharpe ratio in successive periods.

In table 7.9, we present the results (in terms of the Sharpe ratio obtained 1 year later) of purchasing the top three funds, the bottom three funds, and the top third, middle third, and bottom third of funds ranked by their standard deviation. On average and in 4 out of 5 years, the best Sharpe ratio is obtained by purchasing the funds with the lowest standard deviation. There does appear to be information present in these rankings.

Both the association of standard deviation in one period with standard deviation in the next and the association of standard deviation and the Sharpe ratio in the next period suggest that standard deviation might be useful in picking good commodity funds. Examining table 7.8 suggests that standard deviations of .07–.14 might be possible by selecting a low or high standard deviation fund in the prior period. Substituting this range into equation (1) gives the break-even return necessary to include a commodity fund ranging from .0067 to .0075 for the 6-year 100% stock case with similar results for the other scenarios. Thus the predictability of standard deviations results in almost no change in the break-even rate.

Furthermore, it is ambiguous whether a high or low standard deviation fund is desirable. Examining equation (1) shows that, for returns below the risk-free rate, a high standard deviation is desirable.

An investor can probably select a fund with a standard deviation different from the average. Furthermore, low standard deviations have some association with higher Sharpe ratios. However, given the minimal impact on the break-even rate and the ambiguity whether small or large standard deviations are desirable, the predictability of standard deviation is unlikely to affect the basic decision whether commodity funds should be selected in the first place.

IV Conclusion

This paper is the first comprehensive review of publicly traded commodity funds.[17] The returns on these funds are highly variable, with a standard deviation two to three times that of bonds or common equity indexes. This variability was fairly consistent from year to year, and we expect that estimates from our 6-year period will be sustained in the future. The correlation structure is also fairly stable from year to year. Calculating a break-even expected return and comparing it with actual returns make it doubtful that public commodity funds should be included in an investor's portfolio.

When we examined whether we could select a superior commodity fund on the basis of past performance the answer was probably not. Using the past value of the Sharpe ratio as a predictor led to almost no improvement in performance. This was true whether we used the full set of funds or just the extremes. A similar result was obtained with returns. However, there is predictability in standard deviation. A fund with a lower or higher standard deviation than the average can probably be selected on the basis of past values. However, this has minimal impact on the break-even rate and hence has little impact on the desirability of commodity funds.

Appendix A

The condition for a security to enter an optimal portfolio is easy to derive using the simple rules of Elton, Gruber, and Padberg (1976). Consider an asset and a portfolio. Since there is a single portfolio and a single asset, there is a single correlation coefficient of interest. Thus the assumption of a constant correlation coefficient can be made without loss in generality. As Elton et al. (1976) have shown, a security will enter in a positive amount if

$$\frac{(\bar{R}_i - R)_F}{\sigma_i} - \frac{\rho}{1 - \rho + N_k \rho} \sum_{j \in k} \frac{\bar{R}_j - R_F}{\sigma_j} > 0,$$

where $\bar{R}_i$ is the expected return on asset i, R_F is the riskless rate of interest, ρ is the correlation coefficient, N_k is the number of securities, and k is the set of included securities. With a single asset and a single portfolio, N_k and K are both one and the condition becomes

$$\frac{\bar{R}_i - R_F}{\sigma_i} - \rho\left(\frac{\bar{R}_p - R_F}{\sigma_p}\right) > 0.$$

This is equation (1) above. The same condition can be derived in a more cumbersome fashion using first-order conditions.

Appendix B

To estimate the variance, we ran the following single-index model for each year y:

$$R_{ity} = \alpha_{iy} + \beta_{iy} I_{yt} + \varepsilon_{ity},$$

where R_{ity} is the return in month t of year y for commodity fund i; I_{yt} is the value of the index in month t of year y, in which the index is an equally weighted index of all commodity funds; β_{iy} is the responsiveness of commodity fund i to changes in the index in year y; ε_{ity} is a random variable for fund i in month t of year y and represents unsystematic return; and α_{iy} is a constant in year y for fund i.

The total variance of fund i in year y is given by

$$\sigma_{iy}^2 = \beta_{iy}^2 \sigma_{Iy}^2 + \sigma_{\varepsilon iy}^2,$$

where σ_{Iy}^2 is the variance of the index in year y and $\sigma_{\varepsilon iy}^2$ is the residual variance for fund i in year y.

Since the residuals are independent over time and the removal of the average fund performance makes them very close to cross-sectionally independent, the best estimate of the average variance of the residuals is

$$\sigma_\varepsilon^2 = \frac{\sum_y \sum_i \sigma_{\varepsilon iy}^2}{266}.$$

Similarly, the best estimate of the market index variance is an average across the 6 years:

$$\sigma_I^2 = \frac{\sum_y \sigma_{Iy}^2}{6}.$$

Our best estimate of the yearly variance for an average fund is the sum of the average beta squared times the variance plus the average unique variance:

$$\bar{\beta}_i^2 \sigma_I^2 + \sigma_\varepsilon^2.$$

Notes

We would like to thank the Institute for Quantitative Research in Finance and the Center for the Study of Business and Government, Baruch College, and a PSC-CUNY research grant for financial support.

1. *Managed Accounts Report* (1979–85). We would like to thank Morton Baratz for helpful comments and information.

2. Prospectus of Dean Witter Reynolds Commodity Partners (April 1985), p. 33.

3. Prospectus of Matterhorn Commodity Partners (April 9, 1981), p. 11.

4. See Elton and Gruber (1987, ch. 20) for a discussion of transaction costs on futures and commodity funds, and see Irwin and Brorsen (1985).

5. Generally, publicly traded commodity funds allow investors to liquidate their holdings on the last day of any month at their net asset value. Risk from these funds is in reality higher relative to other investments than the numbers in subsequent tables indicate because the alternative investments can be liquidated at any time during the month.

6. Eight funds dissolved due to poor performance during our sample period. One more dissolved during the period but was not included in our sample because it did not exist during any June. Three more went bankrupt shortly after our period. Dissolution values were not obtainable for three funds. For these funds we assumed dissolutions at their prior months' asset value. This overstates returns.

7. Actually, the difference in return for these instruments is so small that it makes much less difference whether a 1-month or 1-year holding period is assumed.

8. We computed both Sharpe and Jensen performance measures. For the Jensen performance measures, we used both an index of bonds and an index of stocks. All performance measures had negative values, indicating that commodity funds should not be held. Actually, this result could have been anticipated from the numbers presented in tables 7.1 and 7.2.

9. The standard deviation of mean returns across the 6 years is .0052.

10. An equivalent condition is presented in Blume (1984).

11. This was obtained by solving standard first-order conditions. The calculations are available from the authors.

12. Correlation coefficients were also computed on the unranked (raw) data. The results were so similar to the rank correlations that we have not bothered to report them or to discuss them further in this paper.

13. See Siegel (1956, pp. 211, 212, and table P).

14. See Siegel (1956, pp. 212, 213).

15. See Siegel (1956, pp. 75–83, and table G).

16. In addition, the rank correlations and naive predictions were examined for betas and correlations of the funds with the common stock index, the bond index, and an index of commodity bond performance. No association or predictive power was found.

17. Lintner (1983) discussed results for eight publicly traded funds that existed over a $3\frac{1}{2}$-year period.

Reference

Blume, Marshall. 1984. The use of "alphas" to improve performance. *Journal of Portfolio Management* 11 (Fall): 86–92.

Breeden, Douglas. 1979. An intertemporal asset pricing model with stochastic consumption and investment opportunities. *Journal of Financial Economics* 6 (September): 265–96.

Elton, Edwin J., and Gruber, Martin J. 1987. *Modern Portfolio Theory and Investment Analysis.* 3d ed. New York: Wiley.

Elton, Edwin J.; Gruber, Martin J.; and Padberg, Manfred. 1976. Simple criteria for optimal portfolio selection. *Journal of Finance* 31 (December): 1341–57.

Ibbotson, Roger. 1985. *Stocks, Bonds, Bills and Inflation 1985 Yearbook.* Chicago: Ibbotson.

Irwin, Scott H., and Brorsen, Wade B. 1985. Public futures funds. *Journal of Futures Markets* 5 (Summer): 149–71.

Lintner, J. 1983. The potential role of managed commodity-financial futures accounts (and/or funds) in portfolios of stocks and bonds. Paper presented at the annual conference of the Financial Analysts Federation, Toronto.

Long, John. 1974. Stock prices, inflation, and the term structure of interest rates. *Journal of Financial Economics* 1 (July): 131–79.

Managed Accounts Report. 1979–85. Columbia, Md.: L.J.R. Communications.

Mandelbrot, Benoit. 1966. Forecasts of futures prices, unbiased markets and Martingale models. *Journal of Business* 39, no. 4, pt. 2:242–55.

Sharpe, William. 1966. Mutual fund performance. *Journal of Business* 39, no. 4, pt. 2:119–39.

Sharpe, William. 1981. *Investments.* 2d ed. Englewood Cliffs, N.J.: Prentice-Hall.

Siegel, Sidney. 1956. *Nonparametric Statistics for the Behavioral Sciences.* New York: McGraw-Hill.

8 New Public Offerings, Information, and Investor Rationality: The Case of Publicly Offered Commodity Funds

Edwin J. Elton, Martin J. Gruber, and Joel Rentzler

In a recent issue of this *Journal* (Elton, Gruber, and Rentzler 1987) we analyzed the performance of publicly offered commodity funds. The conclusion of this research was that publicly offered commodity funds were not attractive either as stand-alone investments or as additions to a portfolio containing stocks and/or bonds. A natural question arising from this study, and one that we have often been asked, is, Why do investors continue to choose to purchase commodity funds and why are these funds such a fast growing segment of investors' portfolios?

While one potential explanation is that investors are irrational, a second and more plausible explanation is that potential investors in a fund are systematically given misleading and biased information and have no ability to evaluate its inaccuracies. The resolution of this puzzle has important implications not only for understanding the growth of limited partnerships like commodity funds but also for the kinds of informational assumptions that are plausible in general model building in finance.

The types of commodity funds we examine in this article are limited partnerships that are offered to the public by prospectuses with the investment "opportunity" offered over a specified period of time, usually less than 6 months.[1] The principal information the potential investor has at the time of the purchase decision is the description of the fund and the historic performance of the fund's investment adviser or advisers and pool operators as presented in the prospectus.[2] In this article, we examine whether the evidence provided in the prospectus, which purports to measure the ability of the investment adviser and pool operator, has any relationship to the performance of the fund after it goes public. We also examine the discussion of commodity funds by a sample of the financial press to see whether it corrects or reinforces the general conclusion that investors might draw from examining prospectuses.

Anticipating our result for a moment, we find that the returns reported in the prospectus are so much higher than the subsequent returns earned on the public funds that, not only are the differences statistically significant, but they are also of a sufficient size that the reported data are *misleading* as a basis for an investment decision. We find the reasons for this discrepancy to be in part a function of the selfselection process in going public and in part a function of the regulations concerning what data can and must be included in the prospectus. In addition, the reasons for these discrepancies are unlikely to be detected by investors over time. Thus, the process is unlikely to be selfcorrecting.

While the research in this article concerns publicly offered commodity funds, we believe the implications of the research go far beyond this particular type of investment. The reasons we find for the discrepancy between return data in the prospectus and subsequent earned returns should apply to other types of limited partnerships, such as those found in real estate, venture capital, and oil and gas, and should in general cause prospectus return data to be viewed with extreme caution.

This article is divided into six sections. In the first section we discuss our sample and the regulations governing the inclusion of performance data in the prospectus. In the second section we discuss the relationship between the performance data as reported in the prospectus and subsequent actual public fund performance. In the third section we examine the reasons for the differences found in the second section. In the fourth section we examine whether newspaper and magazine articles reinforce or contradict the information contained in the prospectuses. In the fifth section we examine the improvement in information for the investor due to the passage of time. Finally, in the conclusion we present some policy implications of this research.

I Background

In this section we discuss background material needed to understand the latter analysis. We first discuss the rules concerning the reporting of performance figures in prospectuses. We then discuss the sample used in this study.

Publicly traded commodity funds are offered by prospectus to potential investors. The rules governing the reporting of past performances are clearly delineated.[3] Both the commodity pool operator (CPO) and the commodity trading adviser (CTA) must provide *at least* 3 years of performance history, *if available*, for all pools and accounts that they have operated (or in the case of an adviser, advised) during the previous 3 years. Note that, while at least 3 years of data are required if available, the CPO and CTA are at liberty to include any period of time longer than 3 years. It is also worth noting that performance figures cannot end more than 3 months before the date of the disclosure document.

In order to analyze the performance of public commodity funds compared to prospectus returns, we attempted to obtain prospectuses for all of the 91 public commodity funds examined in Elton, Gruber, and Rentzler (1987).[4]

We were successful in obtaining prospectuses for 79 of these 91 funds. However, two of the prospectuses we obtained were not used because the trading adviser did not have any previous experience, and hence there was no history of past returns. This left us with a sample consisting of 77 of the original 91 funds. The obvious way the 12 missing prospectuses could have biased our sample is if performance were a function of time and if these prospectuses were all issued at or around the same time. This was not problem: the 12 prospectuses were issued in 5 different years.[5]

To prepare our data we used the following procedure. If a prospectus reported performance for only one commodity trading adviser or pool operator, we utilized the return for that adviser. If a prospectus reported returns for more than one commodity trading adviser and/or one or more commodity pool operator, we calculated an equally weighted average of the return for all advisers and pool operators.

II Results

Table 8.1 shows a comparison between the historic returns reported in the prospectuses and the returns on the same set of funds after they went public.[6] The average return shown in the prospectus was 5.59% per month (annualized 92% per year). This is much higher than the return earned by these same funds once they went public. For the first year and the first 2 years after going public, only one fund in our sample had returns above the average return shown in all prospectuses. No fund had average performance above the average prospectus return after 2 years. We also examined how many funds outperformed the return shown in their own prospectuses. The answer is, None after 2 years and only two in the first 2 years after going public. Thus, if prospectus returns are an attempt to convey the mean expected return with some funds having actual performance above and some funds below that shown in the prospectus, they fail. Actual fund performance is almost always below and in

Table 8.1

	N	Average monthly returns	Average monthly returns as % of return in prospectus	No. of funds with returns above own prospectus	No. of funds with returns above the average of all prospectuses
Prospectus	77	5.59			
Public commodity funds:					
First year public*	73	.23	4.1	2	1
First 2 years public†	51	.36	6.4	2	1
First 3 years public	36	.30	5.4	0	0
First 4 years public	25	.54	9.7	0	0

* Four funds were excluded because of missing data in early months.

† Only 51 of the 77 firms in our sample had return data available 2 years after going public. The numbers decrease as we go down the table because funds that went public toward the end of our sample period do not have a long history of performance after going public.

fact substantially below prospectus return. After funds went public, they earned on average a very small fraction (between 4.1% and 9.7%, depending on the time period employed) of the return shown in the typical prospectus.

One possible explanation for the difference in prospectus and public fund return is that performance changed over time, and that the prospectus performance occurred during a period when commodity trading advisers did well and public fund performance was during a period when commodity trading advisers did poorly. The funds in our study went public over a 6-year period, so this is unlikely to be the explanation, but we did test this directly. Our sample contains 54 months in which both of the following conditions are met: (1) we have returns on at least 10 public commodity funds, and (2) we have returns from at least 10 prospectuses.[7] The number of commodity funds over the 54-month common period varied from 11 to 72, with an average of 35. The number of prospectuses with returns in these months varied from 10 to 66 with an average of 48. For each month we calculated both the average return on all public commodity funds and the average return from all the prospectuses. Thus, both commodity fund returns and prospectus returns are subject to the same economic influences. We then examined (1) the size and statistical significance of the difference in these paired observations (prospectus returns minus public fund returns), and (2) a regression of the average return on public commodity funds on the average return shown in the prospectuses in the same month (both stated in percent per month). The results are

$$\text{average (prospectus returns} - \text{public fund returns)} = 2.81, \quad \text{with a } T\text{-value of } 5.15, \tag{1}$$

$$\text{public fund returns} = \underset{(0.59)}{-1.96} + \underset{(.07)}{.79}\ \text{(prospectus return)}, \quad R^2 = .71. \tag{2}$$

The values in the parentheses are standard errors.

These two results clearly point out that, while the pattern of prospectus returns is very similar to the pattern of public fund returns, the means differ. The high and statistically significant R^2 is evidence that the pattern of returns reported in the prospectus is very similar (highly associated with) the pattern of returns earned by public funds. The fact that the public funds earned 2.81% less per month than the returns (in the same month) shown in the prospectus and that the difference is statistically significant clearly demonstrates that prospectus returns are different from the returns on public funds.[8] These results strongly suggest that the difference in public fund return and prospectus return cannot be explained by a different time period or different economic influences.

Our next type of analysis, analogous to a traditional event study in the sense that it examines returns in event time rather than calendar time, examines whether there is a time pattern to the history of returns shown in prospectuses. Once again, to control for conditions in the market we subtract the average return on public funds from each prospectus return in the same calendar month. Thus we will be reporting the average returns shown in the prospectus minus the average returns earned by public funds in the same month. If we require prospectus returns and returns on commodity funds for at least 10 funds, we have 54 months of differential returns.

Figure 8.1 shows the cumulative differential returns. Time zero is the first month of public fund returns. Thus, the number reported for date −1 is the differential return shown in the month before the public fund first reports returns. There are several notable features in the figure. First, of course, is the consistent difference between the returns shown in the prospectus and the returns public funds achieve. The second feature is that the differential return is very high in the early months relative to the later months. This feature will be discussed in some detail in the next section.

These three types of analysis have all indicated that the level of returns reported in prospectuses is not indicative of the level of returns that funds will earn once they are public. Prospectuses might still be useful if they

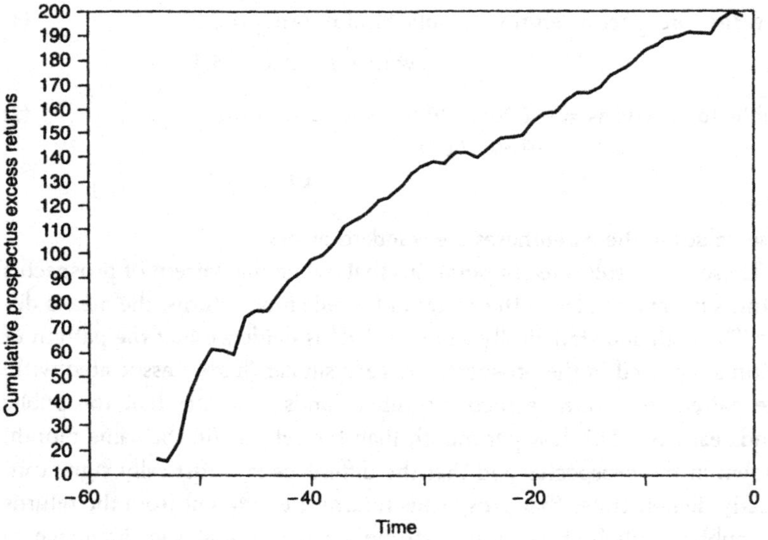

Figure 8.1
Excess returns—prospectus over public

conveyed information about the future relative ranking of commodity funds. For example, if an investor compared a set of prospectuses available at a moment in time, would an investor selecting a fund with the higher prospectus return increase the odds of holding a better performing fund? Table 8.2 provides an answer to this question. This table compares the relative performance reported in a prospectus with relative actual fund performance.

In each year we assumed a potential investor could choose among all funds that went public in that year for which we had prospectuses. Our first analysis was a cross-sectional regression of prospectus returns and subsequent performance. We used four different measures of public fund performance: performance the first year after going public, the first 2 years, the first 3 years, and the first 4 years. Since funds that went public in recent years would have fewer than 4 years of actual returns, we had 14 regressions. Of the 14 regressions, eight have positive slopes and six negative slopes. Only one of the R^2s is significant, and in this case subsequent fund performance was negatively related to prospectus performance.

Our second type of analysis computes the average fund return on the half of the funds with the highest prospectus return minus the average fund return for the funds in the lowest half of prospectus return. The

Table 8.2
Public returns = $a + b$ prospectus returns

Year went public and no. of years of performance*	Intercept a	Slope b	R^2	Returns (upper half minus lower half)†
1983:				
1	−1.29	−.16	.16	−.55
1982:				
1	−1.79	.13	.05	+.59
2	−.65	.10	.02	+.44
1981:				
1	−.92	.15	.09	−.44
2	−.38	−.00	.00	−.47
3	.42	−.08	.10	−1.17
1980:				
1	−.20	.22	.09	1.94
2	−.64	.21	.15	1.57
3	−.58	.11	.08	.46
4	.02	.06	.02	.10
1979:				
1	4.72	−.71	.84	−2.61
2	3.12	−.42	.38	−1.92
3	1.24	−.05	.07	−.73
4	.33	.07	.06	−.70

* Year is from July to June. Thus, 1979 is for funds that went public from July 1979 to June 1980.

† This column shows that difference in returns actually earned once public. The number is the return on the funds that had the highest returns reported in the prospectus minus the funds which had the lowest returns.

results are shown in the last column of table 8.2. In nine of 14 instances, subsequent performance was higher for those prospectuses that showed the poorer history of returns.[9] Table 8.2 does not provide any support to the proposition that an investor could use prospectus returns to select the better performing funds.

In the next section we discuss why the difference in return exists between what is shown in the prospectus and what is actually earned on public funds.

III What Went Wrong

We have now demonstrated that the historic return data reported in the prospectuses of publicly offered commodity funds are not indicative of the return these funds earn once they are public. In fact, the differences in performance figures are so large that the prospectus numbers are seriously misleading. We have shown that this discrepancy cannot be accounted for by a different time period for prospectus returns and public fund returns. The logical question is, What can account for these discrepancies?

There are three reasons why we would expect prospectus return figures to be unrepresentative of future performance.

1. *Transaction Costs and Management Fees.* Public funds in general charge larger commissions and management fees than private pools. While the data as reported in the disclosure document would allow the investor to recalculate some or all of the rates of return based on the new expected commissions, theses corrected rates of return are often not presented.

2. *Self-Selection.* Only commodity advisers with successful track records are likely to go public. To the extent that good performance arose by chance, the superior performance is unlikely to continue over time.

3. *Control over Reported Numbers.* The adviser can choose the length (in excess of 3 years) of the performance period placed in the disclosure document (prospectus) and to some extent the ending date. This allows the most favorable period to be selected.

We now discuss each of these in more detail.

A Transaction Costs and Management Fees

The first reason that the historic returns reported in the prospectus are not indicative of future performance is because transaction costs and management fees will be different after the public offering than they were before. Some prospectuses include a return figure utilizing the new fee schedule. Other prospectuses contain enough data to allow an investor with a calculator and some time to approximate the returns that would have been earned had the new commission costs and management fees been in existence. However, the time period covered by the transaction and management fee data is often different from, and shorter than, the return history in the prospectus. Furthermore, the level of sophistication and the time required to perform the necessary calculations is not insignificant. We have recalculated returns for a sample of 23 prospectuses. If these new fees had been in effect the average monthly return shown in the prospectus would have been lowered by .13% (from 5.59 to 5.46%). Furthermore, only one prospectus had a change in return of more than .75%. Thus the change in the fee schedule as reported in the prospectus accounts for only a small part of the difference in returns before and after going public.

B Self-Selection

There are a large number of commodity trading advisers registered with the National Futures Association. In 1980 there were 1,866 such advisers. As of February 1987, there were 2,080 such advisers. The vast majority of these advisers manage private, as opposed to publicly traded, accounts (there were only 94 public funds in our sample period).

Since the prospectus on any publicly offered account must, by law, contain past performance figures, it is logical that those advisers who have done well over a recent period are the advisers who are going to be selected to manage a public account.

One possible explanation for the results we found is that commodity trading advisers' performance is random and that the ones who are selected as advisers to public funds are the ones who, by pure chance, had a sequence of good returns. To examine this hypothesis we first determine whether the returns shown in the prospectus could have arisen by chance given the actual performance of public commodity funds. Then we examine evidence of randomness.

By law, the disclosure document must include at least 36 months of data if it exists. The average return shown in the prospectus over the last 36 months of reported data is 4.14% per month. In our earlier study we found that public commodity funds had an average return of .73% per month with a standard deviation of 11.30% per month.[10] Assuming that the average return is normally distributed, the probability of finding an average monthly return for any fund over a 36-month period higher than 4.14%, given that the true mean is .73%, is .35.[11] This number is calculated by taking the difference between the mean return shown in prospectuses and the mean return earned by public funds (4.14%–.73%) and dividing by the standard deviation of the mean return ($11.30/\sqrt{36}$). The probability of exceeding this computed value of 1.81 is ascertained from the cumulative normal table to be .035. Given the number of advisers managing private pools (between 1,886 and 2,080), we would expect to find more than 65 advisers at any time who have a return greater than 4.14% over the prior 36 months.[12] The number of funds that went public averaged $15\frac{1}{3}$ per year over our sample period. Thus prospectus performance is consistent with the performance we find for public commodity funds if managers of such funds are selected from the private pools with high performance and performance is random. In fact, the number of prospective managers is much larger than 65. We have computed this number by assuming that each fund going public has an average monthly return greater than 4.14% when all we required was that the average for all funds going public was greater than 4.14%.

Probably the strongest indication that fund performance is random and, hence, that selection bias accounts for the results is provided by examining the random nature of the relative performance of funds. In our prior study, we showed that there was no predictability in the year-to-year performance of publicly traded commodity funds. In the previous section of this study we showed that the relative ranking of prospectus returns could not be used to predict subsequent relative performance of public funds. This evidence of unpredictability is exactly what would be expected if performance were random and prospectus return were the return of managers who performed well by chance in the prior period.

The presence of selection bias has implications for other types of investments offered by prospectus. Due to self-selection by the managers of any type of public offering, the historical data in prospectuses are likely to be highly misleading and inflated indicators of future performance.

C *Control over Reported Numbers*

While the number of months of reported performance data must be no less than 36 months if such data exists, the manager is free to present additional data. We would expect, since the prospectus is in a real sense a sales document, that a length of time would be chosen to make the fund managers have as high a return as possible. There are two ways of demonstrating that this is in fact the case. There were 77 prospectuses in our sample. Their average reported monthly return for the latest 36 months was 4.14%. Of these 77 funds, 69 presented data for more than 36 months. The average monthly return for the added period that was selected voluntarily was 8.85%. Even more dramatic is the average return reported for the first month in the prospectus for all funds reporting more than 36 months of data. Recall that the funds can choose any starting point they desire. The average return in the starting month was 14.6%, or an annualized rate of better than 400%. Clearly, allowing the adviser to select the length of the time series to be included in the prospectus leads to an upward bias in the performance figures. The average monthly return reported by funds was 5.59% while, if they had been restricted to reporting a uniform length of 36 months, it would have been 4.14%.[13]

Once again this has connotations for other public offerings. Any time the issuer is allowed to select the time period over which returns are reported, the result is bound to be on average an overstatement of what the future will bring.

IV Information on Commodity Funds in the Press

The other source of information on commodity funds is articles in the financial and popular press. We performed two computerized searches of references to commodity funds. the first examined references in 34 business magazines from June 1979 through February 1987. The second examined the *New York Times* and the *Wall Street Journal* over the same period.

Our search of 34 business magazines yielded 28 references to commodity funds. Although any classification scheme is somewhat subjective, we divided the articles as follows: 12 articles provide a general discussion about investing in commodity funds, 9 articles presented general performance results, 4 discussed the results of an individual manager, and 3 were classified as miscellaneous.

Almost all of the 12 articles discussing general investment in commodity funds were highly favorable both in the selection of the numbers they reported and in their general comments on commodity funds. Indeed, some of the statements were stronger than anything contained in any of the disclosure statements.[14]

Of the nine articles presenting general results, five were highly favorable. Even those articles that did not present totally favorable results almost always closed with a success story. Typical is an April 26, 1982, story in *Business Week*. After talking about the fact that half of the commodity funds suffered losses in 1981, it explains that the industry is continuing to grow probably because of the outstanding performance of some funds. The article then goes on to discuss in some detail the performance of Heinhold, which earned a 75% rate of return in the prior year. Articles like this provide biased information to the investor because they almost always discuss the performance of the one to five funds that did well over some time period and they almost never discuss the funds that did badly, nor do they ever caution the reader that there is no evidence that past performance of a commodity fund is related to future performance.

Of the seven remaining articles, four discussed the *success* of some individual managers. Of the last three articles, one discussed our study (Elton,

Gruber, and Rentzler 1987), one discussed the Bodie and Rosansky (1980) study on the performance of buying futures long, and one discussed the factors that would lead to a large increase in new money invested in commodity funds.

The second data search was of the *Wall Street Journal* and the *New York Times*. Every month, the *Wall Street Journal* reports the prior month's performance for commodity funds. Separate from this, there were eight articles on commodity funds in the *Wall Street Journal* and the *New York Times*. Four of these were favorable discussions of funds usefulness, three were a discussion of results, of which only one reported poor performance in the prior year, and one discussed the success of a single fund.

While the computerized search may not have located all articles on commodity funds, there is no reason to believe it systematically excluded certain types of articles. Anyone reading these articles as a whole would get the impression that commodity funds had excellent performance and were good investments. Although impressions are necessarily subjective, only one article mentioned that a fund had poor performance and dissolved. The overwhelming majority read like a sales presentation. The newspaper and magazine articles support and reinforce the favorable impression of the prospectuses.

V Information and Time

Much of the analysis in finance assumes that investors learn over time as more and more information is revealed to them. Thus, although investors may be initially misled, eventually they will adjust their decisions.[15]

In prior sections, we showed that the return data in the prospectus provide little guidance in judging the performance of public commodity funds or in choosing between new offerings. Data in the prospectuses may provide useful information to the investor on fund volatility and correlation with other investments, but they do not provide information that would allow an investor to estimate mean returns. Volatility and correlation data can be judged with a few prospectuses, but whether an investor sees one prospectus or a thousand will not lead to an improvement in the ability to forecast subsequent mean returns. Thus, insofar as prospectuses are the principal source of information, investors will not learn over time.

The other principal sources of new information to an investor includes newspapers, magazines, and other investors. Our comments here must be more speculative. As just discussed, general articles on commodity funds in the press primarily support the impression given in the prospectuses. The types of information sometimes reported in the press that should have reflected the poor performance of commodity funds are indices of past performance of commodity funds and data on the actual performance of individual commodity funds. However, the indices we are aware of are upwardly biased due to exclusion of funds that fail and those that get into financial difficulty. This effect should not be underemphasized since, over our sample period (which contained a total of 91 funds and an average of 44 funds), 11 funds dissolved. Likewise, tables of performance figures of individual funds that we have seen have excluded those that dissolved or had suspended trading due to poor performance. Thus, the press, rather than providing useful information to an investor, is reinforcing the image created by the prospectus.

The final source of information is other investors. Given the information in the press, most investors are likely to believe that they had a bad outcome rather than believe that public commodity funds are a poor investment. Thus, we believe that unlike the assumption we usually make that investors learn quickly over time, investors in commodity funds are likely to be misled for a long time. This has serious implications for the assumptions about the rational allocation of resources.

We believe this is a general problem for investments where potential investors are unable to obtain unbiased data on actual performance and must rely on prospectus data and coverage by the financial press. Real estate, oil, gas, and motion-picture limited partnerships are examples of other types of investments where we would expect similar problems to arise.

VI Conclusion

Sales of new publicly offered commodity funds have continued to increase over time. This is true despite the poor performance of publicly offered commodity funds. We believe this growth continues because of the grossly misleading information on performance presented in prospectuses and because of the biased press coverage these funds receive.

A natural question to ask is, How can these funds sell at above their economic value in a world of efficient markets? Markets are made efficient by the existence of arbitrageurs who profit from exploiting inefficiencies. But there is no way to trade against these funds in a manner that earns an arbitrage profit. In Elton, Gruber and Rentzler (1987), we showed that the lack of an economic profit from these funds comes about primarily because of high transaction costs and high management fees, not because of taking the wrong side of futures contracts. Since these partnerships cannot be sold short, there is no way to take an arbitrage position to exploit these inefficient securities.

If arbitrageurs cannot restore efficiency to the market, it is necessary for all potential investors, not just a small group of professional investors, to possess correct information about these funds. While we do not have a plan for obtaining this result, surely the first step is correcting the misleading nature of fund prospectuses. We recommend three policy changes.

1. State all rates of return as they would have existed had the future commission charges and transaction costs been in effect. Although the effect is small, the returns would be more indicative of what the investor would have received had the actual fee schedule been in effect.

2. Include a statement with the return data that any returns beyond 36 months are included at the discretion of the CPO or the CTA.

3. Finally, and most important, provide data on actual performance on the same type of investment vehicle and on the ratio of actual returns to prospective returns for funds that have gone public in the past. The fact that in the past commodity funds that have earned less than one-tenth of the returns they reported in the prospectus after they went public is a warning that any investor should have and should heed.

Notes

We would like to thank the Institute for Quantitative Analysis in Finance and a PSC–City University of New York research grant for providing research support and Kenneth French for his helpful comments.

1. Occasionally funds are reopened after the initial public offering and new capital is sought. However, the normal procedure is to simply start a new commodity fund.

2. The other sources of information an investor has are word-of-mouth and newspaper and magazine articles. We did a search of references in the press. The details are discussed later. However, an idea of how limited this discussion is can be seen from our search of 34 business magazines from June 1979 to February 1987. There were only 28 references. Furthermore, 15 of the 28 references were in the specialized magazines, *Futures* and *Commodities*. While our search surely missed some references, the numbers are suggestive, and for most investors the sole or principal information source is the prospectus.

3. See National Futures Association, "A Compliance Guide: Commodity Pool Operators and Commodity Trading Advisors" (Chicago: National Futures Association, 1986).

4. This includes all public commodity funds that existed over this period except for three. Our sample procedure in Elton, Gruber, and Rentzler (1987) was to include all public funds

that existed in June of each fund. The three excluded funds went public after June of one year and dissolved before June of the next.

5. There is a slight tendency for the missing prospectuses to be associated with the older funds. The missing are five for funds that went public in 1978, two in 1979, two in 1981, two in 1982, and one in 1983. We believe that our results are minimally affected by their exclusion. There is also a slight tendency for the missing prospectuses to be associated with funds that went bankrupt. This exclusion will cause an increase in prospectus performance relative to public fund performance.

6. As discussed in Elton, Gruber, and Rentzler (1987), the reader should not utilize the average monthly return to estimate return over a longer holding period. In our study we found an average monthly return of .73%. However, the average monthly return assuming an annual holding period was negative. The average monthly return is an overestimate of what the investor can expect to receive from investing in commodity funds and holding them for a year. The use of average monthly returns, although inaccurate as a projection of longer run returns, is appropriate for comparing relative performance.

7. The choice of 10 is arbitrary. Only 2 additional months would have been added if we had used a cutoff of five and 6 additional months if our cutoff was one.

8. The reader should note that the mean return shown in the prospectus over the period of this analysis was 4.05%, rather than the 5.59% reported in table 1. This difference comes about because in the months included in the comparative analysis there were almost no prospectus returns longer than 36 months before public offering. As we explain in a later section, prospectus returns tend to be much larger in the period of time longer than 36 months (the voluntary period). When we look at prospectus returns for the 36-month period before the offering we find they average 4.14%, a figure close to the 4.05% found for the regression period.

9. These are not independent observations since the first year's performance is also part of the performance over the first 2 years, etc.

10. Arithmetic means rather than holding-period returns (geometric means) are used throughout this study. This makes comparisons over different horizons easier but overstates all returns. We once again caution the reader not to use average monthly returns as indicative of returns over a longer period. See Elton, Gruber, and Rentzler (1987) for more details.

11. The assumption of normality would follow from the Central Limit Theorem if all funds were drawn from the same distribution. Heterogeneity among fund managers would in general lead to more funds having average returns above the 4.14% cutoff rate.

12. These numbers are approximations because we have not considered new entries and exits from the population of advisers and the overlapping 36 months of data for our calculations. The only simplification that would reduce the number of potential high return advisers is the lack of adjusting for overlaps. But even if we allowed no overlap, there would still be more than a sufficient number of advisers. Thus the prospectus returns, while misleading, are consistent with the true performance of private pools being the much lower return of publicly traded funds rather than that shown in the prospectus, and there is no predictability of future return from past return.

13. We also examined a break at 40 months since some of the latest results shown in the prospectus may be included because of a delay in prospectus issuance. No difference in the type of results was detected.

14. See, e.g., the April 11, 1983, issue of *Industrial Edition of Business Week.*

15. Given the enormous volatility of the returns on public commodity funds, a lengthy time period was necessary before one could be sure that the poor results were not simply a bad sequence of returns but, rather, a very poor mean return. The 6 years of data we analyzed was sufficiently long that the odds that returns are attractive and that we are simply observing a bad sequence was very small.

References

Bodie, Zvi, and Rosansky, Victor. 1980. Risk and return in commodity futures. *Financial Analysts Journal* 36 (May–June): 3–14.

Elton, Edwin J.; Gruber, Martin J.; and Rentzler, Joel. 1987. Professionally managed publicly traded commodity funds. *Journal of Business* 60 (April): 175–99.

9 The Performance of Publicly Offered Commodity Funds

Edwin J. Elton, Martin J. Gruber, and Joel Rentzler

Publicly offered commodity funds are professionally managed limited partnerships, offered to investors by prospectus, that buy and sell futures contracts. While individual funds may differ, the typical fund has the following characteristics.

(1) Most funds have the ability to trade (and do trade) in many futures and forward contracts on financial instruments, foreign currencies and commodities. In addition, they frequently hold financial instruments directly (using them for margin against their futures transactions). Most fund prospectuses stress diversification and the ability to take long as well as short positions in commodities (i.e., to buy or sell futures contracts).

(2) Most funds can only be purchased for a short time after the initial prospectus, but allow investors to liquidate their position at net asset value at monthly (sometimes quarterly) intervals. A monthly rate of return can, however, be computed.

(3) Most funds use technical and trend-following systems to decide whether to take a long or short position with respect to any commodity (futures contract).

(4) Most funds incur high management fees and transaction costs relative to other types of asset management such as mutual funds. Management fees usually exceed 5 per cent of capital a year, while the sum of management fees and transaction costs exceeds 19 per cent of capital per year.

(5) Most fund prospectuses contain a clause that calls for the fund to dissolve if either the net asset value per share falls below a predetermined level (most often 25 to 30 per cent of the initial capital an investor pays in) or the total size of the fund (assets under management) falls below a specific level.

Prior to 1978, there were only three publicly offered commodity funds, but their number has grown rapidly in recent years—from 94 funds with $600 million under management in 1985 to 130 funds with over $2 billion under management in 1988. Their popularity has continued despite two apparent handicaps—extremely high management fees and transaction costs, and almost exclusive reliance on technical analysis. Furthermore, an earlier study of commodity funds in existence from June 1979 through June 1985 found that these funds, on average, experienced relatively low returns and very high risk.

Prior and Current Research

We analyzed the performance of publicly offered commodity funds in an earlier paper published in 1987.[1] That study represented the first comprehensive analysis of what was at the time, and has continued to be, a fast-growing industry. Enough years have passed since that initial study that it is worthwhile examining whether our initial conclusions still hold.

Our initial study used only six years of data—all that were available at that time—and the results of several of those years were dominated by the performance of a few funds. We now have nine years of data to look at, as well as a substantially larger number of funds.

Several criticisms were directed toward our earlier paper, and we have attempted to respond to them here. One was that we looked at investment from June to June. That period was selected because, at the time, it allowed us to use the longest possible set of data. It has been suggested that if we had used the calendar year as the holding period, our results would have been different. With the luxury of more data, we have switched to a calendar year for analysis.

In the original study, when a fund dissolved during a year, we made the assumption that the funds received by investors were reinvested across all remaining funds. Because funds are not in general open for new investment, this procedure is not possible in practice. In this article we make the more conservative assumption that the proceeds from fund dissolution are placed in Treasury bills for the remainder of the year. Because the average return on funds is below the Treasury bill rate, this assumption should improver measured fund performance.

The original paper employed the geometric mean return over a one-year holding period. Objections were raised to our use of one-year returns. This article uses the continuously compounded rate of return (the log of price relatives). The log price relative is the return measure used by most investigators of return distributions. This measure has additive properties that are desirable and approximates long-term returns.

Finally, we have added some analysis, largely in response to comments received from the industry. It had been suggested, for example, that commodity funds might be desirable because, despite poor mean return and high variances, they have attractive skewness (i.e., offer investors the chance of large payoffs). We examine this explicitly.

In addition, we received a number of suggestions about how to select superior funds. In our earlier study we looked at performance year-by-year and found that funds that performed well in one year did not necessarily perform well the next year. It was suggested that superior funds could be selected by analyzing performance over longer time periods (an analysis now possible, given the longer time frame). It was also suggested that superior funds could be selected by looking at the size of the fund or looking at the past record of the general partner. We examine each of these suggestions below.

Data

The basic data consist of monthly returns on all publicly offered commodity funds listed in the MAR reports for the period January 1980 to December 1988. If a fund dissolved, we collected dissolution values, primarily from the final reports to shareholders, obtained from the Commodity Futures Trading Commission. When final reports did not exist in the CFTC files, we contacted sponsoring firms, trading advisers and accounting firms. In a few cases, we relied upon verbal statements from brokerage firms, trading advisers or MAR.

There are three sources of potential inaccuracies in our data. First, although MAR is considered all-inclusive, there may be publicly traded commodity funds that are not included in its reports. Second, in the small number of cases where dissolved values were obtained verbally, inaccuracies may exist.[2] Third, our analyses of the impact of size and the identity of general partners on future returns relied on prospectus data, and prospectuses could be obtained for only 79 our of the 91 funds in our original sample.[3]

Performance

Table 9.1 presents the returns and risks for publicly traded commodity funds for each year 1980 through 1988. We calculated return in two

Table 9.1

Year	Monthly standard deviation[a]	Annual return (per cent)	
		All[b]	Beginning year
1980	12.6[c]	5.8980	2.0748
1981	10.0	0.5452	4.0716
1982	10.1	0.4944	−0.0864
1983	11.7	−16.1568	−15.0768
1984	10.6	7.0620	7.6656
1985	8.7	10.5096	10.8840
1986	10.4	−17.3916	−17.1588
1987	8.7	27.8676	28.3200
1988	10.4	0.4962	0.5568
	10.4	2.2565	2.3612

a. The standard deviation for non-log returns is almost identical.
b. Simple average annual return was 4.4 per cent.
c. This number excludes the firm with the highest standard deviation. This firm existed for only a few months in 1980. Including this firm would result in a value of 24.3 for 1980.

ways. First, we assumed that an investor is equally likely to hold any fund while it exists, hence we included data for all firms that existed at any point in time in the year.[4] This averaging method, which we term "all," is equivalent to assuming that an investor reallocates (for the remainder of the year) any funds he or she obtains from a fund dissolution to the rest of the funds in existence. Second, we assumed a fund was included in a portfolio only if it existed at the beginning of the year. If a fund dissolved during the year, we assumed that the proceeds received by the investor were placed in T-bills. This approach, which we term "beginning year," resulted in slightly higher returns, because commodity fund returns were well below the T-bill rate.

Table 9.2 presents the risks and returns for a broad group of competing investments. A comparison of Tables 9.1 and 9.2 makes clear the low return and high risk associated with investment in commodity funds. The return of 2.3 per cent per year is clearly lower than that offered by competitive investments, and the standard deviation of 10.4 per cent per month is clearly much higher.

Despite our changed definition of return and the longer time period, the results of this more recent study do not differ substantially from the findings of our earlier study. The earlier study ended in June 1985, hence

Table 9.2

	Yearly return (per cent)	Standard deviation of monthly return
Common stocks	14.88	4.91
Long-term corporate bonds	11.80	3.84
Long-term government bonds	11.40	4.17
Shearson Lehman Bond Index	11.40	2.38
Treasury bills	8.64	0.25

SOURCES. Common stock and long-term corporate and government bond returns from R. Ibbotson, *Stocks, Bonds, Bills, and Inflation 1989 Yearbook* (Chicago: Ibbotson Associates, 1989). Shearson Lehman Bond Index data supplied by Shearson American Express.

Table 9.3

Starting year	Percentage return in year 1	2	3	4	5	6	7	8	Lifetime return (per cent per year)
1980	9.45	8.72	−7.43	−6.32	−3.34	−1.19	−5.50	16.24	1.47
1981	−1.74	−7.90	−12.34	7.14	10.40	−9.67	21.16		−1.86
1982	−25.32	−23.74	9.10	23.02	16.18	15.28			−7.17
1983	−6.20	3.67	11.76	−18.38	18.01				−0.54
1984	2.26	19.60	−12.30	8.92					2.73
1985	8.24	−24.66	25.12						−0.08
1986	1.31	21.52							6.31
1987	−0.18								−0.26

the later study includes three complete years of data not analyzed earlier. The average return during these three years was 3.64 per cent. For the six years that overlap with our previous study, the return was 1.56 per cent. Commodity funds have clearly enjoyed a higher rate of return over the last three years. However, the return during this time was still considerably lower than the return from Treasury bills (8.64 per cent) and not sufficiently high to make investment in commodity funds seem worthwhile.

Table 9.3 shows the lifetime performances of the funds. The lifetime returns varied from −7.2 to +6.3 per cent, depending on the year the fund was introduced. This table also shows the average performance in the first year of existence, the second year and so forth. There is no discernible time pattern. The diagonals represent approximately the same calendar time. Note the similarity in returns along diagonals. This shows that overall market performance, and not number of years in existence, is the more important influence on fund returns.

Given the large risk associated with commodity fund returns and the low average level of returns, we should expect to see numerous funds dissolving over time. We examine below the dissolution pattern is the industry.

Dissolution

A large number of publicly traded funds dissolved over our nine-year sample period. Almost all the dissolutions took place for one of two reasons. First, most funds have a clause in their partnership agreement that causes automatic dissolution if the net asset value per share falls to some predetermined level. For example, a fund with an initial asset value of $1,000 might automatically dissolve if net asset value per share drops to $300. This automatic dissolution allows the seller to guarantee that investors will never lose 100 per cent of their investment. The second major reason for dissolution is a decline of total funds under management. Many publicly traded commodity funds have as part of their partnership agreement a clause that results in dissolution if fund size becomes sufficiently small, whether as a result of withdrawals or poor performance. Because withdrawals are likely to be correlated with poor performance, poor performance is the main cause of dissolution. In our sample, only three funds dissolved at a value above their initial issuance price; the average dissolved fund had a rate of return over its lifetime of −19.99 per cent per annum.

Table 9.4 shows in more detail the dissolution experience over our sample period. Over this period, 40 funds dissolved—25 per cent of all funds in existence. The columns in the table show the detailed experience by year of entrance. Note that the percentage of dissolution is very high for firms that entered before 1984, ranging form 25 to 50 per cent. For firms that entered after 1984, the percentage of funds dissolving declined substantially. However, an examination of the columns under year of dissolution shows that funds tend to dissolve after they have been around a while. The lower dissolution rate of funds that entered in later years can thus be explained in part by their limited amount of time in existence.

Table 9.5 explores in more detail the dissolution experience as a function of number of years of existence. Consider the fifth year. There were 67 firms in our sample that had returns in the fifty year of their existence. Of these, five (7.5 per cent) dissolved in that year. The odds of a firm dis-

Table 9.4

	New entrants[b]	Total dissolved	Percent dissolved	Number of funds dissolved in their year								
				1	2	3	4	5	6	7	8	9
Before 1980[a]	13	6	46									
1980	12	4	$33\frac{1}{3}$					1		1	1	1
1981	22	11	50				3	3	2		3	
1982	16	4	25		2	1	1					
1983	18	6	$33\frac{1}{3}$		1		2	1	2			
1984	12	3	25			1	2					
1985	14	2	14		2							
1986	16	2	13		1	1						
1987	21	2	10	1	1							
1988	14	0	0									
	158	40	25	1	7	3	8	5	4	1	4	1

a. We do not show the year of existence in which these funds dissolved because they were started in very different years and the data we have simply tell us they existed as of June 1979.
b. Funds are classified as new funds by the year for which we have the first return data. Thus a fund that started in December would have its first return in January and be classified as a new entrant in January.

Table 5.5

i^{th} year of existence	Number of firms at beginning	Number dissolved in year	Probability of dissolving in year i	Probability of dissolving in or before year i*
1	145	1	0.7%	0.7%
2	130	7	5.4	6.0
3	104	3	2.9	8.7
4	87	8	9.2	17.1
5	67	5	7.5	23.3
6	53	4	7.5	29.1
7	37	1	2.7	31.0
8	24	4	16.7	42.5
9	9	1	11.1	48.8

* The probability of dissolving in a before year i is not simply the cumulative distribution of the previous column but is adjusted for the probability that a fund may already have dissolved before it reached year i.

solving by the end of its fifth year of existence are 23.3 per cent. The probability of it dissolving by the end of the ninth year of existence is 48.8 per cent. If the past is indicative of the future, an investor purchasing a publicly traded commodity fund has close to a 50 per cent chance of having it dissolve within 10 years.

The reader should not be surprised by the large number of funds dissolving each year. Given the low return earned by commodity funds and the high standard deviation of their returns, we would expect a large percentage of the funds to experience performances poor enough to trigger their dissolution clauses.

Arguments for Investing in Commodity Funds

Three arguments can be advanced for placing some money in commodity funds, despite their poor performance. First, while commodity funds are not appropriate as a stand-alone investment, they might be held as part of a portfolio of stocks and bonds. Second, they might be held as a hedge against inflation. Third, they may be attractive because they offer a chance of a very high return (i.e., the returns are positively skewed). We address each of these points in turn.

We developed in great detail in our earlier paper the necessary conditions for commodity funds to be included in a portfolio of stocks and bonds. We showed that, for inclusion, commodity funds must offer a higher return than Treasury bills if the correlation between commodity funds and stocks and bonds is zero or positive. In fact, over our sample period the correlation between commodity funds and stocks and bonds was positive but close to zero and, as already discussed, the return on commodity funds was considerably lower than that on Treasury bills.[5] This evidence would not support the addition of commodity funds to a portfolio of bonds and stocks.

If commodity funds are to provide a hedge against inflation, their returns would need to be highly positively correlated with inflation. That is, commodity fund returns would have to increase when inflation rose. One might initially expect positive correlation, because there tends to be some positive correlation between futures returns and inflation.[6] But commodity funds both buy and sell futures.[7] The average correlation between our commodity funds and the Consumer Price Index was −0.0337. The correlation was also negative over the shorter period of our earlier study. The data indicate that commodity funds do not provide an attractive hedge against inflation.

Table 9.6

Year	Skewness
1980	−1.0470
1981	−0.4564
1982	−1.0988
1983	−1.2860
1984	−0.3882
1985	−0.5407
1986	−0.4160
1987	0.3231
1988	2.5071

Finally, publicly traded commodity funds may be good investments if their payoffs are positively skewed. There are two versions of this argument. The one that has always made more sense to us proceeds as follows. On average, returns on commodity funds are low. Occasionally, however, there is a very large return. Just as people purchase lottery tickets for the opportunity to get a very good return, even though the return on average is negative, they could use commodity funds for the same purpose. This argument would be supported if we observe that the cross-sectional distribution of commodity fund returns was positively skewed. Consider, for example, 1985 returns. The distribution of returns for this year comprises the annual return for each firm. An unusual opportunity for occasional high returns would be signalled by a positively skewed distribution.

To test this, we formed nine different distributions, one for each of our sample years. The entries in the distribution were the continuously compounded annual rates of return. We included all firms that existed at the beginning of the year. If a firm dissolved during the year, the proceeds were assumed to be invested in T-bills. Table 9.6 gives the results. For most years, the distribution is negatively skewed, primarily because of the extremely poor returns for the firms that dissolved in that year. Thus empirical evidence is exactly opposite to the contention of those who defend publicly traded commodity funds on the basis of skewness.

The skewness argument as generally made is really incomplete, however. Even if the returns on publicly traded commodity funds were positively skewed, commodity funds would have to offer this pattern of returns at more attractive rates than alternative investments. One obvious alternative is common stock; Lorie and Fisher have shown that the cross-section of returns on common stock held individually and in portfolios is positively skewed in each and every year.[8]

Lorie and Fisher defined return as ending wealth divided by beginning wealth. Applying this definition of returns to our commodity funds, we found the skewness measures were positive in six years and negative in three years. Over our nine-year sample, three skewness measure were statistically significant at the 5 per cent level, one positive and two negative. Thus common stocks have much more desirable skewness properties, along with higher average returns and lower standard deviations. Empirical evidence rejects cross-sectional skewness as an incentive for investing in publicly traded commodity funds.

A second argument based on skewness assumes that the utility functions of some investors exhibit a preference for positive skewness. Thus an investment that exhibits positive skewness of returns over time is desirable. To test this argument, we looked at the time series of returns for each of the 155 funds with more than six months of data. Of these, 99 were positively skewed (44 significant) and 56 negative (29 significant), with the average skewness slightly negative. This is mild evidence that some funds occasionally have high-return months and exhibit a small degree of positive skewness in the time series of returns.

Predictability of Returns

Can an investor find a way of selecting a fund with above-average performance? If so, what would the return on these funds be? We examined the predictability for two types of data.

Prior Returns

Our earlier paper showed that this year's return for a commodity fund cannot be predicted on the basis of the prior year's return. This should not be surprising in light of studies done on mutual funds. It is nevertheless possible that longer-term performance can be predicted by longer-term past performance. While we still do not have much history, a preliminary examination of this question is possible.

We calculated average continuously compounded returns for all funds with three years of history as of December 1985. We then calculated a rank-order correlation coefficient between the past three-year return and the subsequent three-year return. (If a fund dissolved before three years, we used data through its dissolution.) The rank-order correlation for the

51 firms in the sample was 0.053, which is insignificant at any normal level.

We also divided the sample into three groups on the basis of past performance. The subsequent performance of the one-third with the highest past performance was 8.5 per cent. The middle group returned 2.76 per cent, while the average subsequent performance of the bottom one-third was 7.7 per cent. Both the best and worst-performing funds did considerably better than the funds with average performance. The difference between the best and the worst groups was small.

Prospectus Data

Publicly traded commodity funds are offered by prospectus, and new investment is generally possible only for a few months around the time a fund is offered. Thus an investor desiring returns above the average for all funds needs to base his or her selection on material available at the time of the initial offering. In a prior paper, we showed that the past performance figures contained in the prospectus could not be used to select a fund that would have superior subsequent performance.[9]

For this study, we examined whether there are other items contained in a prospectus that might be useful in selecting a superior fund. We looked at three variables—the offering size for a fund and both the amount of experience and past investment performance (with publicly traded funds) of the fund's general partner.

Size could be related to subsequent performance for several reasons. First, one could argue that funds that attempt to raise more money are run by managers that underwriters have more faith in; this is tantamount to assuming that underwriters can successfully select managers. Also, one could argue that the larger funds can hire better managers.

Most prospectuses contain two measures of size—the minimum needed to start the partnership and the maximum that will be raised. We had prospectuses for most funds for the years 1980 to 1984. For each year, we ranked funds on three measures of size-minimum to start the fund, maximum to be raised and the average of the minimum and maximum. We then calculated for each size measure for each year the Spearman rank-order correlation coefficient with the lifetime return of each fund. None of the correlations was significant on any of the three size measures, and they were all close to zero. With maximum size as the measure, the correlations were −0.11, 0.03, −0.02, −0.05 and 0.11 for the years 1980 to 1984, respectively.[10]

Table 9.7

	Annual percentage return to funds managed by partners with prior experience in		
	4+ funds	1–3 funds	0 funds
1983	−10.04	12.51	−1.96
1984	−1.5	10.19	−7.93
1985	–	4.51	−8.35

The second variable we analyzed was experience. The logic underlying this variable is as follows. New funds are often managed by general partners who are also general partners in existing publicly traded commodity funds. The ability to issue new partnerships can be seen as an endorsement of their prior performance and might be predictive of superior performance for their new funds. Similarly, general partners with more experience might have superior performance.[11]

We examined three years—1983, 1984 and 1985—for which we had a minimum of three years of subsequent performance. (We could have used earlier years, but there were not enough funds in existence to give meaningful experience measures.) For each year, we counted the number of publicly traded commodity funds a general partner was already managing. We then divided the funds issued in each year into three groups according to whether the general partner (1) had no prior experience with publicly traded commodity funds, (2) managed one to three funds or (3) managed four or more.[12] We then examined the average lifetime performance in each of these three categories.

Table 9.7 gives the results. No clear pattern is evident. The only interesting conclusion to be drawn is to avoid funds whose general partners have zero experience. However, the reader should be cautioned that the sample were small. A further caution on the future predictability of these results is that the second-worst-performing group was general partners with a lot of experience.

The final variable we looked at was past performance of other funds managed by the same general partner. We divided newly issued funds into those with general partners whose prior public funds had above-average returns and those whose prior public funds had below-average returns; Table 9.8 gives the results. Here the results were consistent: Funds managed by partners with above-average prior experience outperformed those managed by partners with below-average prior experience.

Table 9.8

	Annual percentage return to funds managed by partners with	
	Above-average prior performance	Below-average prior performance
1983	10.14	−7.67
1984	10.83	0.78
1984	7.57	6.38

The reader should be cautioned that the sample sizes were small. Requiring that the general partner have prior experience resulted in sample sizes of eight or nine in the three years examined. Several funds had returns very close to the average. A small change in past return could have reversed the results. Nevertheless, this is one of the few areas where we found any indication of predictability, and it may be worth pursuing as more data become available in the future.

Notes

1. E. J. Elton, M. J. Gruber and J. Rentzler, "Professionally Managed Publicly Traded Commodity Funds," *Journal of Business*, April 1987.

2. Because there is no incentive for firms to understate dissolution value, using verbal statements of dissolution value might bias our results upward.

3. See Elton, Gruber and Rentzler, "New Public Offerings, Information, and Investor Rationality: The Case of Publicly Offered Commodity Funds," *Journal of Business*, January 1989, for a more detailed discussion of our sample of prospectuses.

4. We averaged across all firms that existed in a month and then across all months. We also averaged all fund months. This latter average differed in a minor way in the first years and is not reported.

5. The correlation with the S&P index was 0.08, while it was 0.05 with the Shearson Lehman Corporate Government Bond Index and 0.07 with the Ibbotson indexes for both corporate bonds and government bonds.

6. Z. Bodie, "Commodity Futures as a Hedge Against Inflation," *Journal of Portfolio Management*, Spring 1983.

7. The correlation between the percentage change in futures prices and commodity funds is positive but small.

8. J. Lorie and L. Fisher, "Some Studies of the Variability of Returns on Investment in Common Stocks," *Journal of Business*, April 1970.

9. Elton *et al.*, "New Public Offerings," *op. cit.*

10. Maximums are probably the most relevant size measure. Minimums have little significant variation, lying generally between one-half million and one million, and this variation hasn't much to do with the amount they hope to raise.

11. The same argument could be used for underwriters or commodity trading advisers. The correlation between general partners and underwriters is almost one, so no new information s contained in this analysis. Commodity trading advisers are frequently changed, and many funds have multiple advisers. There is much less continuity, so analysis here was not seen as fruitful.

12. We counted as of December of the prior year. The general partner could have had additional funds that had dissolved earlier. We wanted to use a rule an investor could potentially use. Earlier dissolved funds would be extremely difficult to trace.

Glossary

Geometric Mean Return The average return that, when compounded, causes the beginning value to equal the ending value.

Continuously Compounded Rate of Return The return earned when interest is assumed to be compounded continuously.

Skewness A measure of the symmetry of a return distribution. Positive skewness would indicate a greater probability of large high returns relative to low returns.

Standard Deviation A measure of the dispersion of the return distribution. For symmetric distributions, 19 of 20 returns should lie between the mean return minus two standard deviations and the mean return plus two standard deviations.

Mutual Funds—Stock Investments

10

Efficiency with Costly Information: A Reinterpretation of Evidence from Managed Portfolios

Edwin J. Elton, Martin J. Gruber, Sanjiv Das, and Matthew Hlavka

The evaluation of professional money management has long been a topic of considerable interest to financial economists. Two developments have stimulated renewed interest in this topic. The first is the work of Grossman (1976) and Grossman and Stiglitz (1980). They argue that trades by informed investors take place at prices that compensate these investors for the cost of becoming informed. Under these conditions, it is possible for informed investment managers to pass on the cost of analysis to their clients and for their clients to be no worse off after reimbursing managers for the cost of becoming informed. Managers who charge higher fees do not necessarily earn lower returns for their clients. Higher fees may or may not be associated with lower returns, depending not on the efficiency of security markets, but rather on the efficiency of the market for money managers.

The second development stems from the work of Roll (1977) and Ross (1977) and its implication for the evaluation of the money manager. Roll's argument against the use of CAPM as a benchmark for performance together with Ross's discovery of arbitrage pricing theory has led to questions about the appropriate benchmarks against which to judge abnormal performance.

Recent work, particularly that of Lehman and Modest (1987), Admati et al. (1986), Conner and Korajczyk (1991), and Grinblatt and Titman (1989), raise further questions about the appropriate benchmark to use in evaluating performance. In particular, Lehman and Modest (1987) stress the sensitivity of performance to the benchmark chosen and the need to find a set of benchmarks that represent the common factors determining security returns. This literature should be contrasted with a set of literature that seems to indicate that a single-index model provides an adequate description of portfolio returns and that the evaluation of the returns is reasonably insensitive to the definition of the index used. For example, Roll

(1971) found that three market proxies provided nearly identical performance measures for randomly selected portfolios. Copeland and Mayers (1982) found that inferences about the Value Line Enigma were unaffected by the choice of a performance benchmark.

Our purpose in this article is to show that even a very parsimonious description of the proxies generating returns on portfolios of bonds and stocks and can lead to very different and superior inferences about the attributes of active portfolio management compared to a single index. We use as an example the data used (and conclusions reached) in a recent study of mutual fund performance by Ippolito (1989). The Ippolito study is important because it is the first test of the expanded (Grossman) definition of market efficiency using data on managed portfolios. In addition, Ippolito's study is interesting because his results and conclusions are different from those reached in a long series of mutual fund studies.

Ippolito has at least two findings that are important and consistent with a theory of efficiency with informed investors.

(1) Estimated risk adjusted return (α) for the mutual fund industry is greater than zero even after accounting for transaction costs and expenses. Ippolito attributes nonnegative α to the existence of informed actions by management.
(2) There does not seem to be any evidence that turnover, management fees, or expenses are associated with inferior returns, net of management fees and expenses.

These results and conclusions are very different from those reached by earlier researchers [see Jensen (1968), Friend, Blume, and Crockett (1970), and Sharpe (1966)]. In particular, they are different from the results presented by Jensen, who found a negative α on average for a broad sample of mutual funds over the periods 1955–1964 and 1945–1964.

In this article, we show that Ippolito's results are primarily due to the difference in the performance of non-S&P 500 assets in the Ippolito period (1965–1984) compared to the performance of these assets in the Jensen period.[1] Furthermore, once we explicitly account for mutual funds holding non-S&P assets, the results of the type of analysis Ippolito performs change and are identical to those found in earlier studies.

In the first section of this article, we examine the effect of holding non-S&P equities and bonds on alphas of mutual funds. Mutual funds have historically held some stocks not in the S&P index and held some stocks in the S&P index in proportions below their weighting in the S&P index.

We shall see that holding non-S&P stocks would cause negative α's for funds over the earlier period studied by Jensen and positive α's for funds over the period studied by Ippolito, *even if* management had no selection ability. In both the earlier period and the latter period, the effect of bonds being part of the portfolio had very little impact on α.[2]

Having documented in the first section of this article two influences that could account for the positive α's found by Ippolito, we then correct for these influences. This is done by introducing two new indexes into the standard one-index performance measurement model. This allows us to examine if funds have a positive α above and beyond that arising from extending holdings beyond the S&P 500.

In the final section, we examine the influence of expenses and turnover on α when we have explicitly taken into account the effect of non-S&P assets.

I The Effect of Non-S&P Assets on Mutual Fund α's

To examine the effect of non-S&P assets on fund performance we considered two non-S&P asset categories commonly held by mutual funds: bonds and non-S&P stocks.[3] The α on a portfolio, which is the Jensen measure of portfolio performance, is a weighted average of the α's on the individual assets that compose the portfolio. Thus, to see the effect of inclusion of an asset category on the portfolio α, one only has to estimate the α for that asset category.

We wish to examine the effect one measured α's when mutual funds hold non-S&P assets and there is *no selection ability*. To do so, we will proxy the performance of non-S&P stocks and bonds by the return on several alternative passively managed portfolios.

1.1 Non-S&P Stocks

The common stocks that compose Standard & Poor's index are selected to guarantee broad industry representation; however, within each industry the larger firms are generally selected. The weight placed on each stock in computing the index is proportional to the total market value of the firm's equity. The result is that the S&P index is primarily comprised of, and affected by, the large firms listed on the NYSE. Thus, indexes of the return on small (low capitalization) stocks should be good proxies for non-S&P stocks. We examine the impact of small stocks on α in two ways. The first uses the return indexes on deciles formed by market size

Table 10.1

	With S&P indexes		With combined indexes[1]	
Decile by size	1945–1964 Jensen period	1965–1984 Ippolito period	1945–1964 Jensen period	1965–1984 Ippolito period
Smallest	−5.03	12.81[2]	−6.58	15.40[2]
2	−4.39	10.64[2]	−5.26	13.15[2]
3	−3.40	9.08[2]	−4.04	11.51[2]
4	−4.42	8.62[2]	−5.11	10.96[2]
5	−3.60	6.87[2]	−4.22	8.99[2]
6	−3.02	5.88[2]	−3.69	7.89[2]
7	−1.73	4.18	−2.41	6.29
8	−1.84	3.88[2]	−2.56	5.74
9	1.14	1.35	.52	2.97
Largest	.19	−1.07	−.12	.43

All α's come from a simple regression of the annual excess return on each decile against the indicated index measured in excess return form. In this and all tables that follow, annual excess returns are used where excess return is defined as the actual annual return minus the annual return from holding 30-day Treasury bills.
1. This is the second index used by Ippolito (1989). It is constructed by equally weighting the S&P index and the Ibbotson-Sinquefield long-term bond index.
2. Indicates t-value >2.1.

constructed by the Center for Research in Security Prices (CRSP) at the University of Chicago. The CRSP return indexes are constructed by ranking all stocks listed on the NYSE by market capitalization, dividing the stocks into 10 equal-sized groups, and then value-weighting the return on individual stocks within each group.[4] Table 10.1 shows the α for each of the 10 deciles in the Jensen period and in the Ippolito period. A manager who had no selection ability and selected part of the portfolio from non-S&P stocks would have shown a negative α in the Jensen period and a strong positive α in the Ippolito period. The average α of the smallest five deciles in the Jensen period is −4.17 percent, while in the Ippolito period it is +9.61 percent. Similar results are obtained when the analysis is repeated employing Ippolito's combined bond stock index as the independent variable defining α's. Negative α's for the small stock index in the Jensen period do not imply that the returns on the small stock index are less than returns on the S&P index. In fact, in the Jensen period they were higher. In Table 10.2, we present another illustration of the same phenomenon. The small stock index is a value-weighted index of the lowest

Table 10.2
α for alternative indexes

Index	With S&P indexes 1945–1964	With S&P indexes 1965–1984	With combined indexes[1] 1945–1964	With combined indexes[1] 1965–1984
CRSP value-weighted	−0.26	0.57	−0.71	2.21
CRSP equal-weighted	−3.13	6.25	−3.91	8.41
CRSP small stock index	−4.04	10.06	−5.07	12.38

All returns are in annual excess return form.
1. Second index used by Ippolito (1989). It is constructed by equally weighting the S&P index and the Ibbotson–Sinquefield long-term bond index.

quintile of the stocks listed on the NYSE. It is the standard small stock index used in many academic studies. In the Jensen period, the small stock index exhibited a negative α of -4.04 percent, while in the Ippolito period the α is $+10.06$ percent.

In Table 10.2, we also present the α's for market-weighted and equally weighted averages of all stocks on the NYSE. These α's reinforce the effects shown by examining deciles. Examination of the α's on the market-weighted CRSP index of all NYSE stocks shows that extending holdings beyond stocks in the S&P index, even when maintaining market weights, results in negative α's for the Jensen period and positive α's for the Ippolito period. The larger negative α's for the Jensen period and positive α's for the Ippolito period associated with the equally weighted index illustrates another influence. Holding stocks in proportions closer to equal rather than market proportions results in large positive α's in the Ippolito period and negative α's in the Jensen period, even with no selection ability.

The results shown in Tables 10.1 and 10.2 are dramatic. Given the extremely large α's, even a small part of the portfolio not being invested in S&P stocks would explain Ippolito's results on average performance (α), even with *zero* forecasting ability.[5]

1.2 Bonds

The second category of assets we examined was bonds. There were three widely used bond return indexes that existed from 1945 to 1984. These are the Ibbotson and Sinquefield (I&S) long-term corporate, intermediate-term government, and long-term government bond indexes. The first question we need to examine is which index is the best proxy for a passively

Table 10.3
Regression results of potential bond proxies versus bond funds and Shearson Lehman index

	With Shearson Lehman[1]			With bond funds[2]		
Bond proxies	α	β	R^2	α	β	R^2
Intermediate govt.	1.61	0.83	.93	.51	0.85	.92
Long-term govt.	−4.61	1.46	.90	−.55	1.57	.90
Long-term corporate	−4.93	1.55	.95	−.42	1.66	.95
80:20 mix[3]	−0.30	0.97	.96	.33	1.01	.94

1. Regressions of the bond proxies versus the Shearson Lehman Government Corporate Index were over the period 1973–1988.
2. Regressions of the bond proxies versus the Bond Funds Index were over the period 1979–1988.
3. The 80:20 mix is made up of 80% of the return on the intermediate-term government bond index and 20% of the return on the long-term bond index.

managed bond fund. The most common index used by passive bond managers is the Shearson Lehman Government Corporate Index. Unfortunately, the Shearson Lehman index has only existed since 1973 and so cannot be examined for our entire sample period. To find a proxy for it, we regressed each of the Ibbotson and Sinquefield indexes as well as a composite I&S index comprised of 80 percent intermediate government and 20 percent long-term corporate bonds against the Shearson Lehman index over the period 1973 to 1988 (the period for which we have data on the Shearson Lehman index). The 80:20 ratio was examined as a possible proxy because its duration closely matched the duration of the Shearson Lehman index.

The results are shown in Table 10.3. As expected, the long duration of the Ibbotson and Sinquefield long-term indexes made these indices much more volatile than the Shearson Lehman index. The 80:20 mixture closely matches the index. The β on the Shearson Lehman index is 0.97 with an α of 0.30. The composite index is a reasonable proxy for a passive bond index fund.

We did one additional test. We have data from 1979 to 1988 on all bond mutual funds that existed in 1979.[6] Although these funds may have under- or overperformed an index fund, our proxy index ought to be highly related to the average active fund. Table 3 shows the results. The β of the 80:20 mixture was 1.01 with an α of 0.33. Thus, the 80:20 mixture has a very similar pattern of return to actual bond funds, but earned in this period an excess return. In subsequent analysis, we will use the 80:20 mixture as a proxy for a passive bond fund.

Table 10.4
Results for 80:20 bond proxy regressed against the S&P index

	α	β	t_α	R^2	Excess return[1]
1945–1964	1.39	−.057	.83	.07	.57
1965–1984	−0.42	.12	−.25	.03	−.19

Regressions were also run using the equally weighted bond stocks index as the dependent variable. Results were substantially unchanged.
1. Excess return refers to the annual return of the 80:20 bond index over and above the annual return of 30-day Treasury bills.

As shown in Table 10.4, the relationship between our proxy for a passive bond fund and the S&P index is insignificant in both periods. In the 1945–1946 period, the adjusted R^2 is 0.07 for the 80:20 mixture; whereas in the 1965–1984 period, the adjusted R^2 is 0.03. Thus, it is difficult to place much confidence in the α values.

If bond funds are unrelated to the S&P index, then it is the return above the riskless rate that determines their α.[7] The return on the bond proxy was 0.57 percent above the riskless rate in the first period and −0.19 percent in the second. The magnitude of the α's and excess returns for bonds are much smaller than the magnitude of the α's and excess returns for other non-S&P assets. Thus, any effects of mutual funds holding debt on the mutual fund α's are likely to be swamped by other influences. However, bonds do mitigate to a limited extent the effect of other non-S&P assets. Although the performance of bonds is unlikely to affect results in the Ippolito period, the reader should be cautious about generalizing. Most studies analyze about 10 years of data. We examined all 10-year periods in our sample. The average α for bonds on the S&P index varied from −2.6 to +1.0. Most recent studies have factor-analyzed stock returns in order to obtain a return generating process. Unless some of the factors that are produced by factor-analyzing equity returns are highly correlated with bond returns, the average α on balanced funds could be heavily influenced by the bond α.

II Adjusting for Other Indexes

In the prior section we showed that inclusion of non-S&P assets in a mutual fund portfolio would result in nonzero α's, even if selection of all assets was random. The magnitude of the impact is a direct function of the fraction of non-S&P assets held. Since the fraction of non-S&P assets held by a fund is correlated with many of the characteristics of funds we wish to examine, it is important to control for this effect. In this section, we will discuss how one can control for the effect of non-S&P assets on mutual fund α's.[8]

One way to view a mutual fund is as a combination of three portfolios: one containing S&P stocks, one containing non-S&P stocks, and one containing bonds. The return on the fund is a weighted average of the return on the three portfolios. Management performance is the extra return earned on the fund compared to holding a combination of three passive portfolios with the same characteristics as the overall fund. The measure of performance developed from this approach can be considered a generalization of the Jensen measure to encompass the situation where managers hold non-S&P stocks and bonds.[9] It could also be considered a measure of performance given a belief in a three-factor return generating process. If a passive portfolio interpretation of the model is employed, one must consider costs.

Mutual fund returns are net of management fees and trading costs. When utilizing indexes as proxies for passive portfolios, these costs are not subtracted. The question that needs to be analyzed is how much lower are the returns on passive portfolios after fees are deducted relative to the indexes they duplicate. Institutional investors have available passive S&P index portfolios and bond portfolios that almost exactly match indexes after all fees and trading costs. For individual investors, index funds such as the Vanguard funds match the index within 25 basis points for the part of the fund not in cash. A number of analysts argue that returns on small stock indexes are unattainable by actual portfolio managers because of high transaction costs [e.g., Fouse (1989) and Stoll and Whaley (1983)]. Sinquefield (1991) examined the returns on the five passive small stock index funds with any substantial history. He found that net of trading costs and management fees, the passive funds earned 2 basis points per month more than the particular small stock index they followed. The worst shortfall was 12 basis points per month. Thus, even for small stocks, index returns may well be reasonable measures of passive returns net of costs, and a deduction of 25 basis points would be a generous adjustment.

The return on an active fund relative to the return on the three passive portfolios is

$$R_i - R_F = \alpha_i + \beta_{iM}(R_M - R_F) + \beta_{iS}(R_S - R_F) + \beta_{iD}(R_D - R_F) + e_i.$$

In this model,[10] R_M is the return on the S&P 500 index, R_S is the return on a non-S&P equity index that has been made orthogonal to the S&P

index, R_D is the return on a bond return index that has been made orthogonal to both the S&P and the non-S&P equity index, β_{ij} is the sensitivity of portfolio i to the relevant index j, and e_i is the residual risk.

We will use two alternative proxies for the returns on non-S&P stocks: the small stock index and a value-weighted index of all NYSE stocks, each with the effect of the S&P removed. By orthogonalizing (removing the effect of another index from) the non-S&P indexes, we lose the interpretation of each index as the return on a passive fund. However, using orthogonalized rather than raw indexes does not affect the explanatory power of α and does highlight the marginal effect of non-S&P assets above that accounted for by the S&P index.[11] The portfolio used to generate a return on a passive debt portfolio is the portfolio consisting of 80 percent intermediate government bonds and 20 percent long-term corporate bonds orthogonalized to remove any effects of the other two indexes. Orthogonalization is performed by running a regression of the non-S&P index (e.g., the small stock index) against the S&P index. A new index is created by using the intercept plus the residual from this regression as the orthogonalized small stock index. This new index captures both the mean effect and the time-series impact of the effect.

Table 10.5 shows the average α in our sample for a number of different definitions of passive portfolios. We present results for the single-index case, the two-index case, and the three-index case. Jensen's results for the time period 1945–1964 are presented in part A of Table 10.5. Our new results and Ippolito's results are presented in part B. Our results on a corrected version of Ippolito's sample are presented in the second row of part B. While the corrections we make lower the average α for mutual funds and lead to estimates that are not statistically different from zero, they do not change the sign of the average α. The corrections we made in his sample are of two types. In checking his data, we found several errors. By far the most frequent error was the omission of the negative sign on individual observations of returns with no corresponding misclassification of positive returns. Correcting individual observations changed the average α from 0.81 to 0.38. The second correction involved a slight redesign of the sample. Ippolito selected all funds that met certain criteria in 1984 and also had data or were formed from a fund that had data in 1965. Twelve of these funds did not meet Ippolito's criteria (e.g., no international funds) in 1965. We formed our sample from all firms that met Ippolito's criteria at the beginning of 1965. By coincidence the sample size was the same but 12 of Ippolito's funds were replaced by different funds. Actually drawing the sample correctly resulted in increasing the

Table 10.5
α's for individual funds

		Significant[1] (5%)				Mean			
	No. pos.	Pos.	Neg.	Mean α	t-value*	Mean S&P β	small stock β	Mean bond β	R^2
A. 1945–1964 (115 firms)									
1. Jensen		3	14	−1.1		.84			
B. 1965–1984 (143 firms)									
1. S&P (Ippolito uncorrected)		12	4	.81		.88			
2. S&P (Ippolito corrected)	87	9	5	.61	.56	.94			.74
3. S&P and small stock	38	0	15	−1.49	−2.11	.94	0.21		.79
4. S&P and value-weighted residual	47	1	11	−.81	−1.25	.94	2.58		.78
5. S&P, small stock, bond	34	0	21	−1.59	−2.35	.94	0.21	0.13	.83
6. S&P, value-weighted residual, bond	44	1	12	−.88	−1.46	.94	2.58	0.15	.83

1. The t-value is calculated using the cross-sectional correlation of α's. The standard error of the mean α is $1/N^2$ times the sum of all the elements in the variance covariance matrix of the residuals. All t's in subsequent tables are calculated the same way.

β from 0.38 to 0.61, which is still below Ippolito's estimate of 0.81. Also note the low t-value that occurs, in part because of the change in α, but also because we corrected t's for cross-sectional correlation and heteroskedasticity.[12]

Once we account for non-S&P stocks or bonds, the α's become negative and the results are similar to Jensen's results. Using any of the two-index or three-index models, the average α is negative. The α's involving the small stock index are significantly different from zero at the 1 percent level; more than two thirds of the funds have negative α's; and the number of negative α's that are significantly different from zero at the 5 percent level far exceeds the number of α's that are positive and different from zero at the 5 percent level. In computing the t-statistics for the α's, the standard error of the mean α was computed taking into account the cross-sectional correlation among α's. The variance of the average α is the vector of proportions (each equal to $1/N$) times the variance-covariance matrix of residuals times the vector of proportions. All subsequent t-statistics on α's were computed in this way. The pattern and significance of the α's are further evidence that Ippolito's results are due to the relative performance of alternative classes of securities rather than the ability of managers to select superior securities from any class.

Since in subsequent analysis we will feature the α's from the three-index model with the small stock index as one index, a few additional comments on this formulation are in order. The F-ratio shows that the addition of the index for non-S&P stocks and bonds improves the explanatory power of the equation. In addition, a substantial number of the sensitivities as significant. In the three-index model using the small stock index, 73 sensitivities are significant for the small stock index and 52 for the bond index.

All studies that employ multiple indexes have a potential problem: by using multiple indexes, they may fail to attribute to management the element of good performance associated with superior sector selection. This is true of our study as well as those of Grinblatt and Titman (1989), Lehman and Modest (1987), Jagannathan and Korajczyk (1986), and Conner and Korajczyk (1991). In our study, given the performance of the indexes, the main concern is the split between S&P equities and non-S&P equities. We will present evidence that shows that investors in 1964 had information that would allow them to determine which funds would have significant small stock exposure. Furthermore, we will show that managers did not successfully time changes in the relative performance between S&P and non-S&P equities. Since at the beginning of the period the investor could duplicate the small stock strategy of any firm with an index fund, and since, as we show, fund management did not improve performance by changes in small stock strategy within the period, we believe the intercept from the multi-index model is the relevant measure of performance.[13]

To examine whether an investor could determine the sector selection of the funds in 1964, we examined the fund descriptions and the stock holdings reported in Wiesenberger in 1964. While the policy description is subjective, it is clear that the majority of the funds with very high (positive) small stock sensitivity were funds that had a policy of investing in high technology, high growth stocks. On the other hand, the funds with low small stock sensitivity tended to be funds that had been established for a longer period of time and stated their objectives as holding larger well-established companies. We computed the percentage of the stock portfolio held in non-S&P stocks as of 1965 for the 10 funds with the largest and the 10 funds with the smallest sensitivity to small stocks. For the funds with high positive sensitivity to small stocks, 56 percent of the stock portion of their portfolio consisted of non-S&P stocks; while for the low sensitivity group, the proportion of non-S&P stock was only 17 percent. These numbers were computed from Wiesenberger reports and thus were data that were available to any investor.[14] Clearly, the investor could have known in 1965 which funds were holding non-S&P equities.

In order to examine the fund managers' ability to sector select, we compared their exposure in periods of good and poor small stock performance. Our sample contained five years in which small stocks underperformed large stocks. If managers are sector timers, and have forecasting ability, then the sensitivity to small stocks should decrease in the years when small stocks did poorly. To test this, we estimate a separate small stock sensitivity measure (small stock β) for the years in which small stocks did poorly. This procedure, which employed a zero-one dummy variable to estimate the new slope, is analogous to the Merton–Henriksson [Henriksson and Merton (1981)] procedure, except that the switching is between S&P stocks and small stocks rather than between stocks and Treasury bills. Our procedure is also similar to that followed by Jagannathan and Korajczyk (1986). If managers are successful timers, then the differential β for years when small stocks did poorly should be negative. In fact, for our overall sample, only 44 out of 143 were negative, indicating some slight tendency for rotation into small stocks to take place at the wrong time. It is possible that timing was only relevant for those funds that had high sensitivity to small stocks. For the 10 percent of the firms with the largest small stock β's, seven had positive differential β's and seven negative. One was significantly positive at the 5 percent level and none significantly negative. For the top 20 percent of the firms ranked by small stock β's, the numbers are 14 positive and 15 negative with 1 significantly positive. These results lead us to believe that management has shown no ability to time the small stock effect. Given the ability of investors to identify the funds with significant non-S&P exposure and the lack of timing demonstrated by these funds, we feel our multi-index approach is appropriate.

Table 10.6 shows the performance of managers when mutual funds are classified in various ways. These classifications were used by Ippolito and are included here because they provide additional evidence on the performance of funds and the linkage between performance and portfolio composition. Ippolito in his analysis eliminated 15 funds because the β in the first 10 years differed from the β in the second 10 years, and we did not eliminate them. We repeated the test he used to determine changing β with the corrected sample. Only two firms were eliminated using his procedure. The difference arose because the data for the other firms he eliminated generally had substantial data errors. We included these firms, although eliminating them would not affect our results.[15]

The first classification is β. The β ranges used in this table are identical to those used by Ippolito. All numbers in the table except for t-values are simple averages across the included funds. The t-values were calculated by the method described in discussing Table 10.5. Examining the one-index model shows that α is positively related to β. This pattern is what should be expected given that non-S&P stocks generally have higher β's. Ippolito found no relationship between α and β when he used a single-index model. The difference is due to data errors in Ippolito's sample. A sign error (which was always a negative return recorded as positive) increases the α. In addition, it lowers β. Thus, the sign errors in Ippolito's sample were concentrated in the low β category. When the three-index model is utilized, the pattern disappears. Adding the additional passive portfolios significantly increases the explanatory power. In addition, the sensitivities to the non-S&P indexes are sensible. The sensitivity to the small stock index increases as the S&P β increases. Mutual funds with high S&P β have high exposure to small stocks. Likewise, the exposure to bonds decreases as the S&P β increases.

The second categorization we utilized is percent of the funds' assets invested in common stock. We utilized the average percent over 20 years. We adopted Ippolito's categories. For the one-index model, the greater the percent in common stock, the greater the α. When the three-index model is examined, the relationship disappears. The β's on the other

Table 10.6
Performance of mutual funds for various criteria

Classification criteria	One-index model[1]					Three-index model[2]						Ippolito[3]
	No. of funds	α	t_α^4	$\beta_{S\&P}$	R^2_{adj}	α	t_α	$\beta_{S\&P}$	β_{SS}	β_B	R^2_{adj}	α
β												
$\beta < .77$	30	−0.31	−.25	0.66	.69	−1.92	−3.76	0.66	.10	.72	.86	0.86
$.77 < \beta < 1.02$	72	0.59	.80	0.91	.81	−0.77	−1.44	0.91	.13	.12	.86	0.85
$\beta > 1.02$	41	1.33	.56	1.19	.65	−2.80	−1.78	1.19	.44	−.29	.77	0.75
Stock share												
<65%	32	0.36	.30	0.70	.67	−1.41	−2.77	0.70	.12	.65	.85	0.44
65–90%	75	0.54	.41	0.98	.75	−1.92	−2.21	0.98	.25	.01	.82	0.99
>90%	36	1.00	.81	1.06	.78	−1.07	−1.16	1.06	.21	−.09	.84	0.88
Wiesenberger type												
1. Common stock												
a. Max capital gain	12	1.63	.42	1.34	.54	−4.59	−1.87	1.34	.69	−.81	.77	0.82
b. Growth	33	0.82	.54	1.05	.73	−1.55	−1.23	1.05	.24	.06	.79	1.28
c. Growth and income	40	0.66	.98	0.92	.86	−0.68	−1.65	0.92	.12	.16	.89	0.45
2. Balanced	31	0.34	.30	0.71	.73	−1.27	−2.73	0.71	.11	.66	.89	0.62

1. The one-index model regresses excess returns of funds on the excess returns on the S&P.
2. The three-index model regresses excess fund returns on the excess returns on the S&P, the excess returns on the small-stock index orthogonalized on the S&P, and the 80 : 20 bond index orthogonalized on the S&P and small stock index returns.
3. The α's shown in this column are those reported by Ippolito (1989).
4. t_α refers to the t-statistic on α.

indexes show why. The small stock β increases with percent in common stock and the bond β decreases.

The third section of the table examines performance by objective and policy as reported by Wiesenberger. Four categories were used. First, firms' investment policy was used to divide funds into groups that either invest only in common stock or as a policy invest in bonds and common stock (balanced). Within the common stock category, we further classified firms according to their stated objective. A number of firms changed their policy or objective over the 20 years. If the firm changed its policy from common stock to balanced or the reverse, it was excluded from this part of Table 10.6.[16] Further, if it changed its objective more than just to an adjacent category or was not in the same category for at least 14 of the 20 years, it was excluded. These procedures led to 27 firms being excluded.

When examining the one-index model, the α declines as the category becomes less aggressive. When three indexes are used, the pattern is reversed for the common stock funds. The pattern of sensitivities is as expected. Sensitivity to the S&P index declines uniformly as the fund's objective becomes less aggressive. The small stock β declines and the bond β increases as the fund's objective becomes less aggressive. Thus, the Wiesenberger objective seems to describe fund behavior accurately on average.

III Market Efficiency Turnover and Expenses

The basic idea underlying the Grossman (1976) and Grossman and Stiglitz (1980) view of efficiency is that informed investors earn a sufficient amount to just compensate for the cost of information gathering. High expenses do not necessarily imply inferior performance, even after expenses have been deducted. Ippolito's article has received much attention because he found no relationship between turnover or expenses and performance net of expenses.This was different than most prior studies and lent strong support to the Grossman view of efficiency.

In this section, we reexamine this question after adjusting for the effect of non-S&P assets. We will examine the relationship between performance and three cost variables: expense ratios, turnover, and load costs.

Recall that mutual fund returns are measured after the deduction of expenses and costs associated with turnover, but before any costs to the investor associated with load charges. Because of the way returns are calculated, load costs should have a different impact on performance statistics than the other costs. Let us start by examining expense ratios and turnover. Expenses are incurred or portfolios changed in an attempt to increase performance. If mutual funds invest money efficiently, there should be no relationship between performance (α) and either expense ratios or turnover. Table 10.7 shows the relationship between performance and both turnover and expenses. Part A of Table 10.7 divides the funds into quintiles by expense ratios. Equally sized quintiles are formed on the basis of average expense ratios for each fund and the α for each quintile is displayed.[17] In addition, we ran a cross-sectional regression between the α on each fund in the sample and their average expense ratio. When a single-index model is employed, there is no statistically significant relationship between performance and expense ratios. When we examine the three-index model, the results change. There is a statistically significant relationship between α and expenses (t-values of -7.12) and a relationship that can clearly be seen by examining the quintiles. Higher expenses are associated with poorer performance. Management does not increase performance by an amount sufficient to justify higher fees. Examination of the individual sensitivities to each of the three indexes shows why the results are different for the single-index model. High expense funds tend to be more sensitive to (place more money in) small stocks and less in bonds than do low expense managers. However, they underperform what an investor could earn by allocating his or her funds to three passive portfolios. When a single-index model is used, this relationship between performance and expenses is obscured by differences in the investment philosophy of funds. This is the same phenomenon we saw earlier when we examined the relationship between α and β in the single-index model.

When we examine turnover, we find the same type of results, although the relationships are not nearly as strong. With the one-index model, performance appears to be very weakly positively related to turnover. With the three-index model, the relationship between performance and turnover becomes negative and significant at the 5 percent level using a two-tailed test. Management does not earn enough excess return to compensate for the full cost of increased turnover.

Our principal test relating performance to either expenses or turnover used the average values for expenses and turnover because there was little variation in year-to-year values. Although we do not have a long history on turnover, we have 20 years of expense ratios. Since Ippolito examined yearly values, we performed a test on yearly values for expenses to be

Table 10.7
Effect of average expenses and average turnover on α

A. Quintiles by expense ratios

Single-index[1] group	Average expenses	α	t^2_α	$\beta_{S\&P}$	R^2_{adj}
High	$.912 < E < 2.020$	0.06	0.06	1.01	.60
2	$.753 < E < 0.912$	1.22	0.90	0.93	.69
3	$.680 < E < 0.753$	1.10	1.08	0.91	.73
4	$.590 < E < 0.680$	0.28	0.34	0.92	.79
Low	$E < 0.590$	0.33	0.47	0.92	.86

Three-index[3] group	Average expenses	α	t_α	$\beta_{S\&P}$	β_{SS}	β_B	R^2_{adj}
High	$.912 < E < 2.020$	−3.87	−3.56	1.01	.40	−.07	.76
2	$.753 < E < 0.912$	−1.68	−2.34	0.93	.27	.23	.83
3	$.680 < E < 0.753$	−0.69	−0.86	0.91	.17	.16	.82
4	$.590 < E < 0.680$	−1.19	−1.93	0.92	.13	.18	.86
Low	$E < 0.590$	−0.59	−0.89	0.92	.08	.13	.89

B. Quintiles by turnover

Single-index group	Average turnover	α	t^2_α	$\beta_{S\&P}$	R^2_{adj}
High	$72\% < T < 162\%$	.75	.46	1.05	.69
2	$51\% < T < 72\%$	.75	.49	0.98	.68
3	$34\% < T < 51\%$	.35	.30	0.93	.74
4	$22\% < T < 34\%$	.64	.69	0.87	.76
Low	$T < 22\%$	.58	.93	0.86	.81

Three-index group	Average turnover	α	t_α	$\beta_{S\&P}$	β_{SS}	β_B	R^2_{adj}
High	$72\% < T < 162\%$	−2.21	−1.94	1.05	.30	−.03	.80
2	$51\% < T < 72\%$	−1.87	−1.60	0.98	.26	−.01	.79
3	$34\% < T < 51\%$	−2.17	−3.39	0.93	.24	.14	.85
4	$22\% < T < 34\%$	−1.11	−2.11	0.87	.15	.34	.86
Low	$T < 22\%$	−0.58	−1.49	0.86	.10	.20	.88

1. The one-index model regresses excess returns of funds on the excess return on the S&P.
2. t_α refers to the t-statistic on α.
3. The three-index model regresses excess fund returns on the excess returns on the S&P, the excess returns on the small-stock index orthogonalized on the S&P, and the 80:20 bond index orthogonalized on the S&P and small stock index returns.

Table 10.8
Performance of load and no-load funds

		From one-index model[1]				From three-index model[2]					
	Number	α	t_α	$\beta_{S\&P}$	R^2_{adj}	α	t_α	$\beta_{S\&P}$	β_{SS}	β_B	R^2_{adj}
Load	90	.48	.49	.92	.74	−1.55	−2.38	.92	.19	.19	.84
No load	19	.86	.78	.96	.72	−0.84	−0.89	.96	.17	.01	.81
Switch	33	.84	.56	.97	.72	−2.17	−3.30	.97	.30	.05	.83

One fund, State Street, was not classified by Wiesenberger.
1. t_α refers to the t-statistic on α.
2. The one-index model regresses excess returns of funds on the excess returns on the S&P.

more comparable with his tests. Each year we regressed α plus the residual for each firm on the yearly expenses for the firm. Of the 20 slopes, 15 were negative and 10 significantly so. Estimating the standard deviation of the mean of the slopes, using the 20 observed slopes, and testing for the difference of the average slope from zero, produced a t-value of −3.28, which is highly significant.

The last cost we examine is the load charge on funds. Since the load cost of purchasing funds is not deducted in calculating returns, load funds need a higher α in order to be an attractive investment. In fact, as seen in Table 10.8, load funds have a lower α whether the single-index or three-index model is used. There is no evidence in the data that mutual funds that charge a load compensate investors for the added cost.

Having examined the relationship between performance and average expenses, average turnover and load, we now examine whether funds change these in response to performance. One view of mutual fund expenses is that mutual fund managers charge what their performance justifies. A large portion of expenses are under the control of managers. That is, they are expenses to a fund's shareholder but they are set by and controlled by management. Successful managers can raise their fees and unsuccessful managers may have to lower them. To examine this question, we divided the sample into two 10-year periods (Table 10.9). In the first 10-year period, we calculate α from our three-index model, rank the firms by α, and divide the sample into 10 equally sized groups. The last column shows the percentage change in average yearly expenses from the first 10 years to the last 10 years for each of our groups. The percentage increase in expenses declines almost linearly, with an increase in performance. Thus, the table does not provide evidence of expenses being changed in relationship to past performance.[18]

Table 10.9
α in two 10-year subperiods and percent change in expenses from earlier subperiod to later (deciles sorted by α during 1965–1974)

Deciles	1965–1974 α	1975–1984 α	% change in expenses
Low	−5.22	−4.37	34.1
2	−2.71	−2.68	34.9
3	−2.01	−2.59	34.2
4	−1.40	−2.02	22.2
5	−1.03	0.18	16.6
6	−0.56	−1.98	27.6
7	0.05	−0.48	16.4
8	0.64	−0.98	17.2
9	1.54	−1.26	17.4
High	3.97	−1.68	9.4

Another way to test the hypothesized interrelationship between expenses and performance is to examine performance over time. If expenses are just sufficient to eliminate the excess return due to being informed, then performance should be unpredictable. To test this, we used the same deciles ranked by α in the first 10 years. For these deciles, we calculated the average α in the second 10 years. This is shown in the second column of Table 10.9. A rank correlation test is highly significant. In addition, a regression of α in the second period on α in the first period is significant at the 5 percent level. Thus, historical performance of managers is somewhat predictive of future performance and superior performance is not simply a reward for the cost of obtaining information.[19]

As a final test, we examined the performance of funds around the time they changed from load to no-load funds. Since load fees are a sales charge and unrelated to the costs of security analysis, we would not expect to see this change affect performance. Table 10.10 shows the non-index-related unique return for all funds that switched from load to no-load compared to the average non-index-related return for the funds that did not switch. Data is arranged in event time. To obtain the entry for −1, we calculate for each switching fund the difference between its unique return in the year before the switch and the average unique return for all nonswitching funds in the same year. The figure in the table is the average of this number across all 33 funds that switched. The data for +1 is the year in which the switch took place. The data around the switch do

Table 10.10

Time	Unique return switches[1] minus average unique return nonswitches
−7	+1.22
−6	−1.91
−5	−3.17
−4	−1.88
−3	−0.61
−2	0.78
−1	0.72
+1	−2.54
+2	−0.42
+3	−4.00
+4	0.66
+5	2.22
+6	−3.38
+7	1.60

1. The data is lined up in event time and is arranged such that the year in which the switch occurred is taken to be +1. The unique return is non-index-related return; that is, in the regression $y = \alpha + \beta x + \varepsilon$, the unique return is $\alpha + \varepsilon$.

not present a clear pattern. There is a slight tendency for funds that switched to do slightly better than the average fund in the two years before the switch and to do worse in the few years after the switch. As shown in Table 10.9, funds that charge a load fee and funds that switched did worse for investors than funds that have been no load over a long period of time.

IV Conclusion

Market efficiency is one of the major paradigms of financial economics. Modern theories of efficiency argue that informed investors in an efficient market will earn just enough to compensate for the cost of obtaining the information. Mutual fund managers are commonly viewed as the prototype of informed investors. Ippolito (1989) found that mutual funds earned a positive α before load charges and that fund performance was unrelated to expenses and turnover as predicted by efficiency arguments. In this article, we show that Ippolito's results are due to using a metric that did not appropriately account for the performance of non-S&P assets.

More specifically, when the performance of non-S&P assets is appropriately accounted for, Ippolito's findings are reversed and the results are consistent with prior literature, Mutual fund managers underperform passive portfolios. Furthermore, funds with higher fees and turnover underperform those with lower fees and turnover. Finally, funds do not adjust expenses over time to reflect their performance.

Ippolito was incorrect in stating that mutual fund performance provides evidence in support of the Grossman view of efficient markets.

Notes

The authors would like to thank Eugene Fama, Andrew Lo, William Sharpe, and the referee (Bruce Lehmann) for helpful comments and suggestions on an earlier version of this article. We have benefited from useful suggestions received at workshop presentations at MIT, the University of Chicago, and the University of Michigan and presentation at the European Finance Association.

1. In part, his results are also due to data errors that led to a particular bias. This will be explored in later sections of the article.

2. Bonds impact α indirectly if the presence of bonds means that the aggregate portfolio has a smaller percentage of non-S&P stocks.

3. All results in this and subsequent sections are based on annual returns. This allows direct comparison with Ippolito's results.

4. If security α's are a function of size as in Table 10.1, the CRSP weighting procedure understates the α compared to equal weighting when α's increase with decreasing size and overstates the α when α decreases with increasing size.

5. Another category of non-S&P assets held by mutual funds is international stocks. Academic literature on the advantages of international diversification first appeared in the late 1960s. This literature plus the availability of ADRs has led to the recent increase in the ownership of foreign assets by mutual funds. The Morgan Stanley index is the most widely used index of international securities and is the index most often matched by passive managers. The α on the Morgan Stanley index from the inception of the index in 1970 until 1984 was 6.97 percent. Thus, international diversification and random selection would have led to a positive α in Ippolito's period. Although the large size of the α associated with international stocks could account for Ippolito's results, the likelihood is that the effect is small. There are no international funds in the corrected sample. Non-U.S. stocks (generally in the form of ADRs) are only a small part of most noninternational mutual funds even today. Thus, the effect on Ippolito's α's of international diversification is likely to be very small over Ippolito's period but is likely to become increasingly important in the future.

6. See Blake (1992) for a detailed description of this data.

7. In the Jensen model, a zero correlation with the index means a zero β. Thus, α is the return above the riskless rate.

8. The other way to control for the effect of the non-S&P assets is the multifactor approach of Lehman and Modest (1987), Grinblatt and Titman (1989), Conner and Korajczyk (1991),

and Jagannathan and Korajczyk (1986), where the factors include bond factors. The disadvantage of this approach is that the factors do not have passive portfolios that are actively traded in the market. Thus, an investor would be unable to replicate this strategy.

9. The Jensen measure is usually stated with an equilibrium interpretation. Another interpretation is that it is the extra return earned by a manager compared to the return on a combination of an index fund and Treasury bills of the same risk.

10. This regression model is consistent with a multifactor asset-pricing model. In independent research. Sharpe (1988) has developed a nine-index model based on asset classes to decompose investment returns.

11. By orthogonalization we leave the β on the S&P index unchanged and the β on other indexes captures the marginal impact of those indexes.

12. We made this replacement since Brown et al. (1992) have shown survivorship bias can be a serious problem in this type of study and Ippolito's sample has a potential survivorship bias.

13. An argument could be made that, while the investor could have matched the funds with passive portfolios, fund management should get credit for showing the investor the way. This is a difficult problem and one that is more general than this study. As an analogy, should the manager of a utility fund who buys exclusively utility stocks be judged against the performance of utility stocks or against the S&P index? We believe the appropriate benchmark is utility stocks, but that gives the manager neither credit (or discredit) for choosing that sector of the market. Having expressed our opinion, we leave the final resolution of this point up to the reader.

14. We do not repeat these numbers for later years because Wiesenberger stopped reporting portfolio composition and other sources are not available until after our period.

15. We utilized a different procedure for analyzing the effect of changing β. The percentage in common stock is highly related to β. In addition, firms that change their investment policy would be expected to change their sensitivities. Thus, we formed a sample that eliminated those firms with a change in policy (the exact method is discussed later in the text when we discuss Wiesenberger classifications) or changed the percentage invested in common stock by more than 50 percent. This eliminated 44 firms. We repeated all the tests and the results were substantially unchanged. Hence, we only report the results for the full sample.

16. Three firms that should have been discarded by this criteria were not. They were listed in a different category their first two years. However, the percent in equity was of the same magnitude in these years so that we judged the policy was not changed but that the category change was to reflect practice more accurately.

17. Ippolito treated each year's expense ratio separately. There are two reasons why we emphasize average rather than year-to-year data. First, there is very little year-to-year variation in expenses. The high expense firms are high throughout and the low are low throughout. Second, there is a fair amount of latitude concerning when expenses are charged and mutual funds time expenses to smooth performance. For example, management fees can and are deferred in years of relatively poor performance. An extra firm was included in each of the three middle quintiles.

18. The results are consistent with expenses having a fixed and variable component and, thus, average expenses increasing for firms with relatively poor performance.

19. The significance is heavily dependent on the poor α for the first category so that the reader should be somewhat cautious concerning these results. The results may indicate simply that there is consistency in a set of inferior managers. The predictability might also simply reflect differences in expenses across categories.

References

Admati, A., S. Bhattacharya, P. Pfleiderer, and S. Ross, 1986, "On Timing and Selectivity," *Journal of Finance*, 41, 715–731.

Blake, C., 1992, "Bond Fund Performance," unpublished dissertation, New York. University.

Brown, S. J., W. Goetzmann, R. G. Ibbotson, and S. A. Ross, 1992, "Survivorship Bias in Performance Studies," *Review of Financial Studies*, 5, 553–580.

Conner, G., and R. Korajczyk, 1991, "The Attributes, Behavior, and Performance of U.S. Mutual Funds," *Review of Quantitative Finance and Accounting*, 1, 4–25.

Copeland, T., and D. Mayers, 1982, "The Value Line Enigma (1965–1978): A Case Study of Performance Evaluation Issues," *Journal of Financial Economics*, 10, 289–322.

Fouse, W., 1989, "The Small Stock Hoax," *Financial Analyst Journal*, July/August, 4–22.

Friend, I., M. Blume, and J. Crockett, 1970, *Mutual Funds and Other Institutional Investors*, McGraw-Hill, New York.

Grinblatt, M., and S. Titman, 1989, "Portfolio Performance Evaluation: Old Issues and Insights," *Review of Financial Studies*, 2, 393–421.

Grossman, S., 1976, "On the Efficiency of Competitive Stock Markets When Traders Have Diverse Information," *Journal of Finance*, 31, 573–585.

Grossman, S., and J. Stiglitz, 1980, "On the Impossibility of Informationally Efficient Markets," *American Economic Review*, 70, 393–408.

Henriksson, R., and R. Merton, 1981, "On Market Timing and Investment Performance II: Statistical Procedures for Evaluating Forecasting Skills," *Journal of Business*, 54, 513–534.

Ippolito, R., 1989, "Efficiency with Costly Information: A Study of Mutual Fund Performance," *Quarterly Journal of Economics*, 104, 1–23.

Jagannathan, R., and R. Korajczyk, 1986, "Assessing the Market Timing Performance of Managed Portfolios," *Journal of Business*, 59, 217–235.

Jensen, M., 1968, "The Performance of Mutual Funds in the Period 1945–1964," *Journal of Finance*, 23, 389–416.

Lehman, B., and D. Modest, 1987, "Mutual Fund Performance Evaluation: A Comparison of Benchmarks and Benchmark Comparisons," *Journal of Finance*, 42, 233–265.

Roll, R., 1971, "Sensitivity of Performance Measurement to Index Choice Commonly Used Indices," working paper, University of California, Los Angeles.

Roll, R., 1977, "A Critique of the Asset Pricing Theory Tests: Part I on Past and Potential Testability of the Theory," *Journal of Financial Economics*, 4, 129–176.

Ross, S., 1977, "Risk, Return, and Arbitrage," in I. Friend and J. Bicksler (eds.), *Risk and Return in Finance*, Ballinger, Cambridge, Mass.

Sharpe, W., 1966, "Mutual Fund Performance," *Journal of Business*, 39, 119–138.

Sharpe, W., 1988, "Determining a Fund's Effective Assert Mix," *Investment Management Review*, June, 5–15.

Sinquefield, R., 1991, "Are Small Stock Returns Achievable?" *Financial Analyst Journal*, Jan/Feb, 45–50.

Stoll, H., and R. Whaley, 1983, "Transactions Costs and the Small Firm Effect," *Journal of Financial Economics*, 12, 57–79.

Wiesenberger, A., 1964, *Investment Companies*, Arthur Wiesenberget and Co., New York.

11 Survivorship Bias and Mutual Fund Performance

Edwin J. Elton, Martin J. Gruber, and Christopher R. Blake

The subject of mutual fund attrition and the effect of survivorship bias on performance has only recently begun to receive attention in the academic literature. Early studies of mutual fund performance were concerned with illustrating new methodologies for measuring performance and were less concerned with biases in the data. Later studies tended to neglect fund attrition: the most commonly used databases do not allow the user to either study it or correct for it.

Mutual fund attrition can create problems for a researcher because the funds that disappear tend to do so either because their performance is very poor over a period of time or because their total market value is sufficiently small that management judges that it no longer pays to maintain the fund. The latter reason for closing a fund is usually associated with the former reason: poor performance. Thus, to study only funds that survive overstates the measured performance. In the vast majority of cases, a fund that disappears is not dissolved but is merged into another fund, often within the same family of funds (sponsoring organization). The effect and perhaps intent of this is that the sponsoring organization continues to earn fees on the investors' capital while the record of the fund's poor performance is deleted from most hard copy and computerized sources of data. For example, drawing a sample from any of Wiesenberger's publications would present a history of return for mutual funds that exist at the time the issue was prepared but would give no details on funds that ceased to exist during the historic time period studied. Most of the classic studies of mutual fund performance ignore attrition and are subject to survivorship bias.[1]

Correction for attrition is important for several reasons. First, samples that do not correct for attrition will overstate the return that mutual funds earn for their investors. Second, ignoring attrition may differentially impact the return reported for mutual funds with different objectives, because funds with different objectives may have different rates of attrition. Finally, some of the other variables studied may also be correlated with attrition and, thus, studying a sample with survivorship bias may introduce spurious correlation between these variables and performance.

The purpose of this study is to examine the impact of survivorship bias. We will examine both the frequency of mutual fund disappearance and the impact of this on investor return. In studying performance we examine raw returns as well as risk-adjusted returns from both a single- and a multi-index model.

This article differs from other studies of mutual fund attrition in that we trace the subsequent performance of all funds that existed at a prior point in time. If a fund disappeared from standard databases, we trace what happened to it by contacting the master trustee or the management group associated with the original fund. Once we know what happened to a fund, we track the return an investor in that fund would earn over time. For example, if a fund merged with a second fund with the same objective, we compute risk-adjusted return by examining return for the original fund prior to the merger, incorporating actual merger terms to compute return in the month of the merger, and computing risk-adjusted return for the combined fund after the merger.[2] Since we track the performance of an investment in any fund that existed at the start of our sample period, our sample is free of survivorship bias. We calculate performance from this sample and from a sample with survivorship bias. We then compute the effect of survivorship bias on performance. In addition, we compute the amount of bias over different horizons to allow the reader to estimate the size of the bias present in the classic studies of performance.

This article contains eight sections. In Section 1, we present a brief review of how articles on mutual fund performance dealt with survivorship bias. In Section 2 we examine estimates of survivorship bias from other authors. In Section 3 we discuss our sample. In Section 4 we discuss our analysis and estimates of survivorship bias. In Section 5 we discuss the characteristics of funds that disappear by merging into other funds as well as the characteristics of the funds with which they merge. In Section 6 we examine the magnitude of survivorship bias over different time horizons and thus the impact of survivorship bias on the results of previous studies. In Section 7 we examine the effect of survivorship on estimates of the relationship between fund characteristics and performance. The final section contains our conclusions.

I Review of the Literature

The majority of mutual fund performance studies selected funds that existed continuously over a period of time and had some stated investment policy or policies (for example, classification as a common stock fund) at the beginning or end of that period. Such a sampling scheme produces survivorship bias, since only funds that existed over the full period are selected and those that failed are omitted. This selection procedure was used by Connor and Korajczyk (1991), Grinblatt and Titman (1988, 1992),[3] Henriksson (1984), Jensen (1968), Lehmann and Modest (1987), Sharpe (1966), and Treynor (1965).

Some studies of common stock mutual funds which estimate or attempt to correct for survivorship bias are Brown and Goetzmann (1994), Carhart (1994), Elton et al. (1993),[4] Grinblatt and Titman (1989), and Malkiel (1994). Grinblatt and Titman (1989) estimate survivorship bias via a simulation study. Brown and Goetzmann (1994) and Malkiel (1994) track all funds and record their returns up to the year they disappear. Elton et al. (1993) track the yearly returns for all funds that existed at the beginning of a sample period, including the year of merger, and the subsequent performance of the funds they merged into. Four of these latter studies provide estimates of survivorship bias for common stock funds, and they will be discussed in the next section of this article.

II Prior Estimates of Survivorship Bias

Five studies have provided some estimate of survivorship bias: Blake, Elton, and Gruber (1993) for bond funds and Brown and Goetzmann (1994), Carhart (1994), Grinblatt and Titman (1989), and Malkiel (1994) for common stock funds. Blake, Elton, and Gruber (1993) estimate that survivorship bias raises return by 27 basis points per annum for bond funds. This estimate is obtained by taking the difference in excess risk-adjusted return (α from a multi-index model) between those funds that survive and those that don't survive. We might expect this number to be larger for stock funds, given the higher variance of the underlying securities.

Grinblatt and Titman (1989) use quarterly equity holdings to try to estimate the effect of survivorship bias. For each fund, they simulate quarterly returns by calculating the return as if the fund held the equity shares shown at the beginning of each quarter to the end of that quarter. Annual return is computed from the quarterly returns. They calculate the return on two equally weighted portfolios of the individual funds in their sample: one with survivorship bias and one they state is without bias.[5] Their estimate is the difference in α between these two portfolios. They produce several estimates of bias ranging between 10 and 30 basis points.

Brown and Goetzmann (1994) present annual returns for the years 1976 to 1988 for two samples. The first sample is all funds that exist as of 1988 and that didn't merge or disappear in the period 1976 to 1988. The second is all funds that existed in Wiesenberger any year for the period 1976 to 1988. Brown and Goetzmann do not track funds that disappear from Wiesenberger where Wiesenberger does not record what happened to them. Some of these disappearances are mergers and some are name changes that Wiesenberger did not record. This problem is recognized by the authors, and they refer to their estimates as coming from an almost survivorship-bias-free sample. Because of the way Brown and Goetzmann select their sample, funds that are included in their sample could have existed for 1 year, 2 years, or up to 12 years. Thus, unlike earlier researchers, they have not used the dual objective of survival and a minimum history. It is therefore difficult to use their results to understand the size of the bias in other studies of mutual fund performance. Brown and Goetzmann's estimates of the bias involved by not including merged funds vary between 20 and 80 basis points per year, depending on the weighting scheme used. Brown and Goetzmann's estimates are based on differences in annual raw returns.

Malkiel (1994), like Brown and Goetzmann, examines the performance of all funds that exist for any time over a period of years. He too reports unadjusted raw returns. He finds that survivorship bias increases the return on the surviving mutual funds by 150 basis points. Finally, Carhart (1994) measures survivorship as the difference in α between these portfolios at 3% to 5% per year. He does not provide a direct estimate of survivorship bias. The studies by Brown and Goetzmann (1994), Carhart (1994), and Malkiel (1994) have gone further to correct for survivorship bias than any previous studies.

Our study differs from those discussed above in one or more ways. First, unlike most studies, we use risk-adjusted returns in addition to raw returns. Risk adjustment is performed using a three-index model, that has been successfully employed in the past, as well as the standard single-index model. Second, we explicitly track every individual fund that existed at the beginning of our sample period to the end of our sample period. We call this technique "follow the money." Most prior studies that looked at bias had funds that disappeared from the sample, with no subsequent tracking of performance. Either funds disappeared from a data set for unknown reasons or, if they merged, they disappeared without accounting for performance in the final period before the merger or accounting for performance after the merger.

III Sample

We initially started with the 361 funds categorized as having a "common stock" investment policy in the 1977 edition of Wiesenberger's *Investment Companies.*[6] This directory lists data for the year 1976. We divided the sample into those funds with $15 million or more in total net assets (207) and those with under $15 million in total net assets (154) as of year-end 1976. It is extremely difficult to track returns for funds that are no longer reported in Wiesenberger. For very small funds it is often impossible.[7] Thus our return calculations will be made using returns on funds that had capital of $15 million or more at the end of 1976. However, when calculating the effect of survivorship bias we will use data on the incidence of survival for the full sample. Having divided our sample by size, we tracked each fund that initially had total net assets of $15 million or more to December 1993. In this process (see Table 11.1) we found that 42 of the 207 funds merged, 146 survived to the end of the sample period, and 19 were restricted funds.[8]

Table 11.1
Distribution (number) of firms by 1976 year-end total net assets

	$15 million or greater	Under $15 million	All[a]
Merged	42[b]	30	106
Survived	146[c]	67	216
Disappeared		37	
Restricted	19	20	39
Total	207	154	361

a. based on allocation of disappearing firms.
b. 12 of the merged funds also changed policy.
c. 15 of the funds that survived to the end of the period changed policy during the period.
Surviving funds are defined as funds that existed from the end of 1976 to the end of 1993; merged funds are those funds that existed at the end of 1976 and subsequently merged into another fund; disappeared funds are funds that were listed in Wiesenberger at the end of 1976 but which disappeared from subsequent wiesenberger listings with no indication of what happened to them; restricted funds are funds that were not available to the general public for investment at the end of 1976.

There were two types of restricted funds. The first type, called variable annuities (like CREF), were listed in earlier editions of Wiesenberger's *Investment Companies* but were primarily available through insurance plans. The second type were restricted as to purchaser (e.g., a fund that could only be held by Lutherans). We eliminated variable annuity funds, because their sale was usually tied to an insurance product resulting in higher fees to cover insurance, because they are taxed differently, and because their objectives may well be different from the objectives of other funds in the sample.[9] We excluded funds that could not be bought by the general public because, once again, they may have special objectives.

Of the remaining 188 funds that make up our sample of funds with initial assets of $15 million or more, 13 disappeared from Wiesenberger with no indication in Wiesenberger of what happened to them.[10] Each was traced: 12 of these merged and 1 had a name change. Applying the same ratio to the funds with net assets under $15 million to allocate the disappearing funds as either merged or survived results in 106 mergers and 216 survivors for the full sample.

We explored the relationship between fund investment objective and survivorship. There was not a monotonic relationship between fund objectives (maximum capital gain, growth, income) and survivorship. Nor was there a meaningful difference in survival probabilities among categories. Thus, within common stock funds, survivorship does not seem to be related to investment objective.[11]

Having determined our sample, we then collected returns for the funds. We calculate return for each fund on a monthly basis. In calculating return, dividends are assumed to be used to purchase additional shares in the fund at the reinvestment price (net asset value) that was available to shareholders of the fund. This is the assumption made by Morningstar and Investment Company Data, Inc. (ICDI) in constructing their databases.

For funds that existed over the entire period, returns were supplied by ICDI. For funds that ceased to exist, returns were calculated from data supplied by Interactive Data Corporation (IDC), supplemented by information from the fund management companies themselves. Merger terms (e.g., merge ratios) were obtained from the fund management companies themselves.

We checked our data by comparing our returns with those calculated from data reported by Wiesenberger on an annual basis and by comparing monthly returns derived from IDC data with monthly returns from ICDI for time periods over which these data were simultaneously available. Although the pattern of returns between Wiesenberger and ICDI was usually similar across funds, differences of several percent in annual returns were not uncommon. The return differences come about because, in calculating returns with Wiesenberger annual data, dividends are assumed to occur at the end of the year, and ICDI assumes reinvestment in shares of the fund at the time the dividends were paid. Differences between returns calculated from IDC data and ICDI returns rarely occurred. In each case where we found a difference, we went to original sources to resolve the differences. This process gave us great confidence in the accuracy of ICDI return data.[12]

IV Analysis

As explained above, to calculate return we start with all funds that were listed in Wiesenberger as of 1977 and that had $15 million or more in total net assets. Each fund was tracked to the end of 1993, recording all name changes, policy changes, and mergers. We could track every fund in our sample, and none dissolved. We measure performance using excess return (α) as described below.

Alpha was calculated in two ways, based on a three-index model and one-index model. Our principal results utilize a three-index model. Alpha is defined by the following equation:

$$R_{it} = \alpha_i + \beta_{iL} R_{Lt} + \beta_{iS} R_{St} + \beta_{iB} R_{Bt} + \varepsilon_{it} \qquad (1)$$

where R_{it} is the excess return on fund i in month t (the return on the fund minus the 30-day T-bill rate); R_{Lt} is the excess return on the S&P 500 Index in month t; R_{St} is the excess return on small stocks in month t, measured by the return on an equally weighted average of the smallest two deciles of CRSP NYSE stocks; R_{Bt} is the excess return on a bond index in month t, measured by a par-weighted combination of the Lehman Brothers Aggregate Bond Index and the Blume/Keim High-Yield Bond Index;[13] β_{ik} is the sensitivity of return on fund i to return on index $k (k = L, S, B)$; and ε_{it} is the random error in period t.

The three-index model compares the performance of the fund to a passive portfolio of large stocks, small stocks, bonds, and T-bills which in combination has similar risk.[14] To help in comparing our results to other studies, and because it has been used historically to evaluate funds, we also present α's calculated from a single-index model where the single index is the S&P 500 Index. Finally, because other authors have done so, we present results using raw (unadjusted) returns in addition to α's.

Table 11.2 presents our estimates of survivorship bias. Note that in Table 11.2 and all subsequent tables our monthly results have been

Table 11.2
Alternative estimates of survivorship bias (annualized)

	Surviving	Merged	Policy changed	Policy changed and merged	All[a]	Bias
Panel A: Assuming investment to earlier of merger and/or policy change						
Common stock investment policy at beginning of sample period	(67.034%)[a]	(32.966%)[a]				
1-index α	0.6712%	−0.2991%			0.3513%	0.3199%
3-index α	−0.1269%	−2.8779%			−1.0388%	0.9069%
Raw return	14.6832%	8.9977%			12.8089%	1.8743%
S&P 500	14.0373%	9.5373%				
Raw return—S&P 500	0.6459%	−0.5396%			0.2551%	0.3908%
Common stock investment policy throughout sample period	(60.147%)[a]	(23.547%)[a]	(6.887%)[a]	(9.419%)[a]		
1-index α	0.6355%	−0.0180%	1.9178%	1.0412%	0.6081%	0.0274%
3-index α	−0.1352%	−2.9052%	−0.0051%	−1.0942%	−0.8688%	0.7336%
Raw return	14.7504%	9.2448%	9.0589%	8.4516%	12.4687%	2.2817%
S&P 500	14.0373%	9.0764%	6.5405%	7.2516%		
Raw return—S&P 500	0.7131%	0.1684%	2.5184%	1.2000%	0.7550%	−0.0419%

Panel B: Assuming reinvestment at earlier of merger and/or policy change						
Common stock investment policy at beginning of sample period	(67.034%)[a]	(32.966%)[a]				
1-index α	0.6712%	−1.5566%			−0.8985%	0.7716%
3-index α	−0.1269%	−2.4575%			−0.8985%	0.7716%
Raw return	14.6832%	12.4684%			13.9531%	0.7301%
S&P 500	14.0373%	14.0373%				
Raw return—S&P 500	0.6459%	−1.5689%			−0.0842%	0.7301%
Common stock investment policy throughout sample period	(60.147%)[a]	(23.547%)[a]	(6.887%)[a]	(9.419%)[a]		
1-index α	0.6355%	−1.5165%	0.4138%	−1.0441%	−0.0447%	0.6802%
3-index α	−0.1352%	−2.3978%	−0.3549%	−1.8085%	−0.8407%	0.7055%
Raw return	14.7504%	13.0762%	14.5171%	12.7555%	14.1522%	0.5982%
S&P 500	14.0373%	14.0373%	14.0373%	14.0373%		
Raw return—S&P 500	0.7131%	−0.9611%	0.4798%	−1.2818%	0.1149%	0.5982%

a. Adjusted to reflect entire population of available common stock funds at end of 1976.

For surviving funds, raw returns and excess returns (α's) are calculated over the full sample period. In panel A, for funds that merged or changed policy, returns are calculated through the month of merger of policy change. In panel B, a "follow the money" approach is used. After a merger, we assume the investor invests in the "partner" fund that the original fund merged into. After a policy change, we assume the investor invests in the average of the remaining funds in the sample. Excess or raw returns are then calculated as a weighed average of the returns in the pre- and post event periods. The category percentages are adjusted to reflect the entire population of available common stock funds at the end of 1976. The returns in the category "All" are weighted averages by percentage in each category. "Bias" is the difference between the value shown for "Surviving" and the value shown for "All."

annualized. All estimates of bias are the difference in performance (α or return) between funds that survive and the full sample that existed at the beginning of the period (labeled all). What varies in the table is the definition of survival and how the performance on the nonsurviving funds is calculated. Both survival and performance are calculated in two ways, resulting in four estimates of bias for the three-index, one-index, and raw-return models.

Panel A of Table 11.2 shows results when performance on funds that do not survive is calculated up to and including the month when the fund ceased to survive. The upper part of panel A presents the results when survival is defined as "did not merge" over the period. The lower part of panel A defines a surviving fund as a fund that meets the dual criteria: no merger and maintaining a common stock investment policy throughout the sample period. The reason for this division is that some researchers draw their sample from funds that list common stock as an investment policy at the beginning of their sample period and survive throughout, while others insist on a common stock policy throughout the sample period. We wanted to measure bias for both sampling procedures.[15] In calculating return for funds that "disappear in merger" (DIM), we calculate return through the month of the merger. If the fund merged midmonth, this includes any dividends plus capital changes where capital changes are calculated using merger terms and end-of-month NAV for the partner fund.

Table 11.2 shows results for both α and raw return. We will first discuss the results using α, then using raw return. As shown in the top half of panel A, the average α using the three-index model for the survivors is −0.1269%, and the average α for those that merge calculated through the month of the merger is −2.8779% per year. Since 32.97% merge and 67.03% survive, the α for the combined sample is −1.0338%; the estimate of bias is equal to the α in the surviving sample minus the α on the full sample, or 0.9069% per year.[16]

The bottom part of panel A in Table 11.2 calculates bias when the researchers used the dual criteria that the fund had data in each year and was a common stock fund throughout. To determine bias, the funds were divided into four groups. For those funds that neither merged nor had a policy change, α was calculated over the 17-year sample period. For those funds that merged or had a policy change, or did both, α was calculated up to the policy change or merger, whichever came first. The average α for funds that survive and are common stock throughout is −0.135%, for those that have a policy change and do not merge it is −0.0051%, for those that merge it is −2.9052%, and for those that both merge and have a policy change it is −1.094%. The fractions in each category are, respectively, 0.6015, 0.0689, 0.2355, and 0.0942. Multiplying the fraction in each group times the α for each group and summing across the four groups, we see that the α for the combined sample is −0.869%. Our estimate of bias is the difference between the α for the full sample and that for the surviving sample (−0.135%), or 0.734% per year.

The disadvantage of this method of determining survivorship bias is that disappearing funds and surviving funds exist over different periods of time.[17] An alternative procedure that does not have this disadvantage is to make an explicit reinvestment assumption that investors stay invested over the entire period and follow the fund with their money. For funds that merge into another common stock fund, we assume the investor continues to hold the new fund. The α is computed for the original and partner funds separately and then weighted by the time the investor held each. For example, if the fund merged in 5 years we would calculate the α for the first 5 years for the original fund and the last 12 years for the partner fund, and then take 5/17 of the α on the original fund and 12/17 of the α on the partner fund to get an average α. If the fund changes policy and becomes a noncommon stock fund before a merger, after a merger, or without a merger, and if policy change is being used to determine the sample, we assume that at the time the policy change is recorded the investor sells the fund and purchases a new fund with a return equal to the average return on the remaining common stock funds. The overall α, following parallel methodology to that described above, is again a weighted average of the two α's before and after the event. All of the results under these reinvestment assumptions are shown in panel B of Table 11.2. Let's first examine the situation where the researcher ignores policy changes and includes funds that changed policy in the surviving category.

If we apply the same methodology to panel B as we applied to panel A, we see that for the three-index model the difference in α between the survivor sample and the full sample is 0.77% per year. If the researcher forming the sample required that the mutual funds both had data over the full period and were listed as common stock in each year, the difference in α between the researcher's sample and the full sample is 0.71% per year.

All of the results discussed to this point measure α from the three-index model. We believe this is appropriate.[18] However, for comparison with earlier studies we also calculated the effect of survivorship bias for a one-index model. These results are also shown in Table 11.2. The estimates of

α for the one-index model are much higher than for the three-index model. This was a period where small stocks performed relatively well. We know from Elton et al. (1993) that this will cause funds with significant exposure to small stocks to appear to have superior performance when a one-index model is used. The estimates of bias for panel A in Table 11.2 are much lower for the one-index model than they are for the three-index model. Examining the regression results used to estimate α's revealed that β's (sensitivity) for merged funds with the small-stock index were generally higher than those for nonmerged funds. This causes the single-index model to confound the small-fund effect with α and thus to underestimate the bias for the one-index model. We feel the estimates shown in panel A for the one-index model are inaccurate and should be ignored. When we consider reinvestment, the same influences are present, but they are dampened by the averaging with the data from the partner fund.

While we believe the three-index model is the appropriate way to measure excess returns and bias, we also present the results in terms of raw (unadjusted) returns and the difference between return and the naive strategy of holding the S&P 500 Index.[19]

Examining panel A, we see that looking at raw returns would lead to a very high estimate of bias (1.875). The reason is easy to see. The S&P 500 Index performed worse in the months when the merged funds were around than it did in the months when the merged funds were not around. Measuring bias from raw returns confounds the effects of merger performance and market performance. Simply measuring each fund's performance net of the return of the S&P 500 Index eliminates the bulk of this problem.[20] Notice that the estimates from these excess returns are close to the estimates arrived at using the one-index model. The reason is that this procedure is the same as assuming a one-index model holds and the β of all funds with the S&P 500 Index is equal to 1. We have already explained why the results using the one-index model are inferior to the results using the three-index model. Forcing the β to be equal to 1 for all funds compounds the error and leads to inferior estimates of bias. It is important to point this out, for using raw returns or excess returns over some index is a procedure that has been using extensively in the literature.

When we move to panel B, we see that the estimate of bias remains unchanged whether we measure returns in raw form or as excess return relative to the market. This is one of the advantages of the "follow the money" approach; it is much more robust to alternative metrics for performance measurement. However, while the alternative measures of bias are closer together, for the reasons given above we believe the three-index model gives the best results.

Before leaving this section, we should address a potential problem with our methodology. It is possible that funds systematically change their behavior prior to a merger. This could show up either as a change in β's (sensitivities) or a change in residual risk. For example, one could hypothesize that a manager observing that a fund is having difficulties may increase risk dramatically by loading up on high-risk securities, reducing diversification, or betting on a type of stock (e.g., small stocks). If a manager were to do any of these, then the variance of the residuals around the three-index (or one-index) model should be higher right before the merger than in earlier proofs. Because we are using a regression over the full sample period (up to the time of the merger), changes in either the regression coefficients or residual risk should be reflected in an increase in the variance of the residuals. To examine this we calculated for all merged funds the variance of the residuals for the 6 months prior to the merger and for the 30 months that preceded this 6-month period. The average number is .0595 and .0591, respectively. The fact that the variances are virtually the same over both periods gives us confidence that our three-index model adequately describes the risk process prior to the merger.[21]

V Characteristics of Funds that Merge into Partner Funds and Their Partner Funds

In this section we will examine the characteristics of funds that disappear in merger (DIM) and the partner funds into which they merge. We examined size (total net assets), expense ratio, load, investment objective, and performance. All analysis is done for the sample of funds over $15 million in size. While characteristics of mutual funds that merge into another fund have been previously studied, no one heretofore has simultaneously analyzed both the characteristics of funds that merge into other funds and the partner funds into which they merge.

Funds that merge into partner funds are smaller than the average of all funds and smaller than the funds into which they merge. The average size of DIM funds in our sample was about $52 million, while the average size of all funds weighted by the year of merger was about $305 million.[22] Twenty-eight of the 42 funds were under $50 million, with 15 under $25 million.

Table 11.3
Total year-end net asset size and annual expenses by decile (each decile constructed by ranking on asset size)

	1976		1992	
Decile	Assets	Expenses	Assets	Expenses
1	$ 16.85	1.25%	$ 5.43	2.38%
2	$ 21.50	1.12%	$ 15.51	1.51%
3	$ 29.93	1.13%	$ 29.27	1.55%
4	$ 38.01	1.10%	$ 45.35	1.55%
5	$ 49.96	0.94%	$ 76.17	1.34%
6	$ 71.23	0.93%	$ 120.91	1.28%
7	$113.09	0.79%	$ 182.47	1.33%
8	$189.39	0.67%	$ 312.55	1.16%
9	$328.47	0.66%	$ 621.88	1.05%
10	$831.70	0.54%	$2,469.14	0.90%

The 1976 data are from the 207 funds with more than $15 million in total net assets as shown in the 1977 edition of Wiesenberger and described in Table 1. The 1992 sample is all common stock funds listed in Morningstar at the end of 1992; that sample size is 773 funds. Total net assets are in millions of dollars; expenses are expressed as a percentage of net assets.

Both the average for the entire sample and for the DIM funds was strongly affected by a few large funds. To control for this we also computed their average rank, where funds were ranked from small to large. The average rank for the DIM funds was the 25% percentile.

The partner funds also tended to be smaller than average. The average size of the partner funds was $155 million, about one-half the size of all funds. On average, the partner funds ranked in the 43% percentile of all funds (43% were smaller).

Before we examine expenses we must consider the interrelationship between size and expenses per dollar invested. Size and expenses are highly related. To examine this we ranked funds in our sample by size decile and computed the average expense ratio in each decile. To examine if our sample was in any way idiosyncratic, we also did the same analysis for the funds listed in Morningstar that had the same objectives as funds in our sample. Our sample contained a maximum of 207 funds with over $15 million in assets at the end of 1976, and Morningstar included 773 funds for the year-end 1992 that we analyzed. Table 11.3 shows the results for the beginning of our sample period and for the 1992 Morning-

Table 11.4
Average annual expense ratios of merged and partner funds

	Sample	Matched pair	Difference	Std. dev. of difference	*t* value of difference
Merged	1.170%	1.210%	−0.040%	0.065%	0.70
Partner	1.240%	0.970%	0.270%	0.075%	4.45
Average	1.025%				

The column labeled "Matched pair" contains the average expense ratio of the matched pair for each of the corresponding sample funds; a sample fund's matched pair consists of the funds with the next smaller and next larger asset sizes surrounding the asset size of the sample fund.

The columns labeled "Difference," "Std. dev. of difference," and "*t* value of difference" contain values computed using pairwise differences of the corresponding sample funds' expense ratios and the average expense ratios of the sample funds' matched pairs.

The row labeled "Average" contains the simple average of the expense ratios for all funds in the sample.

star data. Examining Table 11.3 shows almost a monotonic decrease in expense ratios as size increased. This relationship is significant at the 1% level using a rank correlation test.

Thus, in examining difference in expenses, we need to hold the effect of size constant. To hold size constant we matched each DIM fund as well as each partner fund with the two funds closest in size: one larger and one smaller. The results are shown in Table 11.4. DIM funds have higher expenses than the average fund (1.17% compared to 1.03%). However, the expenses for DIM funds are lower than the matched pairs of similar size, although not significantly so. Thus the expenses of DIM funds are no different than funds of the same size that don't merge. A different pattern emerges for partner funds. Partner funds have significantly *higher* expenses than the matched funds of the same size, 1.24% compared to 0.97%. Furthermore, the partner funds are *higher* in expense than the DIM funds. We also examined what happened to the expenses of partner funds after the merger. We could find no discernible pattern. The higher expenses of partner funds were not due to expenses incurred with the merger, nor did the merger lead to lower expenses in subsequent years.[23]

While we have discussed expense ratios in general, we have not as yet examined one element of expense, the existence of loads. It is possible that funds merge into partners which, while having a higher annual expense, do not have a load. Table 11.5 shows that this is not the case. There is no tendency for funds that merge to select partner funds without

Table 11.5
Change in load policy between merged funds and partner funds

	Actual occurrence	Expected occurrence
No change	29	20.3
Load to no load	4	9.1
No load to load	4	7.6

Expected occurrence is computed by assuming that the probability of a fund ending up in any load category is equal to the fraction of funds in that category in the year of the merger. Actual occurrences do not total 42 (the number of merged funds in our sample) due to unavailability of load policy data for some partner funds.

Table 11.6
Change in investment objective between merged funds and partner funds

	Actual occurrence	Expected occurrence
No change	20	13.5
Riskier	12	11.1
Less risky	8	19.2

Investment objectives were ranked from most risky to least risky as follows: maximum capital gains, growth, growth and income, and income.

Expected occurrence was computed by assuming that the probability of any fund merging into a partner fund with a particular objective was equal to the percentage of funds that followed that particular objective in the merger year.

Actual occurrences do not total 42 (the number of merged funds in our sample) due to unavailability of investment objective data for some partner funds.

loads. There is some tendency for funds to merge into partners with the same load policy as the merged fund.

The next issue to be examined is the investment objectives of the DIM fund and the partner fund. Do funds tend to merge into funds with less risky objective to help out investors who have recently had a bad experience (bad return), or do funds pay no attention to risk in picking partners? Table 11.6 presents some evidence on this. The column labeled "actual occurrence" shows the number of funds that held investment objective constant, became riskier, or became less risky. The entries under "expected occurrence" show the number that would have been in each category if the decision as to merger partner were made at random. This number was calculated by assuming that the chance of picking a partner fund was equal to the percentage of funds that followed each investment objective. The table shows that there is no tendency for funds to pick merger partners that are less risky. One-half of the sample pick partners that have the same risk. Of the remaining group, more than half merge into funds that are more risky. When comparing these results to the expected occurrence, we see that the number of funds that became riskier is about what we would expect, while many fewer funds become less risky that expected, and a larger than expected number merge into funds with the same policy. There is no evidence that funds become less risky; in fact, on average they tend to become more risky after they merge.

The last aspect of DIM funds and partner funds we examine is the excess return (α) from the three-index model. We examined the α for the DIM fund for a 3-year period before the merger and the α for the partner fund both 3 years before and 3 years after the merger. The DIM funds had an average annualized α of -3.6% before merger, while for this same period of time the partner funds had an average annualized α of $+1.7\%$.[24] It appears that funds that are doing poorly are merged into partner funds that have had very good performance relative to the population of funds from which partners can be selected. The next obvious question to ask is whether this excellent performance continues after the merger. The answer is that in the 3 years following the merger the α on the partner fund is actually slightly *worse* than the α for the average fund in our sample.[25]

VI Survivorship Bias and Length of Sample Period

Researchers who have examined mutual fund performance have used sample periods ranging from 10 to 20 years. Clearly, the longer the sample period the greater the survivorship bias. In order to interpret the results contained in the literature, we need to estimate the survivorship bias for different holding periods. Merger activity is clearly a function of economic conditions. Thus to look at survivorship over the first 10 years of our sample is to make the estimate both a function of the shorter time interval and a function of the particular economic conditions that exist over that period. An alternative is to compute an average merger rate and use that average rate as the merger rate in each year. The argument against using the average rate is that each year in our sample we know that funds have existed one more year, and this could affect merger probability. Also, it is possible that mergers are related to market movements and tend to cluster in one year. To test this, we regressed merger rates as a function of time. We found no relationship (a negative adjusted R^2). Figure 11.1 shows the plot of the actual proportion that survived and a plot under the assumption of a constant survival rate when survival is defined as not merging.[26] Figure 11.2 shows the same data when survival

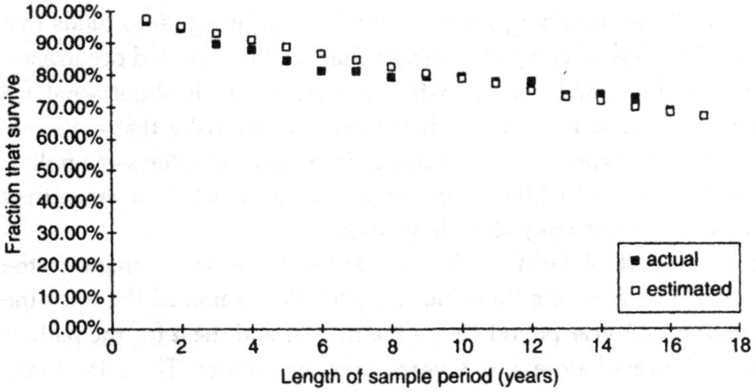

Figure 11.1
Survival as a function of time: common stock at beginning

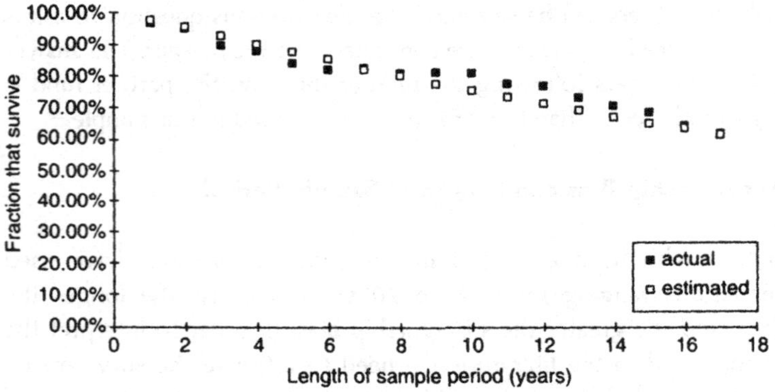

Figure 11.2
Survival as a function of time: common stock throughout

is defined as not merging and with no change in investment policy. The percentage of funds that merge in each year is 2.3%, while when we consider either a merge or a policy change, the percentage becomes 2.9%. As can be seen from the diagrams, the assumption of a constant survival rate closely matches the data for the actual survival rate. These same figures can be used to analyze another issue. Potentially, survivorship can be a function of market conditions. The figures suggest survivorship is not a function of market conditions. A regression of survival rates on the S&P 500 Index also showed no relationship.

Table 11.7
Survivorship bias (α) and length of sample period (three-index model)

Number of years in study	Assuming no reinvestment: Common stock at beginning	Assuming no reinvestment: Common stock throughout	Assuming reinvestment: Common stock at beginning	Assuming reinvestment: Common stock throughout
10	0.489%	0.386%	0.396%	0.348%
11	0.545%	0.431%	0.443%	0.392%
12	0.602%	0.478%	0.493%	0.439%
13	0.660%	0.526%	0.544%	0.487%
14	0.719%	0.576%	0.598%	0.538%
15	0.780%	0.627%	0.654%	0.591%
16	0.843%	0.679%	0.712%	0.647%
17	0.907%	0.734%	0.772%	0.705%
18	0.972%	0.789%	0.834%	0.766%
19	1.039%	0.847%	0.899%	0.830%
20	1.108%	0.906%	0.966%	0.896%

Bias is defined as average α for surviving funds minus average α for all funds when a three-index model is employed.

Table 11.7 for the three-index model and Table 11.8 for the one-index model show the effect of survivorship bias over horizons from 10 to 20 years using each of the measurement techniques discussed earlier.

In Table 11.7 we calculate all results using a three-index model. Bias estimates are presented for 10 to 20 years because this encompasses the time frame of all prior studies. In the columns headed "Common Stock at Beginning" we are presenting bias estimates that are relevant for all studies that insisted that a fund exist for the entire period but only looked at investment policy at the beginning of the period. The failure rate used here is the 2.3% per year that we previously estimated from our database. In the two columns headed "Common Stock Throughout" we present estimates of bias to use in evaluating results from studies that insisted on a fund existing for the entire period and that eliminated funds that changed policy at any point in the study.

Table 11.7 shows us that the amount of bias present in other studies does not vary a great deal whether we measure α up to the month of a merger or policy change or measure α by making specific reinvestment assumptions. In addition, the estimate does not vary much whether researchers examine samples where funds that changed investment policy were included or excluded. For example, consider bias estimates for a 20-year sample. The largest estimate of bias is 1.108% and the smallest is 0.896%. All of the numbers are clearly of economic significance. The largest differences occur between the cases where the researcher rejects funds with investment policy changes and the cases where they are not rejected. The table shows that the bias is smaller when the investor rejects funds (throws out funds) that had a change in policy during a period. Why does this occur? The answer is that a large number of the funds that had policy changes subsequently merged. In fact, 58% of the funds that had policy changes subsequently merged. These funds had very poor performance between the time of the policy change and the merger (that is why they subsequently merged). By assuming the investor stops investing in these funds at the time of the policy change rather than at the time of the merger, we increase the performance of the unbiased sample (labeled "All" in Table 11.2). Therefore the "All" entries are much larger for the case where funds that have policy changes are excluded, and this results in a smaller bias.

Note that while the differences at a point in time across ways of measuring bias are not large, the esitmate of bias varies a great deal with the length of the study regardless of the methodology adopted. For example, when ignoring policy change while assuming reinvestment, the estimate of bias is 0.396% per year in a 10-year study and 0.966% per year in a 20-year study.

The results for the one-index model are shown in Table 11.8. When we assume reinvestment, the bias produced by the one-index model is very similar to the results using the three-index model. A large difference does arise in the case where we assume no reinvestment. This case shows much lower values for bias. Again, the data that leads to this can be clearly seen from Table 11.2, where the estimates of bias without reinvestment for the one-index model are shown to be much smaller than for the three-index model. The reasons for this were discussed earlier. They account for the results in Table 11.8 and explain why we do not consider these cases in Table 11.8 to be appropriate.

VII Survivorship and Fund Characteristics

There is one more aspect of survivorship that deserves discussion. Failure to correct for bias can lead to incorrect inferences about the impact of fund characteristics. Two examples of this are presented in Tables 11.9 and 11.10.

Table 11.8
Survivorship bias (α) and length of sample period (one-index model)

Number years in study	Assuming no reinvestment		Assuming reinvestment	
	Common stock at beginning	Common stock throughout	Common stock at beginning	Common stock throughout
10	0.173%	0.014%	0.378%	0.336%
11	0.192%	0.016%	0.423%	0.378%
12	0.212%	0.018%	0.470%	0.423%
13	0.233%	0.020%	0.519%	0.470%
14	0.254%	0.022%	0.570%	0.519%
15	0.275%	0.023%	0.624%	0.570%
16	0.297%	0.025%	0.679%	0.624%
17	0.320%	0.027%	0.737%	0.681%
18	0.343%	0.029%	0.796%	0.739%
19	0.367%	0.032%	0.858%	0.801%
20	0.391%	0.034%	0.923%	0.865%

Bias is defined as average α for surviving funds minus average α for all funds when a one-index model is employed.

Table 11.9
Size and performance

Size	α (from three-index model)	
	Biased	Unbiased
Smallest decile	−0.342%	−0.718%
Largest decile	−0.394%	−0.308%

The values in this table are the average decile α's, where the α's are calculated from our three-index model over our sample period; funds are assigned to deciles by ranking on size (total net assets) at the start of our sample period (year-end 1976).

Table 11.10
Investment objective and performance

	α (from three-index model)	
	Biased	Unbiased
Max. cap. gain	0.720%	−0.341%
Growth	0.680%	−0.655%
Growth & Income	−0.649%	−1.049%

The values in this table are the average α's within investment objective categories, where the α's are calculated from our three-index model over our sample period; funds are classified according to their investment objectives at the start of our sample period (year-end 1976).

When we examine the performance of the largest 10% of our sample and the smallest 10% of our sample ranked by assets under management, we find very different inferences about the impact of size (at the beginning of the sample) on performance. If we look at the biased sample (see Table 11.9), we find virtually no difference in performance between large funds and small funds. (Actually, small funds appear to perform just slightly better.) These results are consistent with previous findings of the impact of size on fund performance [e.g., Sharpe (1966)]. However, when α's on the largest and smallest funds are examined for the unbiased sample, we find the smaller funds perform much worse, with a negative α more than twice the negative α of the large funds. The results are clearly consistent with the fact that a larger percentage of small funds relative to large funds fail to survive, and funds that fail to survive have poorer performance than funds that do survive.

As a second example of the effect of survivorship bias on the relationship of fund characteristics and α consider Table 11.10. Table 11.10 is a standard table for comparing α across fund investment objective. For the biased sample, the maximum capital gain and growth funds appear to have positive α's. This is consistent with the results reported by Grinblatt and Titman (1989) and Connor and Korajczyk (1991). However, when looking at the results accounting for survivorship bias, a different picture emerges. All fund categories have negative α's. Further, the category "growth," which some prior researchers found had the best performance, has the biggest adjustment in α and no longer has the best performance.

These simple cases illustrate the fact that erroneous conclusions can be reached about the impact of a variable on performance when a sample of mutual funds that contains survivorship bias is examined.

VIII Conclusions

Almost all prior mutual fund studies suffer from survivorship bias. Since funds that merge have worse performance than those that don't, those studies contain estimates of performance that overstate true performance. This study provides estimates of survivorship bias that can be used as benchmarks to determine the amount of bias in studies that do not take survivorship into account. This study also examines the characteristics of funds that disappear through merger and the funds into which they merge. Finally, we have presented two examples of the fact that a failure to eliminate survivorship bias can lead a researcher to spurious conclusions about the effect of fund characteristics on return.

Notes

We thank Robert Korajczyk (the editor), an anonymous referee, and participants at the 1995 European Finance Association meetings (Milan) for helpful comments. We are also grateful to Stephen Brown, Bill Crawford at Micropal (ICDI), Judy Doliner at Ivessco, Betsy Tompkins at Salomon Brothers, Chuck Webster at Lehman Brothers, and Interactive Data Corporation (IDC) for supplying data.

1. This may have occurred for any one of several reasons: (1) The methodology of examining funds was new and the authors of these studies were interested at least as much in illustrating the methodology as in studying mutual funds; (2) The author desired to demonstrate new techniques over a time span with no missing observations, therefore making the application of the techniques straightforward; (3) Computerized databases were in their infancy and the work required to get any data was immense. To correct the data for missing funds would have been a Herculean task; even today it is extremely difficult. Refinement in correcting data should have proceeded step by step with refinement in the methodology of evaluating mutual fund performance. Yet only recently have researchers become concerned with correcting data for survivorship bias.

2. We call this approach "follow the money." In using it, we are careful to correct for differences in risk that might occur before and after the merger.

3. The Lehmann and Modest (1987) sample, also used by Connor and Korajczyk (1991), requires survival over most of, but not all of, the full period.

4. Ippolito (1989) selects all funds that were classified by Wiesenberger as common stock funds at the end of his sample period. He traces these back to the beginning, including funds that merged into each of the funds he selected. However, at the beginning of his sample period the investment policies of many of the funds are not common stock. Thus, no investor interested only in stock funds would have selected the sample.

5. Their samples were affected by an inability to track funds because of name changes. Name changes are highly correlated with mergers and policy changes. Thus it is unclear if the sample is free of survivorship bias.

6. In 1977, Wiesenberger was considered the standard directory for information on mutual funds.

7. Prior to 1985, funds had to have a minimum of 1,000 shareholders to be listed by the NASDAQ. Furthermore, the SEC supplies an annual list to the NASD of mutual funds that must be recertified (after their initial listing) as having a minimum of either 750 shareholders or $15 million in total net assets in order to be included in the NASDAQ listing supplied to newspapers. Although the NASDAQ now provides a supplemental listing to so-called level-one quote vendors (such as IDC) that includes funds with under $15 million in net assets, for return data in earlier years the NASDAQ newspaper listing is the basic source of return data for all newspapers and firms, and hence investors, that collect data on mutual funds.

8. In the process we recorded all name changes, mergers, investment policy changes (e.g., common stock to bond), and restrictions (including changes in variable annuity status). The source of these data was Wiesenberger's *Investment Companies*, supplemented by information from the funds themselves.

9. In 1982, the IRS issued a series of so-called wrap-around annuity rulings, designed to prevent tax avoidance. The results is that, since 1982, a fund cannot be both an open-end mutual funds available through direct purchase and a variable annuity fund medium.

10. A substantial number of others "disappear" in that they are not listed in the next issue of Wiesenberger. However, they reappear in subsequent issues of Wiesenberger or have a name change that can be traced through other data recorded in Wiesenberger.

11. In general, survival seems to be a function of risk. Commodity funds have much greater failure rates than common stock funds, and bond funds have lower failure rates than either. Studies that included balanced funds may well have survival related to objective.

12. One must be very careful when calculating returns involving dividends and reinvestment net asset values (NAVs) shown in IDC. While IDC is an excellent source of data, we occasionally found discrepancies in dividend reinvestment dates, dividends, and other dividend-related data. These tended to happen around the time of a merger or share change. We checked all data around the time of these events with the funds and examined NAVs surrounding dividend reinvestment dates to ensure accuracy.

13. See Elton, Gruber, and Blake (1994) for details on the construction of the bond index.

14. In Blake, Elton, and Gruber (1993) we showed that estimated β's closely matched the weights of the asset groups in the portfolio. This type of evaluation was first discussed in Sharpe (1988). For most funds in our sample the bond β is close to 0. However, some funds with common stock as an investment policy still hold some bonds and hence have a positive β with respect to the bond index.

15. More funds disappear from the sample because they merge than because of policy changes. The only other reason we found for funds disappearing is because they are variable annuities (like CREF). Variable annuities were no longer available for direct purchase after 1982; thus they would disappear from all data sets that encompass this period. This affects three funds in our sample.

16. Measuring the statistical significance of the difference in mean α's between the groups is a more complex issue when the data for all funds are not over the same time period (as in panel A of Table 2) or when α's over the entire sample period are calculated as weighted averages of α's from two or more funds over different time periods (as for the nonsurviving funds in panel B). To test for significance, for each group we calculated the variance-covariance matrix of the residuals, utilizing only the data over the common time frame for each pairwise residual covariance for nonsurviving funds in panel A and utilizing the complete set of "spliced" residuals for nonsurviving funds in panel B, and assumed stationarity of the $(X'X)^{-1}$ matrix of the regressors to obtain an estimate of standard error of mean α. The advantage of this technique is that it utilizes actual correlation patterns, both cross-sectionally and over time, to adjust for both heteroskedasticity and cross correlation. Using the results from this procedure, the difference in mean α between surviving funds and the merged funds is statistically significant for the three-index model, where the t values are 2.69, 2.57, 2.14, and 1.90, proceeding from top to bottom in Table 11.2. (For the one-index model, no difference are significant at or below the 10% level.)

17. While differences in length of life is a problem in itself, it can bias the results even more if there is a time pattern to α. The bias occurs because funds that don't exist for the entire sample period have more of their observations in early years. We examined the return of surviving funds over different periods and found a slight tendency for higher α's in early years. Thus, if there is a bias because of differential performance across time it will result in an overstatement rather than understatement of the performance of funds that don't exist for the entire period.

18. To examine the robustness of our estimate of bias, we also used a four-index model employing a value versus growth index. Researchers have shown that value-growth and market-to-book are potentially interesting additional indexes. We used a value versus

growth index based on growth and value indexes produced by Prudential Bache. This index was extremely highly correlated with an index measuring the difference between high and low market-to-book ratios [similar to the index employed by Fama and French (1992)], and thus it may in part capture market-to-book influences. The estimates of bias using the four-index model were for panel A in Table 11.2: 1.4789% for merger only and 1.3181% for merger and policy change; and for panel B were 0.8388% and 0.7326%, respectively. These estimates are very close to the estimates using three indexes.

19. In panel A, since our nonsurviving funds exist for different numbers of months, each fund was paired with an investment in the S&P 500 Index over the months it existed. The overall return for the S&P 500 Index is a weighted average of these paired returns. The effect of this is to weight the monthly S&P 500 return by the number of funds in our sample in any month. Since panel B represents a "follow the money" approach and the investor is always fully invested, the appropriate value for the S&P 500 is its average return over the full sample period.

20. We use the S&P 500 Index for comparison with, and adjustment of, raw returns. Comparison with an index fund is also interesting and can be done easily. Index funds available to individuals exist with a correlation of .99 with the S&P 500 Index and an annualized α of -0.30%, which is just about equal to the expense ratio for these funds. The comparison with an index fund simply lowers the appropriate index returns by about 30 basis points and leaves the estimate of bias unchanged.

21. When using the one-index model, the average variance for the 6 months prior to the merger is .0671, and the average variance for the 30 months preceding that 6-month period is .0722. These numbers are also fairly close and indicate, if anything, a reduction in risk prior to the merger.

22. The average for all funds in our sample was computed by taking the average asset size in each year and multiplying by the fraction of funds that merged in that year. This averaging was done to correct for an increase in size of the average fund over time.

23. For a few funds the merger year seemed to be a local maximum. This pattern was not strong enough to show up for the average of all DIM funds.

24. The α for merged funds is slightly different from that reported in Table 11.2. The reason is that funds that merged did slightly worse in a 3-year span prior to the merger than they did in earlier periods.

25. We got similar results when performance was computed over a 1-year period (before and after) the merger.

26. Brown and Goetzmann (1994) explore the relationship between funds disappearing from Wiesenberger and fund characteristics. They find that fund disappearance from Wiesenberger is a function of size, expenses, age, and relative performance. We do not find the same relationship with age. Malkiel (1994) has a sample where new funds enter as they are formed. He was concerned that the different life of his funds might affect his results. The survivorship pattern in our data indicates that this is not likely to be a problem in his sample.

References

Blake, C. R., E. J. Elton, and M. J. Gruber, 1993, "The Performance of Bond Mutual Funds," *Journal of Business*, 66, 371–403.

Brown, S., and W. Goetzmann, 1994, "Attrition and Mutual Fund Performance," working paper, New York University; forthcoming in *Journal of Finance*.

Carhart, M. M., 1994, "On Persistence in Mutual Fund Performance," working paper, University of Chicago.

Connor, G., and R. Korajczyk, 1991, "The Attributes, Behavior and Performance of U.S. Mutual Funds," *Review of Quantitative Finance and Accounting*, 1, 5–26.

Elton, E. J., and M. J. Gruber, 1995, *Modern Portfolio Theory and Investment Analysis* (5th ed.), John Wiley, New York.

Elton, E. J., M. J. Gruber, and C. R. Blake, 1994, "Fundamental Economic Variables, Expected Returns, and Bond Fund Performance," working paper, New York University, forthcoming in *Journal of Finance*.

Elton, E. J., M. J. Gruber, S. Das, and M. Hlavka, 1993, "Efficiency with Costly Information: A Reinterpretation of Evidence for Managed Portfolios," *Review of Financial Studies*, 5, 1–22.

Fama, E. F., and K. R. French, 1992, "The Cross-Section of Expected Stock Returns," *Journal of Finance*, 47, 427–465.

Ferson, W., and R. Schadt, 1993, "Measuring Fund Strategy and Performance in Changing Economic Conditions," working paper, University of Washington School of Business Administration.

Grinblatt, M., and S. Titman, 1988, "The Evaluation of Mutual Fund Performance: An Analysis of Monthly Returns," working paper, John E. Anderson Graduate School of Management, UCLA.

Grinblatt, M., and S. Titman, 1989, "Mutual Fund Performance: An Analysis of Quarterly Portfolio Holdings," *Journal of Business*, 62, 393–416.

Grinblatt, M., and S. Titman, 1992, "Performance Persistence in Mutual Funds," *Journal of Finance*, 47, 1977–1984.

Henriksson, R. D., 1984, "Market Timing and Mutual Fund Performance," *Journal of Business*, 57, 73–96.

Henriksson, R. D., and R. C. Merton, 1981, "On Market Timing and Investment Performance II: Statistical Procedures for Evaluating Forecast Skills," *Journal of Business*, 54, 513–553.

Ippolito, R. A., 1989, "Efficiency with Costly Information: A Study of Mutual Fund Performance," *Quarterly Journal of Economics*, 104, 1–23.

Jensen, M. C., 1968, "The Performance of Mutual Funds in the Period 1945–1964," *Journal of Finance*, 23, 389–416.

Lehmann, B. N., and D. Modest, 1987, "Mutual Fund Performance Evaluation: A Comparison of Benchmarks and Benchmark Comparisons," *Journal of Finance*, 42, 233–265.

Malkiel, B., 1994, "Returns from Investing in Equity Funds," working paper, Princeton University; forthcoming in *Journal of Finance*.

Sharpe, W. F., 1966, "Mutual Fund Performance," *Journal of Business*, 39, 119–138.

Sharpe, W. F., 1988, "Determining a Fund's Effective Asset Mix," *Investment Management Review*, June, 5–15.

Treynor, J., 1965, "How to Rate Management of Investment Funds," *Harvard Business Review*, 44, 63–75.

Wiesenberger Financial Service, 1977–1992, *Investment Companies*, Warren, Gorham & Lamont, Inc., Boston.

12 The Persistence of Risk-Adjusted Mutual Fund Performance

Edwin J. Elton, Martin J. Gruber, and Christopher R. Blake

There is overwhelming evidence that, post expenses, mutual fund managers on average underperform a combination of passive portfolios of similar risk.[1] The recent increase in the number and types of index funds that are available to individual investors makes this a matter of practical as well as theoretical significance. Numerous index funds, which track the Standard and Poor's (S&P) 500 Index or various small-stock, bond, value, growth, or international indexes, are now widely available to individual investors. These same choices have been available to institutional investors for some time. Given that there are sufficient index funds to span most investors' risk choices, that the index funds are available at low cost, and that the low cost of index funds means that a combination of index funds is likely to outperform an active fund of similar risk, the question is, why select an actively managed fund?

An investor could rationally select an actively managed fund if he or she had the ability to select a fund that outperforms the average fund by a sufficient amount to beat a passive portfolio. The principal study to find results that might support this view is that of Hendricks, Patel, and Zeckhauser (1993), who find a "hot hands" effect in short-term predicted returns. Brown, Goetzmann, Ibbotson, and Ross (1992) have shown that survivorship bias can produce an appearance that performance is predictable even when there is no predictability and discuss the results of the Hendricks, Patel, and Zeckhauser study in this context.

This article examines mutual fund predictability for common stock funds, using a sample free of survivorship bias, and measures performance using risk-adjusted returns. We reconfirm the hot hands result that high return can predict high return in the short run. Like Hendricks, Patel, and Zeckhauser, we find that this is short-run phenomenon. However, using *risk-adjusted* returns to rank funds, we find that past performance is predictive of future risk-adjusted performance in both the short run *and* longer run. Furthermore, when we utilize modern portfolio theory (MPT) techniques to allocate capital among funds, we can construct a portfolio of funds based on prior data that significantly outperforms a rule based on past rank alone and that produces a positive risk-adjusted excess return. In addition, we demonstrate the improvement in performance using MPT by selecting a combination of actively managed portfolios that has the same risk as a portfolio of index funds but has higher mean return. While consistent with past studies, our study finds that expenses account for only part of the differences in performance across funds. We find that there is still predictability even after the major impacts of expenses have been removed. Throughout our study we are able to construct portfolios of funds that have small but statistically significant positive risk-adjusted returns during a period where mutual funds in general have negative risk-adjusted returns.

The article is divided into six sections. In the first section we review the literature. In the second section we discuss our sample selection. This is followed by a section discussing how performance is evaluated and a section discussing our results. In the fifth section, we examine expenses and performance. The last section contains the conclusion.

I Review of Literature

Many of the mutual fund studies have briefly looked at predictability of performance as part of a larger study of mutual fund performance. These include Lehmann and Modest (1987), Grinblatt and Titman (1989), Blake, Elton, and Gruber (1993), and Elton, Gruber, Das, and Hlavka (1993). Recently, however, there have been several articles that have directly examined persistence in mutual fund performance. These include Grinblatt and Titman (1992), Hendricks, Patel, and Zeckhauser (1993), Carhart (1994), Brown and Goetzmann (1995), Malkiel (1995), and Sharpe (1995).

Several issues are present in these studies. First, as Brown et al. (1992) show, survivorship bias causes an appearance of persistence even when none exists, and there is substantial potential for survivorship bias in common stock mutual funds (see Elton, Gruber, and Blake, in press). As the authors of the studies recognized, this affects the results reported in Lehmann and Modest (1987) and Grinblatt and Titman (1989) and the results for the larger of the two samples in Blake, Elton, and Gruber (1993). Second, results are not always risk-adjusted (see Hendricks, Patel and Zeckhauser 1993; and Malkiel 1995), or when they are risk-adjusted, the technique used is often inappropriate. For example, one technique that is used by several authors to adjust for risk is to regress returns on a portfolio composed of the top-performing funds, or the difference in return between portfolios of the top- and bottom-performing funds, on a set of indexes and to use the intercept from this regression as a measure of superior performance. The problem with this procedure is that the characteristics of the top-performing funds change significantly over time. In some periods, small-stock funds do best; in other periods, growth funds do best. This implies that the sensitivity of the portfolio of top-performing funds with a single- or multiple-index model is temporally unstable, and therefore a time-series estimate of the intercept on the portfolio is meaningless.

While the methodologies of Carhart (1994) and Sharpe (1995) differ significantly from ours, those studies are closest in spirit to our analysis. Sharpe employs a sample consisting of the 100 largest mutual funds. That sample includes bond funds and international funds, as well as stock funds. Sharpe uses quadratic programming to determine the sensitivities (betas) of a fund to 15 indexes. (This technique has become known as "return style analysis.") He then ranks on risk-adjusted excess return (alpha) and examines whether past alphas are related to future alphas. Carhart employs a sample of stock mutual funds. He uses a four-index model in a manner similar to ours to select high-performing funds. The four indexes he uses are different in definition and, in some cases, in spirit from the four indexes we employ. His methodology for evaluating performance is also different from ours. While both Sharpe and Carhart reach conclusions broadly similar to ours regarding the fact that past performance contains information about future performance, the samples and methodologies used differ among the three studies. Of major importance is that all three articles measure (evaluate) performance in very different ways.

In addition, our article differs from past articles on performance by including three important issues not generally discussed in prior studies. First, authors have not directly addressed the fundamental question of whether a portfolio of actively managed funds can be constructed that consistently beats index funds. Second, how much of the difference in stock fund performance is simply due to expenses? Blake, Elton, and Gruber (1993) find that, for bond mutual funds, a regression of risk-adjusted performance (alpha) on expenses has a slope of about minus one and an insignificant intercept, implying each percentage-point increase in expenses lowers performance by about 1 percentage point and that underperformance is primarily due to expenses. Given the great divergence in stock fund expenses, do those expense differences explain performance differences? Third, can any of the tools of modern portfolio theory be used to select a portfolio of mutual funds that will outperform index funds?

II Sample

To examine predictability, it is important to construct a sample that is free of survivorship bias. The necessity for this has been pointed out by Brown et al. (1992) and Elton, Gruber, and Blake (in press). Failing to account for survivorship bias can introduce the appearance of predictability when none exists. We designed a sample that is free of survivorship bias.

Our initial sample consisted of all funds that were categorized as "common stock" funds in the 1977 edition of Wiesenberger's *Investment Companies* and that had $15 million or more in total net assets under management at the end of 1976. We excluded restricted funds from this sample. There were two types of restricted funds. The first type, called "variable annuities" (like the College Retirement Equities Fund), were listed in Wiesenberger but were primarily available through insurance plans. We eliminated these because their purchase was usually tied to an insurance product. The second type were restricted as to purchaser (e.g., a fund that could only be held by Lutherans). These were excluded because a general investor could not purchase them. After excluding funds with less than $15 million in assets and the restricted funds, 188 funds remain in our sample. All 188 are followed from 1977 to the end of 1993, through name changes and mergers. Thus, our sample is free of survivorship bias.

Having determined our sample, we then collected returns for the funds. We calculate return for each fund on a monthly basis. In calculating return, dividends are assumed to be used to purchase additional shares in the fund at the reinvestment net asset value that is available to shareholders of the fund. This is the assumption made by Morningstar and Investment Company Data, Inc. (ICDI), in constructing their databases.

For funds that existed over the entire period, returns were supplied by ICDI. For funds that ceased to exist, returns were calculated from data supplied by Interactive Data Corporation, supplemented by information from the funds themselves. Merge terms (e.g., merge ratios) were obtained from the funds themselves. (For a more complete discussion of our sample, see Elton, Gruber, and Blake, in press.)

III Measurement of Performance

In order to measure and compare performance, it is necessary to adjust for the risk of the fund. This is illustrated in Elton et al. (1993), where they showed that failure to include an index of firm size as a risk index leads to a substantial overestimate of the performance of funds that hold small stocks and an incorrect inference concerning average performance. They used a three-index model, including the S&P Index, a size index, and a bond index, to capture the relevant characteristics of performance. In this article, we continue to employ these influences, but we introduce one more index to account for the performance of growth versus value stocks. This new index has been added because of the establishment of a number of mutual funds that state either growth or value as an objective and because the growth and value distinction is highly correlated with book-to-market ratios, which have been shown by Fama and French (1993, 1994) to be empirically important in explaining common stock returns. A failure to account for this influence might result in our confounding the temporary performance of a type of fund (e.g., a "value" fund) with management skill. We have made one additional change to the performance model employed in Elton et al. (1993). In that article, the size index was orthogonalized with the S&P 500 Index. In this article, we measure size as the differential return between a portfolio of small stocks and large stocks, and we measure value or growth as the differential return between a portfolio of growth stocks and a portfolio of value stocks. Using differential returns has two benefits. First, this method produces indexes that are almost completely uncorrelated with each other. Second, the impact of these indexes on risk-adjusted performance is easy to understand, since they are zero-investment portfolios.

In this article, a fund's risk-adjusted performance is based on the intercept (a_i) from a four-index model. The model is

$$R_{it} = a_i + \beta_{iSP} R_{SPt} + \beta_{iSL} R_{SLt} + \beta_{iGV} R_{GVt} + \beta_{iB} R_{Bt} + \varepsilon_{it}, \tag{1}$$

where

R_{it} = the excess return on fund i in month t (the return on the fund minus the 30-day Treasury-bill rate);

R_{SPt} = the excess return on the S&P 500 Index in month t;

R_{SLt} = the difference in return between a small-cap and large-cap stock portfolio,[2] based on Prudential Bache indexes in month t;

R_{GVt} = the difference in return between a growth and value stock portfolio based on Prudential Bache indexes in month t;

R_{Bt} = the excess return on a bond index in month t, measured by a par-weighted combination of the Lehman Brothers Aggregate Bond Index and the Blume/Keim High-Yield Bond Index;[3]

β_{ik} = the sensitivity of excess return on fund i to excess return on index $k (k = SP, SL, GV, B)$; and

ε_{it} = the random error in month t.

We distinguish between two time periods: the period where we rank and select funds (the "selection period"), and the period following the selection period, where we evaluate our selections of funds (the "performance period"). We use equation (1) to calculate both 1-year and 3-year risk-adjusted performance measures, which we will refer to as "alphas." The way alphas are calculated depends on which of the above 2 periods is being considered.

In order to calculate alpha in the selection period, we first calculate betas using 3 years of data. For example, if we were selecting funds on January 1, 1980, we would use the 3 years beginning January 1, 1977, through December 31, 1979, as our selection period to calculate betas. If we were ranking on 1-year alphas as of January 1980, we would estimate equation (1) over the prior 3 years and add the average monthly residual during 1979 to the estimated value of a_i to get a 1-year alpha. If we were ranking on 3-year alphas as of January 1980, we would simply use the value of a_i, estimated over the prior 3 years, for a 3-year alpha.

The alphas in the performance period were computed over each fund's full history if the fund existed over the full time frame or through the month of merger or policy change if the fund merged or changed investment policy. The alpha in the performance period is the value of a_i plus the average of the monthly residuals over the performance period. For example, if the performance period is 1 year, the alpha in the performance period is the overall a_i plus the average monthly residual during 1 year. If a fund that merges or changes policy is selected, the alpha in the performance period is a weighted average of the alpha and residuals on the selected fund through the month of merger or policy change and the average alpha plus average residuals on the surviving funds for the remaining months in the evaluation period. This is the return that would be earned by an investor who buys a fund at random from the population of funds that have existed since 1977 if the fund they own merges or changes policy.[4]

IV Results

The first set of results involves ranking funds into 10 deciles each year according to a measure of past performance and then observing how well the deciles perform in subsequent periods. Does past performance (ranking) contain information about performance in future periods? While we start by examining whether ranking tends to be preserved over time, we quickly turn to questions about whether information in the extremes of the ranking is both economically and statistically significant.

A Ranking Results

The funds ranked at each point in time are the funds available for purchase at that point in time. If a fund merges or changes investment policy (is no longer classified as a "common stock" fund) prior to or at that point in time, it is not a candidate for selection.

Each column of table 12.1 and table 12.2 shows the average risk-adjusted excess return (performance alpha) realized in subsequent periods when mutual funds are ranked and placed in deciles using a particular criterion. The column headings show the criteria used to rank funds. "Total Return" is ranking on annual total return calculated for 1-year selection periods; "3-Year Alpha" is ranking on 3-year selection alpha; "1-Year Alpha" is ranking on 1-year selection alpha; "*t* Alpha" is ranking on 3-year selection alpha divided by the standard error of 3-year selection alpha (the *t*-value of the intercept in eq. [1] using a 3-year selection period). Before examining performance predictability, it is worth noting that the average performance of funds is negative. Furthermore, then we examine the full sample, the average underperformance is statistically significant at the 1% level for the 3-year results and statistically significant at the 5% level for the 1-year results.

Let us examine whether information about past ranking tells us anything about future ranking. Table 12.1 presents the results where performance alphas are calculated over 3-year periods and reported as average monthly risk-adjusted return. The first four columns present results when we do not further restrict the group of funds being ranked. Note that, except for total return, any other ranking criterion studied (3-year selection alpha, 1-year selection alpha, or *t*-value on 3-year selection alpha) leads to a rank correlation coefficient that is significant at the 1% level. Ranking by total return is significant at the 10% level. We used two rules for eliminating certain funds from our sample to study the impact of

Table 12.1
Average realized 3-year alpha by deciles for different ranking criteria (reported on a monthly basis, in %)

	Deciles formed on the basis of:										
	Full sample				High expenses eliminated*	Low R^2 eliminated†			High expenses and low R^2 eliminated‡		
Decile	Total return	3-year alpha	1-year alpha	*t* alpha	Total return	3-year alpha	1-year alpha	*t* alpha	3-year alpha	1-year alpha	*t* alpha
Bottom 1	−.327	−.437	−.390	−.351	−.151	−.359	−.310	−.273	−.180	−.158	−.144
2	−.078	−.101	−.112	−.144	−.040	−.077	−.081	−.129	−.055	−.051	−.075
3	−.053	−.058	−.058	−.107	−.028	−.052	−.054	−.092	−.060	−.040	−.090
4	−.057	−.076	−.072	−.066	−.026	−.075	−.088	−.063	−.057	−.099	−.038
5	−.051	−.039	−.062	−.044	−.061	−.044	−.074	−.045	−.017	−.045	−.051
6	−.042	−.047	−.020	−.054	−.017	−.055	−.023	−.058	−.043	−.021	−.021
7	−.070	−.009	−.024	−.023	−.047	−.003	−.013	−.027	−.010	−.008	−.040
8	−.007	−.038	−.011	.012	−.016	−.043	−.018	.023	−.028	−.013	.034
9	−.016	.034	−.026	−.004	−.010	.042	−.012	.007	.036	.008	.001
Top 10	−.059	.009	.015	.023	−.049	.028	.038	.026	.019	.036	.029
Average	−.076	−.076	−.076	−.076	−.044	−.064	−.063	−.063	−.040	−.039	−.040
Rank correlation	.552	.952	.879	.976	.394	.915	.927	.976	.891	.927	.891
p-value	.0984	.0001	.0008	.0001	.2600	.0002	.0001	.0001	.0005	.0001	.0005

NOTE. Shown is the average realized monthly risk-adjusted return (alpha computed for 3-year performance periods), where the deciles were formed using the ranking criteria shown at the top of each column and for the four samples shown above the columns.

* The top decile of funds with the highest past 3-year average expenses was eliminated each year.

† All funds for which the multi-index model explained less than 80% were eliminated.

‡ All funds for which the multi-index model explained less than 80% were eliminated, and then from the resulting sample the top decile of funds with the highest past 3-year average expenses was eliminated each year.

Table 12.2
Average realized 1-year alpha by forecast deciles for different ranking criteria (reported on a monthly basis, in %)

	Deciles formed on the basis of:										
	Full sample				High expenses eliminated*	Low R^2 eliminated†			High expenses and low R^2 eliminated‡		
Decile	Total return	3-year alpha	1-year alpha	t alpha	Total return	3-year alpha	1-year alpha	t alpha	3-year alpha	1-year alpha	t alpha
Bottom 1	−.391	−.469	−.467	−.388	−.183	−.402	−.401	−.318	−.189	−.230	−.191
2	−.103	−.043	−.133	−.142	−.053	−.030	−.083	−.129	−.051	−.057	−.074
3	−.093	−.095	−.085	−.096	−.067	−.123	−.083	−.098	−.109	−.071	−.096
4	−.089	−.105	−.086	−.101	−.064	−.081	−.094	−.095	−.054	−.104	−.093
5	−.089	−.051	−.062	−.041	−.100	−.058	−.064	−.050	−.058	−.019	−.039
6	−.052	−.058	−.017	−.025	−.033	−.030	−.010	−.014	.001	−.026	.032
7	−.039	.056	.023	.000	−.024	.060	.030	.021	.061	.029	.031
8	.011	−.028	.049	.005	−.002	−.020	.024	.025	−.014	.034	.043
9	.014	.012	−.070	−.045	.000	.027	−.034	−.021	.032	−.015	−.018
Top 10	.051	−.004	.065	.050	.052	.030	.098	.051	.019	.107	.044
Average	−.078	−.078	−.078	−.078	−.047	−.063	−.062	−.062	−.036	−.035	−.036
Rank correlation	1.000	.770	.867	.867	.891	.806	.867	.927	.806	.903	.879
p-value	.0000	.0092	.0012	.0012	.0005	.0049	.0012	.0001	.0049	.0003	.0008

NOTE. Shown is the average realized monthly risk-adjusted return (alpha computed for 1-year performance periods), where the deciles were formed using the ranking criteria shown at the top of each column and for the four samples shown above the columns.
* The top decile of funds with the highest past 3-year average expenses was eliminated each year.
† All funds for which the multi-index model explained less than 80% were eliminated.
‡ All funds for which the multi-index model explained less than 80% were eliminated, and then from the resulting sample the top decile of funds with the highest past 3-year average expenses was eliminated each year.

elimination on the usefulness of rankings. First, we eliminated funds for which our risk model had low explanatory power in the selection period (adjusted R^2 below 0.8). We felt that an investor might recognize that funds for which the model fit poorly in the selection period might be less predictable in subsequent periods. A low R^2 could result from market timing or from very low diversification. Eliminating these funds had very little effect on the ranking results but did improve the performance of the upper and lower deciles. Second, after first eliminating funds with low adjusted R^2, from the resulting reduced sample we eliminated funds with high expenses (funds in the top decile of expense ratios in the reduced sample) to see if we were only picking up differences in expenses rather than differences in management performance. This had almost no effect on the rank correlations but improved average risk-adjusted returns and dramatically improved the risk-adjusted returns for the lowest deciles.

Figure 12.1 plots expenses by decile when funds are ranked on 3-year alpha. Figure 12.1 shows that expenses are high in the low decile when we eliminate the 10% of the funds with the highest expenses. Expense differ-

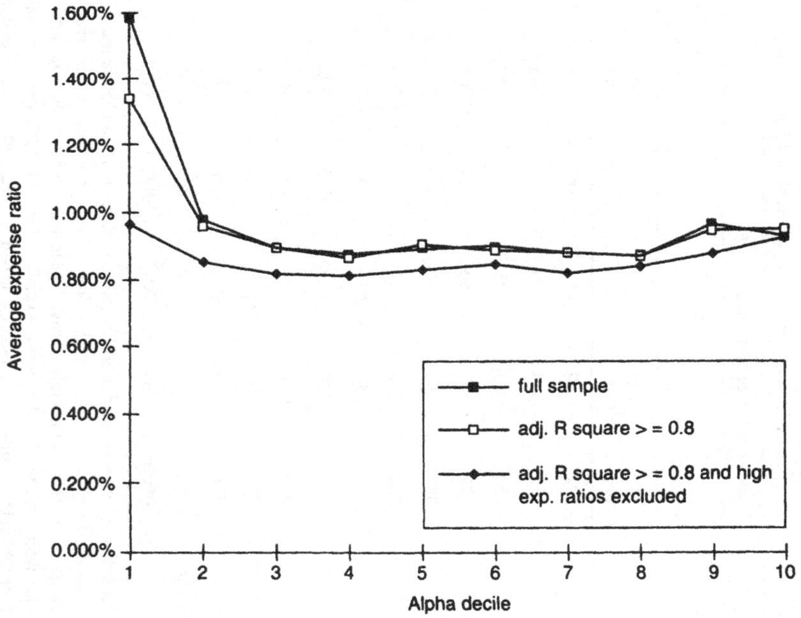

Figure 12.1
Performance and expenses

ences are minimal across all deciles, although the lowest decile has slightly higher expense ratios than other deciles. Thus, while high expenses cause common stock funds to be in the lowest performance decile, they do not explain ranking across other deciles.

Table 12.2 presents the same analysis where average performance alpha (excess return) is measured for a period of 1 year after the rankings. The major difference between table 12.2 and table 12.1 is that, when using the 1-year performance evaluation period, ranking techniques involving 1 year of past data generally perform much better than ranking techniques involving 3 years of past data. Total return provides the best ranking technique (as opposed to risk-adjusted return), although, as we will see shortly, it does not do as good a job at forecasting the tails of the distribution.

Comparing table 12.1 and table 12.2 shows that deciles formed on the basis of total return are highly correlated with future performance alpha when performance alpha is measured over a 1-year period, but the relationship deteriorates when future performance alpha is measured over 3 years. This is similar to the result in Hendricks, Patel, and Zeckhauser (1993). However, when ranking is done on a risk-adjusted basis, the predictability is increased when performance is measured over the longer (3-year) period.

B Performance Results Using Ranks

While the preservation of rank across time is interesting, of perhaps more practical significance is an answer to the question, "Can information about past performance help earn a positive alpha in the future?" Tables 12.3 and 12.4 repeat the postselection performance alphas shown in tables 12.1 and 12.2 for the average fund and for deciles 1 and 10 and present the statistical significance of some differences. Table 12.3 presents the results for a 3-year holding period, while table 12.4 presents the 1-year holding period results.

We start by examining the section of panel A labled "full sample." Starting with the predictions based on selection alphas computed over the previous 3 years, we find that the top decile (decile 10) produces a positive excess return of 0.9 basis points per month if it is held for the following 3 years, while the bottom decile produces an excess return of −43.7 basis points per month. An investor selecting an equally weighted average of the funds in the top decile earns a positive (albeit tiny) excess

Table 12.3
Comparison of realized 3-year alphas using deciles and simple rules for different ranking criteria (reported on a monthly basis)

	Deciles formed on the basis of:										
	Full sample				High expenses eliminated[a]	Low R^2 eliminated[b]			High expenses and low R^2 eliminated[c]		
	Total return	3-year alpha	1-year alpha	*t* alpha	Total return	3-year alpha	1-year alpha	*t* alpha	3-year alpha	1-year alpha	*t* alpha
A. Averages (in %):											
Average decile	−.076	−.076	−.076	−.076	−.044	−.064	−.063	−.063	−.040	−.039	−.040
Bottom decile	−.327	−.437	−.390	−.351	−.151	−.359	−.310	−.273	−.180	−.158	−.144
Top decile	−.059	.009	.015	.023	−.049	.028	.038	.026	.019	.036	.029
Simple rules	...	.066	.060	...	...	.065	.064	...	.058	.065	...
B. Differences (in %):											
Top vs. bottom	.267*	.446*	.405*	.374*	.102	.387*	.348*	.299*	.199*	.194*	.173*
Top vs. average	.017	.085*	.091*	.099*	−.004	.092*	.101*	.089*	.059	.075*	.068*
Simple rules vs. top	...	.057*	.044*	...	...	.037**	.026	...	.039*	.029	...
C. Number of 3-year periods (out of 12) that first listed group beat second listed group:											
Top vs. bottom	10	11	12	12	9	12	12	12	10	9	10
Top vs. average	5	9	9	12	5	10	11	11	9	11	9
Simple rules vs. top	...	10	10	...	...	9	7	...	...	...	...

Note. Simple rules solutions to optimization are applied to the top decile of either 3-year or 1-year alphas calculated in selection periods.
a. The top decile of funds with the highest past 3-year average expenses was eliminated each year.
b. All funds for which the multi-index model explained less than 80% were eliminated.
c. All funds for which the multi-index model explained less than 80% were eliminated, and then from the resulting sample the top decile of funds with the highest past 3-year average expenses were eliminated each year.
* Significant at the 1% level.
** Significant at the 5% level.

Comparison of realized 1-year alphas using deciles and simple rules for different ranking criteria (reported on a monthly basis)

	Deciles formed on the basis of:										
	Full sample				High expenses eliminated[a]	Low R^2 eliminated[b]			High expenses and low R^2 eliminated[c]		
	Total return	3-year alpha	1-year alpha	*t* alpha	Total return	3-year alpha	1-year alpha	*t* alpha	3-year alpha	1-year alpha	*t* alpha
A. Averages (in %):											
Average decile	−.078	−.078	−.078	−.078	−.047	−.063	−.062	−.062	−.036	−.035	−.036
Bottom decile	−.391	−.469	−.467	−.388	−.183	−.402	−.401	−.318	−.189	−.230	−.191
Top decile	.051	−.004	.065	.050	.052	.030	.098	.051	.019	.107	.044
Simple rules	...	.073	.139	...	...	.083	.134	...	.069	.135	...
B. Differences (in %):											
Top vs. bottom	.442*	.465*	.532*	.439*	.235**	.431*	.498*	.369*	.208**	.337*	.235*
Top vs. average	.129**	.074	.143**	.128*	.099	.092**	.159**	.112*	.055	.142	.080**
Simple rules vs. top	...	.077*	.074*	...	...	.053*	.036	...	.050**	.028	...
C. Number of years (out of 12) that first listed group beat second listed group:											
Top vs. bottom	10	11	12	11	9	11	12	12	8	9	10
Top vs. average	9	9	8	11	7	10	9	10	9	9	8
Simple rules vs. top	...	10	10	...	...	10	8	...	9	8	...

Note. Simple rules solutions to optimization are applied to the top decile of either 3-year or 1-year alphas calculated in selection periods.

a. The top decile of funds with the highest past 3-year average expenses was eliminated each year.

b. All funds for which the multi-index model explained less than 80% were eliminated.

c. All funds for which the multi-index model explained less than 80% were eliminated, and then from the resulting sample the top decile of funds with the highest past 3-year average expenses was eliminated each year.

* Significant at the 1% level.

** Significant at the 5% level.

return in an environment where most funds (and the average fund) earned a large negative excess return.

It is interesting to examine the performance of the top-ranked decile (portfolio) compared to both the bottom-ranked decile and the average fund. However, to see if these differences are statistically significant, differences in the mean return in each decile can be computed each year and a t-test performed for differences of the mean from zero. The results of this type of test are recorded in panel B. In addition, we can examine the number of time periods (out of a possible 12 times) that decile 10 (the top decile) outperforms decile 1 (the bottom decile) or the average fund. This is done in panel C. In interpreting this panel, it is useful to know that the chances of one decile having a higher estimated alpha 11 out of 12 times if the deciles being compared have the same true alpha is less than 1%; 10 of 12 times is statistically significantly different from zero at the 2% level, and nine out of 12 times is statistically significantly different from zero at the 6% level.

Returning to our analysis of ranking on 3-year selection alpha, we see that selecting the top decile is better (at the 1% significance level) than selecting either the bottom decile or the average fund. It also outperforms the bottom decile 11 times and the average fund nine out of 12 times.

If we forecast 3-year performance alphas using the past 1-year selection alpha rather than the past 3-year alpha, we find results which are perhaps slightly improved. The top decile goes up slightly in return form 0.9 basis points to 1.5 basis points per month. This is an improvement, though the bottom decile also improves by about 4 basis points. The differences in risk-adjusted return between the top decile and either the bottom decile of average fund continue to be significant at the 1% level.

When we rank by t-value of the 3-year selection alpha, the return on the portfolio of the top decile funds is higher and is equal to 2.3 basis points per month. The differences in performance between the top decile and the average or bottom deciles are statistically significant at the 1% level. Here the top decile outperforms both the bottom decile and the average fund 12 out of 12 times.

The final selection metric we examined was total return in the year preceding the prediction. Unlike the cases with the other selection metrics, when we form deciles on total return we get a negative performance alpha over the following 3 years. While the top decile outperforms both the average fund and the bottom decile, differences from the average fund are no longer statistically significant.

The next section of tables 12.3 and 12.4 examines results when we have eliminated all funds in the selection period with an adjusted R^2 less than 0.8 on our four-index model. In all cases the risk-adjusted excess return on the top decile increases. It increases by a much smaller percentage for rankings on t-values, probably because the funds with low adjusted R^2's also had large standard errors and so were unlikely to be in the top decile for the t-value criterion when the full sample was used. When we discard funds with adjusted R^2 less than 0.8, the risk-adjusted return for the average fund also increases, indicating that funds with low adjusted R^2 tended to have negative risk-adjusted performance.

The last section of tables 12.3 and 12.4 shows performance when we delete the 10% of the funds with the highest expenses from the sample of funds having an adjusted R^2 not less than 0.8. The effect of removing these funds on the performance of the top decile is mixed, hurting performance when ranking with 3-year selection alphas and helping with the other ranking criteria. The major effect of removing the high-expense funds is to improve average performance and the performance of the lowest decile. Note that the performance of the bottom decile increases by more than 2.0% per year when the high-expense funds are deleted. This causes the differences between the top and bottom deciles to shrink; however, the differences are still statistically significant at the 1% level.

So far we have discussed ranking funds when the results of holding a decile (portfolio) is evaluated over a 3-year performance period. We now turn to an examination of results when the performance evaluation (holding) period for a portfolio is 1 year. While many of the results for the 1-year performance period are similar to those for the 3-year performance period, there are some interesting differences.

The first point to note from table 12.4 is that when evaluating performance over a 1-year period, the performance of the top decile based on 1-year ranking criteria improves markedly compared to forecasts prepared on the basis of 3 years of past data. Also note that whether one selects on the basis of total return, 1-year alpha, or t alpha, the top decile (portfolio) has fairly large monthly returns. For example, selecting on the basis of 1-year selection alphas gives a positive return of 78 basis points per year. Note that for all ranking techniques using the full sample, the top decile outperforms the bottom decile at the 1% level of statistical significance. In contrast to the 3-year performance evaluation period, total return seems to carry real information as a ranking criteria, though it does not perform as well as 1-year selection alpha.

Other results in table 12.4 are similar to those presented in table 12.3. Eliminating funds with a poorer fit (low adjusted R^2) during the selection period (when deciles are formed) results in a higher return for the top decile but decreases the difference between the top and bottom deciles. Eliminating high-expense funds sometimes lowers and sometimes raises the performance of the top decile but definitely raises the performance of the bottom decile.

In order to be sure that our results were not due to unusual and persistent high performance of one or two funds, we eliminated the two funds that appeared most often in the top decile of the selection periods and recalcualted the performance period averages. The resulting average performance alpha for the remaining funds in the top decile sometimes increased and sometimes decreased, but all changes were negligible.

C *Performance Results Employing Modern Portfolio Theory*

Up to now we have compared the performance of deciles (portfolios of funds) formed on the basis of alternative ranking criteria. In examining performance, the fraction of investor capital invested in each of the funds in a portfolio was assumed to be the same. But the literature of MPT gives us great insight into what optimal weights should be within a decile. In this section we examine two alternative evaluation schemes. Both use MPT to find the optimal weight on each fund in the top decile or top two deciles of funds. The first evaluation scheme compares performance on the basis of alpha. The second scheme evaluates on the basis of total return while holding risk constant.

Optimal Portfolio Weights

We start by assuming that the investor is going to hold a portfolio composed of the funds found in the top decile in the selection period. We then draw on the modern portfolio theory literature to find the optimal weighting of funds in that decile. It is well known that, if we assume returns are described by a model such as that shown in equation (1), then the optimal weight (fraction of money) to place in any fund is given by

$$X_i = \frac{(a_i/\sigma^2_{\varepsilon_i})}{\sum_i (a_i/\sigma^2_{\varepsilon_i})}, \tag{2}$$

where $\sigma^2_{\varepsilon_i}$ is the variance of the random error term in equation (1). This is a generalization of the Treynor and Black (1973) and Elton, Gruber, and

Padberg (1976) criteria and is derived for a multi-index model in Elton and Gruber (1992).

The results of employing this weighting across all securities in the top decile are shown in tables 12.3 and 12.4 under the row labeled "simple rules."[5] Note that employing a technique that optimizes weights leads to a large improvement in performance. Examining the results using a 3-year evaluation period, the optimal portfolio (selected on the basis of past performance) earns between 70 and 80 basis points per year in excess return. Note that eliminating funds with low adjusted R^2 over the selection period makes almost no difference in return. This comes about because funds with low adjusted R^2 tend to have high residual risk and thus receive lower weights in the optimal portfolio. Removing high-expense funds has, at most, a marginal effect on the performance of the optimal portfolio, since high-expense funds are normally not in the top decile.

If we turn to the results employing a 1-year performance evaluation period, we find that the results are even more dramatic. Employing the 1-year selection alpha to form deciles from which a portfolio is selected results in a portfolio that produces risk-adjusted excess return of more than 1.50% per year in the performance evaluation period.

In every case, both for the 1-year and 3-year performance evaluation periods, employing optimal weights results in a large increase in performance relative to using equal weights. In addition, in most cases the results obtained with optimal weights are statistically significantly better than the results obtained with equal weights.

Before leaving this section we should comment on one more issue: the magnitude of the weights when a portfolio optimization technique is used. The percentage of time that each weight occurs is shown in figure 12.2. This figure makes it clear that while there are deviations of the weights from an equal-weighting scheme, the results do not come about by holding an extremely concentrated portfolio of funds. If we held equally weighted portfolios, the percent invested in any fund would average $6\frac{2}{3}$%. The weights depicted in figure 12.2 show a high concentration in the 2%–11% range, with very few weights above 15%.

Active versus Passive Funds

We have one final way to test whether past mutual fund performance can be used to select funds that subsequently produce superior risk-adjusted returns. This involves a comparison of active and passive portfolios with the same risk. We select a set of risk levels (target betas) that seem relevant for investors in actively managed stock mutual funds. We then select

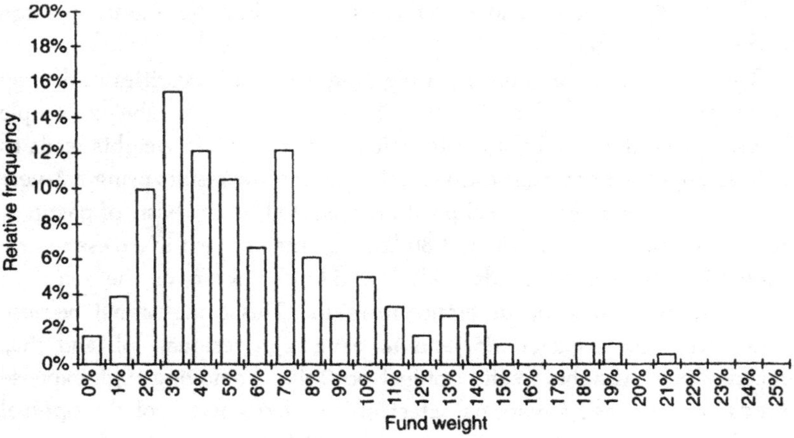

Figure 12.2
Frequency of composition weights in simple rules fund portfolios

both a portfolio of active funds and a portfolio of index funds that have the same target betas. Finally, we compare the return of the portfolio of active funds to that of the index portfolio to see which has a higher mean return.

Although an investor currently has a large number of index funds to select from, these funds are a recent phenomenon. Thus, we do not have actual fund histories for a large number of different types of index funds. For the S&P Index fund we selected the Vanguard S&P 500 Index fund, both because it has a long history and because it has the lowest expenses of the available S&P Index funds. To represent the return on other types of index funds, we had to use actual indexes as proxies. The indexes we chose were

1. the Wilshire Large Capitalization Value Portfolio for a value portfolio;
2. the S&P Barra Growth Portfolio for a growth portfolio;
3. the Wilshire Small Cap Growth Portfolio for a small-cap growth portfolio;
4. the Ibbotson Associates Small Capitalization Portfolio for a small-cap index;
5. the Ibbotson Associaties 30-day Treasury bill as a short-term money market portfolio; and
6. the Lehman Brothers Government Corporate Index as a bond index.

We first decided on a set of target betas that our hypothetical investor in index funds might choose. We used as our target betas the four average sensitivities to each of the indexes in our four-index model across all mutual funds in the sample and across all 3-year selection periods. These are the expected sensitivities for an investor who randomly selects from our population of funds. The average sensitivities are 0.86 on the S&P Index, 0.30 on the differential size index, 0.32 on the value-growth index, and 0.07 on the bond index. We constructed a portfolio of index funds that had these target betas as the passive portfolio for a hypothetical investor.[6]

We tried two alternative techniques for selecting portfolios from among active funds, one using maximization of 3-year selection alpha as an objective and one maximizing the average 3-year selection alpha over residual risk. The first criterion was chosen because it was a criterion investors might logically try and because it is consistent with much of the research in this area. We chose the second because Elton and Gruber (1992) show this criterion is optimal for selecting an active portfolio when security returns of follow a multi-index model. To ensure that the results were realistic, short sales were not allowed. We initially selected funds using data from 1978 through 1980. The active portfolios were then reformed at the beginning of every year from 1982 through 1991 using the prior 3 years of data. Performance was measured over the period 1981–93.

We used an upper bound constraint of 10% investment in a fund. This forced some diversification. This upper bound constraint had to be relaxed on occasion in order to find a solution. The maximum upper limit was 20%, and even when this came into play there was a fair amount of diversification. Finally, we limited our choices to funds in the upper two deciles, since restricting choices to the top decile did not allow a solution in several of the selection periods.

The reason that we used the upper two deciles and occasionally had to allow the maximum fraction of capital invested in any fund to rise to 20% was because of the changing nature of stocks in the top two deciles. In certain years, the stocks in the top decile and in the top two deciles had sensitivities (betas) that differed considerably from the average sensitivities in our sample. For example, in 1 or more years high growth stocks may be good performers (have high predicted alphas), while in other years value stocks end up as the best performers.[7]

Our portfolio of active funds outperformed our passive-fund portfolio in each case. In terms of total return, the average outperformance was 22 basis points per year using 3-year selection alpha as an objective, and 71 basis points per year when funds were selected by maximizing the average 3-year selection alpha divided by the residual risk. The Vanguard S&P Index fund's return is reduced by fees and expenses; the returns on the other indexes are not. If we assume 30 basis points in fees and expenses for the index funds other than the Vanguard S&P fund, the return differences described above should be increased by 29 basis points per year.

While we were able to find a combination of active funds that outperformed a combination of index funds with average characteristics in each case we tried, this might not have been possible if the target betas had deviated considerably from the average sensitivities of the top-performing funds.

V Size and Expenses

While we have found predictability in this study, an argument has been made that predictability should not exist. This argument proceeds from the assumption that successful managers subsequently raise fees in order to increase their income. The increase in fees could thus eliminate subsequent excess return, resulting in no continuity of performance even when managers have an ability to construct superior portfolios.

Managers' fees are almost universally stated as a fraction of total net assets. Thus, a manager's total compensation is equal to a stated percentage of total net asset value. Furthermore, growth in total net asset value is a function of prior performance (see Sirri and Tufano 1992). An increase in the fee percentage would hurt postexpense performance and therefore reduce subsequent growth in assets. If the relationship between asset growth and performance is strong enough, a successful manager might increase manager revenue more by not raising management fees and thereby having higher asset growth. Which of the above two behavioral models best describes actual performance is an empirical question.

To examine this question, we must control for the relationships between asset size and expenses and time and expenses. Table 12.5 shows the regression between expense ratios and the log of total net asset value for each year between 1977 and 1991. There is a significant negative relationship in each year, with the slope varying from −0.14 to −0.20 and an R^2 of between 0.24 and 0.44. Thus, expenses decline as size increases. The right-hand half of table 12.5 shows the predicted expense in percent for funds of different asset size. The numbers in the right part of the table are obtained by substituting the log of the size shown at the top of the

Table 12.5
Annual expense ratios and fund total net asset sizes (cross-sectional regression results by year; annual expense ratio regressed on constant and log of size)

Year	Adjusted R^2	Intercept (%)	*t*-intercept	Slope	*t*-slope	Predicted expense ratios based on regression results (in %) (total net assets in millions $)				
						50	100	200	400	1,000
1977	.41	1.72	24.44	−.19	−11.93	.99	.87	.74	.61	.44
1978	.44	1.70	26.44	−.19	−12.71	.97	.85	.72	.59	.42
1979	.36	1.75	22.23	−.19	−10.62	1.01	.87	.74	.61	.44
1980	.29	1.75	18.77	−.18	−8.90	1.04	.91	.79	.66	.49
1981	.37	1.70	22.26	−.17	−10.53	1.04	.92	.81	.69	.53
1982	.35	1.79	19.55	−.19	−9.84	1.04	.91	.78	.65	.47
1983	.35	1.83	19.80	−.18	−9.79	1.11	.99	.86	.73	.56
1984	.30	1.71	18.25	−.16	−8.76	1.08	.97	.86	.75	.61
1985	.35	1.63	21.16	−.14	−9.52	1.07	.97	.87	.77	.64
1986	.31	1.98	16.24	−.20	−8.75	1.20	1.06	.93	.79	.60
1987	.37	1.74	20.06	−.16	−9.98	1.12	1.01	.90	.79	.64
1988	.23	1.70	15.19	−.14	−7.08	1.13	1.04	.94	.84	.71
1989	.24	1.78	16.03	−.15	−7.27	1.21	1.11	1.01	.91	.78
1990	.28	2.05	15.62	−.18	−8.04	1.33	1.21	1.08	.95	.78
1991	.31	2.00	16.94	−.17	−8.47	1.32	1.20	1.08	.96	.80

Table 12.6
Comparison of average size and average actual and predicted annual expense ratios (for top decile ranked by alphas calculated during 3-year selection periods)

Year t	Predicted expense ratio (%)	Actual expense ratio (%)	Difference (%)	Asset size (millions $)
Prior	.89	.89	.00	189.87
1	.87	.87	.00	239.67
2	.86	.90	−.05	294.40
3	.86	.91	−.05	346.87
4	.86	.92	−.05	405.20
5	.88	.92	−.04	457.87

NOTE. Prior year is the end of the last year prior of the selection period, year 1 is the end of the first year after selection period, year 2 is the end of the second year after the selection period, etc.

column along with the corresponding parameter values shown in the left portion of the table into the equation described at the top of the table. There is a clear pattern of increasing expense ratios over time.

To analyze whether successful managers increase their expense ratios over time, we used the equation described at the top of table 12.5 along with each fund's asset size to determine predicted expense ratios. These predicted expense ratios are shown in table 12.6 in the first column. The table analyzes expenses for all funds in the top decile using 3-year alphas in the selection period. Actual expense ratios are in the second column, and the differences is in the third column. The first row is expense ratios at the time of selection. For example, if we were selecting on January 1, 1980, the expense ratios are for the end of 1979. Rows 2–6 are the expense ratios at the end of the 5 years subsequent to selection (1980–84 in the above example). The expenses at the time funds are selected are exactly what would have been predicted given the fund size and year of selection. In the first year of the evaluation period, their expense ratios are again exactly what would be predicted given the fund size and year of selection. Expense ratios increase slightly in subsequent years, although the magnitude of the increase is small. Furthermore, examining the second column of table 12.6, and examining table 12.5 to note how expenses increase with time, shows that, ignoring the increase in size, selected funds increase fees no more than the average fund. However, the increase in fees is faster than their increase in size would suggest. Fees could also be increased by imposing loads. Although 19 funds changed from no-load to load funds, none of these funds were in the top selection decile in the year before the change. In fact, the greatest number of these funds were in the *bottom* selection decile in the year before the change! In conclusion, the fees of top-performing funds exhibit at most a slight increase in years subsequent to their top ranking, and clearly not enough to affect performance. On average then, managers of successful funds increase their total revenues by having the sizes of their funds increase, not by increasing expenses.

VI Conclusions

There are a number of lessons that can be learned from this study.

1) The past carries information about the future. Funds that did well in the past tend to do well in the future on a risk-adjusted basis.

2) Both 1- and 3-year alphas convey information about future performance.

3) When future performance is evaluated over 3-year periods, selection on prior 3-year alpha conveys no less, and perhaps more, information about future performance than selection using other time horizons.

4) When future performance is evaluated over a 1-year period, selection of funds based on the prior year's data conveys much more information about performance than selection based on data from the prior 3 years.

5) There is definite information about future performance conveyed by past performance, and this information works for periods 3 years into the future as well as 1 year into the future. "Hot hands" may be an important phenomenon, but there is a longer persistence in performance than noted in the hot hands literature.

6) Employing modern portfolio theory to form optimal portfolios based on past information leads to the selection of portfolios of mutual funds that have a positive and both economically and statistically significant return compared to a portfolio that places an equal amount in each fund that is considered.

7) The very bad performance of the lowest decile is largely accounted for by the fact that it contains the majority of the funds with very high expenses. Expense ratios are about the same for all other deciles. When high-expense funds are removed from the sample, we see that past

performance still tells us a lot about future performance. Differences in risk-adjusted return between the top and bottom decile are partially differences in selection skill and partially differences in expenses.

8) Successful funds do not increase their fees compared to less successful funds.

Notes

We thank Douglas Diamond and Eugene Fama for helpful comments. We are also grateful to Investment Company Data, Inc., and to Interactive Data Corporation for supplying data used in this study. This research was supported in part by a grant from Fordham University's Graduate School of Business Administration.

1. Of the few studies that find that managers or a subset of managers with a common objective (such as growth) out-perform passive portfolios, most, if not all, would reach opposite conclusions when survivorship bias and/or correct adjustment for risk are taken into account.

2. The small-large index was formed by averaging the small-cap value index and the small-cap growth index and subtracting the average of the large-cap growth index and the large-cap value index. The growth-value index was formed by averaging the large-cap, mid-cap, and small-cap stock growth indexes and subtracting the average of the large-cap, mid-cap, and small-cap stock value indexes. Note that both of these indexes are in excess-return form. Since these indexes are based on differences, the riskless rate cancels out. Therefore, we do not subtract the riskless rate from these indexes, because doing so would in effect be double-counting the riskless asset.

3. See Elton, Gruber, and Blake (1995) for a detailed description of the bond index.

4. We considered and examined other rules for what happens when a fund merges or changes policy. Alternative choices had no significant effect on the results. This is in part because few of the selected funds merged or changed policy in the subsequent evaluation periods. For example, only 0.8% of 1,875 selected funds merged or changed policy in the first year after selection. In fact, among the top decile of selected funds, which we focus on in the next section, only five funds merged in the performance evaluation periods, none in the first year after selection and most near the ends of the 3-year performance evaluation periods, and none changed policy. Thus, our procedure for handling nonsurviving funds has virtually no effect on our results.

5. None of the optimal portfolios selected by this rule involve short sales since all selection alphas in the top decile are positive. Note that a fund's 3-year selection alpha is the a_i appearing in eqq. (1) and (2). When 1-year selection alphas are used, we substitute the 1-year selection alpha for the a_i appearing in eq. (2). The residual variances in eq. (2) are those obtained from a 3-year selection period in either case.

6. We solved a linear programming problem to minimize the difference between the betas on the portfolio of index funds and the target betas. The program was able to match the target betas exactly in 8 of 11 years and almost exactly in the other 3 years.

7. This intertemporal instability of betas over time in each decile casts some doubt over numerous other studies that measure alpha from a particular decile (or octile) over time by running a single- or multiple-index model on the returns of a particular decile over time.

Since the betas are unstable, the results are not meaningful. This contrasts with the methodology used throughout this article, where alphas are estimated for individual funds and then aggregated for portfolios. As an example, for the four-index model we employ in this article, the sensitivity of the difference in return between the top and bottom performing decile on the small-stock index varies between +0.74 and −0.51.

References

Blake, C. R.; Elton, E. J.; and Gruber, M. J. 1993. The performance of bond mutual funds. *Journal of Business* 66 (July): 371–403.

Brown, S. J., and Goetzmann, W. N. 1995. Performance persistence. *Journal of Finance* 50 (June): 679–98.

Brown, S. J.; Goetzmann, W. N.; Ibbotson, R. G.; and Ross, S. A. 1992. Survivorship bias in performance studies. *Review of Financial Studies* 5 (Winter): 553–80.

Carhart, M. M. 1994. On persistence in mutual fund performance. Working paper. Chicago: University of Chicago.

Elton, E. J., and Gruber, M. J. 1992. Portfolio analysis with non-normal multi-index return-generating process. *Review of Quantitative Finance and Accounting* 2 (March): 5–17.

Elton, E. J.; Gruber, M. J.; and Blake, C. R. 1995. Fundamental economic variables, expected returns, and bond fund performance. *Journal of Finance* 50 (September): 1229–56.

Elton, E. J.; Gruber, M. J.; and Blake, C. R. In press. Survivorship bias and mutual fund performance. *Review of Financial Studies.*

Elton, E. J.; Gruber, M. J.; Das, S.; and Hlavka, M. 1993. Efficiency with costly information: A reinterpretation of evidence for managed portfolios. *Review of Financial Studies* 6 (Spring): 1–22.

Elton, E. J.; Gruber, M. J.; and Padberg, M. 1976. Simple criteria for optimal portfolio selection. *Journal of Finance* 31 (December): 1341–57.

Fama, E. F., and French, K. R. 1993. Common risk factors in the returns on bonds and stocks. *Journal of Financial Economics* 33 (February): 3–53.

Fama, E. F., and French, K. R. 1994. Size and book-to-market factors in earnings and returns. Working paper. Chicago: University of Chicago.

Grinblatt, M., and Titman, S. 1989. Mutual fund performance: An analysis of quarterly portfolio holdings. *Journal of Business* 62 (July): 393–416.

Grinblatt, M., and Titman, S. 1992. Performance persistence in mutual funds. *Journal of Finance* 47 (December): 1977–84.

Hendricks, D.; Patel, J.; and Zeckhauser, R. 1993. Hot hands in mutual funds: Short-run persistence of performance, 1974–88. *Journal of Finance* 48 (March): 93–130.

Lehmann, B. N., and Modest, D. 1987. Mutual fund performance evaluation: A comparison of benchmarks and benchmark comparisons. *Journal of Finance* 42 (June): 233–65.

Malkiel, B. G. 1995. Returns from investing in equity funds. *Journal of Finance* 50 (June): 549–72.

Sharpe, W. F. 1995. The styles and performance of large seasoned U. S. mutual funds. Working paper. Palo Alto, Calif.: Stanford University.

Sirri, E. R., and Tufano, P. 1992. The demand for mutual fund services by individual investors. Working paper. Cambridge, Mass.: Harvard Business School.

Treynor, J., and Black, F. 1973. How to use security analysis to improve portfolio selection. *Journal of Business* 46 (January): 66–86.

Wiesenberger Financial Service. 1977–92. *Investment Companies*. Boston: Warren, Gorham & Lamont.

Mutual Funds—Bond Investments

13 The Performance of Bond Mutual Funds

Christopher R. Blake, Edwin J. Elton, and Martin J. Gruber

I Introduction

The subject of mutual fund performance has received a great deal of attention in the literature of financial economics. Alternative metrics for performance have been proposed, and mutual fund performance has been examined extensively.[1] However, almost all of the empirical work on mutual fund performance has involved either common stock funds or funds that invest in both common stock and debt instruments (e.g., balanced funds). In this study, we will examine the performance of mutual funds that restrict their investments almost exclusively to debt instruments: bond funds.

There are several reasons why this study is important. First, bond funds constitute a major part of the mutual fund industry, yet we have almost no information on their performance.[2] The present and potential importance of bond funds can be judged by looking at some historical data. At the end of 1978, there were 600 mutual funds registered in the United States, and they had total net assets of $58.1 billion. Of those funds, only 84 were bond and U.S. government security funds, and they held only 10.1% of the total net assets of mutual funds. By the end of 1990, there were 2,679 mutual funds with total net assets of $990.2 billion. Of those, 914 were bond funds representing 34.1% of the total number of funds, and those bond funds held 27.3% of the total net assets held by all mutual funds.[3] Given the importance of bond mutual funds in both size and growth, it is important to know more about how well they perform and what factors account for differences in their performance.

A second reason for studying bond funds is that most stock mutual fund performance studies include a large number of balanced funds. In those studies, all mutual funds, including balanced funds, are analyzed as if the portfolios consisted solely of common stock and Treasury bills. This study will aid in understanding whether the failure to explicitly incorporate one or more indexes for other types of debt instruments in the analysis can affect the interpretation of mutual fund performance results and will develop appropriate performance evaluation models for the bond portion of balanced funds.

A third reason for studying bond funds is that there are fewer influences affecting bond funds, and therefore the likelihood of measuring and understanding their performance is greater. Empirical evidence indicates that bond returns can be explained by no more than three and possibly two factors, while most studies of common stocks find that five to seven factors are necessary.[4] We know that the evaluation of stock and balanced mutual funds is extremely sensitive to the index or indexes that are used to measure performance.[5] Different indexes result in very different inferences about a fund's ability to outperform a passive strategy and result in very different rankings of funds. In this article, we will show that modeling is much simpler for bond mutual funds than for stock mutual funds and that bond fund performance is robust across a wide range of models.

A final reason for studying bond funds is to see if the multi-index models we use can explain the investment strategy followed by bond fund managers. That is, can we infer the types of securities held by a bond fund manager simply by studying the time-series return pattern? This type of analysis has been applied by both Elton, Gruber, Das, and Hlavka (1992) and Sharpe (1992) to bond-stock portfolios with some success; if it applies to bond portfolios, it will allow us to infer management style without having full access to composition data.

II Samples

In this study we employ two very different samples of bond fund data. The first of these consists of the 46 nonmunicipal bond funds identified as having a "bond" or "specialized" investment policy in the 1979 edition of Wiesenberger Financial Services' *Investment Companies.*[6] This sample excludes money market funds. End-of-month net asset values (NAVs), distributions, and reinvestment NAVs were obtained from Interactive Data Corporation (IDC) for most of these funds. The IDC data were supplemented by data from the funds themselves for those funds not listed by IDC and for the many missing data points in the IDC data set.[7] The missing data were primarily reinvestment NAVs. The IDC data were then analyzed and compared to Wiesenberger data and data obtained from the funds themselves to check for any errors. Monthly returns were calculated by computing the value at the end of the month minus the value at the beginning of the month divided by the value at the beginning of the month. If the firm paid a distribution during the month, we assumed the investor used the distribution to purchase additional shares at the reinvestment NAV, and the ending value was calculated including these shares.[8]

Our initial sample period is the 10-year period from the beginning of 1979 to the end of 1988. Ten of the 46 sample funds did not survive during the sample period, due to either liquidation, merger, or change in investment policy. For those funds that ceased to exist during a month, we assumed reinvestment to the end of the month at the Treasury-bill rate. For five of the 10 nonsurviving funds (two of which liquidated and three of which merged into other funds during our sample period), we were able to obtain only annual data.

In the final section of this article, we examine performance using a second, much larger, sample of funds. This sample consists of all bond funds that existed at the end of 1991 and was obtained from Investment Company Data, Incorporated (ICDI). This latter sample obviously has survivorship bias. Survivorship bias is less important for bond funds than it is for stock funds since bond fund performance is less variable and, consequently, fewer funds merge or dissolve. Furthermore, the smaller sample, which we analyze extensively, does not have this problem. Thus, we can obtain a rough measure of the magnitude of the problem by comparing the results for the funds that survive in that sample with the results for those that do not survive in that sample. As latter sections will show, survivorship bias causes bond fund performance to appear better than it actually is; thus, it cannot explain the underperformance we find for the larger sample.

We use several indexes to measure performance in this study. These include the return on 30-day Treasury-bills from Ibbotson and Associates; various government, mortgage, and investment-grade corporate bond indexes from Lehman Brothers; and the Blume/Keim high-yield bond index.[9] The Lehman Brothers indexes are comprehensive market-weighted indexes and were chosen because they are the most widely used indexes for bond portfolio evaluation and are widely used by passive bond portfolio managers.

III Models

In the previous section of this article, we mentioned a set of bond indexes that will be used in this study. The return on any of those indexes can be considered the return on a corresponding passive portfolio. The simplest comparison to make for a fund is to compare its rate of return to that of a passive portfolio represented by one or more indexes. However, this comparison neglects the differentials in risk that may exist between a fund and an index. A more sophisticated approach is to compare a fund to a passive portfolio that is a mixture of the selected benchmarks and a risk-free asset and that has the same risk as the fund. This can most easily be done when that fund's excess return (the fund's return minus the riskless rate) is related linearly to the excess return on an appropriate index.

More specifically,

$$R_{it} = \alpha_i + \beta_i I_t + \varepsilon_{it}, \tag{1}$$

where

R_{it} = the continuously compounded excess return on the ith fund during month t,

α_i = the average risk-adjusted excess return for the ith fund,

I_t = the continuously compounded excess return on an appropriate index during month t,

β_i = the sensitivity of the excess return on the ith fund to the excess return on the index, and

ε_{it} = the residual return of the ith fund during month t not accounted for by the model.

There are two ways to think about this model. First, this time-series regression model can be thought of as a single-index model similar to the market model used in the evaluation of common stocks. The β_i's in this characterization are the sensitivities (risk) of the funds to the selected market index. An alternative interpretation is that the manager of fund i has a choice of holding various combinations of a riskless asset and an active bond portfolio and that β_i is the fraction of the manager's money that, if invested in the *passive* portfolio with excess returns (above the riskless asset) I, along with the remainder in the riskless asset, would provide a total return that best matched the return on the manager's portfolio.[10]

To use this model, we have to define the appropriate index. One choice is the Lehman Brothers (LB) government/corporate bond index. The Lehman Brothers government/corporate bond index is a market-weighted index of government and investment-grade corporate issues that have more than 1 year remaining until maturity and is the one most often used as a basis of comparison for bond portfolios. Both because it is so widely used and because it is likely to be the index that most closely matches the aggregate of all funds in our sample of mutual funds, we employ this index as one single-index model and call it Market-1.

For a second one-index model, we used the single index that seemed most appropriate given the objectives and policies of the fund as described by Morningstar in their winter 1989 *Sourcebook*.[11] We call this model Own-1. Examining Morningstar descriptions led us to divide our fund sample into six categories or groups. The intent was not to search for an optimal index for each fund but to see if an investor looking at a single issue of Morningstar could select an index that supplied more information about performance than did the overall index used in the first single-index model. To the extent that looking at only one date does not provide a description of a fund's typical behavior over the full period, or that the funds are not classified in a meaningful way, our results will tend to understate the real performance of Own-1 relative to Market-1.

The groups we used, the members of each group, and the index selected for each group for model Own-1 can be seen by examining table 13.1. (Each index is shown in parentheses.) The choices of the indexes, given the stated objectives of the funds and our groupings, are fairly obvious. The Lehman Brothers mortgage-backed securities index was used for funds that had as an objective government mortgage, the Blume/Keim high-yield index was used for funds that had high yield as an objective, and the Lehman Brothers government/corporate index was used for funds that had high quality as an objective. The Lehman Brothers corporate index was used for the three remaining groups that had general investment objectives involving corporate bonds. There was a group of funds that were not classified by Morningstar. The Lehman Brothers government/corporate index was used for this group.

The next set of models we employed was designed to see if introducing more indexes allowed us to explain more of the mutual fund returns or to gain more insight into their performance. These models can be described, in general, as

$$R_{it} = \alpha_i + \sum_{j=1}^{K} \beta_{ij} I_{jt} + \varepsilon_{it}, \tag{2}$$

where

R_{it} = the continuously compounded excess return on the ith fund during month t,

α_i = the average risk-adjusted excess return for the ith fund,

I_{jt} = the continuously compounded excess return on an the jth index during month t,

β_{ij} = the sensitivity of the excess return on the ith fund to the excess return on the jth index,

K = the number of indexes employed (three or six in our analysis), and

ε_{it} = the residual return of the ith fund during month t not accounted for by the model.

In a manner analogous to the single-index model, we can consider equation (2) as a multiple-index model with the β_{ij}'s representing sensitivities or risks. Alternatively, we can think of the β_{ij}'s as the weights on sets of passive portfolios that best represent (reproduce the return series of) the fund under study.

We employed both three-index and six-index models in our analysis. Two different three-index models were employed. The first, called Risk-3, used the Lehman Brothers government/corporate bond index, the Lehman Brothers mortgage-backed securities index, and the Blume/Keim high-yield index. The government/corporate bond index was used to capture the influence of a large population of investment-grade bonds. The high-yield bond index was introduced to examine the effect of holding low-quality bonds. The mortgage index was introduced to capture the specific effect of a class of government securities that act differently because of the particular option features found in mortgages.[12]

A second three-index model, called Maturity-3, was also used. The Lehman Brothers government/corporate bond index was replaced by both the Lehman Brothers intermediate government bond index and the Lehman Brothers long-term government bond index, and the mortgage index was deleted.[13] This model was used to see if sensitivity to different portions of the maturity spectrum was more important than including the different attributes of mortgages.

A six-index linear model, called Reg-6, was introduced to allow us to capture both the differences in maturity range and the differences in risk premiums between securities. We used both the Lehman Brothers intermediate and long-term government bond indexes to capture maturity. The Lehman Brothers intermediate corporate index, long-term corporate index, and mortgage-backed index and the Blume/Keim high-yield index were used to capture risk and option differences.[14]

The β's in all of the linear index models are estimated via regression analysis. While this optimizes the explanatory power of the models, it sometimes results in negative weights for (implied investment in) some asset categories. In the latter section of this article, after examining performance, we wish to examine our ability to infer investment policies of mutual funds. Since funds do not short sell, we would like to have a solution involving a replicating portfolio with no short sales. Sharpe (1992) has shown that such solutions can be obtained by formulating a quadratic programming problem. To find the best replicating portfolio, we solved the following quadratic programming problem for each fund, using the same indexes that we used for Reg-6:

$$\min_{\beta} \sum_{t=1}^{N} \left[(R_{it} - \bar{R}_i) - \sum_{j=1}^{6} \beta_{ij}(I_{jt} - \bar{I}_j) \right]^2 \qquad \beta_{ij} \geqslant 0, \forall j \tag{3}$$

The β_{ij}'s in equation (3) are the appropriate sensitivities or portfolio weights given that all weights are greater than zero. $\bar{R}$ and $\bar{I}$ represent sample means. We will compare this model (called QPS-6) to the regression model primarily to see if it yields similar results and thus is a reasonable model for examining correspondence between sensitivities and managers' portfolio choices. This represents our final model.

IV Overall Performance

In the prior section, we discussed the models we use to examine performance of bond mutual funds. In this section, we will apply these models to our sample. Initially, we will restrict our analysis to the 41 funds for which we have monthly data; we will end the section by examining the performance of the five funds that cease to exist early in our sample period and for which we have only annual data. Throughout this section, we present data grouped into categories as previously discussed.

A Performance and Alternative Methods of Measurement

Table 13.1 shows the difference in return between each fund and the 30-day Treasury-bill rate, between each fund and the Lehman Brothers government/corporate index, and between each fund and the single index most closely matching its investment objective as described by Morningstar. For each fund for which we had monthly data and that exited early (indicated by a dagger in the table), the returns are over the period before

Table 13.1
Mean differences (continuously compounded monthly returns in %)

		Mean difference		
CUSIP*	Number of months	Fund return—T-Bill	Fund return—government/corporate	Fund return—own index
Group 1: Government mortgage backed (LB mortgage-backed securities index):				
00168210	120	.100	−.046	−.080
35349660	120	−.023	−.169	−.203
36079910	120	.019	−.126	−.161
Group 2: High quality (LB government/corporate index):				
09787310	120	.205	.060	.060
26188010	120	.148	.003	.003
31617Q10	120	.209	.063	.063
46623610	120	.088	−.057	−.057
49344010	120	.069	−.076	−.076
62830210	120	−.009	−.155	−.155
82657010	120	.044	−.101	−.101
92203110	120	.110	−.035	−.035
Group 3: Investment grade (LB corporate index):				
31614610	120	.030	−.115	−.128
44919810	120	.115	−.030	−.043

48841210	120	.109	−.037	−.050
77957010	120	.073	−.072	−.085
81429110	120	.057	−.089	−.102
91045020	120	.134	−.012	−.025
Group 4: General (LB corporate index):				
40975210	120	.054	−.092	−.105
49344020	120	.172	.027	.013
57564010	120	.126	−.020	−.033
63762370	120	−.037	−.182	−.196
81727040	120	.059	−.086	−.099
Group 5: General with significant high yield (LB corporate index):				
02490310	120	.092	−.053	−.067
31739010	120	.101	−.045	−.058
Group 6: High yield (Blume/Keim high-yield index):				
02501010	120	.137	−.008	−.151
24661710	120	.184	.039	−.103
31419610	120	.195	.050	−.092
32057310	120	.087	−.059	−.201
48841110	120	.347	.202	.059
49344030	120	.100	−.046	−.188
54400410	120	.189	.043	−.099
57564710	120	.294	.149	.006

Table 13.1 (continued)

CUSIP*	Number of months	Mean difference: Fund return—T-Bill	Mean difference: Fund return—government/corporate	Mean difference: Fund return—own index
68379610	120	.096	−.049	−.191
74678210	120	.260	.114	−.028
92203120	120	.228	.082	−0.60
Group 7: Not listed in Morningstar (LB government/corporate index):				
01852830	120	−.061	−.207	−.207
02629810†	18	−.216	.077	.077
02630010†	107	.046	−.097	−.097
55057410†	59	−.139	−.053	−.053
57564810†	22	−.633	.074	.074
78643610†	73	−.061	−.067	−.067
Overall statistics:				
No. of positive mean differences		33	13	8
No. of negative mean differences		8	28	33
Average mean difference		.076	−.029	−.073

* CUSIP = Committee on Uniform Security Identification Procedures number.

† Indicates a fund that exited early for which we have monthly data. Returns are over the period before exit.

it exited. Positive numbers indicate the fund outperformed the index. Examining the last two columns shows the average fund underperformed the overall index or the one that most closely matched its policy. This monthly underperformance was −0.029% and −0.073%, respectively. These numbers are presented to give a historical perspective. For a meaningful analysis of the contribution of active management, we need to utilize the models developed in the prior section. Those models take account of the fact that the results shown in table 13.1 could arise because fund investment policies did not match the composition of the index in either asset mix or maturity.

Table 13.2 shows the average monthly alpha (across all funds) for each of the models discussed in the last section.[15] The average alphas across models are very similar, varying from −0.023% to −0.069%. The only model that does not account for the high-yield effect (Market-1) is a possible outlier with an alpha of −0.023%, while the range of the remaining alphas is −0.046% to −0.069%. The number of funds with negative alphas is also similar across models, varying from 27 to 33. The importance of the number of negative alphas would be overstated if the residuals from a performance model were highly correlated across funds. They are not. For example, for the six-index models, the average correlation across funds is less than 0.10. Thus, correlation among residuals cannot account for the large number of negative alphas.

If we examine average performance for each of our subgroups, we see that group performance is negative across all models except for the high-yield group. For this group, alpha is positive for Market-1 and negative for all of the other models. We consider this to be evidence of the failure of Market-1 as a measure rather than evidence of superior performance of high-yield bond fund managers.

Another way to see if the alternative models lead to the same performance conclusions is to ask if the same funds are ranked as having the manager provide value across alternative models. Thirty-one funds out of 41 have the same sign for alpha (24 negative and seven positive) across all measures. Six additional funds (five of which are high yield) have the same sign for alpha except for Market-1. Thus, once we account for the effect of high yield, we would reach the same conclusions concerning performance across measures for 37 out of 41 firms.

The rankings across funds with positive alphas are also very similar. Table 13.3 provides the rankings for those funds with positive alphas on any measure. A dagger indicates that the alpha was negative for the fund.

Table 13.2
Fund performance by groups and models: average monthly alpha (in %)

	Models					
	One-index		Three-index		Six-index	
CUSIP*	Market-1	Own-1	Risk-3	Maturity-3	Reg-6	QPS-6
Group 1: Government mortgage backed:						
00168210	−.039	−.020	−.048	−.063	−.036	−.036
35349660	−.155	−.147	−.148	−.203	−.165	−.166
36079910	−.149	−.142	−.166	−.248	−.190	−.173
Group 1 average	−.114	−.103	−.121	−.171	−.130	−.125
Group 2: High quality:						
09787310	.068	.068	.040	.045	.067	.066
26188010	.040	.040	.034	.063	.078	.063
31617Q10	.120	.120	.120	.127	.131	.134
46623610	−.084	−.084	−.077	−.041	.003	−.040
49344010	−.069	−.069	−.088	−.076	−.060	−.058
62830210	−.090	−.090	−.093	−.077	−.084	−.077
82657010	−.115	−.115	−.149	−.169	−.138	−.139
92203110	−.039	−.039	−.045	−.054	−.024	−.025
Group 2 average	−.021	−.021	−.032	−.023	−.003	−.009
Group 3: Investment grade:						
31614610	−.121	−.099	−.126	−.136	−.112	−.112
44919810	−.020	−.002	−.019	−.042	−.015	−.030
48841210	−.038	−.019	−.050	−.068	−.043	−.045

77957010	−.001	.010	.008	.037	.037	.010
81429110	−.038	−.027	−.069	−.040	−.028	−.050
91045020	−.045	−.022	−.083	−.093	−.063	−.061
Group 3 average	−.044	−.027	−.056	−.057	−.037	−.048
Group 4: General						
40975210	−.109	−.088	−.131	−.148	−.115	−.109
49344020	.072	.084	.023	.082	.082	.045
57564010	−.030	−.009	−.045	−.063	−.036	−.036
63762370	−.171	−.155	−.243	−.237	−.223	−.223
81727040	−.074	−.055	−.077	−.060	−.042	−.039
Group 4 average	−.062	−.045	−.094	−.085	−.067	−.072
Group 5: General with significant high yield:						
02490310	−.049	−.034	−.116	−.110	−.078	−.092
31739010	−.017	−.002	−.031	−.002	−.019	−.006
Group 5 average	−.033	−.018	−.073	−.056	−.030	−.049
Group 6: High yield:						
02501010	.013	−.106	−.098	−.094	−.067	−.091
24661710	.046	−.049	−.023	−.018	.020	−.009
31419610	.062	−.047	−.031	−.047	−.016	−.025
32057310	.015	−.112	−.134	−.116	−.135	−.112
48841110	.220	.114	.126	.117	.136	.125
49344030	.001	−.107	−.107	−.083	−.044	−.099
54400410	.078	−.042	−.044	−.031	−.033	−.042
57564710	.186	.079	.083	.103	.130	.087
68379610	−.032	−.158	−.153	−.163	−.149	−.159

Table 13.2 (continued)

CUSIP*	Models					
	One-index		Three-index		Six-index	
	Market-1	Own-1	Risk-3	Maturity-3	Reg-6	QPS-6
74678210	.119	−.002	.012	−.009	.021	.007
92203120	.113	.017	.030	.029	.053	.041
Group 6 average	.075	−.038	−.031	−.028	−.008	−.025
Group 7: Not listed in Morningstar:						
01852830	−.207	−.207	−.234	−.211	−.157	−.224
02629810†	−.074	−.074	−.089	−.133	−.167	−.108
02630010†	−.063	−.063	−.065	−.101	−.082	−.082
55057410†	−.042	−.042	−.071	−.091	−.113	−.106
57564810†	−.142	−.142	−.298	−.316	−.154	−.177
78643610†	−.065	−.065	−.060	−.096	−.097	−.099
Group 7 average	−.099	−.099	−.136	−.158	−.128	−.133
All groups:						
Positive alphas	14	8	9	8	12	9
Negative alphas	27	33	32	33	29	32
Average alpha	−.023	−.046	−.067	−.069	−.046	−.055
t average alpha	−.214	−1.230	−1.280	−1.115	−.900	−1.175
Average adjusted R^2	.722	.786	.803	.792	.824	.817

NOTE. *t*-values are for average alphas of the 36 surviving funds and reflect adjustment for heteroscedasticity and correlation across those funds; for all models, the average alphas of the five nonsurviving funds is more negative than the average alpha across all funds.

* CUSIP = Committee on Uniform Security Identification Procedures number.

† Indicates a fund that exited early for which we have monthly data. Returns are over the period before exit.

Table 13.3
Performance ranking by models

CUSIP*	Market-1	Own-1	Risk-3	Maturity-3	Reg-6	QPS-6
48841110	1	2	1	2	1	2
31617Q10	3	1	2	1	2	1
57564710	2	4	3	3	3	3
49344020	7	3	7	4	4	6
09787310	8	5	4	6	6	4
26188010	11	6	5	5	5	5
92203120	5	7	6	8	7	7
77957010	†	8	9	7	8	8
74678210	4	†	8	†	9	9
24661710	10	†	†	†	10	†
31739010	†	†	†	†	11	†
46623610	†	†	†	†	12	†
54400410	6	†	†	†	†	†
31419610	9	†	†	†	†	†
32057310	12	†	†	†	†	†
02501010	13	†	†	†	†	†
49344030	14	†	†	†	†	†

* CUSIP = Committee on Uniform Security Identification Procedures number.
† The alpha was negative for the fund.

Except when using the first measure (the alpha from Market-1), an investor interested in examining which managers provided the most value added would reach similar conclusions no matter which measure was used, as long as the measure contained a high-yield index.

Studies that have analyzed common stock or balanced fund returns have increasingly found that utilizing multi-index models results in very different rankings that using single-index models (see Lehmann and Modest 1987; Grinblatt and Titman 1989*b*; Connor and Korajczyk 1991; and Elton, Gruber, Das, and Hlavka 1992). Further, different multi-index models result in very different rankings. As we have just seen, single-index models that include an index for high-yield bonds and mortgages (Own-1) and various multi-index models result in virtually the same ranking for bond funds.

Finally, returning to table 13.2, we see that there is an increase in explanatory power (adjusted R^2) with any model that includes a high-yield index and a mortgage index over any model that does not. However, even the simple one-index model explains over 70% of the return variation. Also, the reader should note that imposing the added restrictions of the QPS model leads to almost no change in results.

In this section, we have shown that the implied performance of bond funds is not very sensitive to the method used to measure it. Whether one is concerned with evaluating overall performance, ranking funds, or simply selecting the best funds, one reaches similar results with any one of several reasonable models. There is evidence that funds that hold a large percentage of their assets in high-yield securities are better measured by a model that explicitly accounts for these securities.

Before turning to other uses of our models, it is worth examining the effect of exiting funds on our analysis.

B *Exiting Funds and Bias*

A number of funds ceased to exist during our sample period. Those for which we had monthly return data are shown in table 13.2 under "Not Listed" and are marked with a dagger. The average alphas are all negative, where the alphas are calculated over the period before the fund ceased to exist.[16] The average alpha for these funds using Reg-6 is −0.123%. Annualized, this is about 1.02% below the average alpha for our sample of funds that existed through the entire sample period. Table 13.4 shows annual returns for the three funds that exited early for which we have annual data but not monthly data.[17] These three funds underperformed the average fund in our sample in each year. The underperformance varied between 2.8% and 4.3% per year.[18] From the monthly and annual data, it is clear that failed funds underperform other funds.

Table 13.4
Annual returns for exiting funds (in %)

Fund ID	1979	1980	1981
0186001	−3.5	−2.2	3.6
7123001	2.8	−2.6	1.5
9001001	−1.1	...	...
Average	−.6	−2.4	2.5
All sample funds	2.7	1.9	5.3

NOTE. These funds exited early and only annual data are available.

Analyzing the total return on all funds (including those which dissolved) showed that the average fund underperformed a passive portfolio by 75–95 basis points annually.[19] The average expense ratio at the end of 1983, obtained from Wiesenberger's *Investment Companies*, for our sample funds still in existence at that time is 83 basis points, and this is a good estimate for the full 10-year sample period. Thus, the managers of funds that do not dissolve do better before transaction costs than random selection, while for the group as a whole, the performance before transaction costs is about equal to that achieved by random selection.

Most studies of mutual fund performance ignore in their analyses the part of a fund's portfolio invested in bonds. This is especially critical for those studies that include balanced funds. Unless bond returns are correlated with the indexes used for stocks, the presence of bonds will impact the fund's alpha by the difference between the return on the bond portion of the portfolio and the Treasury-bill rate times the percentage invested in bonds.[20] Table 13.1 shows that for most funds this difference is positive and on average about .076% per month for all funds and .123% per month for those that survived.

We regressed our indexes on the Standard and Poor's (S&P) 500 index, and the R^2, except for the high-yield index, ranged from .04 to .09. For the high-yield index, the R^2 was .25. Thus, studies that include balanced funds and do not include indexes that pick up the bond component produce upward-biased estimates of alphas.

V Forecasting

Up to this point, we have examined whether alternative index models tend to produce different estimates of performance. The purpose of this section is to examine whether past alphas are predictive of future alphas. To accomplish this, our 10-year sample was divided into two 5-year periods and three 3-year periods (based on the last 9 years of data). For the six models under study, alphas were computed for each subperiod. Rank correlations were calculated between the alphas computed from each model and the alphas computed for the same model in adjacent periods. The results are shown in table 13.5. The first thing to notice is that all of the rank correlations are small, and only one is statistically significant at the 2.5% level. Across the 5-year subperiods, and on average across the 3-year subperiods, the single-index model based on the government/corporate index (Market-1) produces the highest rank correlation. This is

Table 13.5
Rank correlations across adjacent time periods

	5-year subperiods	First pair 3-year subperiods	Second pair 3-year subperiods
Market-1	.234	.090	.378*
Own-1	−.111	−.046	−.037
Risk-3	.063	−.025	.059
Maturity-3	−.010	.145	.019
Reg-6	.010	.046	.074
QPS-6	−.001	−.068	.083

* Significant at the 2.5% level; the critical value at the 2.5% level (one tail) varies from .319 to .328 across the pairs of subperiods.

because the single-index model does not capture high-yield bond performance and high-yield funds had positive alphas with respect to Market-1 over much of the period. It should not be interpreted as indicating a superior index. The result we see here is similar to finding that stock funds that contain a large proportion of small stocks tend to produce consistently positive alphas using a single-index model based on the S&P index.[21]

As another test of the predictability of alpha, we examined the difference in squared forecast error from predicting alpha from each model using a fund's past alpha compared to a naive forecasting model that assumed that the future alpha was equal to the average historic alpha (across all funds) produced by that model. In all cases across all time periods, the naive model produced superior forecasts, indicating that there was no information produced by the ordering of historical alphas.

While it appears that none of the models produce useful information about future performance for funds in general, it is possible that the models produce useful information about funds that are unusually good or bad performers. To check on this, we selected the four funds with the highest alphas and the four funds with the lowest alphas (from each model) and examined how well these funds performed in the subsequent period. The results for the 5-year subperiods are shown in table 13.6. The only measures in which the best performing funds continued to outperform the worst performing funds and the average fund were those obtained from Market-1 and Maturity-3. Even here the results are not very encouraging. The magnitude of the difference is small (less than .06% per month). Also, in the case of Maturity-3, the worst performing funds

Table 13.6
Persistence in performance for extremes (average monthly alphas in second subperiod; 5-year subperiods; in %)

Model	Best four	Worst four	All funds
Market-1	.032	−.027	−.006
Own-1	−.245	−.081	−.140
Risk-3	−.046	−.023	−.080
Maturity-3	−.035	−.068	−.077
Reg-6	−.103	−.115	−.092
QPS-6	−.147	−.129	−.085

(in addition to the best performing funds) outperform the average fund. Furthermore, in the case of Market-1, even this very weak evidence of consistency is most likely due to the failure to consider relevant influences on bond returns. In addition, when 3-year subperiods were examined, there was no model where the best performing funds beat both the worst performing funds and the average fund in both of the 3-year subperiods.

All of these tests indicate strongly that, while all of the models produce broadly similar ranking of funds, none is useful in selecting funds that have higher alphas in subsequent periods.

VI Sensitivity Coefficients and Investment Policy

In this section, we will show that the historic return series for a fund can be used to infer its investment policy. The sensitivity of a fund's return to an index is determined by the proportion of the portfolio invested in the asset class represented by the index and the duration of bonds in that asset class relative to the duration of the index.[22] In equation form, this is

$$\beta_{ij} = \frac{D_{ij}}{D_j} X_{ij}, \tag{4}$$

where

β_{ij} = the sensitivity of fund i to the index used for asset class j,

D_{ij} = the duration of bonds in fund i that are classified as belonging to asset class j,

D_j = the duration of the index used for asset class j, and

X_{ij} = the proportion of bonds in fund i invested in asset class j.

End-of-year (fourth-quarter) data on fund composition for the 6 even years between 1978 and 1988 were provided by Lipper Analytical Services.[23] The data we obtained were aggregated by type (government, corporate investment grade, corporate low grade) and by maturity (1–5 years, 5–10 years, ect.).[24] The classifications used by Lipper do not directly correspond to the indexes in QPS-6 in the sense that Lipper's maturity breakdown is for the portfolio as a whole and not for each type of bond. Thus, we reestimated the QPS model using indexes that conform to Lipper's classifications. Two divisions are possible. One is by bond type, divided into governments, investment-grade corporate, and high-yield corporate (represented by the LB government and corporate indexes and the Blume/Keim high-yield index). The second is by maturity. In this case, the indexes available (the LB intermediate and long-term government/corporate indexes) split maturity between 1 and 10 years and greater than 10 years, and we can arrange Lipper data to conform to this grouping.

We ran a QPS analysis with each of the two divisions for the 34 funds in our sample for which we could obtain Lipper data. We aggregated data within Morningstar groups. Aggregating the data should cause the aggregate duration to be closer to the index duration and thus make the slope in equation (4) closer to unity. Panel A of table 13.7 shows the QPS betas and average Lipper proportions (over the 6 years) for each of the six Morningstar groups (where the betas and proportions are scaled to add to one). An examination of panel A shows a very close correspondence between QPS betas and Lipper weights, except for the government mortgage funds. The lack of correspondence for the mortgage group is likely to be due to Lipper not disaggregating governments into mortgages and nonmortgage governments over the full period. However in 1988, Lipper split government bonds into mortgages and nonmortgage governments. For the government mortgage group, we reran the QPS as a four-index model by including the LB mortgage index and compared the resulting betas to the Lipper weights shown for December 1988.[25] The results are shown in panel B of table 13.7. There is much greater correspondence between QPS weights and Lipper proportions.

Table 13.8 shows the breakdown in proportions by maturity. The correspondence between QPS weights and Lipper weights is very good except for the government mortgage and high-yield categories. For both of these categories, the QPS weights show much shorter maturities. During this period, Lipper primarily classified mortgages and high-yield debt by their nominal maturities. Given expected prepayments, the *effective* maturity for mortgages is much shorter. Given default probability

Table 13.7
Lipper and QPS proportions by bond type (in %; proportions scaled to add to 100%)

	Bond type					
	Government agency		Corporate		High yield	
Group	QPS	Lipper	QPS	Lipper	QPS	Lipper
A:						
Government mortgage backed	23.16	90.32	75.32	8.95	1.52	.73
High quality	43.72	39.30	48.92	54.62	7.36	6.08
Investment grade	24.42	30.04	68.65	66.42	6.92	3.54
General	18.89	14.43	61.74	66.36	19.36	19.21
General with significant high yield	12.56	23.84	61.37	51.82	26.07	24.34
High yield	.00	4.93	25.69	24.40	74.31	70.67

	Bond type							
	Government agency		Mortgage		Corporate		High yield	
	QPS	1988 Lipper	QPS	1988 Lipper	QPS	1988 Lipper	QPS	1988 Lipper
B. Government mortgage backed	14.03	22.55	54.54	77.45	25.97	.00	5.46	.00

Table 13.8
Lipper and QPS proportions by bond maturity (in %; proportions scaled to add to 100%)

	Bond maturity			
	1–10 years		Greater than 10 years	
Group	QPS	Lipper	QPS	Lipper
Government mortgage	80.1	23.5	19.9	76.5
High quality	32.9	37.2	67.1	62.8
Investment grade	46.1	43.5	53.9	56.5
General	40.1	34.5	59.9	65.5
General with significant high yield	21.1	33.1	78.9	66.9
High yield	59.5	25.4	40.5	74.6

and the prepayment option almost always included in high-yield debt, it is not surprising that their return behavior is also more like a shorter term instrument.

Since we do not have individual fund duration measures for each of the various investment categories, we cannot test equation (4) directly. However, since we obtained Lipper proportions for two subdivisions of each maturity investment category, we can do an approximate test of equation (4). We formed the following two ratios:

$$\frac{X_{1-5i}}{X_{ij}} \tag{5}$$

and

$$\frac{X_{11-20i}}{X_{ik}}, \tag{6}$$

where X_{1-5i} is bond fund i's Lipper weight in the 1–5-year subcategory, X_{ij} is the fund's weight in the total intermediate-term category (1–10 years), X_{11-20i} is the fund's Lipper weight in the 11-20-year subcategory, and X_{ik} is the fund's weight in the total long-term category (greater than 11 years). The larger the equation (5) or (6), the more the fund invested in shorter duration bonds and the smaller should be the relative duration measure in equation (4). Thus, we should find an inverse relationship between (5) and β_{ij} divided by X_{ij}, and between (6) and β_{ik} divided by X_{ik}. To test this, we ran Spearman's rank correlation tests. For the intermediate-term category, the resulting rank correlation coefficient was

−0.374, and for the long-term category it was −0.414, both significant at the .025 level.

In this section, we have shown that the past return series can be used to determine management's investment policy. While this is useful by itself, it should also increase the reader's confidence in the models employed in the prior analysis.

VII Large-Sample Tests

Investment Company Data, Incorporated, provided us with total monthly return data on all bond funds that existed as of December 1991. We formed two samples. The first sample consisted of all funds that had at least 2 years of data. It contained returns from each fund's inception (or first listing by ICDI), or from January 1977 if the fund existed prior to that date, until December 1991. The second sample consisted of return data for the full 5-year period from January 1987 through December 1991 for all funds that had such data. The latter sample was formed to control for any time-series pattern in alphas. We eliminated funds in the ICDI data set that were not listed by Wiesenberger as having either a "bond" or "U.S. government securities" investment policy during any year in the two sample periods (which eliminated 61 and 36, respectively), funds not open to investment by the public (which eliminated 4 and 2, respectively), funds not listed in Wiesenberger (which eliminated 8 and 4, respectively), and one duplicate fund (from the since-inception sample). This left us with 361 funds in the since-inception sample and 223 funds in the 5-year sample.[26]

In any data set, there is a possibility of inaccurate data points. To examine this, we compared the alphas for Market-1 and Reg-6 for the 33 funds that existed in both the ICDI data set and our own data set (which has been carefully screened for errors and is described in earlier sections). The average difference in alphas (ICDI minus our own) was −0.004% for Market-1 and −0.003% for Reg-6. Given ICDI's belief that the accuracy of their data improves as the data become more recent and the small differences over the earlier period in average alphas, we feel comfortable with the accuracy of the ICDI data base.

All of the empirical results in this section are reported for our two samples (since inception and 5 year) aggregately and for each of four Wiesenberger investment objective subclassifications as of December 1990, as reported in the 1991 edition of Wiesenberger's *Investment Companies*. These four subgroups are corporate bond, high-yield bond, government mortgage, and government securities.[27]

Given what we have learned from the first part of this study, we chose to explore performance in this section by employing four of our earlier models. We continue to employ Market-1 because it is the most widely used and simplest measure of performance. We learned from our earlier results that incorporating an index for high-yield bonds improved the results. Therefore, we also employ Own-1. Because of the importance of high-yield bonds and because we could not clearly see the impact of mortgage securities in our earlier sample (given that we only had three mortgage funds in that sample), we employ Risk-3 as our third model. Finally, we employ Reg-6 to examine whether term and risk premium effects are jointly important in affecting fund performance measures.

The results from applying these four models to the ICDI returns data are shown in table 13.9 for the 5-year sample and table 10 for the since-inception sample. The results are striking. No matter which model is applied to either sample, the average alphas for the overall samples (appearing in the rows labeled "All bond funds") and for each Wiesenberger subgroup are negative. Furthermore, except for Market-1, average alphas in the 5-year sample are statistically different from zero at better than a 0.01 level of significance.[28] Bond funds as a whole and subclassifications of bond funds underperform any reasonable set of passive portfolios.[29] While examining these results, keep in mind that our performance estimates are upward biased. The samples constructed from ICDI data do not contain funds that ceased to exist (due to either liquidation, merger, or change in investment policy) prior to December 1991. We know on the basis of logic and from our empirical work in an earlier section of this article that funds that cease to exist tend to have poorer performance than those that survive.

Panel A of table 13.11 shows the average annual expense ratios and average maximum annual 12b-1 fees for 209 of the funds in our 5-year sample as of December 1989.[30] The 12b-1 fees are maximum annual fees; thus, total expenses are overstated if these fees are added directly to the expense ratios. The mortgage and government securities groups had average negative performance approximately equal to their average expense ratios. The corporate bond group had average performance slightly less negative than its average expense ratio. If these three groups had actually charged the maximum 12b-1 fees, they would have underperformed our benchmark portfolios by less than the amount of total expense ratios. Thus, on average, the underperformance of our sample of bond funds is primarily due to expenses. For the funds that survived, there is some weak evidence of slight overperformance pre-expenses for these three groups.[31] The average expense ratio and average maximum 12b-1 fee for the high-yield group are higher than for the other three groups. If the maximum 12b-1 fees were charged, it could account for the much poorer performance of that group.[32]

Panel B of table 13.11 shows the results of regressing alphas on expense ratios. The coefficients of the expense ratio for all four models are close to negative one, indicting that a percentage-point increase in expenses reduces performance by about 1 percentage point. Thus, on average, an investor is better off selecting a low-expense fund. After accounting for expenses but not 12b-1 fees, the intercepts are negative but very close to zero. Expenses account for the major portion of the amount by which mutual funds underperform passive bond portfolios.[33]

Before leaving this discussion on overall performance, a few additional remarks are in order. First, examining the average betas in each of the four groups (in table 13.9 and table 13.10) shows that the weightings on the indexes strongly reflect the group membership. For example, consider the three-index model in table 13.9. For the mortgage group, the beta on the mortgage index is .62, the beta on the government/corporate index is .33, and the beta on the high-yield index is .01. For the government securities group, the beta is .95 on the government/corporate index, .10 on the mortgage index, and 0 on the high-yield index. The same reasonableness in pattern is true for the other groups and the six-index model.

In earlier sections of this article, we have shown that performance measurement was robust across models, after we accounted for high-yield bonds. We now repeat this analysis recognizing that, with the larger samples, it is also necessary to account for mortgages. (There were only three mortgage funds in our smaller sample.) Table 13.12 presents comparisons of relative performance results for the four models used in this section applied to the 5-year sample. Compare the performance classifications of Risk-3 and Reg-6. Reg-6 classifies 32 funds as having positive alphas, and Risk-3 has 28 of those same 32 funds classified as positive. In addition, seven of the top 10 are common to the two models. Thus, an investor using either model would come to similar conclusions regarding which funds are the top performers.

As shown in table 13.12, Market-1 and to a lesser extent Own-1 classify many more funds as having positive alphas than do the multi-index models. The vast majority of the funds classified as positive by Risk-3 and Reg-6 are also classified as positive by Market-1 and Own-1. Market-1 and Own-1 miss four out of 44 compared to Risk-3, and they miss five or six our of 32 compared to Reg-6. Then of the top 15 ranked funds

Table 13.9
Regression results for ICDI funds: ICDI funds from January 1987 through December 1991 (5 years)—223 funds (continuously compounded monthly excess returns)

A. Market-1 model
Return = Constant + Government/Corporate

Fund objective	Average alpha (%)	Average beta	Average adjusted R^2	No. of funds	No. of negative alphas	No. of significant alphas: Positive	No. of significant alphas: Negative
Corporate	−.033	.89	.81	49	34	2	3
High yield	−.129	.45	.08	42	31	0	1
Government mortgage	−.020	.91	.88	30	19	0	2
Government securities	−.096	.94	.87	96	68	3	35
All bond funds*	−.077	.87	.71	223	157	6	43
	(−1.245)						

B. Own-1 model
Corporate or unlisted: return = constant + government/corporate
High yield: return = constant + high yield
Government mortgage: return = constant + mortgage
Government securities: return = constant + government

Fund objective	Average alpha (%)	Average beta	Average adjusted R^2	No. of funds	No. of negative alphas	No. of significant alphas: Positive	No. of significant alphas: Negative
Corporate	−.033	.89	.81	49	34	2	3
High yield	−.160	.73	.74	42	31	0	9
Government mortgage	−.123	.96	.90	30	30	0	17
Government securities	−.081	1.05	.86	96	63	3	29
All bond funds*	−.090	.93	.84	223	163	6	60
	(−3.740)						

C. Risk-3 model

Return = Constant + Government/corporate + Mortgage + High Yield

Fund objective	Average alpha (%)	Average Beta: Government/corporate	Average Beta: Mortgage	Average Beta: High yield	Average adjusted R^2	No. of funds	No. of negative alphas	No. of significant alphas: Positive	No. of significant alphas: Negative
Corporate	−.045	.76	.10	.07	.85	49	34	2	7
High yield	−.153	−.13	.06	.74	.76	42	31	0	8
Government mortgage	−.090	.33	.62	.01	.92	30	29	0	15
Government securities	−.107	.95	.10	.00	.89	96	80	2	39
All bond funds*	−.099 (−3.859)	.61	.16	.16	.86	223	179	5	72

D. Reg-6 model

Return = constant + intermediate government + long-term government + mortgage + high yield + intermediate corporate + long-term corporate

Fund objective	Average alpha (%)	Average beta: Intermediate government	Average beta: Long-term government	Average beta: Mortgage	Average beta: High yield	Average beta: Intermediate corporate	Average beta: Long-term corporate	Average adjusted R^2	No. of funds	No. of negative alphas	No. of significant alphas: Positive	No. of significant alphas: Negative
Corporate	−.051	.24	.10	.05	.05	.26	.20	.87	49	38	1	14
High yield	−.225	−1.11	−.06	−.16	.63	1.81	−.20	.78	42	38	0	11
Government mortgage	−.098	.40	−.07	.53	.00	−.16	.28	.92	30	30	0	15
Government securities	−.089	.44	.22	.17	.01	−.03	.14	.90	96	80	2	42
All bond funds*	−.107 (−4.171)	.10	.10	.13	.13	.36	.11	.87	223	191	4	85

NOTE. Significance level for alphas is .05 (two tail). *t*-values for average alphas across all bond funds in the sample appear in parentheses and reflect adjustment for both heteroscedasticity and cross correlation of residuals.

* Figures in rows labeled "All bond funds" include funds in the Investment Company Data, Incorporated (ICDI) sample that are not classified by Wiesenberger; six funds are not classified by Wiesenberger in the 5-year sample.

Table 13.10
Regression results for ICDI funds: ICDI funds since inception or January 1977—361 funds (continuously compounded monthly excess returns)

A. Market-1 model

Return = constant + government/corporate

Fund objective	Average alpha (%)	Average beta	Average adjusted R^2	No. of funds	No. of negative alphas	No. of significant alphas	
						Positive	Negative
Corporate	−.033	.85	.82	92	60	3	10
High yield	−.053	.59	.21	54	30	0	1
Government mortgage	−.011	.77	.78	40	21	2	3
Government securities	−.095	.94	.82	162	113	6	43
All bond funds*	−.064	.84	.72	361	234	13	58

B. Own-1 model

Corporate or unlisted: Return = constant + government/corporate
High yield: return = constant + high yield
Government mortgage: return = constant + mortgage
Government securities: return = constant + government

Fund objective	Average alpha (%)	Average beta	Average adjusted R^2	No. of funds	No. of negative alphas	No. of significant alphas	
						Positive	Negative
Corporate	−.033	.85	.82	92	60	3	10
High yield	−.065	.73	.74	54	34	4	3
Government mortgage	−.104	.84	.84	40	36	1	20
Government securities	−.079	.94	.81	162	104	8	35
All bond funds*	−.069	.87	.81	361	244	18	69

C. Risk-3 model

Return = constant + government/corporate + mortgage + high yield

Fund objective	Average alpha (%)	Average beta: Government/ corporate	Average beta: Mortgage	Average beta: High yield	Average adjusted R^2	No. of funds	No. of negative alphas	No. of significant alphas: Positive	No. of significant alphas: Negative
Corporate	−.036	.77	.04	.05	.84	92	60	3	18
High yield	−.066	−.04	.05	.71	.75	54	38	2	3
Government mortgage	−.088	.19	.65	.01	.85	40	35	1	17
Government securities	−.110	.82	.14	.00	.84	162	131	3	61
All bond funds*	−.083	.60	.16	.12	.83	361	275	12	102

D. Reg-6 model

Return = constant + intermediate government + long-term government + mortgage + high yield + intermediate corporate + long-term corporate

Fund objective	Average alpha (%)	Average beta: Intermediate government	Average beta: Long-term government	Average beta: Mortgage	Average beta: High yield	Average beta: Intermediate corporate	Average beta: Long-term corporate	Average adjusted R^2	No. of funds	No. of negative alphas	No. of significant alphas: Positive	No. of significant alphas: Negative
Corporate	−.041	.27	.14	−.01	.03	.27	.14	.86	92	65	3	17
High yield	−.116	−.86	−.08	−.15	.61	1.26	.06	.78	54	41	1	11
Government mortgage	−.102	.29	−.07	.53	.00	−.01	.18	.85	40	37	1	22
Government securities	−.093	.46	.17	.16	.00	−.03	.12	.86	162	134	0	63
All bond funds*	−.101	.20	.04	.10	.08	.21	.23	.83	361	288	6	118

NOTE. Significance level for alphas is .05 (two tail).

* Figures in rows labeled "All bond funds" include funds in the Investment Company Data, Incorporated (ICDI) sample that are not classified by Wiesenberger; 13 funds are not classified by Wiesenberger in the since-inception sample.

Table 13.11
Management fees (5-year sample—209 funds)

A. Annual management fees as of December 1989 (in 1990 Wiesenberger)

Fund objective	Average expense ratio (%)	Average maximum 12b-1 fee (%)
Corporate	.882	.130
High Yield	1.147	.257
Govt. mortgage	1.062	.166
Govt. securities	1.018	.165
All bond funds	1.027	.179

B. Alpha regressed on expense ratio

Model	Average intercept (%)	t Average intercept	Average slope	t Average slope
Market-1	−.005	−.124	−.834	−.1953
Own-1	−.012	−.497	−.891	−3.063
Risk-3	−.024	−1.213	−.859	−2.952
Reg-6	−.014	−.843	−1.086	−4.160

NOTE. Only 209 of 223 funds in the 5-year Investment Company Data, Incorporated (ICDI) sample were listed by Wiesenberger in 1990. Averages are calculated from 60 monthly time-series regressions.

according to Reg-6 are also in the top 15 according to Own-1. Finally, Market-1 has nine of the top 15 according to Reg-6 also in the top 15. The similarity in ranking between Reg-6 and Risk-3 is greater than that between Reg-6 and Own-1, which is in turn greater than that between Reg-6 and Market-1.

Table 13.13 examines how well the alpha calculated over the first 3 years of the 5-year sample predicts the alpha calculated over the subsequent 2 years, and it shows significantly positive rank correlations for most of our models and subclassifications. However, Brown, Goetzmann, Ibbotson, and Ross (1992) have shown how selection bias induces a correlation between past and future performance measures, and this could explain our results. Table 13.14 shows how the best and worst performing funds did in the subsequent period, where the best or worst funds were the top or bottom 10% or five funds, which ever was larger. The higher performance of the upper tail could be explained by high-performing funds in the first subperiod that did poorly in the second subperiod not being included in the sample due to survivorship bias. However, the persistence of underperformance in the lower tail cannot

Table 13.12
Comparison of performance classification across models: number of positive and negative alphas (5-year ICDI sample)

	Joint ranking							
	Market-1		Own-1		Risk-3		Reg-6	
	Positive	Negative	Positive	Negative	Positive	Negative	Positive	Negative
Market-1:								
Positive	66							
Negative		157						
Own-1:								
Positive	55	5	60					
Negative	11	152		163				
Risk-3:								
Positive	40	4	40	4	44			
Negative	26	153	20	159		179		
Reg-6:								
Positive	26	6	27	5	28	4	32	
Negative	40	151	33	158	16	175		191

Note. Each number in the table indicates how many of the funds that are classified as positive or negative by the model in the corresponding column are classified as having the same or opposite sign by the model in the corresponding row. ICDI = Investment Company Data, Incorporated.

Table 13.13
Spearman rank correlations for ICDI alphas: 3-year subperiod 1 and 2-year subperiod 2

Group	*N*	Cutoff	Market-1 correlation	Own-1 correlation	Risk-3 correlation	Reg-6 correlation
All bond funds*	223	.132	.451	.445	.212	.403
Corporate	49	.283	−.085	−.085	.186	−.099
High yield	42	.306	.387	.449	.391	.444
Government securities	96	.201	.618	.582	.181	.401
Government mortgage	30	.362	.582	.547	.326	.297

NOTE. Cutoff is for rejecting null of zero correlation at significance level of .025 (one tail). ICDI = Investment Company Data, Incorporated.
* Figures in the row labeled "All bond funds" include the six funds not classified by Wiesenberger in the 5-year sample.

Table 13.14
5-year ICDI sample: alphas ranked in first 3-year subperiod; averages calculated in second 2-year subperiod: best and worst 10%

	Best	Worst	Average
Overall (22 and 22):			
Market-1	.024	−.384	−.068
Own-1	.034	−.371	−.091
Risk-3	−.145	−.247	−.093
Reg-6	−.011	−.428	−.117
Corporate (5 and 5):			
Market-1	−.091	−.146	−.035
Own-1	−.091	−.146	−.035
Risk-3	−.105	−.134	−.037
Reg-6	−.026	−.032	−.047
High yield (5 and 5):			
Market-1	.127	−.422	−.112
Own-1	.081	−.540	−.163
Risk-3	.034	−.452	−.102
Reg-6	−.010	−1.029	−.386
Government (10 and 10):			
Market-1	.056	−.505	−.104
Own-1	.031	−.480	−.089
Risk-3	−.292	−.256	−.136
Reg-6	.001	−.090	−.058
Mortgage (5 and 5):			
Market-1	.116	.006	.049
Own-1	.003	−.133	−.098
Risk-3	.017	−.090	−.040
Reg-6	.060	−.082	−.026

Note. ICDI = Investment Company Data, Incorporated.

be explained by survivorship bias.[34] Given the lack of persistence in our unbiased sample in the earlier sections of this article and the Brown et al. (1992) results, we must be cautious in drawing conclusions. A more detailed analysis must await a subsequent study.

VIII Conclusion

Bond mutual funds are a major investment vehicle, and yet there has been no serious analysis of their performance heretofore. This study represents the first major analysis of the performance of this important investment vehicle.

Overall and for subcategories of bond funds, we found that bond funds underperformed relevant indexes. For most models and fund subgroups, this underperformance was approximately equal to the average management fees, indicating that, pre-expenses, the surviving funds performed about on par with the indexes.

The regressions of alphas on expense ratios for the ICDI sample indicated that, on average, a percentage-point increase in expense leads to a percentage-point decrease in returns, so that investors without forecasting ability should select low-expense funds.

There appear to be fewer available bond index mutual funds than stock index mutual funds. The results in our article strongly indicate that the introduction of more bond index funds would be very useful to individual investors. Individual investors are likely to pay large bid-ask spreads for purchases of small numbers of bonds. Thus, the lack of available index funds for individual investors, coupled with the high transactions costs that accompany small purchases, might account for the past appeal of actively managed bond funds, despite substantial underperformance.

Our results were robust across a wide choice of models. In the small sample, the inclusion of the high-yield index was sufficient to result in models with similar results. In the larger samples of the previous section, it was necessary to include a separate mortgage index as well as a high-yield index. It did not affect ranking to allow for a term or corporate-risk (other than high-yield) effect. This is in contrast to the common stock area, where the choice of factors crucially affects performance.

We could find no evidence of predictability using past performance to predict future performance for our unbiased sample. When we examined this issue for the larger biased samples, we found some evidence of predictability. However, whether this is due to bias or to the larger sample sizes must await further study.

Finally, we showed that our QPS procedure produced weights on the passive portfolios that closely matched the actual fund holdings in their respective investment categories. This provides both confidence in our procedure and a method of determining management policy from the fund returns themselves.

Notes

We are grateful to Marshall Blume, Donald Keim, Interactive Data Corporation, Investment Company Data, Incorporated, Lehman Brothers, Lipper Analytical Services, Salomon Brothers, and numerous management companies for supplying data used in this study. We also thank Bill Sharpe, Bill Greene, Stephen Brown, Doug Diamond, and an anonymous referee for helpful comments and suggestions. All remaining errors are our own.

1. See, e.g., Treynor (1965), Sharpe (1966), Jensen (1968), Grinblatt and Titman (1989a), Cumby and Glenn (1990), and Elton, Gruber, Das, and Hlavka (1992).

2. The exception to this is Cornell and Green (1991), who study high-yield bond funds. While theirs is an excellent study, the authors have appropriately, given the intention of their study, restricted themselves to a small segment of the bond mutual fund population.

3. See Wiesenberger Financial Services, *Investment Companies* (1979, 1991). The above figures understate the growing importance of bonds in the mutual fund industry since those figures exclude so-called balanced funds, flexible funds, and international bond funds, which hold large percentages of bonds in their portfolios.

4. See Elton, Gruber, and Nabar (1988) and Roll and Ross (1980).

5. See Lehmann and Modest (1987) and Elton, Gruber, Das, and Hlavka (1992).

6. Four of the funds listed as having a "bond" investment objective are excluded, either because they were variable-annuity backing funds or because investment was limited to a particular group of investors; not all "specialized" funds are included, only those that involved bonds (primarily U.S. government securities).

7. Interactive Data Corporation obtains its historical mutual fund data from NASDAQ. Missing mutual fund data in the IDC databases are primarily due to NASDAQ listing requirements or to funds not reporting to NASDAQ in time for NASDAQ listing.

8. We were unable to obtain all reinvestment NAVs. When we were unable to obtain a reinvestment NAV for a distribution, we estimated the value of the distribution at the end of the month. This value was determined by compounding the actual distribution to the end of the month using an estimate of the fund's monthly return. The estimated return for the fund was determined by assuming that the distribution came at the end of the month if the distribution occurred in the last half of the month or by deducting the distribution from the prior month-end NAV if the distribution occurred in the first half of the month. The resulting estimated return was then assumed uniform over the month for the purposes of compounding the distribution to the end of the month. Also, for so-called daily accrual funds, which pay daily distributions, only "accumulation factors" representing the total accumulation from one reinvestment date to the next were available for distribution data. In a month where daily distributions had been declared and accrued but not yet reinvested or paid, we adjusted the actual month-end NAV by first calculating the average daily distribution for the accrual

period and then adding the total amount accrued since the last reinvestment data to the month-end NAV.

9. See Blume and Keim (1987) and Blume, Keim, and Patel (1991) for descriptions of the Blume/Keim high-yield index.

10. Estimating this regression is equivalent to finding the pair of weights for the index and the riskless asset that minimizes the squared difference in return between this weighted combination of the passive portfolios and the portfolio that the manager actually holds.

11. Alternatively, this model can be thought of as a multi- or four-index model where each fund is loaded on only one index. The use of the recent date was necessitated by the fact that Morningstar did not publish a description of bond mutual funds at the start of our sample. The result of taking a data outside of our sample period biases the results in favor of Market-1.

12. The Lehman Brothers government/corporate bond index does not include mortgage-backed securities.

13. The Lehman Brothers intermediate government bond index is a market-weighted index of government bonds with maturities between 1 and 10 years. The long-term index contains bonds with maturities beyond 10 years.

14. A second six-index linear model was run employing the Lehman Brothers government/corporate index instead of the long-term government index. The results were virtually the same, so we will not report them here.

15. The average alphas for this sample are not significantly different from zero, although they are for the larger samples discussed later. Standard deviations of average alphas across the 36 surviving funds were computed using the full variance/covariance matrix of the residuals in order to correct for both heteroscedasticity and cross correlations of the residuals.

16. we examined performance of other funds over these subperiods. The magnitude of the negative alphas are not due to all funds doing poorly in the subperiods.

17. Two additional funds failed almost immediately on forming. We do not have any return data for those funds.

18. The annual data assume all interest income is received at the end of the year, whereas monthly data use reinvestment rates. This could overstate the underperformance. To examine the magnitude of this effect, consider the following. The average fund in this period had approximately 10% interest income. Assuming all interest was received at the beginning of the year and using a 10% short-term rate would add 1% (10% of 10%) to the return. However, given the generally poor returns of these funds, assuming instead that interest income was reinvested into the funds (as we did for the funds with monthly data) might well result in greater underperformance.

19. These numbers were computed assuming that the funds for which we do not have any return data were similar to the three funds for which we have only annual return data. Estimates of the impact of the 10 funds that exit our sample on overall results are made by calculating average return with and without those 10 funds included in the sample. Differentials in average return are translated directly into differences in average alphas.

20. If a study has identified the correct equilibrium model for both bonds and stocks, then analyzing balanced funds does not introduce a bias.

21. See Elton, Gruber, Das, and Hlavka (1992). In table 13.5, we are implicitly assuming that residuals are uncorrelated. For the multi-index models, that is a reasonable assumption since

the average correlation between residuals is less than 0.10. Furthermore, correlated residuals would bias results in favor of finding rank correlation, and thus that cannot explain the results shown in table 13.5 for the multi-index models.

22. See Elton and Gruber (1991), pp. 557–58, for a proof.

23. For a number of firms, end-of-year composition data were missing. In those cases, we used adjacent quarters: third quarter of the prior year or first quarter of the next.

24. Lipper has finer classifications for corporate bonds.

25. We also ran the above four-index QPS over just the last 2 years in our sample period (1987 and 1988) and obtained similar results.

26. Differences between these numbers and those discussed in the introduction are due primarily to the exclusion of municipal bond funds from our sample (there were more than 500 municipal bond funds in 1990) and the exclusion of funds that do not have a minimum of 2 years of data.

27. Beginning with the 1991 edition of *Investment Companies*, Wiesenberger no longer classifies funds by investment policy; instead, the investment objective categories have been greatly expanded. We repeated all of the above analyses using Morningstar and ICDI classifications and obtained very similar results.

28. Market-1 produces nonsignificant alphas partly because it results in slightly less negative alphas but primarily because it results in very large increases in the standard error of alpha. This is not surprising since Market-1 does not fit the data (explain bond fund performance) nearly as well as the other models. We do not report t-statistics for the since-inception sample. The problem with that sample is that the length of data (the time series) varies across funds. Normal corrections for heteroscedasticity and cross correlation require the same time series for each fund. We tried several approximations to the normal tests by utilizing estimates of the correlations of residuals, variances of residuals, and means and variances of the independent variables from the time-series data that were available. All approximations resulted in standard errors for alpha that were very similar to those found in the 5-year sample. Since the average alphas are basically the same in both samples, the t-values are essentially unchanged in the 5-year and since-inception samples.

29. The fund returns are after expenses and management fees, while index returns are not. The Vanguard Bond Market Fund (a bond index fund) reports total fees of 16 basis points in their 1992 prospectus. On a monthly basis, this is a little over 1 basis point. Thus, even after adjusting for fees, active funds significantly underperform indexes.

30. Elton, Gruber, Das, and Hlavka (1992) have shown that relative expense ratios are fairly constant across funds (funds with higher expense ratios in one year tend to have the higher ratios in subsequent years). Also, any linear time trend would be mitigated by using the middle year in a sample period. Thus, we believe 1989 expense ratios provide good expense measures for our 5-year sample.

31. In an earlier section, we found that 10 of 46 funds failed in a 10-year period. A conservative estimate of the effect of failure is to assume that only half would fail in a 5-year period. Failed funds had an average alpha about .204 less than the surviving funds. Including failed funds should lower average alphas by about 5/46 of .204, or about 27 basis points per year. Including failed funds means that average performance was approximately equal to or slightly worse than expenses for the above three groups.

32. To make sure the performance of the high-yield group was not a function of the index we selected, the tests were rerun using the Salomon Brothers long-term high-yield index in place of the Blume/Keim index. The results were virtually unchanged.

33. Note in table 13.11, panel B, that the intercepts are not significantly different from zero while the slope coefficients are all significantly different from zero at the 1% level, except for the slope for Market-1 (which is almost significant at the 5% level). The statistical results reported in this table were derived using a series of monthly cross-sectional regressions, similar to the methodology employed by Fama and MacBeth (1973). The relationship between alphas and expenses was also examined using ordinary least squares and weighted least squares. The regression coefficients were substantially unchanged, but the t-values of the slope coefficients were larger negative numbers under either alternative methodology. We also ran the regression including maximum 12b-1 fees. The slopes are flatter when those 12b-1 fees are added to expense ratios, while the intercepts are lower. This is probably due to the fact that those 12b-1 fees maximums that are not always charged.

34. It might be due to either funds with higher fees not performing significantly better or worse (before fees) than funds with low fees or bad managers continuing to remain bad managers.

References

Blume, M. E., and Keim, D. B. 1987. Lower grade bonds: Their risks and returns. *Financial Analysts Review* (July–August), pp. 26–33.

Blume, M. E.; Keim, D. B.; and Patel, S. A. 1991. Returns and volatility of low-grade bonds, 1977–1989. *Journal of Finance* 46, no. 1 (March): 49–74.

Brown, S.; Goetzmann, W.; Ibbotson, R.; and Ross, S. 1992. Survivorship bias in performance studies. *Review of Financial Studies* 5, no. 4:553–80.

Connor, G., and Korajczyk, R. A. 1991. The attributes, behavior, and performance of U.S. mutual funds. *Review of Quantitative Finance and Accounting* 1:5–26.

Cornell, B., and Green, K. 1991. The investment performance of low-grade bond funds. *Journal of Finance* 46, no. 1 (March): 29–48.

Cumby, R. E., and Glen, J. D. 1990. Evaluating the performance of international mutual funds. *Journal of Finance* 45, no. 2 (June): 497–521.

Elton, E. J.; and Gruber, M. J. 1991. *Modern Portfolio Theory and Investment Analysis.* 4th ed. New York: John Wiley & Sons.

Elton, E. J., Gruber, M. J.; Das, S.; and Hlavka, M. 1992, in press. Efficiency with costly information: A reinterpretation of evidence from managed portfolios. *Review of Financial Studies.*

Elton, E. J.; Gruber, M. J.; and Nabar, P. 1988. Bond returns, immunization, and the return-generating process. In M. Sarnat and G. Szego (eds.), *Studies in Banking and Finance, Essays in Memory of Irvin Friend.* New York: North Holland.

Fama, E., and MacBeth, J. 1973. Risk, return, and equilibrium: Empirical tests. *Journal of Political Economy* 71 (May/June): 607–36.

Grinblatt, M., and Titman, S. 1989a. Mutual fund performance: An analysis of quarterly portfolio holdings. *Journal of Business* 62, no. 3:393–416.

Grinblatt, M., and Titman, S. 1989*b*. Portfolio performance evaluation: Old issues and new insights. *Review of Financial Studies* 2:393–421.

Jensen, M. 1968. The performance of mutual funds in the period 1945–1964. *Journal of Finance* 23, no. 2 (May): 389–416.

Lehmann, B. N., and Modest, D. 1987. Mutual fund performance evaluation: A comparison of benchmarks and benchmark comparisons. *Journal of Finance* 42, no. 2 (June): 233–65.

Lipper Analytical Securities Corporation. 1978–1988. *Lipper—Portfolio Analysis Report on Fixed Income Funds*. New York: Lipper Analytical Services, Inc.

Morningstar, Inc. 1989. *Mutual Fund Sourcebook, Winter 1989*. Chicago: Morningstar, Inc.

Roll, R., and Ross, S. 1980. An empirical investigation of the arbitrage pricing theory. *Journal of Finance* 35, no. 5 (December): 1073–1103.

Sharpe, W. F. 1966. Mutual fund performance. *Journal of Business* 39, no. 1 (January): 119–38.

Sharpe, W. F. 1992. Asset allocation, management style, and performance measurement. *Journal of Portfolio Management* (Winter), pp. 7–19.

Treynor, J. 1965. How to rate management investment funds. *Harvard Business Review* 44. no. 1 (January/February): 63–75.

Wiesenberger Financial Service. 1979–1991. *Investment Companies*. Boston: Warren Gorham & Lamont, Inc.

14 Fundamental Economic Variables, Expected Returns, and Bond Fund Performance

Edwin J. Elton, Martin J. Gruber, and Christopher R. Blake

One of the major research topics in the recent literature of financial economics is the estimation and testing of relative pricing models. The purpose of this study is to develop and test relative pricing models for bonds utilizing a variety of different types of bonds. This study is important for several reasons. First, despite the economic importance of bond markets, very little attention (compared to that paid to common stocks) has been paid to relative bond pricing models. Second, recent developments in the methodology of the testing of relative pricing models (based on the Arbitrage Pricing Theory (APT) of Ross (1976)) have yet to be applied to the pricing of bonds. Third, this study is important because it uses fundamental economic variables as well as return indexes to explain both returns and expected returns on bonds. While the inclusion of fundamental variables along with return indexes has been used to explain relative prices for common stocks (see Chen, Roll, and Ross (1986) and Burmeister and McElroy (1988)), the importance of the variables has not been demonstrated for bonds. Fourth, this study is important because it is the first study to employ forecasts prepared by economists and investment professionals to measure unexpected changes in the fundamental economic influences that affect returns. Finally, this study is important because it is the first time relative pricing models parameterized on passive portfolios have been used to examine the performance of actively managed bond portfolios. This will both give us additional evidence on the performance of the models on a separate sample of returns and insight into the contribution of active management.

Bonds are an important asset category, having an aggregate market value many times that of equities. In 1992, the Federal Reserve estimated that U.S. bond markets had an aggregate value of $9.1 trillion for publicly traded issues. This was almost twice the aggregate value of the stock market. Adding nonpublicly traded issues would make this difference even larger.

There have been tests of equilibrium models based on bond data. However, the tests have either been restricted to government bonds or have utilized a very limited set of bond portfolios in conjunction with a much larger set of stock portfolios. The principal type of test of equilibrium models derived for the bond market involves estimating the parameters of a variant of the Cox, Ingersoll, and Ross (CIR) (1981) model (see Brown and Dybvig (1986), Pearson and Sun (1994), Longstaff and Schwartz (1992), and Gibbons and Ramaswamy (1993)). Tests of variants of the CIR model only utilize Treasury securities and involve estimating properties of the term structure of Treasury securities. Parameters to capture risk differentials of nonTreasury instruments have not been included in published models to date. The structure and testing of the CIR model are very different from the structure and types of tests that have been performed on relative pricing models for common stocks.[1] Tests of relative pricing models using stock return data have been two-pass (time-series and cross-sectional) tests popularized by Fama and MacBeth (1973) (e.g., Fama and French (1992)) or joint-estimation (constrained time-series) tests (e.g., Gibbons (1982), Stambaugh (1982), Burmeister and McElroy (1987 and 1988), Gibbons *et al.* (1989), Snow (1991), and Bansal and Viswanathan (1993)).

To the extent that these types of tests have been applied to bond data, the tests have been primarily limited to Treasury bonds. The reasons for this are the dearth of bond return data on non-Treasury instruments and the inability to use time-series data to estimate sensitivities because of the changing risk characteristics of most bonds as maturity changes. To get around the second difficulty, most researchers have used return data on pure-discount Treasury instruments that allow both maturity and duration to remain constant over time. Relative pricing models have been tested using data on Treasury bills with short maturities (see Fama and Bliss (1987) and Stambaugh (1988)). Similarly, Elton, Gruber, and Mei (1993) have tested a relative pricing model using McCulloch (1990) estimates of the prices of pure-discount instruments for longer maturities. Finally, the few researchers who have not limited their analyses to Treasury instruments have utilized a few bond portfolios in conjunction with a much larger set of stock portfolios (Fama and French (1992) and Gibbons (1986)).

In this study we fit a relative pricing model for bonds using test methodology developed in the common stock area and employing a large set of bond portfolios. Our basic data are the returns on a set of indices (portfolios) of Treasury, corporate, and mortgage securities compiled by

Lehman Brothers, Merrill Lynch, and Ibbotson and Associates.[2] These indexes are calculated in a manner exactly parallel to the way the Center for Research in Security Prices (CRSP) stock indexes are calculated. The treatment of interest paid during a month is identical to the way dividends paid are treated by CRSP, and the prices used are the prices an investor would pay for purchasing a debt security (quoted price plus accrued interest).

Our technique for estimating a relative pricing model is constrained time-series regression. This technique has been popularized in a series of articles by Burmeister and McElroy and others. Its main advantage is that betas and relative prices are simultaneously estimated so that estimated parameters of the relative pricing model are not affected by estimation error in the estimated sensitivities as in the two-pass (Fama and MacBeth) procedure.

In constructing relative pricing models, we have a choice as to how factors are obtained. In the stock area, three methods have been used. Several authors (e.g., Roll and Ross (1980)) have employed factor analysis to develop underlying variables; several have used portfolios to represent hypothesized underlying influences (e.g., Fama and French (1992)); and several have used unexpected changes in hypothesized economic variables to represent the factors (e.g., Chen, Roll, and Ross (1986)).[3] The advantage of using the last approach is that it relates returns to fundamental influences in the economy rather than to other returns (which are themselves driven by economic influences). In this paper we not only employ a combination of returns on a set of portfolios that have been shown to affect bond returns, but we also employ unexpected changes in some economic variables to see if they add additional explanatory power. In our study we examine the ability of our model not only to explain the time series of returns, but also cross sectional differences in average returns. Because we examine cross sectional differences, we can determine whether the influences we hypothesize are priced by the market.

Two of the three methods that were used in the stock area to develop the factors driving returns have been employed in studying fixed-income returns. Gutelkin and Rogalski (1985), Litterman and Scheinkman (1991), and Knez, Litterman and Scheinkman (1994) use factor analysis to identify a set of indices to explain the time series behavior of the return on debt instruments. In addition, Litterman and Scheinkman form mimicking portfolios for their factors and examine how well linear combinations of these mimicking portfolios seem to be associated with a set of hypothesized economic influences.[4] The second approach is used by Blake, Elton, and

Gruber (1993), who employ portfolios of debt instruments to explain the behavior of mutual funds over time. None of these studies (nor to the best of our knowledge, other studies) examines whether adding unexpected changes in economic variables to the types of factors (portfolios) described above produces a model that has greater ability to explain the time series behavior of bond returns. None of these articles examines the ability of the models tested to explain relative prices in an APT sense (the cross-sectional behavior of returns on alternative bonds), and thus none can supply information on whether any of the influences in the model are priced. That is, none of these studies tells us whether the investor requires a higher (or lower) return for taking on some of the systematic variability associated with a factor. While there are papers that accomplish these goals in the stock area, this is the first article to do so in the bond area.

Like many current APT models, our models use unanticipated changes in economic variables to explain, in part, expected return. However, unlike others who estimate unanticipated changes in economic variables from time-series analysis, we utilize publicly available forecasts to measure unexpected changes in expectations. Changes in expectations have been shown to be the driving force in security prices (see Elton, Gruber, and Gultekin (1981)). Using expectational data directly has the dual advantage of focusing on the variable that directly affects returns and allowing us to easily define "unexpected changes."

After developing and parameterizing relative-pricing models on bond indexes, we apply the models with these parameters to analyze the performance of a sample of bond mutual funds with data over a different time period. We find that the model with out-of-sample parameters is useful in evaluating bond mutual fund behavior. Bond mutual funds have realized returns below our models' estimates of expected returns. This underperformance is about equal to transaction costs. These results provide additional support for our models, as they are consistent with previously published results that did not involve equilibrium models (see Blake, Elton, and Gruber (1993)). In addition, we find that the discrepancies in performance among different styles of managers disappear when we correctly account for economic variables.

The article is divided into four sections. In the first section, we discuss our general methodology, the sample, and the variables we use. In the second section, we present the alternative forms of the models we test, and present the estimation and tests of the models. In the third section we apply the models developed in the second section to the examination of the performance of bond mutual funds. The last section contains our conclusions.

I Model Specifications

In this section of the article we will develop a plausible set of models to see how well they explain both the time series of returns and expected returns. The financial economics literature gives us some guidance as to the set of variables that might enter into these models and explain expected returns. Previous studies (e.g., Chen, Roll, and Ross (1986) and McElroy, Burmeister, and Wall (1986)) have shown that both the time series of individual returns and the cross section of expected returns used in common-stock studies are explained by:

1. market returns (the excess return on the stock market)
2. default risk (the difference in return between corporate bonds and government bonds)
3. term risk (the difference in returns between long-term and short-term government bonds)
4. unexpected changes in inflation
5. unexpected changes in a measure of economic performance.

It has been shown that these variables are significant in explaining expected and actual equity returns. Therefore, they should be important in explaining bond returns. The first variable, the excess return (net of the riskless rate) on the stock market, can be viewed as a measure of expectations about general economic conditions. Our second variable is a measure of default risk. Default risk should affect corporate bond returns. Several authors (e.g., Brennan and Schwartz (1983) and Nelson and Schaefer (1983)) have used a form of our third variable, a term premium, in constructing models of interest rates and bond prices. Our fourth and fifth variables are measures of macro-economic influences. Changes in both of these variables should affect the level of interest rates (and hence bond returns) and could affect the certainty of cash flows on different types of bonds (e.g., corporate bonds and mortgage debt). Evidence to support this is found in Ederington and Lee (1993), who show that similar variables impact Treasury bill futures prices and, hence, short-term interest rates.[5] We examine two additional variables. The first is simply an index of aggregate bond returns. If one were looking for the single factor that best explains individual bond returns, the single variable that would probably do the best job is a market index of bond returns. This is analogous to a market index for stock returns being the single index that best explains the performance of individual stocks. The aggregate index should also be included because it serves as the benchmark against which to measure the importance of other indices. We also add one more index, a measure of the return on mortgage securities relative to the return on government bonds. This index is added because options are an important element in bond returns. Mortgages are chosen to represent this influence because of the importance of the option effects on mortgage returns. In the remainder of this section, we discuss a more exact formulation of our variables, the sample to be used in our empirical work, and our statistical methodology.

A *Measuring The Variables*

One of the innovations of this study is the use of survey data on expectations to measure unanticipated changes in expectations. Previous studies such as Chen, Roll, and Ross (1986) and Burmeister, Wall, and Hamilton (1986), have used changes in realizations of economic variables or differences between realizations and historical extrapolation of past data to measure unexpected changes. In another context, we have shown that expectations determine (are captured in) prices and that changes in expectations represent unexpected influences. Treating changes as unexpected is consistent with a rational expectations view of economic decision-making and is consistent with a large body of empirical evidence.[6] We use changes in expectations about an economic variable as a measure of unexpected changes in that variable. The use of survey data has the advantage of focusing directly on expectations rather than depending on an unspecified link between the measure used and expectations as justification for the measure.[7]

Our models of expected return utilize two fundamental expectational variables. The first fundamental expectational variable is a measure of unanticipated changes in inflation. The variable is based on monthly data provided by the Survey Research Center of the University of Michigan. The data are obtained by surveying consumers on inflation over the next year. We use the coincident change in the forecast as our first fundamental expectational variable.

The other fundamental expectational variable we utilize is a measure of general economic conditions. This variable is the unexpected change in the forecast of real Gross National Product (GNP) (nominal GNP with inflation removed). The variable is derived from monthly forecasts of nominal GNP growth rates provided by Eggert Enterprises.[8] The Eggert data are based on a survey of professional forecasters from financial intermediaries, companies, and brokerage firms, as well as on output from major econometric models. We regressed the coincident change in this series on our inflation variable and used the residuals with the sample mean added back (to leave the mean of the variable unchanged under the orthogonality transformation) as our second fundamental expectational variable.

Consistent with other studies, we use return series to measure default risk, term risk, and stock market return. The default-risk variable is the difference in return between the Blume/Keim (B/K) high-yield series and the Lehman Brothers (LB) intermediate government index. We chose this government return series because the coefficient in a regression between the returns on the B/K high-yield series and LB intermediate government series was close to one. This ensures that differences in the return between the two series are due to default risk rather than term structure risk. The term-risk variable is the difference in return between the Ibbotson and Associates long-term government bond index and their intermediate bond index. For the stock market variable, we use the return on the S&P 500 index with dividends as reported by Ibbotson and Associates. As mentioned earlier, we also use a mortgage return series to capture option elements in bond returns and an index of aggregate bond returns. The option series is the difference in return between the Lehman Brothers Government National Mortgage Association (GNMA) index and a government bond series with the same duration.[9] The aggregate return series we use is the return on a modified Lehman Brothers aggregate bond index. The modified aggregate index was created by combining the LB aggregate bond index with the Blume/Keim high-yield series to obtain a return series encompassing all bonds in the marketplace. The weights used in developing the index represent relative par value weights at the middle of each year. Monthly weights are approximated by linear interpolation of the annual weights. The modified Lehman Brothers aggregate series is used both to measure the impact of general bond returns and as a proxy for omitted variables.

B Sample

Throughout most of this study we employ publicly available bond return indices (passive bond portfolios) as the independent variables utilized in fitting the equilibrium models. The Appendix lists the bond indices used.

These include indexes of government bonds, corporate bonds, and mortgages. One of the advantages of using indices is that their durations remain fairly constant over time, unlike durations for individual bonds. We would have liked to use high-yield indices also, but a sufficient number of these indices were not available.[10] The sample period covers February 1980 through December 1992 (155 monthly observations).

We obtained data from three sources (Merrill Lynch, Lehman Brothers, and Ibbotson and Associates). The Ibbotson indices are return indices constructed from the return on a small number of bonds of a particular maturity. The basic price data for these indices comes from Salomon Brothers, and the composition of the indexes changes frequently to maintain an approximately constant maturity. The Merrill, Lynch, and Lehman indexes are comprehensive return indices covering a subset of all bonds that have certain characteristics (e.g., 1- to 3-year governments). Within each category, only the return on actively traded bonds is calculated from market prices. Returns on inactive bonds are calculated in each index as a function of the active bond prices. The net effect is a return series of actively traded bonds, but the portfolio return is computed not by using the weight of each of the actively traded bonds in the category, but rather the weight that bonds with the same characteristics as the actively traded bond represent of the population. In calculating return, both the Merrill and Lehman indices correctly incorporate accrued interest. The Lehman indices assume reinvestment of coupon income in the index at the end of the month. This is the same assumption made in calculating returns in the CRSP monthly stock files. Thus, the return calculations for the Lehman indices are exactly the same as the return calculations for the CRSP size indices that are widely used in testing equity asset pricing models. The Merrill indices assume coupons are reinvested in the index at the time of the disbursement of the interest. These indices are comparable to portfolios constructed from the CRSP daily stock files.

In the next section and the final section we utilize samples of bond funds. The data were supplied by Investment Company Data, Inc. (ICDI) and consist of the full history of monthly returns of all funds that existed as of December 1991. The sample obviously has survivorship bias. The impact of this will be discussed in a later section. In evaluating funds, we utilize data beginning in January 1986. This six-year period involved a tradeoff. We obviously would like a long history, to be more confident in the overall results, and to make comparisons across subperiods. However, the number of bond funds grew dramatically in the 80s. Thus, each year we go back decreases the sample size considerably. The six-year period selected is a compromise between a large sample and a long history.

In the rest of the analysis we use three different samples of the returns on bond portfolios. The first is a sample of 20 bond indices that are used as passive portfolios. The second sample is a group of 36 bond funds stratified into three sub-groups (12 corporates, 12 governments, and 12 mortgages), which are used to examine alternative choices of variables. Our final sample is 123 bond mutual funds that are used to examine the performance of actively traded bond portfolios.

We now examine the general methodology used to estimate relative pricing models.

C *Methodology of Model Specifics*

We hypothesize, in the tradition of Chen, Roll, and Ross (1986), that returns are generated by a mixture of tradeable portfolios and fundamental economic factors. In general, we can write the return generating process as

$$r_{it} = \mathrm{E}[r_i] + \sum_{j=1}^{J} \beta_{ij}(R_{jt} - \mathrm{E}[R_j]) + \sum_{k=1}^{K} \gamma_{ik} g_{kt} + \eta_{it} \tag{1}$$

where

1. r_{it} is the return on asset i at time t $(i = 1, \ldots, N)$;
2. R_{jt} is the return on tradeable portfolio j at time t;
3. g_{kt} is the unexpected change in the kth fundamental variable at time t;
4. β_{ij} is the sensitivity of asset i to the innovation of the jth tradeable portfolio;
5. γ_{ik} is the sensitivity of asset i to the innovation of the kth fundamental variable;
6. η_{it} is the time-t return of asset i that is unrelated to either tradeable portfolios or fundamental variables;
7. $\mathrm{E}[\cdot]$ denotes expectation;
8. $\mathrm{E}[g_k] = \mathrm{E}[\eta_i] = 0$.

Note that g_k represents unexpected changes in a fundamental economic variable, and, since the expected value of an unexpected change is by definition zero, $\mathrm{E}[g_k] = 0$.

From the Arbitrage Pricing Theory (APT) of Ross (1976), equation (1) leads to the following expression for the expected return of asset i:[11]

$$E[r_i] = \lambda_0 + \sum_{j=1}^{J} \beta_{ij}\lambda_j^* + \sum_{k=1}^{K} \gamma_{ik}\lambda_k \tag{2}$$

where

1. λ_0 is the return on the riskless asset (R_F) if it exists. (We will assume it does.)
2. λ_j^* is the market price of sensitivity to the jth tradeable portfolio;
3. λ_k is the market price of sensitivity to the kth fundamental variable.

When variables in the return-generating process are tradeable portfolios, the APT market price of risk associated with such a portfolio is the portfolio's expected return minus λ_0. Thus, $\lambda_j^* = E[R_j] - \lambda_0$ for $j = 1, \ldots, J$. Substituting this expression into equation (2) and recognizing that $\lambda_0 = R_F$ yields:

$$E[r_i] = R_F + \sum_{j=1}^{J} \beta_{ij}(E[R_j] - R_F) + \sum_{k=1}^{K} \gamma_{ik}\lambda_k \tag{3}$$

Substituting equation (3) into equation (1) and allowing R_F to vary over time yields:

$$r_{it} - R_{Ft} = \sum_{j=1}^{J} \beta_{ij}(R_{jt} - R_{Ft}) + \sum_{k=1}^{K} \gamma_{ik}(\lambda_k + g_{kt}) + \eta_{it} \tag{4}$$

Rearranging equation (4) yields:

$$r_{it} - R_{Ft} = \alpha_i + \sum_{j=1}^{J} \beta_{ij}(R_{jt} - R_{Ft}) + \sum_{k=1}^{K} \gamma_{ik}g_{kt} + \eta_{it} \tag{5}$$

where

$$\alpha_i = \sum_{k=1}^{K} \gamma_{ik}\lambda_k \tag{6}$$

This structure allows us to test the performance of any APT model.[12] Equation (6) will fail if we have misspecified the return-generating process or the APT does not hold. Thus, our tests are joint tests of the return-generating process and APT.

First, equation (5) can be estimated. Second, it can be estimated with restriction (6) imposed. Imposing (6) and comparing the results with the unconstrained equation (5) allows us to test whether imposing the APT restriction on a multi-factor model results in a statistically significant decrease in explanatory power. The constrained-form equation (4) can be estimated using iterated non-linear seemingly unrelated regressions (ITNLSUR) (see Gallant (1987)).

In the next section of this article we will employ this methodology to test descriptions of relative pricing models for bonds. Before doing so, we will use canonical correlation both to find out more about the structure of bond returns and to examine which of our variables are related to bond returns.

II Empirical Results

A number of the variables we analyze have been used primarily in common-stock studies. Thus, before performing tests of index and relative pricing models, it is useful to get an idea of how much of the movement in bond returns is picked up by the seven explanatory variables considered. To do this, we formed a stratified sample of mutual funds. From our full sample of 123 bond funds, we select 12 funds that are classified by ICDI as government bond funds, 12 that are classified as corporate bond funds, and 12 that are classified as government mortgage funds. The funds are also selected to span the full spectrum of maturity ranges contained in our sample. For each bond fund we add expenses incurred to the monthly return series. This should approximate the return on a set of passive bond funds.[13]

The matrix of excess returns (the fund returns minus the 30-day T-bill rate from Ibbotson and Associates) on the sample (6 years of monthly returns for each of the 36 funds) was correlated with the set of explanatory variables under study. Canonical correlation is used to examine the relationship between fund returns and the seven variables under study (an aggregate bond return index, an aggregate stock index, indices representing default, term, and option effects, and two observable expectational variables). Canonical correlation determines the linear combination of the seven variables and the linear combination of the 36 funds that are most highly correlated. It then determines the second linear combinations of the seven variables and the 36 funds that are most highly correlated, given that the effect of the first canonical correlate has been removed. The process continues until a number of linear combinations equal to the smaller of the number of funds or the number of variables has been found (in this case, seven). The *F*-test can be used to determine the number of correlations that are significantly different from zero. Only the first three linear combinations of the seven variables under examination are significantly different from zero at the 5 percent level. They are able to account for 89 percent of the variance in the fund return series. The variable measuring term spread does not appear to play an important role in the first three canonical variates. Consequently, the canonical correlation analysis was repeated, deleting the term-spread variable from the list of seven variables. When the analysis is done with six variables, once again, only three canonical combinations (this time of the six variables) show up as statistically significant at the 5 percent level. In addition, the proportion of the variance explained by the first three variates is unchanged. Because of this, subsequent analysis is restricted to a study of six variables: an aggregate bond index, an index of stock returns, a default index, an option index, a series of unexpected changes in real GNP growth, and a series of unexpected changes in inflation. A possible explanation for the term variable not having explanatory power is that its influence may in fact be captured by two other variables. The aggregate bond index minus the risk-free rate is in part a measure of the term premium. Likewise, it has been shown that the excess return on the S&P index is related to the term premium (see Fama and French (1992), and Chen, Roll, and Ross (1986)). Thus, term premium effects could have been captured by the other two variables.

Having selected the set of variables of interest, we investigate the performance of a model containing the six variables. We also investigate three models containing logical subsets of the six variables. By doing so we can judge the impact of including different types of variables on our ability to explain returns and expected returns. The four models we investigate are:[14]

1. A single-index model based on an aggregate bond index (index-1).

2. A four-index model employing not only an aggregate bond index, but also an aggregate stock index and two indices representing default and option effects (index-4).

3. A four-index model that, in addition to an aggregate index of bond returns and an aggregate index of stock returns, incorporates unexpected changes in macro-economic measures of inflation and real GNP (fundamental-4).

4. A six-index model that incorporates all the influences contained in the second and third models (fundamental-6).

In all of the models, we treat expectational variables (unexpected changes in macro-economic measures of inflation and economic growth) as observable variables. These are denoted by g_{kt} in equation (5). We treat the return series for aggregate bonds, stocks, default risk, and option risk as proxies for unobservable variables. These are denoted by R_{jt} in equation (5). The first model (index-1), relating returns to an aggregated bond index, is included because it is the simplest model and because it is analogous to the single-index model most often used to examine stock returns. Index-1 is a naive model. A more complex model must at the very least, outperform the single-index model to be considered for further use. Index-4 contains two aggregate return indices for stocks and bonds, plus two return indices for subsets of bond returns to capture default and option effects. The idea is to see if the inclusion of a stock index plus default and option indices leads to better results. The fundamental-4 and fundamental-6 models incorporate the two fundamental expectational variables.[15] The third model adds these two influences to the return index for bonds and the return index for stocks to see if the fundamental variables improve performance more than adding additional bond indices. The fourth model adds the fundamental indices to the four-variable return model to see if expectational data capture influences not captured by our set of return data. Tests in the remainder of this section are performed on the sample of 20 bond indices (passive portfolios) discussed in section I.*B*.

The time over which we fit the model involves a trade-off between wanting a long-term period to estimate the relative pricing models and losing additional bond portfolios. Both Merrill Lynch and Lehman introduced additional indices over time. We chose to go back to a point in time where we had twenty indices. Incorporating any earlier years would have involved a serious decrease in the number of indices that were available. (Eight of the twenty indices we employ were started in February 1980.) Our time frame for the APT tests is from February 1980 to December 1992. The first test we perform for each of the models is to test whether the cross-sectional (APT) restrictions can be rejected. This is equivalent to asking whether imposing the APT cross-sectional restrictions (6) on equation (5) results in an estimation of the residuals from the model that is inferior at a statistically significant level from that produced by equation (5) with no restrictions. To do this, we employ a test methodology described in Gallant (1987). Our tests utilize the following likelihood-ratio test statistic, recommended by Gallant for maximum-likelihood estimators:

$$L = n(\ln|\tilde{\Sigma}| - \ln|\hat{\Sigma}|) \tag{7}$$

where n is the number of time-series observations (155), $\tilde{\Sigma}$ is the estimate of the variance-covariance matrix of the residual errors from the restricted equation (4), and $\hat{\Sigma}$ is the estimate of the variance-covariance matrix of the residual errors from the unrestricted equation (5). L is asymptotically distributed as chi-squared with q degrees of freedom, where q is the number of parametric restrictions. For small samples, Gallant (1987) recommends the use of the F distribution with degree-of-freedom corrections instead of the chi-squared distribution. The small-sample adjustment is simply to compare L to qF_α, where F_α is the F statistic at significance level α with q numerator degrees of freedom and $nM - p$ denominator degrees of freedom, and where M is the number of equations estimated (20) and p is the number of parameters. If L is greater than qF_α, then the null hypothesis that the restrictions hold is rejected.

When we perform this test, we find that the APT restrictions cannot be rejected at the 5 percent level for any of the four models under study.[16] Since we can not reject the cross-sectional restrictions for any model, it is appropriate to continue to study and to compare the *APT-restricted* form of the four models. Comparisons can be made between several pairings of the four models because some models are nested within others. For example, the index-1 model can be viewed as the index-4 model with the added constraints that the sensitivities of returns to the S&P return, the default index, and the option index are all equal to zero. Similarly, pairwise comparisons can be made between all other combinations of the models except between index-4 and fundamental-4 (because they cannot be nested). In all other cases (shown in Table 14.1), the model that contains fewer variables can be considered a constrained form of the model with more variables, and the constraints (betas on additional indexes equal to zero) can be tested by a variation of the method described in the preceding paragraph. As an illustration, return to the comparison of the models index-1 and index-4. Recall that we are testing these models with expected return equal to the historical average. Thus, the index-4 model contains eighty parameters to estimate while the index-1 model constrains sixty of these parameters to be zero. The null hypothesis is that the sixty parameters are zero and rejection of the null implies that the index-4 model was significantly better at the 5 percent level in explaining returns.

Table 14.1
Likelihood ratio test statistics

Pairwise test (involves APT-restricted models only)

Models	L^a	p^b	q^c	$qF_{0.05}$	$L - qF_{0.05}$	Reject null?
Fundamental-4 vs. fundamental-6	519.36	122	40	55.92	463.43	yes
Index-4 vs. fundamental-6	68.54	122	42	58.30	10.24	yes
Index-1 vs. fundamental-6	659.54	122	102	127.14	532.53	yes
Index-1 vs. fundamental-4	140.30	82	62	81.67	58.64	yes
Index-1 vs. index-4	591.12	80	60	79.36	511.77	yes

a. $L = n(\ln|\tilde{\Sigma}| - \ln|\hat{\Sigma}|)$, where $\tilde{\Sigma}$ is the variance-covariance matrix of restricted residuals and $\hat{\Sigma}$ is the variance-covariance matrix of unrestricted residuals.
b. p = total number of estimated parameters.
c. q = number of restrictions.
All models are in APT-constrained form (equation (4) in the text), and, for each pair of models shown below, the model that contains fewer variables is a restricted form of the other model. The number in each model's name (e.g., "index-1") refers to the number of variables used in the model. "Index" in a model's name means that the model utilizes only return indices; "fundamental" in a model's name means that the model utilizes both indices and fundamental expectational variables. The dependent sample consists of twenty passive bond indices (see Appendix). The sample period is from February 1980 through December 1992 (155 monthly observations). Null hypothesis: restrictions hold; alternative hypothesis: restrictions do not hold. Small-sample adjustment (see Gallant (1987)): Reject null when $L > qF_\alpha$, where F_α is F statistic at α level of significance with q degrees of freedom in numerator and $nM - p$ degrees of freedom in denominator. n = 155 observations, M = 20 equations, and $\alpha = 0.05$.

All pairwise tests that could be performed are shown in Table 14.1. The results clearly show that adding return indexes (S&P, default, and option) improves the ability to explain the time-series pattern of returns and expected returns, and that adding the fundamental variables (GNP and inflation) also improves performance. It is clear that both the added return indexes and the fundamental variables are important influences in explaining the time series of returns and expected returns. The importance of unexpected changes in fundamental data in explaining differences in expected returns across different types of bonds has not previously been documented in the financial economics literature. Although Table I indicates that fundamental-6 is the preferred model, we will continue to examine the other models to understand better the reason for its dominance.

Another type of evidence that shows the importance of the fundamental variables is contained in Table 14.2. In this table we present the λs (prices of risk) and statistical significance of the λs associated with each of the two fundamental variables. λ_1 is the price of risk for unexpected changes in real GNP, and λ_2 is the price of risk for unexpected changes

Table 14.2
Market price of risk associated with fundamental variables

Model	λ_1	$t_{\lambda 1}$	λ_2	$t_{\lambda 2}$
Fundamental-4	0.262%	2.68	−0.642%	−3.01
Fundamental-6	0.201%	2.64	−0.551%	−3.22

λ_1 is the estimated market price of risk for unexpected changes in real gross national product (GNP); λ_2 is the estimated market price of risk for unexpected changes in inflation. The percentages are expressed in monthly terms. The dependent sample consists of twenty passive bond indices (see Appendix). The sample period is from February 1980 through December 1992 (155 monthly observations). The entries are derived from equation (4) using the returns on twenty passive portfolios.

Table 14.3
Adjusted R^2 for restricted regressions

Model	Mean	Maximum	Minimum
Index-1	0.904	0.965	0.786
Index-4	0.921	0.979	0.810
Fundamental-4	0.909	0.966	0.788
Fundamental-6	0.923	0.980	0.808

Mean, maximum, and minimum adjusted R^2 for the explanatory power of the restricted model (equation (4)) for the twenty passive portfolios. These values indicate the ability of the model to explain the time series of monthly returns for the passive bond portfolios.

in inflation. Note that in both the fundamental-6 model and in the fundamental-4 model, the market price of risk (λ) associated with each fundamental variable is significantly different from zero at the 1 percent level.[17] So far the evidence points to the importance of a model that includes fundamental variables. Tables 14.3, 14.4 and 14.5 provide additional evidence on the importance of fundamental variables.

The numbers in Table 14.1 are affected by the ability of a model to explain both the time series and cross-section of returns. Tables 14.3 and 14.4 attempt to decompose this into explanations of the time series and of the cross-section of returns. Table 14.3 presents the average of the time-series explanatory power of each model (averaged across all portfolios). It is clear that most of the adjusted R^2 is associated with the aggregate index of bond performance. While adding return indices for other securities or fundamental variables increases the ability of a model to explain the *time-series* behavior of the average passive bond portfolio, the increase in explanatory power is small. This should not be surprising. Interest rate changes are the dominant cause of changes in returns on bond portfolios.

Table 14.4
Percentage of cross-sectional variation explained by various models

Model	Percentage explained
Index-1	40.62%
Index-4	31.21%
Fundamental-4	87.05%
Fundamental-6	82.47%

The "percentage explained" is calculated by taking 1 minus the sum of the squares of the differences between expected return and estimated expected return from equation (4) divided by the sum of the squares of the differences between expected return and the mean (across all passive portfolios) of expected return.

Table 14.5
Percent of expected return explained by various indexes

Model	S&P	Default	Option	Aggregate	GNP	Inflation
Index-4	4%	3%	4%	89%		
Fundamental-4	3%			73%	7%	17%
Fundamental-6	3%	2%	3%	73%	5%	14%

The entries in this table are calculated by first taking the absolute value of the sensitivity times the risk premium for each index divided by the sum of the absolute values across all indices in the model. This number is then averaged across all passive portfolios. Sensitivities are estimated by time-series regressions of the passive portfolio returns on the indices; risk premiums are the lambdas shown in Table II for the fundamental variables and the average excess returns for the other indexes. "S&P" is the S&P 500 index; "Default" is the difference between the Blume/Keim high-yield bond index and the Lehman Brothers intermediate government bond index; "Option" is the difference between the Lehman Brothers GNMA index and a weighted average of the Lehman Brothers intermediate and long-term government bond indexes; "Aggregate" is a weighted average of the Lehman Brothers aggregate bond index and the Blume/Keim high-yield bond index; "GNP" is the change in expected real Gross National Product (GNP) growth; "Inflation" is the change in expected inflation.

Thus any bond index will explain a large percentage of the time series of bond returns. However, when we look at the ability of our alternative models to explain differences in the *expected return* of different passive bond portfolios (Table 14.4), a very different result emerges. Table 14.4 reports the percentage of the total variance (across our sample) of average bond returns that is explained by each model. To compute this statistic, the squared error in the estimate of expected return (average return for each bond fund minus expected return from equation (4) squared), is computed, then summed over all firms. This sum is divided by the sum of squared deviations of the difference between the mean return for each fund and the average of the 20 means. This is the unexplained variation. This number is subtracted from one, and the result is multiplied by 100 to compute the percentage of cross-sectional variation explained by each model. We see from the table that adding the two fundamental variables to either a two-index or four-index return model markedly increases the power of the model to explain the cross-sectional differences in average returns. This evidence indicates that in explaining the *pattern* of returns over time, return indices are of key importance, while in explaining the cross-section of *expected* returns, fundamental variables play a key role. Table 14.4 reinforces the more formal tests shown in Table 14.1. In Table 14.1 we show that the index models are rejected when compared to the relative pricing fundamental models as models explaining expected return. Table 14.4 shows that the differences in explaining expected return are large.[18]

The impact of these two effects can be seen in Table 14.5. The amount any variable contributes to explaining mean return can be found for any security by multiplying the sensitivity of that security to that variable times the market price of that sensitivity. In order to aggregate these results across securities, the absolute value of each contribution is taken. To determine the percentage of expected return explained by each variable, we sum the absolute values of the amounts explained by each variable and then divide each absolute value by that sum and multiply by 100. The contribution of each variable is then averaged over all firms in the sample. The results in Table 14.5 can be interpreted as the average percent of explained mean return that is contributed by each variable.

The most striking point that can be seen from Table 14.5 is the influence of fundamental variables in explaining expected returns. When the aggregate bond index is employed with our three other security indices (no fundamental variables), it accounts, on average, for 89 percent of the estimate of expected return. When the fundamental variables are employed, the fraction of returns explained by fundamental variables is substantial and much greater than that explained by the non-aggregate return indices. Note that when the fundamental-6 model is used, the contribution of the two fundamental variables average 19 percent, while the contribution of the two security sub-indices average 5 percent. Similarly, when we compare the two four-variable models, we find that, in index-4, the two subindices used (default and option) account for 7 percent of return explained. In contrast, when the fundamental variables are used, the two fundamental variables account for 24 percent of expected return. Once again, we see evidence of the importance of using fundamental expectational variables to explain mean returns.

III Evaluation of Mutual Funds

Blake, Elton, and Gruber (1993) present the first systematic evaluation of bond mutual funds. They perform the evaluation by comparing the performance of actively managed funds with the performance of index (passive) funds of comparable risk. This procedure is one approach to mutual fund evaluation. Its principal advantage is that the evaluation is based on a comparison of mutual fund performance with the performance from a feasible strategy that could be followed by an investor. The procedure does not make use of or depend on the accuracy of any particular equilibrium model. The alternative to evaluating mutual fund performance by comparing actively managed fund performance to index funds is to evaluate performance using an equilibrium or relative pricing model. While these results are interesting in terms of what they show about mutual fund performance, they are perhaps more interesting because they provide an additional test of the type of relative pricing model we are examining by seeing if the model leads to plausible conclusions. Keep in mind that we are parameterizing the model (estimating the prices of risk) from the passive portfolios and applying this to getting expected returns for bond mutual funds. The mutual funds can be thought of as a holdout sample over a partially nonoverlapping time period. These empirical results not only test the model; they test whether the parameters hold over a fresh sample.

The initial sample consists of all bond funds that are in the ICDI data set as of December 1991, have data available from January 1986, and are not classified as high-yield funds by ICDI as of December 1991. High-yield funds are not examined because, as explained earlier, there are not sufficient data to fit a relative pricing model to high-yield funds. Thus, the model might well be missing variables necessary to explain the expected return of high-yield funds. Four funds are subsequently deleted from the sample because management fees cannot be obtained and we want to study investment performance before and after fees.[19]

The sample of 123 mutual funds examined in this paper does suffer from survivorship bias. The ICDI data excludes funds that change from bonds to a nonbond investment policy, or went out of business (normally merger) between 1986 and 1991. The data reported in Blake, Elton, and Gruber (1993) allow an estimate of the order of magnitude of this bias. It is of the order of magnitude of 27 basis points per year (see footnote 31 in Blake, Elton, and Gruber (1993)).

In this section we evaluate bond mutual funds using the relative pricing models developed in earlier sections of this paper. The sensitivity of each of the 123 bond funds to the explanatory variables is obtained by regressing excess returns against the appropriate variables for each of the four models discussed earlier (time-series regression). The return-index variables are all calculated in excess-return form, although the risk-free rate cancels out for the default risk and option indexes (which are calculated as differences in primary indexes). The risk-free rate is not subtracted from the fundamental economic variables. The λs or prices of risk are set at the values estimated in the previous section of this article.

Table 14.6 shows the average sensitivity of the 123 funds for each of the four models. In addition, we examine average sensitivities of the funds grouped into corporate, mortgage, and government categories. The grouping is the one used by ICDI and reflects the investment policy of the fund. Insofar as there are inaccuracies in the classification, the differential results across groups will not be as clean. When we examine the results across alternative models we see that the sensitivities to the aggregate index and to both the default and option indexes remain reasonably constant and independent of the number of indices utilized in the regressions. There is more variation in the sensitivities to the fundamental variables. This variation is more extreme when comparing models that include the default and option variables with models that exclude these variables. This indicates that the fundamental variables act in part as proxies for default and option effects when these influences are not measured directly. For each model there are differences in the sensitivities of funds to the indexes across different objectives. However, the pattern of sensitivities is generally consistent with what is expected. For example, corporate bonds have greater positive sensitivity to the S&P index and to default risk than do other categories. Mortgage funds have greater sensitivity to the option index than do the other categories of funds. For almost all funds and models, the sensitivity coefficient for inflation surprises is negative. Thus, bond funds have lower returns when anticipated inflation unexpectedly increases. This result is plausible, since we would expect an increase in anticipated inflation to be associated with an increase in interest rates and, hence, a decrease in returns. However, researchers who have measured surprises from a time-series regression often find the opposite result (e.g., Burmeister and McElroy (1988)). These results provide some support for the use of expectational data instead of time-series regressions. The sign of the sensitivity to GNP is positive for corporate bond funds but negative for the other categories. Interest rates tend to rise in a recovery,

Table 14.6
Average sensitivities for the mutual fund sample

Group	S&P	Default	Option	Aggregate	GNP	Inflation
Panel A: Index-1						
Corp				0.9143		
Morg				0.8423		
Gov				1.0526		
All				0.9649		
Panel B: Index-4						
Corp	0.0111	0.0039	0.0386	0.9056		
Morg	−0.0071	−0.0679	0.6045	0.9639		
Gov	−0.0001	−0.0704	0.0234	1.0691		
All	0.0021	−0.0457	0.1465	0.9946		
Panel C: Fundamental-4						
Corp	0.0100			0.9048	0.1004	−0.0585
Morg	−0.0198			0.8652	−0.0852	0.0538
Gov	−0.0109			1.0492	−0.2386	−0.0018
All	−0.0059			0.9649	−0.0972	−0.0089
Panel D: Fundamental-6						
Corp	0.0101	0.0011	0.0425	0.9102	0.0847	−0.0642
Morg	−0.0047	−0.0661	0.6104	0.9496	−0.1240	−0.0445
Gov	0.0016	−0.0689	0.0266	1.0594	−0.0905	−0.0196
All	0.0031	−0.0456	0.1504	0.9885	−0.0403	−0.0391

The sensitivities are estimated from a time series regression of each fund's returns on the returns or changes in fundamental values of the indicated indices. The sensitivities are then averaged across all funds and within each category of fund: corporate bond, government mortgage, and government bond.

which would hurt returns. However, the unexpected increase in GNP lowers the risk of corporate bonds. The positive sign for corporate bonds indicates that the lower risk, and hence lower spread, more than compensates for the general increase in interest rates.

Table 14.7 shows the average percentage of expected return explained by each factor. For each firm, it is constructed exactly as in Table 14.5, by taking the absolute value of the sensitivity times the risk premium for each factor and dividing by the aggregate of the absolute values across all factors. Note that for the fundamental variables, these risk premiums are those presented in Table 14.2 and are estimated from a sample of returns

Table 14.7
Percentage of mean return explained by each variable

Group	S&P	Default	Option	Aggregate	GNP	Inflation
Panel A: Index-4						
Corp	5.30%	0.49%	3.16%	91.05%		
Morg	3.01%	0.48%	9.72%	86.78%		
Gov	3.59%	0.54%	5.83%	90.04%		
Avg	4.03%	0.51%	5.75%	89.70%		
Panel B: Fundamental-4						
Corp	4.24%			70.48%	12.09%	13.19%
Morg	4.73%			73.36%	7.31%	14.61%
Gov	3.53%			67.65%	13.84%	14.99%
Avg	4.00%			69.73%	11.94%	14.32%
Panel C: Fundamental-6						
Corp	3.98%	0.37%	2.54%	73.18%	7.43%	12.49%
Morg	2.36%	0.41%	8.58%	74.70%	4.68%	9.26%
Gov	3.27%	0.41%	4.69%	71.64%	8.66%	11.33%
Avg	3.31%	0.40%	4.78%	72.77%	7.45%	11.29%

The entries in this table are calculated by first taking the absolute value of the sensitivity times the risk premium for each index divided by the sum of the absolute values across all indices in the model. This number is then averaged across all funds. Sensitivities are estimated by time-series regressions of the bond fund returns on the indices; risk premiums are the lambdas shown in Table II for the fundamental variables and the average excess returns for the other indexes. "S&P" is the S&P 500 index; "Default" is the difference between the Blume/Keim high-yield bond index and the Lehman Brothers intermediate government bond index; "Option" is the difference between the Lehman Brothers GNMA index and a weighted average of the Lehman Brothers intermediate and long-term government bond indexes; "Aggregate" is a weighted average of the Lehman Brothers aggregate bond index and the Blume/Keim high-yield bond index; "GNP" is the change in expected real Gross National Product (GNP) growth; "Inflation" is the change in expected inflation.

on passive portfolios. The results for each fund are then averaged within each category and across all firms. Consider the fundamental-6 model. About 73 percent of the expected return is explained by the aggregate index. However, a substantial proportion is explained by the two fundamental variables, 7.5 percent from the GNP variable and 12 percent from the inflation variable. The remaining 8 percent is explained by the other three indices. Thus fundamental variables are important determinants of expected returns for active as well as passive funds.[20] While the importance of variables in the fundamental-6 model does not seem to change much across types of bond funds, there are some interesting differences.

For example, the S&P index explains the greatest amount of expected return for corporates, and the option index is most important in explaining expected returns for mortgages.

Table 14.8 shows the performance of our sample of mutual funds after all expenses are paid (except load charges).[21] This is the performance of the return series an investor would receive if all funds were no load funds. The average intercept (alpha) *across all funds* is negative for each of the models under study. Depending on the model used, the average intercept across all funds varies between a negative 6.4 basis points to a negative 11.6 basis points per month. Annualized, this is on the order of $\frac{3}{4}$ percent to $1\frac{1}{3}$ percent per annum. There is no reason to believe managers that manage a certain type of fund (such as a mortgage fund) are superior to managers of other types of funds. When fundamental-6 is used to evaluate performance, the same average performance is computed for managers of corporate, government, or mortgage bond funds. When the other models are used, very different estimates are obtained. This gives support to the use of fundamental-6 (and in particular the use of fundamental economic variables) as an appropriate relative pricing model.[22]

Table 14.9 shows the same analysis where the return series have expenses added back. Expenses are annual expenses as reported in Wiesenberger's *Investment Companies* for December 1989 divided by twelve and added to each month's return.[23] The alphas pre-expenses are very small, varying from minus 3.5 basis points to plus 1 basis point on average. There is no evidence that managers, on average, can provide superior returns on the portfolios they manage, even if they provide their services free of cost.

When we regress alphas (computed after expenses) for the fundamental-6 model on expenses, we get an insignificant intercept (−0.06 percent) and a slope of −0.784 with a t statistic of −1.686. Thus, on average for every $1 of expenses, performance decreases by $0.78. The small and insignificant intercept indicates that the major cause of underperformance is expenses and that an investor with no forecasting ability should select a low-expense bond fund.[24]

In this section we have seen that the relative pricing models examined earlier seem to do a good job of explaining mutual fund performance. The reasonableness of the results supplies additional evidence on the reasonableness of the models we have developed, and the market prices of risk we have estimated are applicable to sets of fixed-income securities not included in our original sample.

Table 14.8
Performance (alphas) of mutual funds after all expenses except load charges

	Panel A: Corp (40 funds)		Panel B: Morg (25 funds)		Panel C: Gov (58 funds)		Panel D: All (123 funds)	
Model	Avg (%)	t	Avg (%)	t	Avg (%)	t	Avg (%)	t
Fundamental-6	−0.1184	−2.30	−0.1196	−3.29	−0.1124	−3.57	−0.1158	−3.72
Fundamental-4	−0.1241	−2.18	0.0154	0.16	−0.0582	−1.19	−0.0647	−1.47
Index-4	−0.0724	−2.27	−0.1105	−4.89	−0.1129	−5.81	−0.0992	−5.17
Index-1	−0.0635	−2.02	−0.0433	−0.83	−0.1081	−3.79	−0.0804	−3.35

The column labeled "Avg" contains the average alpha (model intercept) of the funds in the indicated group; the column labeled "t" contains t-values that are adjusted to correct for both heteroscedasticity and cross correlation of the residuals. Funds are grouped by investment policy: "Corp" is corporate bond; "Morg" is government mortgage; "Gov" is government bond.

Table 14.9
Performance (alphas) of mutual funds with expenses added back

	Panel A: Corp (40 funds)		Panel B: Morg (25 funds)		Panel C: Gov (58 funds)		Panel D: All (123 funds)	
Model	Avg (%)	t	Avg (%)	t	Avg (%)	t	Avg (%)	t
Fundamental-6	−0.0436	−0.85	−0.0443	−1.22	−0.0259	−0.82	−0.0354	−1.14
Fundamental-4	−0.0493	−0.87	0.0907	0.96	0.0283	0.58	0.0158	0.36
Index-4	0.0024	0.08	−0.0352	−1.56	−0.0264	−1.36	−0.0188	−0.98
Index-1	0.0113	0.36	0.0320	0.62	−0.0216	−0.76	0.0000	0.00

The column labeled "Avg" contains the average alpha (model intercept) of the funds in the indicated group; the column labeled "t" contains t-values that are adjusted to correct for both heteroscedasticity and cross correlation of the residuals. Funds are grouped by investment policy: "Corp" is corporate bond; "Morg" is government mortgage; "Gov" is government bond. Monthly fund expenses are added to fund returns before alphas the calculated.

IV Conclusion

In this article, we have developed relative pricing (APT) models that are successful in explaining expected returns in the bond market. In value, the bond market is several times larger than the equity market, yet it has received relatively little attention heretofore from researchers developing models of expected return.

Modern relative pricing models utilize unanticipated changes in economic variables as factors driving security returns. An innovation in this article is the measurement of those factors as changes in forecasts. When we compare the four alternative APT models, those that do not contain the fundamental expectational variables are rejected at the 5 percent level in favor of models that do contain those variables. The return indices are the most important variables in explaining the *time series* of returns. However, the addition of the fundamental variables leads to a large improvement in the explanation of *expected* returns. Furthermore, when we examine the percentage of expected returns explained by each of the variables, the fundamental variables are much more significant than all indices with the exception of the aggregate index.

We utilize our fundamental relative pricing models to examine the performance of bond funds. Bond funds underperform the returns predicted by the relative pricing models by the amount of expenses on average, and the models using fundamental variables do a better job than other models in accounting for the difference in performance between types of bond funds.

Appendix

Bond indices used as passive portfolios

Lehman Brothers	Ibbotson and Associates	Merrill Lynch
1–3 Govt.	Int. govt.	M0A0 (mortgage master)
Int. treasury	Long govt.	C8F0 (15+ yr. med. qual. industrials)
Int. agency		C8I0 (15+ yr. med qual. utilities)
Long agency		C8K0 (15+ yr. high qual. finance)
Industrial		G802 (15+ yr. treasuries)
Finance		G8P0 (15+ yr. govt. agencies)
Int. Aaa		GVPO (1–5 yr. govt. agencies)
Long Aaa		
Int. Baa		
Long Baa		
FHLMC*		

* Federal Home Loan Mortgage Corporation.

Notes

We would like to thank Stephen Brown, Bent Christensen, Jacob Boudoukh, René Stulz, an anonymous referee, and participants at the 1994 European Finance Association meetings (Brussels) for helpful comments.

1. In this discussion we differentiate between relative pricing models and equilibrium models. Relative pricing models are not equilibrium models. The absence of arbitrage is a necessary condition for equilibrium but only guarantees that the assets studied have relatives prices (not absolute prices) consistent with equilibrium.

2. The Lehman Brothers and Merrill Lynch indices are value-weighted with the returns calculated using actively traded bonds. For example, Lehman Brothers and Merrill Lynch have a number of bonds that traders actively price on a daily basis. All other bonds are priced by formulas utilizing prices on the active bonds. The net effect is to calculate return using the actively traded bonds but weighting each bond's return by the proportion that bond type represents of the market. Returns are calculated from prices that take account of (include) accrued interest and are adjusted for coupon payments. The Ibbotson data were obtained from the Center for Research in Security Prices (CRSP) SBBI files.

3. A discussion of the relative strengths and weaknesses of each is beyond the scope of this manuscript. The reader is referred to Elton and Gruber (1995) or Peazy (1994) for a detailed discussion of the appropriateness of each approach.

4. None of these articles examined changes in economic influences or portfolios that mimic economic influences to explain the return on debt instruments. In addition, our analysis also differs from the studies cited above in the data analyzed. Gultekin and Rogalski (1985) and Litterman and Scheinkman (1991) only examine government bonds and thus cannot detect factors related to issuer risk. Knez, Litterman, and Scheinkman (1994) only look at money market instruments and thus cannot detect influences (including types of credit risk) that are present in longer maturity instruments.

5. Evidence is also presented by Chen, Roll, and Ross (1986) and Burmeister *et al.* in Peazy (1994), who find that unexpected changes in these variables impact common stock returns. The unexpected changes do so because, as Chen *et al.* (1986) point out, they impact both future cash flows and discount rates. They should have a similar but less marked effect on discount rates and the uncertainty of realized cash flows for non-government bonds.

6. See Elton *et al.* (1981).

7. We utilize expectational inflation data from the Survey Research Center (SRC) of the University of Michigan and expectational GNP growth data from Eggert Enterprises. The SRC data have been extensively analyzed. Rich (1989) and Baghestani (1992) both analyze the SRC inflation series and conclude that the estimates are rational expectations. Unlike the SRC data, there is not the same lengthy time series for estimates from Eggert Enterprises, so these estimates have not been analyzed for rationality; however, given that the Eggert data are derived from surveys of well-known professional economists, while SRC estimates are derived from surveys of individual consumers, and that economists have been trained in ideas of rationality, the Eggert data are likely to be no worse than SRC estimates with respect to rationality.

8. We examined a number of other candidates for measuring general economic conditions and inflation. We selected the series that showed the greatest correlation with factors extracted from the bond return series.

9. We use the return on a mixture of 75 percent of the intermediate and 25 percent of the long-term LB government bond indexes. The mixture we use was determined by equating the duration of the combined two government indices with the duration of the GNMA index and also by regressing the GNMA index on each of the two government bond indices and then finding the weights that made the combination of the regression coefficients equal to one.

10. We know of only four indices that existed over our sample period (one Merrill Lynch, two Salomon Brothers, and the Blume/Keim index). Furthermore, the Blume/Keim index is identical to one of the Salomon indices over part of our sample period, so that we only have three independent indices. Since we use the return on one of the high-yield indices (the Blume/Keim index) as an independent variable, we are left with only two high-yield indices. Furthermore, the remaining Salomon index suffers from postselection bias over part of our sample period (see Blume and Keim (1987)), leaving us with only the Merrill Lynch index. If high-yield bonds were affected by the same influences as all other bonds, the inclusion of the Merrill Lynch index could improve our estimation. However, our concern is that influences other than those that affect government, corporate, or mortgages might affect high-yield bonds. In that case, the inclusion of a high-yield index would likely hurt the estimation, so we exclude that index.

11. While we refer to this model throughout as an APT model, since we prespecify the factors we employ, the model can also be viewed as a linear factor model. In fact, some researchers prefer this terminology. See Connor (1984) and Hansen and Jagannathan (1991) for sufficient conditions for such models to hold.

12. Huberman, Kandel, and Stambaugh (1987) point out that, in tests of a model such as the one under consideration, the market price of risk for a tradeable portfolio is the portfolio's excess expected return (over the riskless rate). We have incorporated this expression for the market price of risk directly in our model, so, to the extent that it does not hold (APT does not hold), equation (6) will be violated even if the fundamental economic variables are correctly priced. In addition, Huberman, Kandel, and Stambaugh show that, if mimicking portfolios can be found for the economic influences, stronger statements can be made about the size of the λs. This is an interesting avenue of research to pursue. However, as they point out in their conclusion, given that the weights in the mimicking portfolios must be estimated, it is an open question whether the additional restrictions result in increased power for the tests of the model.

13. In a later section we show that after expenses are added back, bond funds have essentially a zero alpha. Thus, they can be used as proxies for passive portfolios. Alternatively, we could have performed the analysis in this section utilizing the passive indices over which we later fit the model. We choose not to do so for two reasons. First, we want to look at the relevancy of variables on a set of data that is different from the data over which we fit the model. Second, we want a larger spectrum of maturities within each bond type classification and more observation on mortgage bonds than we have in our passive-index sample.

14. A fifth model is also investigated to explore the reliability of the methodology used to detect differences in models. This model is a zero-factor model that allows us to examine whether our methodology can determine if the means of our twenty-bond index series are different at a statistically significant level.

15. An alternative way to view these models is as follows: The single-index model can be considered as analogous to a simple duration model with risk differentials between types of bonds ignored. The four-index model, because it contains proxies for wealth, can be considered as a form of Merton's (1973) intertemporal asset pricing model. The models

fundamental-4 and fundamental-6 are in the spirit of the APT models hypothesized and tested by Chen, Roll, and Ross (1986) and Burmeister *et al.* in Peazy (1994).

16. When we examine the zero-factor model, we find that equality of means can be rejected at the one percent level. The maximum-likelihood ratio associated with this hypothesis is 41.95, while the critical value at the one percent level is 37.69.

17. The reader should note that for non-linear models, *t*-tests on individual parameters are only asymptotically valid. Thus, Table 14.2 should be viewed with caution. The results in Table 14.2 are consistent with the results in Table 14.1.

18. Both Table 14.1 and Table 14.4 demonstrate the importance of adding fundamental variables. However, the relative importance of adding the variables varies from Table 14.1 to Table 14.4. The test values shown in Table 14.1 are affected by the model's ability to explain both the time series and cross-section of returns. The values in Table 14.4 are only affected by the model's ability to explain the cross-section of returns. We examined the individual observations. There were no significant outliers. Thus, our results are not due to the ability of the fundamental variables to explain the expected return on only one or two of our portfolios.

19. We examined the performance of these four funds. The inclusion of these funds in the after-fee sample makes no difference in our results.

20. Like Burmeister and McElroy (1988), we do not make aggregate return orthogonal to the other indexes. Thus we are likely to be understating the performance of the fundamental variables in explaining expected return.

21. For each average alpha shown in Tables 14.8 and 14.9, the reported *t* value has been adjusted using the full variance/covariance matrix of residuals across the funds in a given group in order to correct for both heteroscedasticity and cross correlations of the residuals.

22. In our prior study of bond mutual funds, we compare bond funds to a set of passive portfolios. The results of this earlier study concerning aggregate performance are very similar to those reported above. In that study, overall performance varies from minus 8 basis points to minus 11 basis points depending on the measure used, which is almost identical to the results we find using our equilibrium models.

23. Elton *et al.* (1993) show that relative expense ratios are fairly constant across years; i.e., funds with higher expense ratios in one year tend to have the higher ratios in subsequent years. Also, any linear time trend would be mitigated by using expense ratios from the middle of the sample period. Thus, we believe 1989 expense ratios are good measures for our six-year sample.

24. This is consistent with Blake *et al.* (1993). The intercepts and slopes (with *t* statistics in parentheses) for the other three models are as follows. Index-1: −0.02% (−0.849) and −0.733 (−2.507); index-4: −0.03% (−1.199) and −0.922 (−3.806); fundamental-4: −0.02% (−0.396) and −0.530 (−0.822).

References

Baghestani, Hamid, 1992, On the formation of expected inflation under various conditions: Some survey evidence, *Journal of Business* 65, 281–293.

Bansal, R. and S. Viswanathan, 1993, No-arbitrage and arbitrage pricing: A new approach, *Journal of Finance* 48, 1231–1262.

Blake, Christopher R., Edwin J. Elton, and Martin J. Gruber, 1993, The performance of bond mutual funds, *Journal of Business* 66, 371–403.

Blume, Marshall E., and Donald B. Keim, 1987, Lower grade bonds: Their risks and returns, *Financial Analysts Journal* 43, 26–33.

Brennan, Michael, and Eduardo Schwartz, 1983, Duration Bond Pricing and Portfolio Performance, in Bierwag, Kaufman, and Toevs, eds., *Innovations in Bond Portfolio Management: Duration Analysis and Immunization* (JAI Press, Greenwich, CT).

Brown, Stephen J., and Philip H. Dybvig, 1986, The empirical implications of the Cox, Ingersoll, Ross theory of the term structure of interest rates, *Journal of Finance* 41, 617–630.

Burmeister, Edwin, and Marjorie B. McElroy, 1987, APT and multifactor asset pricing models with measured and unobserved factors: Theoretical and econometric issues, paper presented at the November meetings of the Southern Finance Association, Washington, D.C.

Burmeister, Edwin, and Marjorie B. McElroy, 1988, Joint estimation of factor sensitivities and risk premia for the arbitrage pricing theory, *Journal of Finance* 43, 721–733.

Burmeister, Edwin, and Kent D. Wall, 1986, The arbitrage pricing theory and macroeconomic factor measures, *The Financial Review* 21, 1–20.

Burmeister, Edwin, Kent D. Wall, and James D. Hamilton, 1986, Estimation of unobserved expected monthly inflation using Kalman filtering, *Journal of Business and Economic Statistics* 4, 147–160.

Chen, Nai-Fu, Richard Roll, and Stephen Ross, 1986, Economic forces and the stock market, *Journal of Business*, 59, 383–404.

Connor, Gregory, 1984, A unified beta pricing theory, *Journal of Economic Theory* 34, 13–31.

Cox, John C., Jonathan E. Ingersoll, and Stephen A. Ross, 1981, A reexamination of traditional hypotheses about the term structure of interest rates, *Journal of Finance* 36, 769–799.

Ederington, Louis H., and Jae Ha Lee, 1993, How markets process information: News releases and volatility, *Journal of Finance* 48, 1161–1191.

Elton, Edwin J., and Martin J. Gruber, 1995. *Modern Portfolio Theory and Investment Analysis*, 5th ed., (John Wiley & Sons, New York).

Elton, Edwin J., Martin J. Gruber, Sanjiv Das, and Matt Hlavka, 1993, Efficiency with costly information: A reinterpretation of evidence from managed portfolios, *Review of Financial Studies* 5, 1–22.

Elton, Edwin J., Martin J. Gruber, and Mustafa Gultekin, 1981, Expectations and share prices, *Management Science* 27, 43–76.

Elton, Edwin J., Martin J. Gruber, and Jianping Mei, 1993, Return generating processes, expected returns, and term premiums, Working paper, New York University.

Fama, Eugene F., and Robert Bliss, 1987, The information in long-maturity forward rates, *American Economic Review* 77, 680–692.

Fama, Eugene F., and Kenneth R. French, 1992, The cross-section of expected stock returns, *Journal of Finance* 47, 427–465.

Fama, Eugene F., and James D. MacBeth, 1973, Risk, return, and equilibrium: Empirical tests, *Journal of Political Economy* 71, 607–636.

Callant, Ronald A., 1987, *Non-linear Statistical Models* (John Wiley & Sons, New York).

Gibbons, Michael R., 1982, Multivariate tests of financial models: A new approach, *Journal of Financial Economics* 10, 3–27.

Gibbons, Michael R., 1986, Empirical examination of return generating processes of arbitrage pricing theory, Unpublished Manuscript no. 881, Stanford University.

Gibbons, Michael R., and Krishna Ramaswamy, 1993, A test of the Cox, Ingersoll and Ross model of the term structure, *Review of Financial Studies* 6, 619–659.

Gibbons, Michael R., Stephen A. Ross, and Jay Shanken, 1989, A test of the efficiency of a given portfolio, *Econometrica* 57, 1121–1152.

Gultekin, N. Bulent, and Richard J. Rogalski, 1985, Government bond returns, measurement of interest rate risk, and the arbitrage pricing theory, *Journal of Finance* 40, 43–61.

Hansen, Lars P., and Ravi Jagannathan, 1991, Implications of security market data for models of dynamic economies, *Journal of Political Economy* 99, 225–262.

Huberman, Gur, Shmuel Kandel, and Robert Stambaugh, 1987, Mimicking portfolios and exact arbitrage pricing, *Journal of Finance* 42, 1–9.

Knez, Peter J., Robert Litterman, and Jose Scheinkman, 1994, Explorations into factors explaining money market returns, *Journal of Finance* 49, 1861–1882.

Litterman, Robert, and Jose Scheinkman, 1991, Common factors affecting bond returns, *Journal of Fixed Income* 1, 54–61.

Longstaff, Francis, and Eduardo Schwartz, 1992, Interest rate volatility and the term structure: A two-factor general equilibrium model, *Journal of Finance* 47, 1259–83.

McCulloch, J. Huston, 1990, U.S. term structure data, 1946–1987, in *Handbook of Monetary Economics*, Vol. I, 672–715.

McElroy, Marjorie B., Edwin Burmeister, and Kent D. Wall, 1985, Two estimators for the APT model when factors are measured, *Economics Letters* 19, 271–275.

Merton, Robert C., 1973, An intertemporal asset pricing model, *Econometrica* 41, 867–880.

Nelson, J., and S. Schaefer, 1983, The dynamics of the term structure and alternative portfolio immunization strategies, in Bierwag, Kaufman, and Toevs, eds., *Innovations in Bond Portfolio Management: Duration Analysis and Immunization* (JAI Press).

Pearson, Neil D., and Tong-Sheng Sun, 1994, Exploiting the conditional density in estimating the term structure: An application to the Cox, Ingersoll, and Ross model, *Journal of Finance* 49, 1279–1304.

Peazy, John, ed., 1994, *Practitioner's Guide to Factor Models* (Research Foundation of the Institute of Chartered Financial Analysts, Charlottesville, Va).

Rich, Robert, 1989, Testing the rationality of inflation forecasts from survey data: Another look at the SRC expected price change data, *Review of Economics and Statistics*, 71, 682–686.

Roll, Richard, and Stephen Ross, 1980, An empirical investigation of the arbitrage pricing theory, *Journal of Finance* 35, 1073–1103.

Ross, Stephen A., 1976, The arbitrage pricing theory of capital asset pricing, *Journal of Economic Theory* 13, 341–360.

Snow, Karl, 1991, Diagnosing asset pricing models using the distribution of asset returns, *Journal of Finance* 46, 955–984.

Stambaugh, Robert, 1982, On the exclusion of assets from tests of the two-parameter model: A sensitivity analysis, *Journal of Financial Economics* 10, 237–268.

Stambaugh, Robert, 1988, The information in forward rates: Implications for models of the term structure, *Journal of Financial Economics* 21, 41–70.

Wiesenberger Financial Service, 1986–1991. *Investment Companies*, (Warren, Gorham & Lamont, Inc., Boston).

III Debt Markets

This section contains four chapters dealing with debt securities. The first two deal with questions of the efficiency of the Treasury bill futures market, while the second two deal with bond returns and immunization.

The studies of efficiency and arbitrage in the T-bill markets are interesting for a number of reasons. If markets are generally efficient, we might still find inefficiency in new markets where participants have not as yet been fully educated. Second, it is interesting for efficiency of T-bill markets can be tested without the use of a valuation model. Most tests of efficiency require a prespecified model of valuation and are therefore joint tests of the valuation model and efficiency.

This study differs from previous studies of efficiency in futures markets in that 1) we use intra-day prices to measure efficiency, taking care that all trades take place at times subsequent to those that triggered the trading strategy; 2) we examine efficiency from the viewpoint of different players in the market, each of whom is subject to different types of transaction costs; and 3) we examine the difference in performance caused by treating futures contracts as if they were forward contracts.

In the second chapter we examine whether T-bill futures can be used to increase the return on a Treasury bill portfolio without affecting the risk of the portfolio. Given the inefficiencies documented by us and others in the T-bill market, the potential for a profitable trading strategy exists. We develop a dynamic programming model (this is another of the type of models discussed in volume 1) to represent an optimum trading strategy. We parameterize the model using past data. Applying the dynamic programming model in real time leads to excess return.

In the next two chapters we examine a model that allows immunization of a set of liabilities and forecasts unexpected changes in spot rates. The emphasis in the first chapter is on immunizing a liability. One difference between this and previous articles in this area is that we select a liability which is traded in the market so that the time path of immunization in terms of cash flow and market prices can be observed. The assets we employ to immunize the liability are a set of constant duration portfolios. Sets of one- and two-index models are tested. In some models both the indexes and sensitivities are specified from theory (e.g., Macaulay's duration); in others the indexes are specified a priori and the sensitivities are estimated via regression analysis. In still others, both the indexes and sensitivities are estimated empirically (factor analysis). Comparisons in performance are made between these techniques. In all cases, we measure performance by examining the difference in changes in the value of assets and liabilities.

The second chapter in this section attempts to understand the evolution and prediction of unexpected changes in spot rates. Models are constructed and evaluated for predicting these changes.

15

Intra-Day Tests of the Efficiency of the Treasury Bill Futures Market

Edwin J. Elton, Martin J. Gruber, and Joel Rentzler

This paper examines the efficiency of the Treasury bill futures market. This subject has been examined before by Capozza and Cornell (1979), Cornell (1981), Lang and Rasche (1978), Rendleman and Carabini (1979), Vignola and Dale (1979), Poole (1978), and Puglisi (1978). There are a number of reasons why this paper makes an important contribution to the literature.

The first reason is that by using trade by trade futures prices we can make more realistic assumptions about the prices at which trades could have taken place. This paper uses intra-day prices to examine efficiency. Prior studies at best used closing prices to examine apparent inefficiencies and assumed that transactions took place at these closing prices. There are two problems with this procedure. First, simultaneous transactions cannot actually occur at closing prices. There is almost an hour difference between the closing of the Chicago futures and New York spot markets. Thus when the closing spot market price is observed the futures market has been closed for about an hour. Closing prices could be used to judge apparent discrepancies. However, it would be necessary to execute trades at the open. Making decisions based on closing prices and then assuming trades can take place at these prices is an approximation which could significantly affect results. In addition, using only closing prices ignores any intra-day trades which could lead to profits.

In this study we match in time intra-day prices in the spot and futures market. These matched prices are used to identify apparently profitable trading rules. We then assume trades take place at prices which are observed later in the day. This is a test of a trading rule which an investor could actually follow. As we discuss later in the paper, our results differ from prior studies. These differences are primarily due to using intra-day prices and carefully matching times so that information used to initiate trades would actually be available to the investor at the time of the trade.

The second reason is that we examine more complex trading strategies than those which have been employed in other studies. The random walk literature provides a useful analogy. The original random walk studies simply correlated past and future prices or returns. Later studies examined filter rules and other more complicated trading rules. In this study we employ alternative trading rules of increased complexity to test for the existence of trading profits.

Finally, we explicitly examine the consequence of T-bills futures contracts being futures rather than forward contracts. Futures contracts, unlike forward contracts, involve flows every settlement day. The intermediate cash flows on futures contracts can affect the profitability of any strategy. The only prior study that even considered this effect is the one by Rendleman and Carabini (1979). They used the theoretical model of Cox, Ingersoll and Ross (1981) to try to estimate whether the difference between forward and futures prices was likely to be large enough to affect the payoff from alternative trading strategies. This is a useful first attempt. However, ultimately the effect of daily settlement or "marking-to-the-market" has to be examined directly as part of trading strategies to see if it affects the outcome of these strategies. There are other problems with prior studies. These involve gross estimates of prices and averaging data in a way that can mask inefficiencies. Since these problems are discussed in some detail in Rendleman and Carabini, there is no reason to review them further here.

Probably no area in finance has received more attention than the efficiency literature. The reader may well wonder why, even given the approximations used in prior studies, another paper is worthwhile. Efficiency in the futures area is especially interesting for two reasons. First, futures prices are used in estimating future spot rates. Estimates of future spot rates are useful for testing interest rate theories, for developing bond valuation models and in regulatory proceedings. If systematic inefficiencies exist, then estimates from the futures markets are biased. In addition, the market for T-bill futures is a new market and as such allows for the study of the degree of efficiency and changes in the efficiency as a market evolves. Second, most of the literature on the efficiency of capital markets has used common equity returns. These studies are really a simultaneous test of efficiency and the appropriateness of a prespecified valuation model. The arbitrage we analyze does not require a valuation model and thus is one of the few pure tests of efficiency.

This paper has three sections. In the first section we outline the market equilibrating mechanisms (termed strategies), in the second section we present our test of these alternative strategies and in the third section we present the results.

I Market Equilibrating Strategies

The Treasury bill futures market enables the creation of a portfolio consisting of a Treasury bill futures contract and a cash Treasury bill which has the same characteristics as a cash Treasury bill of a different maturity. If we call this portfolio of a bill and a futures contract a *pseudo T-bill,* then in an efficient market the cash T-bill and the pseudo T-bill having the same maturity should sell at the same price.[1] Assume the investor is considering purchasing an N day T-bill with a maturity between 1 and 91 days. The investor can purchase such an N day T-bill in either of two ways:

(1) purchase an N day T-bill in the cash market (cash T-bill instrument)

(2) purchase a $(91+N)$ day T-bill in the cash market and sell a T-bill futures contract which expires in N days. Deliver the $(91+N)$ day bill against the futures contract (pseudo T-bill instrument).

A similar strategy exists for an investor who wishes to purchase an N day T-bill with a maturity between 92 and 182 days. The results reported in this paper are for the 1 to 91 day period but are equally applicable for the 92 to 182 day period.[2]

In an efficient market if there were no transaction costs the cash bill and the pseudo bill instruments should sell at the same price. However, with transaction costs differences can exist. Three strategies with varying transaction costs are examined. First, "pure arbitrage" could take place. In this strategy the cash or pseudo bill with the lower price is purchased and financed by shorting the higher priced instrument. Second, a bill swap strategy could be employed where holders of the higher priced instrument would liquidate their position and purchase the lower priced of the two instruments. Third, an investor wishing to hold a T-bill could simply purchase the lower priced of the two instruments.

The arbitrage strategy involves three transaction costs. The transaction costs are the purchase of a cash T-bill, the shorting of a cash T-bill and a transaction cost in the futures market. The shorting of the cash T-bill involves not only immediate transaction costs but also a differential interest cost payable over the life of the bill. This differential interest cost exists since borrowing is at the repo-rate which is higher than the rate earned on the T-bill by about 1/2%. Thus if the equilibrating mechanism is pure arbitrage the price of the T-bill instrument and pseudo T-bill instrument could differ by as much as three transaction costs and the differential interest rate. The swap strategy involves three transaction costs, two on the purchase or sale of the pseudo T-bill and one on the purchase or sale of the cash T-bill. Thus if swapping were the equilibrating mechanism, the prices of the T-bill and pseudo T-bill instruments could differ by as much as these three transaction costs. Finally, the strategy of purchasing the lower priced instrument involves a differential transaction cost only if the purchase is the pseudo bill rather than the cash bill and this differential is the transaction cost on the sale of a future.[3] Thus the pre-transaction price of the pseudo T-bill could be below the pre-transaction price of the cash T-bill by the amount of the transaction cost on the futures contract if new purchases are the equilibrating mechanism. From this discussion it is obvious that if the market is efficient with respect to purchasers it must be efficient with respect to swappers and arbitrageurs. Similarly if it is efficient with respect to swappers it must be efficient with respect to arbitrageurs.

II Tests of Alternative Strategies

In this section we discuss in detail the tests conducted for each of the strategies outlined above. Before presenting the tests it is worthwhile describing the data used.

A Data

Intra-day quotes on cash T-bill prices were obtained from the Federal Reserve Bank of New York for the period January 6, 1976 through December 22, 1982. These contain the closing bid and ask prices, the opening change from the previous closing bid price and three other changes from this bid price at approximately hourly intervals. The impact of average bid-ask spreads are accounted for in calculating transaction costs. For each day in this period, these intra-day prices were recorded for each of two cash bills. One was for the cash bill deliverable on the near futures contract (maturing 91 days after the maturity of the futures contract). This is the bill held in the 1 to 91 day pseudo T-bill instrument. The other cash bill price used was the price for the bill maturing when the futures contract matured. This is the price for the 1 to 91 day cash T-bill instrument. T-bill futures prices were obtained from a tape supplied by the International Monetary Market of the Chicago Mercantile Exchange. This tape contained the price and time of every T-bill futures trade over the same January 6, 1976 through December 22, 1982 period. There were a total of 28 futures contracts traded over this period.

B Tests

Our first set of tests involves examining the differential profit resulting from the equilibrating strategy of purchasing the lower priced instrument (cash bill or pseudo bill) and holding it until maturity. For each cash T-bill price, the price of the appropriate futures contract which traded just prior to the cash market quote is used to create the expected price of a pseudo T-bill. The anticipated differential in profit from purchasing the lower cost strategy (cash bill or pseudo bill) is then recorded. these profits are anticipated assuming trades take place at these prices and there is no effect due to marking-to-the-market. Whichever instrument has the greatest expected profit is assumed to be purchased using one of two trading rules. The first trading rule assumes that the cash T-bill is purchased at the price used in calculating the expected profit while the futures transaction takes place at the first futures price following the cash market price. In the rest of the paper this is referred to as *immediate execution*. The second trading rule assumes that the cash T-bill is purchased at its next quoted price and the futures transaction takes place at the next trade after the cash T-bill is purchased. This will be referred to as a *delayed execution*. The first trading rule simulates the trading of an investor who can quickly determine the profit of the strategy and reacts accordingly. The second trading rule is feasible even for a slow reacting investor since approximately an hour elapses between the cash T-bill quotes. Both of these trading rules assume that a position once taken is held until maturity of the futures contract. The effect of daily settlement is determined for the pseudo bill over the life of the futures contract. Daily balances are assumed to earn the overnight rate on certificates of deposit. For each trade we calculate the expected profit and the actual profit. The difference between these numbers is separated into the effect of the actual trade and the effect of marking-to-the-market. This strategy is appropriate for an investor who wishes to invest money short term and purchases the cash bill or pseudo bill whichever has the highest expected increase in value. If this is the equilibrating mechanism then the differences in actual profit from buying the instrument which appears most profitable should be very small. In a market which is efficient with respect to this strategy, the differences should be bounded by a very minor transaction cost (a round trip on a T-bill futures contract is less than $25), compensation for risk associated with marking-to-the-market, and compensation for risk associated with having actual trade prices different than expected prices.

The second possible equilibrating strategy comes from a bill or pseudo bill holder observing a difference in return between the bill and pseudo bill and swapping to the lower cost instrument. We examined the profitability from swaps in several ways. Our results show that the pseudo bill strategy is almost always more profitable than the bill strategy. Thus, when strategies involving only single swaps were analyzed, the only swap that needed to be examined was the swap of a bill for a pseudo bill. We initially examined this strategy with various filter rules. We assumed the investor held the bill and would swap into the pseudo bill if some difference in expected profit existed. Filter sizes from $0 to $1,200 above transaction costs were tried. In examining the swap, transaction costs were estimated at $175 on each swap. This is a larger estimate of transaction costs than used by (1) or (7) and probably overestimates the size of transaction costs.[4] By overestimating transaction costs we ensure that any estimates we make of trading profits are conservative. One swap rule using a changing filter size was tried. In this rule we used whatever swap size was most profitable for the prior contract. All the swap rules were examined assuming there were 90, 75, 60, 45, and 30 days left before the contract expired.[5]

The third possible equilibrating mechanism is pure arbitrage. We examined the profitability of pure arbitrage for various filter rules. To be precise, at each point in time we examined if pure arbitrage would be expected to yield a profit above some level ranging from $0 to $800. Pure arbitrage would be expected to be profitable if the difference in expected profit between the two instruments exceeded transaction costs. Transaction costs included not only the cost of trading but also the differential interest cost on shorting the bill. The cost of shorting the bill was assumed to be 1/2% per year over the interest the bill earned.[6] Thus the transaction costs used were $175 plus 1/2% of principle multiplied by the number of days until the maturity of the futures contract divided by 365.

III Test Results

As discussed above, the tests in this paper examine efficiency with respect to three different equilibrating mechanisms (or strategies); the profit from purchasing the lower priced instrument, the differential profit from swapping between cash bills and pseudo bills, and finally the profit from engaging in an arbitrage position involving cash bills and pseudo bills. We will now present our empirical tests of these three equilibrating mechanisms.

A The Profit from Purchasing the Apparently More Profitable Contract

Table 15.1 presents the differential profits from purchasing a cash T-bill or a pseudo T-bill where the instrument which appears most profitable is purchased and held until the maturity of the futures contract (which is the same date as the maturity of the shorter term T-bill). While the differential investment is zero, the investment in either case is equal to the price of a $(91 + N)$ day cash T-bill with a value at maturity of one million dollars.[7] The first column lists the interval of profit which was expected when a trade was initiated. These profits were calculated using every observed cash T-bill price in the data set. The expected profit differential from investing in the lower priced strategy is calculated using the observed T-bill prices and the previous futures trade. The columns headed immediate execution present results if the cash T-bill is purchased at the price used to calculate expected profits and the futures contract is sold at the next observable futures price. The columns headed delayed execution present results when the cash T-bill is bought at the next hourly quoted price and the futures contract is sold at the price immediately after this next T-bill quote. Note that the delayed execution columns have fewer observations. For delayed execution we did not include the trades after the last cash T-bill price of the day since execution would be delayed overnight.

We can see from this table that in those cases where it appears to be profitable to buy a cash T-bill rather than a pseudo T-bill, the average profit earned from purchasing the former instrument was \$259 per contract if executions are made immediately or \$219 per contract if executions are delayed. In those cases where it appeared to be profitable to purchase a pseudo T-bill the extra dollar profit earned from following this action was \$961 if action was taken immediately and \$958 if execution was delayed.[8] Table 15.1 shows that

(1) The anticipated and actual profits from buying the pseudo T-bill are much higher than the profits from buying the cash T-bill. If one were forced to choose one instrument at all points in time the pseudo T-bill would dominate.

Table 15.1
Distribution of profits from purchasing the apparently more profitable contract

Interval of expected profit	Buying cash T-bill: Immediate execution: Number of cases	Buying cash T-bill: Immediate execution: Expected profit	Buying cash T-bill: Immediate execution: Actual profit	Buying cash T-bill: Delayed execution: Number of cases	Buying cash T-bill: Delayed execution: Expected profit	Buying cash T-bill: Delayed execution: Actual profit	Buying pseudo T-bill: Immediate execution: Number of cases	Buying pseudo T-bill: Immediate execution: Expected profit	Buying pseudo T-bill: Immediate execution: Actual profit	Buying pseudo T-bill: Delayed execution: Number of cases	Buying pseudo T-bill: Delayed execution: Expected profit	Buying pseudo T-bill: Delayed execution: Actual profit
$ 0– 200	292	$ 84	$ 80	226	$ 83	$ 63	912	$ 112	$ 113	679	$ 112	$114
200– 400	120	280	274	87	279	245	1006	296	294	764	295	292
400– 600	62	469	469	47	474	440	742	500	499	557	500	506
600– 800	38	695	677	26	699	675	534	691	692	384	689	683
800–1000	16	883	878	9	870	790	376	898	897	293	895	897
1000–1200	8	1078	1065	7	1082	858	290	1085	1090	220	1089	1104
1200–1400	3	1245	1284	1	1273	587	272	1302	1298	203	1303	1288
1400–1600	2	1426	1454	1	1395	1373	227	1514	1505	178	1511	1517
1600–1800							199	1713	1702	141	1709	1710
1800–2000							200	1910	1904	158	1916	1906
2000–2200							166	2103	2096	118	2107	2095
2200–2400							150	2297	2290	113	2292	2259
2400–2600							106	2484	2490	77	2480	2497

2600–2800							85	2665	2684	66	2660	2604
2800–3000							54	2897	2906	46	2890	2901
3000–3200							61	3081	3093	44	3079	3054
3200–3400							43	3304	3324	30	3309	3364
3400–3600							39	3489	3485	27	3485	3523
3600–3800							24	3689	3680	17	3694	3628
3800–4000							16	3959	3920	11	3949	3875
above 4000							36	4463	4452	82	4489	4331
Average profit		264	259		251	219		962	961		960	958

(2) Despite (1), the profits from buying the cash T-bill rather than the pseudo T-bill are positive when prices lead us to expect these profits to be positive.

(3) When executions take place assuming no trade delay, the differences between expected profits and actual profits are small. Another way of saying this is that expected profits are an excellent predictor of the profits which will be earned.

(4) When a trade delay is assumed, the expected profits are still good indications of the actual profits but the differences are much greater particularly when cash T-bill are bought.

(5) The number of times when acting on the basis of observed price information makes one type of purchase much more profitable than the other type is surprising. For example, there are 219 times when buying a pseudo T-bill rather than a T-bill had an expected profit over $3,000. The actual average profit in these instances was $3,557 in the case of immediate execution. In the case of delayed execution for 211 cases it was $3,541.

There are two more associated points of interest which cannot be seen directly from table 15.1. First, the profit from purchasing the apparently profitable instrument has become larger on more recent bills than it was on earlier bills. One might have expected these profits to diminish as the market became more established. On the other hand, interest rates were more volatile in the later period. Second, expected and actual profits show only a slight and uncertain tendency to decrease as maturity approaches. The relationship between profit and time to maturity was sometimes positive, sometimes negative and never very strong.

Let's now examine more closely the relationship between expected profit and actual profit. Differences exist because of the effects of marking-to-the-market and the delay in trading. Each of these will now be examined. Table 15.2 presents the frequency distribution for the interest gained or lost on having to mark-to-the-market given that the pseudo T-bill is purchased.[9] When purchasing the pseudo T-bill position (which means being short the futures contract) marking-to-the-market involved, on average, a minus $4 cash flow. This is small relative to the average profits reported in table 15.1. The adjustment for marking-to-the-market ranged from −$221 to +$158 but over three quarters of the observations were in the range of −$31 to +$31. While we continue to adjust the return on all trading rules for the effect of marking-to-the-market, the magnitude is so small that it is unlikely to have anything but a second order effect.

Table 15.2
Effect of marking-to-the-market

Dollar size	Percentage of occurrences
150 to 158	0.21
100 to 150	1.83
50 to 100	5.98
30 to 50	4.61
11 to 31	15.79
−11 to +11	43.16
−31 to −11	17.10
−50 to −31	4.63
−100 to −50	3.31
−150 to −100	2.30
−200 to −150	0.68
−221 to −200	0.41
Average effect = −$4.00	

Table 15.3 displays the difference between the expected differential profit from buying a pseudo T-bill rather than a cash T-bill and the actual differential profit that would subsequently have arisen from this action under the two execution scenarios but ignoring marking-to-the-market. We refer to this difference as the adjustment. Table 15.3 shows clearly that this average adjustment is small. It is $4 when there is no delay and $0 when there is delay in executing the preferred purchase. Examining similar data on the individual contracts also showed that the average adjustment for any single contract was small. There is no systematic tendency for actual profits to be lower (or higher) than expected profits.

Despite the absence of any systematic difference over all contracts or even any significant adjustment on a single contract, the adjustment for any one trade can be quite large. Assuming immediate executions it is in the range −$45 to +$35 more than 80% of the time. However, adjustments as large as −$278 and +$379 occur. Assuming delayed executions, only 32% are in the range of −$45 to +$35 and adjustments as large as −$2,152 and +$1,797 are present. The same phenomenon can be seen from examining the standard deviations. With no delay in execution the average standard deviation of the adjustment for an individual contract is $38 while with a delay in execution it is $225.

Table 15.3
Probability distribution of adjustments

Size of adjustment	Delayed execution	Immediate execution
Above $1000	0.34%	
600 to 1000	0.93	
400 to 600	2.09	
195 to 400	7.21	0.05%
175 to 195	1.71	0.07
155 to 175	0.36	0.00
135 to 155	2.10	0.02
115 to 135	3.07	0.10
95 to 115	3.70	0.54
75 to 95	4.83	1.73
35 to 75	7.89	6.95
−5 to 35	22.14	49.04
−45 to −5	10.06	32.53
−85 to −45	12.26	8.16
−105 to −85	3.45	0.51
−125 to −105	0.44	0
−145 to −125	2.69	0.15
−165 to −145	2.39	0.07
−185 to −165	1.86	0.03
−400 to −185	7.35	0.07
−400 to −1000	2.89	
Below −1000	0.23	
Average adjustment	$0	$4
Standard deviation of adjustment	$225	$38

While the variability of the adjustment represents risk in any trading strategy, the risk is less than it might at first appear. There are three reasons for this. One is that an investor should be able to trade at the observed T-bill price and the next futures price (the immediate execution case). Second, the profits indicated in table 15.1 are so much greater than the entries in table 15.3 that an investor who will purchase either the pseudo T-bill instrument or the cash T-bill instrument bears almost no risk of doing worse by purchasing the one with the higher expected value. The third reason applies to the analyses discussed below. Many of the

Table 15.4
Mean profit from single swaps immediate execution

Filter size on expected profits	Days to maturity				
	90 days	75 days	60 days	45 days	30 days
$ 0	$1351	$1313	$1230	$1113	$1067
100	1367	1321	1239	1150	1087
200	1391	1340	1267	1170	1104
300	1416	1363	1274	1193	1141
400	1429	1364	1302	1228	1151
500	1406	1335	1295	1208	1109
600	1347	1318	1219	1159	1072
700	1374	1310	1238	1182	1086
800	1394	1304	1196	1144	1052
900	1349	1263	1198	1148	1056
1000	1276	1233	1127	1099	1009
1100	1262	1237	1122	1092	977
1200	1284	1247	1142	1109	985

trading rules examined call for multiple trades, and risk will diminish as more positions are taken over time.

B *The Profit from Swapping*

In this section we examine the profits which can be earned from swapping between a cash T-bill instrument and a pseudo T-bill instrument. All of the swaps we consider are appropriate for an investor who holds a position in cash T-bills but is willing to hold pseudo T-bills when it appears to be more profitable to do so. The first set of tests involves a single swap from cash T-bills to pseudo T-bills.[10] Tables 15.4 and 15.5 present the results of a swap from a T-bill to a pseudo T-bill of the same maturity when varying size filters are used to trigger the action.[11] The difference between these tables is that in table 15.4 once a swap is indicated it is executed immediately while in table 15.5 it is executed with a delay. The analysis is initiated when T-bills have a varying number of days to maturity. For example, consider the entry in the row labeled 400 and the column labeled 75 days in table 15.4. The $1,364 is the extra (after transaction costs) profit which would have been earned on average by

Table 15.5
Mean profit from single swaps delayed execution

Filter size on expected profits	Days to maturity				
	90 days	75 days	60 days	45 days	30 days
$ 0	$1379	$1224	$1113	$1061	$1219
100	1395	1237	1125	1109	1217
200	1404	1250	1177	1140	1211
300	1436	1264	1159	1148	1207
400	1446	1274	1249	1176	1248
500	1397	1248	1227	1120	1167
600	1361	1223	1211	1101	1185
700	1352	1221	1202	1080	1176
800	1372	1188	1215	1084	1089
900	1350	1186	1207	1021	1061
1000	1314	1209	1196	1008	1097
1100	1291	1226	1172	974	1070
1200	1300	1236	1125	926	1030

switching out of a T-bill into the pseudo T-bill at the first point in time when such a switch had an expected profit greater than $400, given that the analysis begins 75 days before maturity. In both tables the profit from employing the $400 filter rule performs best across all maturities. While an investor could not have known this ahead of time, selecting any filter rule presented in these tables leads to extra profits. In fact, marked decreases in profit occur only at very large filter levels.

Tables 15.4 and 15.5 show that the shorter the maturity of the bill when the filter is applied, the smaller the profit earned by the filter. Despite this the application of reasonable size filters to bills with as little as 30 days to maturity produces sizeable profits. For example, returning to the $400 filter rule under immediate execution the profit from applying it to a 30 day period rather than a 90 day period only decreases by 15%. A comparison of these tables shows that while the delay in execution on a swap with a high expected profit does decrease the profit actually earned, the decrease is small relative to the size of the profit. Even assuming delayed execution the use of filter rules yields meaningful profits. Another way to view the significance of these profits is to see how many standard deviations from zero each entry is in tables 15.4 and 15.5. Every entry is at least four standard deviations from zero.[12]

Table 15.6
Pure arbitrage strategy

	Immediate execution				Delayed execution			
Size of filter rule	Number of trades	Expected profit	Actual profit	Standard error	Number of trades	Expected profit	Actual profit	Standard error
$ 0	2304	$ 894	$ 889	$15	1725	$ 893	$ 880	$18
100	2093	980	975	16	1569	977	964	19
200	1902	1064	1058	16	1428	1059	1041	19
300	1738	1142	1135	16	1301	1137	1117	20
400	1595	1212	1206	17	1206	1199	1176	20
500	1469	1279	1271	17	1107	1267	1244	21
600	1332	1352	1346	18	1005	1339	1315	22
700	1190	1437	1432	18	890	1429	1401	23
800	1063	1519	1516	18	789	1517	1490	24

C *Pure Arbitrage*

Table 15.6 shows the profits from a pure arbitrage strategy. The first column shows the filter that initiated the trade. For example $200 means that if an expected profit net of transaction costs (including the differential interest cost) greater than $200 was observed an arbitrage was initiated. Column 2 shows the number of times an expected profit of that magnitude was observed, assuming immediate execution. For example, in 1,902 instances arbitrages with an expected profit greater than $200 were observed over the 28 contracts. The next column shows the expected profit that initiated the trade and the following column the actual profit. Actual profit differs from expected profit due to marking-to-the-market and trading at different prices. The differences between expected profit and actual profit are small. The standard error is the standard error of the mean. The results of table 15.6 are surprising. They are indications of rather substantial profits to arbitrage in a market where swappers and initial purchasers have substantially lower transaction costs than the arbitrageurs.

IV Conclusions

This paper presents an empirical investigation of the efficiency of futures markets. It is different from previous papers in the futures area in that (1) intra-day prices were used for both cash T-bills and futures contracts, (2) all decision rules tested are formulated in terms of observable variables and are executed at prices which existed after the decision rule indicated a course of action, and (3) all results are adjusted for the effect of marking-to-the-market.

Our results indicate that the T-bill futures market is not perfectly efficient. Buying either the cash T-bill or pseudo T-bill and selling the other instrument short when the anticipated profit is larger than transaction costs leads to positive profits. Profits occurred in all contracts and were larger in general for successive futures contracts. Given that the market is not perfectly efficient with respect to pure arbitrage it is not surprising that inefficiencies exist with respect to investors who are considering swaps or an initial purchase of the cheaper of the cash T-bill instrument or the pseudo T-bill instrument.

Notes

The authors would like to thank the Center for the Study of Futures Markets at Columbia Business School for financial supports.

1. Marking-to-the-market makes the pseudo T-bill slightly different from the cash T-bill.

2. To purchase an N day T-bill with a maturity between 92 and 182 days an investor could either

(1) purchase an N day T-bill in the cash market (cash T-bill instrument).

(2) purchase an $(N - 91)$ day T-bill in the cash market and purchase a T-bill futures contract which expires in $(N - 91)$ days. Delivery is then taken on the futures contract (pseudo T-bill instrument).

Note that the cash T-bill held as the 1 to 91 days instrument has the same maturity (i.e., is the same) as the cash T-bill held in the 92–182 day pseudo T-bill instrument. Similarly the cash T-bill held in the 1 to 91 day pseudo T-bill instrument has the same maturity as the cash T-bill held as the 92 to 182 day cash T-bill instrument. Also in both the 1–91 day and 92–182 day cash T-bill instruments the same T-bill futures contract is traded, being sold in the shorter term pseudo instrument but purchased in the longer term pseudo instrument. Since the instruments used for the 1 to 91 day test are the same as those for the 92 to 182 day test, similar results apply concerning efficiency.

3. The longer term T-bill normally has a slightly higher bid-ask spread than the shorter term T-bill. This is also a differential transaction cost.

4. A more realistic estimate of transaction costs over the period of this study would be $30 on the sale of the near T-bill and $40 on the purchase of the more distant T-bill. These costs are estimated from the normal bid-asked spreads of $60 and $80, respectively. In addition, the round trip on the futures contract could be accomplished for less than $25.

5. One more complex swapping rule was tested. Even though it was almost never profitable to swap from the pseudo bill to the bill, multiple swaps are still potentially profitable. For example, it might be profitable to incur a $100 loss in swapping from the pseudo bill to the bill in anticipation of a much higher profit in swapping back to the pseudo bill.

6. See Capozza and Cornell (1979) for a justification of this rate.

7. When comparing the profits from an investment in the cash T-bill instrument with the profits from an investment in the pseudo T-bill instrument, it is necessary to compare the profits from equal amounts of dollars invested. Since T-bills of different maturities sell at different prices, one cash T-bill cannot simply be compared with one pseudo T-bill. However, the adjustment process for equal dollar investment is calculated as follows. The cost of one pseudo T-bill is simply the price of a $(91 + N)$ day T-bill. Define this to be C_{N+91}. The sale of the future requires no cash flow since no money is paid on establishing the initial purchase or sale of a futures contract. If an N day T-bill sells for C_N then one only must buy C_{N+91}/C_N of these to insure that the same sum of money is invested in each instrument.

8. This table has not been adjusted for transaction costs since only differential transaction costs are relevant in calculating net profit. These differential transaction costs are the costs of round tripping (selling and delivering) the futures contract and any difference in the transaction costs for shorter T-bills versus longer T-bills. These costs are small (the round trip for the futures contract is less than $25) and should be subtracted from the pseudo T-bill profits.

9. We computed two frequency distributions. The distribution in table 15.2 is computed assuming the investor is always long the pseudo T-bill (and so sells the future). The conditional distribution which assumes the investor holds the pseudo T-bill or actual T-bill, whichever appears more profitable, was also computed. This is not presented since for all intents and purposes it is the same as shown in table 15.2.

10. Only one direction was used. The pseudo T-bill strategy was the more profitable in most cases. The rules discussed in this section can be considered those that could be used by an investor who has just been introduced to the concept of using the futures markets to construct a pseudo T-bill.

11. The entries are actual profits including the effect of marking-to-the-market and differences due to change in prices between the formation of expectations and the execution of purchases and sales assuming the two different execution scenarios.

12. As mentioned earlier (see footnote 5), we also tried multiple swap rules using a dynamic programming formulation. These produced average profits per futures contract of $2,002 with no delay in execution and $1,475 when execution was delayed.

References

Capozza, Dennis, and Bradford Cornell, "Treasury Bill Pricing in the Spot and Futures Market," *Review of Economics and Statistics* 61 (Nov. 1979), 513–520.

Cornell, Bradford, "Taxes and the Pricing of Treasury Bill Futures Contracts: A Note," *Journal of Finance* 36 (Dec. 1981), 1169–1177.

Cox, John C., Jon Ingersoll, and Steve A. Ross, "The Relation between Forward Prices and Futures Markets," *Journal of Financial Economics* 9 (Dec. 1981), 321–346.

Lang, Richard W., and Robert H. Rasche, "A Comparison of Yields on Futures Contracts and Implied Forward Rates," *Federal Reserve Bank of Saint Louis Monthly Review* 50 (Dec. 1978), 21–30.

Poole, William, "Using T-bill Futures to Gauge Interest Rate Expectations," *Federal Reserve Bank of San Francisco Economic Review* (Spring 1978), 7–18.

Puglisi, Donald J., "Is the Futures Market for Treasury Bills Efficient?," *The Journal of Portfolio Management* (Winter 1978), 64–67.

Rendleman, Richard J., and Christopher E. Carabini, "The Efficiency of the Treasury Bill Futures Market," *Journal of Finance* 34 (Sept. 1979), 895–914.

Vignola, Anthony J., Charles J. Dale, "Is the Futures Market for Treasury Bills Efficient?," *Journal of Portfolio Management* (Winter 1979), 76–81.

16

Employing Financial Futures to Increase the Return on Near Cash (Treasury Bill) Investments

Edwin J. Elton, Martin J. Gruber, and Joel C. Rentzler

Most financial institutions and many industrial corporations invest funds in short-term Treasury bills as a temporary liquidity reserve. T-bills are selected because they are among the safest and most readily marketable financial instruments. In this article we present and test a multiperiod dynamic programming trading rule which exploits previously identified inefficiencies in the futures market to increase the return on a T-bill portfolio.

In the past few years a number of articles have appeared which examine inefficiencies in the futures market.[1] Most recently the authors (1984) in an exhaustive study of the short term T-bill market have shown that

(1) futures on T-bills tend to be systematically overpriced and

(2) when discrepancies between cash T-bill and T-bill futures prices are observed trades can be initiated which allow an excess return to be earned.

The purpose of this article is to develop a decision model for exploiting potential excess profits and to test how well this model performs.

In the first section of this paper we will describe how futures might be used by a treasurer to modify the return on a position in cash T-bills. In the second section we discuss the decision model developed to use futures to earn an increased return. In the last section, we discuss the empirical results of applying this model.

I Using T-Bill Futures

In order to illustrate the use of T-bill futures by a corporate treasurer we shall start with a simple example which will then be generalized. To avoid complexity we will assume away the problem of indivisibility, transaction costs, and daily settlement of gains and losses (marking to the market). The effect of these latter two influences will be explained below and will be considered in the empirical section of this paper. Indivisibility is not a problem as long as the amount of money invested is sufficiently large.

Assume that a treasurer is considering buying a T-bill which matures in 30 days and is now valued at \$990,000. Since T-bills are pure discount instruments this bill will be worth 1,000,000 at maturity. This is a return of 10/990 or 1.01% over the 30 days.

Now assume that a futures contract exists calling for delivery of a 91-day T-bill in 30 days. No money changes hands when a futures contract is bought (or sold) but an agreement is entered into requiring the holder to purchase (and the seller to deliver) a particular maturity T-bill at a particular price on a particular date. Assume that the current price of this futures contract is \$969,700. Also assume that a 121-day T-bill now exists with a price \$960,000.[2]

The treasurer could manufacture a 30-day investment by buying the 121-day T-bill and selling a futures contract now and in 30 days at the maturity of the futures contract, delivering the then 91-day T-bill to fulfill the futures contract. This would return \$9,700 dollars (969,700–960,000) on an investment of 960,000 for a return of 1.01%. Thus whether the treasurer invests in a 30-day bill directly or manufactures one by selling a futures contract and buying a 121-day T-bill, the same return is earned.

In this paper we will analyze the case where the treasurer is assumed initially to be holding a T-bill but considers switching to a longer bill and a futures contract and perhaps back again if the expected return warrants it. In general a switch may be profitable anytime the following instruments offer a different rate of return:

(1) an N-day T-bill,

(2) a $(91 + N)$-day T-bill combined with the sale of a futures contract on a 91-day bill for delivery in N days. We shall call this a pseudo T-bill.

There are two influences which may limit the ability of a treasurer to make a profit when the return on the cash T-bill and pseudo T-bill are not the same. The first of these is transaction costs. If a treasurer held T-bills he would incur transaction costs when switching into pseudo T-bills and prices could differ by the amount of these transaction costs without a swap being profitable. These costs involve the sale of a T-bill, the purchase of another T-bill, and the sale of a futures contract. Reasonable estimates of these transaction costs are \$40 on a one way transaction for the short-term bill, \$60 on a one way transaction for the long-term bill and a \$25 round trip for the futures contract. In all tests in this paper we use \$175 as our estimate of transaction costs in switching from a pseudo T-bill to a cash T-bill or vice versa. This is an overestimate of transaction costs which have an average value of \$82.50 $(30 + 40 + 25/2)$. Our estimates of transaction costs are conservative. If we find positive trading profits with these overstated values, we can be sure they will be even larger under a more realistic estimate.

The second influence affecting the profitability of a swap is the cash flows associated with futures contracts being marked to the market daily. Marking-to-the-market is one of the basic differences between a futures contract and a pure forward contract. Under daily marking to the market at the end of each trading day the holder of a futures contract must compensate the seller (or be compensated by the seller) for any change which takes place in the settlement price. Fortunately this results in a very small cash flow. Cox, Ingersoll, and Ross (1981) have argued on theoretical grounds that it should be extremely small and the authors (1984) have demonstrated empirically that it is quite small having an average value of −\$4 on the one million dollar futures contract.

Just considering a single swap, it would not pay a manager to swap if the T-bill and pseudo T-bill differ by less than transaction costs and the effect of marking to the market. However, empirical studies (Rendleman and Carabini 1979 and the authors 1984) have shown that there are much larger price differences between the two instruments. If large price discrepancies exist but tend to disappear over time one should be able to earn an excess return by trading against these discrepancies. This paper will test whether the differences which have been noted are sufficiently large to allow a profit to be earned by trading against them. The viewpoint taken is that of a corporate treasurer who starts with a sum of money committed to T-bills but is willing to switch between T-bills and pseudo T-bills with the same effective maturity. Likewise if the treasurer has swapped to the pseudo T-bill we assume a willingness to swap back if the differential shrinks sufficiently. Since the T-bill has a finite life this is a case of repetitive decision making over a fixed horizon. As such the problem is amenable to modeling via dynamic programming.

II Optimum Swap Rules

We assume that the decision maker starts with a position in cash T-bills. Several times a day he or she is able to observe prices on cash T-bills and

T-bill futures contracts and based on these observations calculates an expected profit from a swap into the pseudo T-bill. Once the treasurer swaps into the pseudo T-bill he or she continues to examine prices to see if a swap back into bills is profitable.

Even though the analysis of prices in Elton et al. (1984) shows that if one is going to hold only one instrument the pseudo T-bill is the generally more profitable instrument, multiple swaps are still potentially profitable. For example, it might be profitable to incur a $100 loss in swapping from the pseudo bill to the bill in anticipation of a much higher profit in swapping back to the pseudo bill as the difference between the prices of these two instruments once again widens. It is the potential for multiple swaps that makes this a dynamic programming problem.

A The Model

In order to be as realistic as possible we examined two trading rules which differed with respect to the timing of trades. The first trading rule assumes that the cash T-bill is purchased at the price used in calculating the expected profit while the futures transaction takes place at the first futures price (trade price) following the cash market price. In the rest of the paper this is referred to as *immediate execution*. The second trading rule assumes that the cash T-bill is purchased at its next quoted price (about 1 hour later) and the futures transaction takes place at the next trade after the T-bill is purchased. This will be referred to as a *delayed execution*. The first trading rule simulates the trading of an investor who can quickly determine the profit of the strategy and reacts accordingly. The second trading rule is feasible even for a slow reacting investor since approximately an hour elapses between the cash and T-bill quotes.

The optimum swap rules are determined using the following dynamic programming equations. If holding a cash bill

$$B(t,d) = \max \begin{bmatrix} \left(d - \text{adjustment} - \text{transaction costs} + \right. & \\ \left. \dfrac{1}{1+r}\bar{P}(t+1,\cdot)\right) & \text{swap} \\ \dfrac{1}{1+r}\bar{B}(t+1,\cdot) & \text{don't swap.} \end{bmatrix} \tag{1}$$

If holding a pseudo bill

$$P(t,d) = \max \begin{bmatrix} \left(-d + \text{adjustment} - \text{transaction costs} + \right. \\ \left. \frac{1}{1+r}\bar{B}(t+1,\cdot)\right) \quad \text{swap} \\ \frac{1}{1+r}\bar{P}(t+1,\cdot) \quad \text{don't swap.} \end{bmatrix} \tag{2}$$

where

(1) d = the dollar difference in expected profit from holding the pseudo bill compared to a cash bill with the same maturity.

(2) adjustment = the expected change in d from the time the decision is made to swap until the swap is executed assuming the investor holds the cash bill. The adjustment was estimated using the prior contract and in general it was negligible.

(3) transaction costs = the transaction costs of the trade estimated at \$175.

(4) r = the overnight rate of interest on certificates of deposit.

(5) $B(t+1,\cdot)$ = the expected profit of holding a bill at $(t+1)$ and following the optimum course of action from $(t+1)$ to the horizon. It is calculated by taking the expected value over d of $B(t+1,d)$ calculated at time t. At the horizon it is zero.

(6) $P(t+1,\cdot)$ = is parallel to $B(t+1,\cdot)$ except the investor is assumed to hold a pseudo T-bill at $t+1$.

(7) $B(t,d)$ = expected profit from period t to the horizon given that the investor holds a bill at t, observes a differential in expected profit between the pseudo bill and cash bill of size d and follows an optimum course of action from $(t+1)$ to the horizon.

(8) $P(t,d)$ = is parallel to $B(t,d)$ except that the investor is assumed to hold a pseudo T-bill at t.

Several comments on the equations are in order. Consider the equation for an investor holding a cash bill. The first term in brackets represents the expected profit if the investor swaps, while the second term represents the expected profit if the investor doesn't swap. If the investor swaps, the immediate expected profit on the swap is the differential observed plus the expected adjustment to the profit due to the delay in executing the trade less transaction costs. If the investor swaps the cash bill for a pseudo bill, he or she will be holding a pseudo bill at $(t+1)$. Thus the total expected profit consists of not only the profit on the immediate swap but also present value of profits from following the optimum course of action from $(t+1)$ to the horizon given that a pseudo bill is held at $(t+1)$. If the investor doesn't swap then the expected profit is the present value of the expected profit from following the optimum course of action from $(t+1)$ to the horizon given that a cash bill is hold at $(t+1)$. The equation when the investor holds a pseudo bill at t is analogous. Note that both d and the adjustment term have the opposite sign they had in the previous equation. Both d and the change in d have the opposite sign if an investor swaps a cash bill for a pseudo bill rather than swapping a pseudo bill for a cash bill.

B *Parameterizing the Model*

In this section, we discuss in detail the method used to derive the parameters needed in the dynamic programming problem. Before discussing the parameterization it is worthwhile describing the data used.

1 Data

Intra-day quotes on cash T-bill prices were obtained from the Federal Reserve Bank of New York for the period January 6, 1976 through December 22, 1982. These contain the closing bid and ask prices, the opening change from the previous closing bid price and three other changes from this bid price at approximately hourly intervals.[3] The impact of average bid-ask spreads are accounted for in calculating transaction costs. For each day in this period, these intra-day prices were recorded for each of two cash bills. One was for the cash bill deliverable on the near futures contract (maturing 91 days after the maturity of the futures contract). This is the bill held in the 1 to 91 day pseudo T-bill instrument. The other cash bill price used was the price for the bill maturing when the futures contracted matured. This is the price for the 1 to 91 day cash T-bill instrument. T-bill futures prices were obtained from a tape supplied by the International Monetary Market (IMM) of the Chicago Mercantile Exchange. This tape contained the price and time of *every* T-bill futures trade over the same January 6, 1976 through December 22, 1982 period.[4] There were a total of 28 futures contracts traded over this period which includes all data from the inception of the T-bill futures market. One additional point should be noted. The data to compare the cash and pseudo bills were available over the last 91 days of the life of the futures contract. This translates into approximately 65 trading days. However, in the last week to week and a half before maturity of a futures contract volume may be low and it is unrealistic to assume that additional trades can be executed at the actual trade prices. Thus, to be conservative we did not allow a position to change during the last 7 days and analyzed only 58 trading days.

2 Parameterization

The expected profit on each contract (the *d*'s in equations (1) and (2)) were estimated in two ways. First the *d*'s for each contract were estimated using the differentials observed in the immediately prior contract. This is an assumption of a constant dollar profit from one contract to the next. By estimating *d*'s from the immediately prior contract, we are using information that was available to the investor before the period in question. Assume we had 4 observations each day.[5] Then we had 4 times 58 or 232 different values for dollar profit from each contract. In developing the cut off rates we would draw 4 times a day from this distribution of expected profits where each of the 232 values was equally likely.

The second method used to estimate the *d*'s was to assume that the returns that would be observed on any contract were the same as the returns that were observed on the immediately prior contract. For example, to determine cut off rates on the fifth contract we would first determine all observed returns on the fourth contract. Returns were calculated using return $= (1 + d/1{,}000{,}000)^{1/t} - 1$ where t is the number of trading days until expiration. At each point in time it was assumed that the distribution of possible returns was the distribution of the actual returns from the prior contract. Once the return was determined it was reconverted into dollar profits and equations (1) and (2) were applied. The same return would lead to different dollar profits depending on the time to expiration.

The two techniques for estimating *d* make different assumptions concerning the size of the expected profit over the life of the contract. Using constant returns implies a decrease in expected dollar profit over the life of the contract. Assuming constant dollar profits implies the same expected dollar profit on day one as on day 58. We analyzed several contracts to see if the data were more consistent with either assumption. The analysis involved regressing expected dollar returns on time. While on average the slopes of the regressions were negative, they were very unstable from contract to contract and the coefficients were not statistically significant. Thus empirical evidence did not support either assumption as clearly superior and hence both were used. However analyzing the data on the first contracts showed that in the last 10 trading days, large profits were not observed.[6] To partially compensate for this we set the cut off rate for switching to pseudo T-bills at $400 over the last 10 days when parameterizing the model.[7]

In determining the optimum swap rules, we used the adjustment in profit computed from the prior contract. The adjustment was the change in expected profit from the time of the average observed price difference to the time of the execution. This was done for both immediate and delayed executions. For immediate execution the adjustment is small since the only change that can take place is in the futures price. For the delayed execution the size of the adjustment is potentially much larger. Intuitively it seems that the higher the expected dollar profit the greater the adjustment toward zero that might be expected. We regressed expected dollar profit against adjustment for a number of contracts. The relationship was insignificant. The final variable needed is the interest rate. The interest rate used was an overnight rate on certificates of deposit. This rate approximates what an investor could obtain on short term funds.

Given the estimated parameters of the dynamic programming model the optimum value of d at which to switch from a pseudo bill to a cash bill and the optimum point to switch from a cash bill to a pseudo bill can be estimated at each point in time. Cut offs were established using the data on one futures contract and then these cut offs were used to make decisions on the following futures contract.[8]

III Empirical Results

The results of applying the dynamic programming algorithm to make optimum switches between T-bills and pseudo T-bills are shown in Table 16.1. The entries in this table represent the increase in profits (over simply holding cash T-bills) which results from applying the dynamic programming algorithm outlined in the previous section. The first point worth noting is that the application of the algorithm seems to lead to profits under all variations in parameterizing the model. From past research we know that there are inefficiencies in the capital market. This paper shows that a decision model can be formulated which, even in the presence of transaction costs and a delay in responding to information, earns a positive profit.

The assumption of constant dollar return leads to slightly higher profits in both the immediate execution and delayed execution cases. However, the differences in profits are very small. Delayed execution results in lower profits than immediate execution. Profits decline by more than 20%. However the profits are still positive. This is inconsistent with profit opportunities which tend to disappear over time.

Perhaps the most striking aspect of Table 16.1 is that for immediate execution one never loses money on any futures contract. There was only

Table 16.1
Acutal increase in dollar profit from applying the dynamic programming algorithm

	Immediate execution		Delayed execution	
Futures contracts maturity dates	Constant rate of return	Constant dollar profit	Constant rate of return	Constant dollar profit
Jun 1976	$ 255	$ 250	$ 255	$ 233
Sep 1976	154	890	129	357
Dec 1976	394	194	348	194
Mar 1977	0	49	0	100
Jun 1977	438	546	370	545
Sep 1977	455	414	602	358
Dec 1977	565	242	358	90
Mar 1978	411	1051	412	726
Jun 1978	639	870	840	840
Sep 1978	1301	1574	1427	1449
Dec 1978	1560	1159	1432	1696
Mar 1979	577	993	295	991
Jun 1979	570	795	731	941
Sep 1979	1390	1484	1568	1789
Dec 1979	3085	3676	1548	2472
Mar 1980	8050	7366	3290	5114
Jun 1980	13872	11592	10862	6835
Sep 1980	422	1542	624	482
Dec 1980	1760	1760	1271	1271
Mar 1981	4313	4778	3145	2252
Jun 1981	2877	5214	2352	4546
Sep 1981	2463	2463	2124	2124
Dec 1981	816	3372	−176	4854
Mar 1982	6866	5551	6405	4471
Jun 1982	2638	2091	1871	2400
Sep 1982	4594	3735	3958	3370
Dec 1982	4788	4939	4777	4532
Average	$ 2417	$ 2540	$ 1882	$ 2038

one futures contract out of the 27 tested where the profit was not positive. In this it was zero. No trades were made on this futures contract. Any time one or more trades were made on a futures contract, profits were positive. The results were almost as good in the case of delayed execution. Here there was one contract (December 1981) where parameterizing by rates of return produces trades with a loss. There was one case with zero profits and all other contracts had positive profits.

The evidence indicates that a dynamic programming algorithm can produce profits. Alternative simpler decision models might be formulated in terms of single trades. To get some idea of the value of multiple trades we examined the following two rules.

(1) Trade from T-bills to pseudo T-bills at the expected profit level which produced the largest actual profit on the previous bill.

(2) Trade from T-bills to pseudo T-bills at the expected profit level which produces the largest profit on the bill being examined.

Rule 1 is the simple swap equivalent to our multiple swap rule. Rule 2 is an unrealistically tough standard and is impossible to execute in practice. It answers the question of whether the dynamic programming model produced better results than taking the optimal single swap based on perfect knowledge.

Rules 1 and 2 led to profits of $1371 and $1600 under immediate execution. The two dynamic programming algorithms tested in this paper produced profits of $2417 and $2540 under immediate execution. For delayed execution the simple swap rule assuming perfect information lead to an average profit of $1621 while our algorithms led to profits of $1882 and $2038. Thus the dynamic programming algorithm applied using only available information produces profits which are not only positive but are higher than a single swap rule would produce if perfect information were available. Since we have overestimated transaction costs and since the dynamic programming algorithm on average leads to slightly less than eight transactions per futures contract, the real difference should be even greater.

IV Conclusion

In this paper we develop a dynamic programming model which optimizes the use of T-bill futures in cash management. T-bill futures enable a manager to change the effective maturity of a debt instrument. They allow the creation of a pseudo bill with the same maturity as a cash bill. Prior research shows that inefficiencies exist in the pricing of futures contracts. In this paper we show that these inefficiencies are sufficiently large that multiple swaps are profitable even after fully accounting for transaction costs. These profits are higher than just using single swaps.[9]

Notes

1. See Capozza and Cornell (1979), Lang and Rasche (1978), Poole (1978), Puglisi (1978), and Vignola and Dale (1979).

2. These represent actual cash prices not discount prices quoted by financial services.

3. These quotes were obtained from surveys of government security dealers. The accuracy of this data was cross checked by comparing it with the actual trade data of a major financial intermediary. No significant differences were found.

4. This tape was created by pit observers relaying trades via walkie-talkie to terminal operators who recorded the information into the exchange's data banks. The IMM estimates the time lag between an actual trade and its computer time stamp as being 1–10 seconds.

5. There were either 4 or 5 observations each day depending on whether we assumed delayed execution or immediate execution and depending on the time period under study.

6. Recall that we did not assume that trades could take place in the last 7 days. Thus the $400 expected profit is being used 8 to 17 days from the maturity of the futures contract.

7. We also used a value of $250. The results are virtually identical under either rule so we will not present this additional set of results.

8. The cut off or optimal values of *d* at which the switch between instruments was well behaved had the properties one would expect given the nature of the problem For the switch to pseudo bills, the critical value started high ($1203 for the last contract) and decreased continuously over the life of the contract. For the switch to the cash bill, the cut off started with the switch being signaled even though the switch initially led to a large loss ($829 at the start of the last contract). The size of the loss at which such a switch should be made decreased continuously over the life of the contract until near expiration a switch was indicated only if the switch itself was profitable.

9. The authors would like to thank the Center for the Study of Business and Government at Baruch College and the Center for the Study of Futures Markets at Columbia Business School for financial support.

References

Capozza, D. and B. Cornell, "Treasury Bill Pricing in the Spot and Futures Market," *Rev. Econom. Statist.*, 61 (November 1979), 513–520.

Cornell, B., "Taxes and the Pricing of Treasury Bill Futures Contracts: A Note," *J. Finance*, 36, 5 (December 1981), 1169–1177.

Cox, J. C., J. Ingersoll and S. A. Ross, "The Relation Between Forward Prices and Futures Markets," *J. Financial Econom.*, 9 (December 1981), 321–346.

Elton, E. J., M. J. Gruber and J. Rentzler, "Intra-Day Tests of the Efficiency of the Treasury Bill Futures Market," *Rev. Econom. Statist.*, 66, 1 (February 1984), 129–137.

Lang, R. W. and R. H. Rasche, "A Comparison of Yields on Futures Contracts and Implied Forward Rates," *Fed. Reserve Bank of St. Louis Monthly Rev.*, 50 (December 1978), 21–30.

Poole, W., "Using T-Bill Futures to Gauge Interest Rate Expectations," *Fed. Reserve Bank of San Francisco Econom. Rev.*, (Spring 1978), 7–18.

Puglisi, D. J., "Is the Futures Market for Treasury Bills Efficient?," *J. Portfolio Management*, (Winter 1978), 64–67.

Rendleman, R. J. and C. E. Carabini, "The Efficiency of the Treasury Bill Futures Market," *J. Finance*, 34 (September 1979), 895–914.

Vignola, J. and C. J. Dale, "Is the Futures Market for Treasury Bills Efficient?," *J. Portfolio Management*, (Winter 1979), 78–81.

17

Bond Returns, Immunization and The Return Generating Process

Edwin J. Elton, Martin J. Gruber, and Prafulla G. Nabar

I Introduction

Recently a large amount of attention has been devoted to understanding how common stock returns are generated. Arbitrage pricing theory (APT) has provided a framework for examining both the return generating process for individual securities[1] and the differential in mean return between securities.[2] Despite the large and growing body of literature applying a new theory and new technology to explaining stock returns, very little work has been done using the insights we have gained from APT to explain bond returns.[3] The purpose of this study is to explore these insights to increase our understanding of bond returns. This paper examines three issues important in understanding bond returns: the return generating process, immunization, and differential returns across bonds. We will briefly discuss each of these in turn.

1.1 The Return Generating Process

A return generating process is a function relating a bond's return to one or more factors that are common across bonds plus a term unique to the bond in question. In the common equity area, the most commonly used return generating process is the single-index model.

Return generating processes have rarely been directly examined in the bond area. Instead, researchers have concentrated on estimating duration, a theoretically derived measure of the sensitivity of any bond to a change in interest rates (usually the first period's rate). Duration can be utilized in a single-factor model, and it should work well if the assumptions underlying its derivation do not represent serious distortions of reality. Alternative duration measures have been formulated and tested in an immunization framework but they have not been tested in the framework of a return generating process. The simplest definition of duration, Macaulay's duration, has worked about as well as any of the more complex measures which have been proposed.

In this paper we will test Macaulay's duration in a single-factor model of the return generating process. This will be used as the standard against which to test other single-factor and multi-factor models of the return generating process. We use Macaulay's duration as a standard because in previous immunization studies multi-factor models and more complex single-factor models have not been shown to be superior to this simple measure.[4] Our results differ. We believe our results come about because we view the problem as one of choice among alternative return generating processes, leading us to the design of different testing procedures. These procedures show the superiority of multi-index models compared to single-index models.

1.2 *Immunization*

The second area of interest is immunization. An immunized liability is usually defined as one where the duration of the assets is the same as the duration of the liabilities. We view this concept in a much more general way. Immunization is really the formation of a portfolio with zero sensitivity to each of the factors in the return generating process. If duration is the appropriate sensitivity measure, then an immunized portfolio is constructed in the standard way by equating the duration of the assets to the duration of the liabilities. With this construction, the immunized portfolio (the portfolio of assets and liabilities) has zero sensitivity to the factor. However, if a multi-index model is a better description of reality, then an immunized portfolio involves setting the sensitivity of the portfolio of the assets and liabilities equal to zero for each of the indexes. In contrast to previous work we find that portfolios immunized using multiple factors perform statistically better than portfolios immunized using a single-index model with duration as a sensitivity measure. We believe our results come about because of the design of our testing procedures.

Prior tests of immunization assumed that the liability was a single payment at some fixed time in the future.[5] Then a spot rate was estimated for that fixed date. The portfolio which produced a realized rate that most closely matched this spot rate was then judged to be the superior portfolio. This test procedure was sufficiently weak that the investigator could not differentiate between alternative duration measures, or in many cases between an immunized portfolio and one with simple maturity matching.

The latter, of course, has no theoretical justification and was employed simply as a naive model.

In contrast, we employ an actual portfolio as a lability. This means that we can observe monthly prices and cash flows on that portfolio. We construct immunized portfolios using the arbitrary portfolio as the liability. If we truly have an immunized portfolio, the period by period return on the assets less that on the liabilities should be mean zero random noise. With this alternative design, Macaulay's duration is statistically dominated by alternative immunized portfolios utilizing multiple factors, and a clear ranking among alternatives exists.

1.3 Differential Returns

The final area examined is differential returns. Having found that multifactor models are more appropriate as return generating models and for constructing immunized portfolios, we examine whether they do a better job of explaining the differential return between bonds.

The paper is divided into five sections. In the second section we discuss the data. In the third section we discuss alternative return generating models. In section four, we present tests of return generating models, immunization, and differential expected return. Section 5 concludes.

II Sample

Our sample consists of all non-callable government bonds, bills and notes (except for flower bonds) listed on the CRSP (Center for Research in Security Prices) Tape for the period from January 1963 to December 1982. The data were divided into four five-year samples. In each month the bonds were divided into eight groups by maturity. The maturities of the eight groups are shown in column 4 of table 17.1. For each of the eight maturity groups we constructed a portfolio of the bonds within the group. As described below, each portfolio was constructed to have a constant maturity over time. Some of our tests involved using historical data to estimate the sensitivity to a particular factor. The ideal portfolio would be a portfolio where the sensitivity to the factor was constant. This would involve constructing a different portfolio for each model or biasing the results in favor of one model by using a portfolio most appropriate for one model to test all models. Using constant maturity portfolios (CMP) was a compromise. CMP's are a good proxy for the optimum portfolio for each of our techniques without containing an obvious bias in favor of

Table 17.1
Characteristics of constant maturity portfolios (CMP's).

Constant maturity portfolio number	Maturity range in years		Target maturity	Average number of bonds	Number of negative weights[a]
	At or above	Less than			
1	1/6	1/2	0.329	21.76	0
2	1/2	1	0.732	12.05	0
3	1	2	1.438	12.87	3
4	2	3	2.493	8.20	4
5	3	4	3.562	7.03	20
6	4	5	4.466	5.27	19
7	5	7.5	6.055	6.18	28
8	7.5		12.877	10.98	66

a. Recall that we have 240 observations. To calculate the fraction of bond observations that receive negative weights, divide this column by the previous column multiplied by 240. Thus, for portfolio 8 the percentage receiving negative weights is 2.5%. Across all groups the percent is 0.69%.

any one model we estimate using historical data. Note that since the estimation of duration does not involve the use of historical return data, if our grouping is imperfect it will bias our results against the models that do require historical estimation and in favor of duration.[6]

There are two reasons for using portfolios rather than bonds. First, the sensitivity of a bond to basic factors clearly changes over time and any time-series estimation for individual bonds is inappropriate.[7] Second, the pricing errors on single bonds can be substantial; portfolios reduce the impact of pricing errors. The portfolio weights changed on a monthly basis in order to maintain a constant maturity for the group. The portfolios were constructed to maximize diversification. Each month for each group, the following programming problem was solved:

$$\text{minimize} \sum_{i \in G} X_i^2,$$

subject to

$$\sum_{i \in G} M_i X_i - M_G$$

$$X_i \geqslant 0 \qquad \text{for all} \qquad i \in G,$$

where

X_i is the proportion in bond i,

M_i is the maturity of bond i,

M_G is the target maturity of group G.

There were some groups where there was no target maturity that was feasible over the full 20 years without allowing negative weights. For these limited number of months we allowed negative weights. The number of negative weights is shown in the last column of table 17.1. Negative weights are infrequent and small in magnitude and do not introduce the instability found by other studies. Take the worst case CMP, group 8. The percentage of weights that were negative was $[66/(10.98 \times 240)] \times 100 = 2.50\%$ and the median negative weight was approximately -0.04. Finally column 5 shows the average number of bonds in each CMP.

The return series we analyze in the rest of the paper are the returns of these eight CMP's.

III Models of the Return Generating Process

A return generating model relates the return on a security to a set of factors that affect the return. For example, a two factor return generating process would be

$$R_i = a_i + b_{i1}F_1 + b_{i2}F_2 + e_i,$$

where

R_i is the return on bond i,

F_j is the jth factor,

b_{ij} is the ith bond's sensitivity to the jth factor,

e_i is the non-factor-related or unique return on bond i.

There are four reasons for estimating return generating models: for use in estimating expected return, for immunization, to estimate the covariance structure, and for use in event studies. The appropriate model can vary across these uses. For purposes of estimating equilibrium returns only priced pervasive influences are important. For estimating the variance-covariance structure or for immunization, non-priced pervasive influences are also important. Finally, for event studies, unique security influences separate from the event being studied could be important to include in the return generating process if these other unique influences could affect returns at the time the event takes place. The first three of these reasons are the subject of this paper.

We will be analyzing six different forms (models) of the return generating process, both comparing them to one another and to two naive models. Each of these will be discussed in turn.

3.1 *Single-factor Duration Model*

The one period return on a bond can be split into the expected return and the unexpected return. The expected return includes interest income and any expected capital appreciation. The unexpected return includes return due to a price change caused by pervasive influences such as an unexpected shift in the yield curve or a change in the general perceived value of a differential coupon. The unexpected return also includes the return due to unique influences such as the change in the relative pricing of a particular bond. The initial model we will examine assumes that the only pervasive unexpected return is the return due to a shift in the yield curve.

The standard measure of the return sensitivity due to an unanticipated shift in the yield curve is duration. There are at least a dozen different duration measures. Despite the compelling logic of the more recently derived duration measures, the original Macaulay duration measure seems to do just as well as the more complex models in explaining price changes due to shifts in the yield curve.[8] In this paper we will be working with returns over discrete periods of time. It is convenient to think in terms of one such discrete period of time. Take the tth period from t to $t+1$. The change in the price of any bond over this period can be separated into its expected and unexpected components as follows:

$$\tilde{P}_{i,t+1} - P_{i,t} = (\tilde{P}_{i,t+1} - \bar{P}_{i,t+1}) + (\bar{P}_{i,t+1} - P_{i,t}),$$

where

$\tilde{P}_{i,t+1}$ is the actual price of the security at time $t+1$ (unknown at time t),

$P_{i,t}$ is the actual price at t,

$\bar{P}_{i,t+1}$ is the expected price at $t+1$, the expectation being taken at t.

Let us examine the unexpected component. Assume for the moment that the only variable subject to uncertainty is the interest rate and that it will be subject to a random shock at the end of the discrete period t (the beginning of period $t+1$). Then the change in price due to this random shock is simply

$$\frac{\tilde{P}_{i,t+1} - \bar{P}_{i,t+1}}{\bar{P}_{i,t+1}} = -D_{i,t+1}\frac{\Delta_{t+1}}{1+r},$$

where Δ_{t+1} is the shock to the interest rate at time $t+1$, $D_{i,t+1}$ is the duration of the bond at the time the shock takes place, and r is the interest rate before the shock takes place. Multiplying and dividing the right hand side of the above equation by $P_{i,t}$, and recognizing that $\bar{P}_{i,t+1}$ divided by $P_{i,t}$ equals $1+r$ we get the following:

$$\frac{\tilde{P}_{i,t+1} - \bar{P}_{i,t+1}}{P_{i,t}} = -D_{i,t+1}\Delta_{t+1}.$$

Dividing the earlier price equation by $P_{i,t}$ and substituting from the above equation we get

$$R_i = \bar{R}_i - D_i\Delta + e_i \tag{1}$$

where

R_i is the actual return on bond i,

$\bar{R}_i$ is the expected return on bond i,

D_i is the duration of bond i,

Δ is the change in the interest rate,

e_i is the random unexpected return of bond i not due to interest rate shifts.

Now consider an arbitrary portfolio of bonds. Let X_i be the proportion of bond i in the bond portfolio. Let the return on the portfolio be R_p. Then

$$R_p = \sum_i \{X_i\bar{R}_i - X_iD_i\Delta + X_ie_i\},$$

$$R_p = \bar{R}_p - D_p\Delta + \sum_i X_ie_i.$$

For a bond portfolio with a large number of bonds $\sum X_ie_i$ should be approximately zero. This follows if the e_i are independent of one another. Thus

$$R_p = \bar{R}_p - D_p\Delta.$$

Substitution into eq. (1) yields

$$R_i = \bar{R}_i + \frac{D_i}{D_p}(R_p - \bar{R}_p) + e_i. \tag{2}$$

Using standard APT methodology and recognizing that R_{30} is a riskless rate, the model for expected return from equation (2) is

$$\bar{R}_i = R_{30} + \frac{D_i}{D_p}(\bar{R}_p - R_{30}).$$

Substituting into eq. (2) and simplifying yields[9]

$$\text{(Dur-1)} \quad R_i = R_{30} + \frac{D_i}{D_p}(R_p - R_{30}) + e_i.$$

This form of the single-factor duration model is the model that will be estimated and tested. D_i was determined by calculating duration for each individual bond and then using the same weights as used in determining the return on the CMP to determine the sensitivity of the portfolio. The choice of portfolio p is to some extent arbitrary; any widely diversified portfolio would be appropriate. We choose to use an equally weighted portfolio of our eight CMP's. This portfolio had an average maturity of 3.994 years.

3.2 *Two Factor Duration Model*

In appendix A we derive an expression for the reaction of a bond's price to a shift in the yield curve that depends on two factors. The shift in the yield curve depends on both a change in short rate and a change in long rate. The expression derived in appendix A is analogous to the one derived by Ingersoll (1983). Our model differs from his in that we have used the discrete analogy of the continuous interest rate process he used and we have developed our model using multiperiod spot rates rather than forward rates. The shift in the t period spot rate is assumed to be given by

$$\frac{d(1+r_t)}{(1+r_t)} = \begin{cases} \left(1 - \dfrac{t-1}{T-1}\right)\dfrac{d(1+r_1)}{(1+r_1)} + \dfrac{(t-1)\,d(1+r_T)}{(T-1)(1+r_T)} & \text{for } t \leqslant T \\[2ex] \dfrac{d(1+r_T)}{(1+r_T)} & \text{for } t > T, \end{cases} \tag{3}$$

where

r_t is the t period spot rate,

r_1 is the short rate that other rates are dependent on,

r_T is the long rate that other rates are dependent on. T is the maturity of the long rate.

This model links shifts in spot rates with shifts in a short and long rate. For all periods between the short and long, the shift is a simple weighted average of the two shifts with the weights a function of the maturity of the rate. For example, if the short rate is the one period rate and the long rate is a seven period rate, then the shift in the four period spot rate would be half of the shift in the one period rate and half of the shift in the seven period rate.[10]

Incorporating all the unexpected returns except the shift in the yield curve in the random error term, we have for the return on bond i,[11]

$$R_i = \bar{R}_i - D_{1i}\frac{d(1+r_1)}{(1+r_1)} - D_{Ti}\frac{d(1+r_T)}{(1+r_T)} + e_i, \tag{4}$$

where

$\bar{R}_i$ is the expected return on bond i,

D_{1i} is the sensitivity of bond i to changes in the short rate,

D_{Ti} is the sensitivity of bond i to changes in the long rate,

$\frac{d(1+r_1)}{(1+r_1)}$ is the percentage change in the one period spot rate (one period is taken to be the 60-day T bill rate),

$\frac{d(1+r_T)}{(1+r_t)}$ is the percentage change in the T period spot rate,

e_i is a random error term.

In appendix B we use a procedure analogous to that employed earlier for the single duration case to derive the expression for expected returns. Substituting this into the above equation and simplifying yields

$$\text{(Dur-2)} \quad R_i = R_{30} + \frac{D_{Ti}D_{1L} - D_{1i}D_{TL}}{D_{1L}D_{TS} - D_{1S}D_{TL}}(R_s - R_{30}) + \frac{D_{1i}D_{TS} - D_{Ti}D_{1S}}{D_{1L}D_{TS} - D_{1S}D_{TL}}(R_L - R_{30}) + e_i,$$

where the subscripts S and L refer to a short portfolio and a long portfolio respectively.

Once again the choice of the index is to some extent arbitrary. We choose as our short index the average of the first three portfolios. These are bonds with less than two years to maturity. As the long index we choose an average of our two longest portfolios. These are bonds with maturities greater than five years.

3.3 *One and Two Factor Time Series Regressions*

The one and two factor models just developed specify the relationship between the return on a bond and return on a diversified portfolio based on an analytical derivation. However, the assumptions behind these derivations are rather stringent.[12] An alternative approach is to estimate the sensitivities of a bond to the return on a diversified portfolio directly via regression analysis. Recall that in our sample, each bond (unit of observation) is really a constant maturity portfolio. Duration for each of these portfolios will change to some extent over time. To the extent that duration is the appropriate sensitivity measure, the regression estimate, which is constant over time, should prove inferior to the duration model. On the other hand, to the extent that the theoretical assumptions of duration are not met and sensitivity is related to maturity, the regression estimate should prove superior to the duration model.

An analogous set of arguments can be made with respect to the two duration return model. In this case we shall also try a time series regression model. The form of the one factor and two factor regression models, our third and fourth models, are given below. Our third model is the regression form of the one factor duration model or

(Reg-1) $R_i - R_{30} = a_i + b_i(R_p - R_{30}) + e_i,$

where

P_{30} is the 30-day T-bill rate,

a_i and b_i are parameters,

Other terms as before.

In fitting the model, we used the same index used in the one factor duration model, an equally weighted portfolio of the eight bond portfolios.

Our fourth model is

(Reg-2) $R_i - R_{30} = a_i + b_{i1}(R_S - R_{30}) + b_{i2}(R_L - R_{30}) + e_i,$

where

R_S is the return on an index of short bonds,

R_L is the return on an index of long bonds.

We used the same two indexes to fit the two index regression model as we did in Dur-2.

3.4 *Factor Analysis*

In the previous parts of this section we have discussed models of the return generating process where we have specified the sources of risk (indexes) exogenously. An alternative is to let the data provide the sources of risk in the return generating process. Methods of accomplishing this have been presented by Roll and Ross (1980) and, more recently, by Gibbons (1983).

The technique we used was to factor analyze the correlation matrix of standardized excess returns.[13] Both a one and a two factor solution were obtained. Note that Fact models force a_i to be equal to zero, but the Reg models do not. The estimates of a_i from Reg models were extremely close to zero.

The one factor model is

(Fact-1) $R_i - R_{30} = b_i F_1 + e_i,$

where

b_i is the factor loading,

F_1 is the factor.

The two factor model is

(Fact-2) $R_i - R_{30} = b_{i1} F_1 + b_{i2} F_2 + e_i,$

where

b_{ij} are the factor loadings,

F_1 and F_2 are the factors.

The factor models have the largest number of parameters estimated empirically. In the regression model, the sensitivity is determined empirically, but the indexes are prespecified. In the factor analysis model, both the sensitivity and the indexes are determined empirically.

Insofar as the return generating process is stable over time, the factor analysis technique should provide reasonable estimates of it. Furthermore, if theory is sufficiently inaccurate in specifying the appropriate structure, the factor analysis technique might well be the superior technique.

We estimated the factor structure using maximum likelihood factor analysis. Maximum likelihood factor analysis requires normally distributed excess returns. We performed a Kolmogorov-Smirnov test on our excess returns and we could not reject normality at any reasonable level. Thus, the data fit the assumptions surprisingly well.

3.5 *Naive Models*

While in one sense Macaulay's duration model is an appropriate benchmark, given its robust performance in previous tests, it is useful to develop even more naive models to see if we are capturing elements of the return generating process. One sensible naive model we could construct is one which simply assumes that the sensitivity of any bond portfolio to interest rates is the same as the sensitivity of any other bond portfolio to interest rates. This model which we have labelled Naive is simply,

$$\text{(Naive)} \quad R_i - R_{30} = (R_p - R_{30}) + e_i,$$

where

R_p is the return on the equally-weighted portfolio used for both Dur-1 and Reg-1.

In the common stock area, the assumption of constant sensitivity (all betas equal one) is very difficult to beat. Thus, the Naive model is a reasonable alternative.

The second naive model we examined simply used maturity as a proxy for duration. It is analogous to Dur-1.

$$\text{(Mat)} \quad R_i - R_{30} = \frac{m_i}{m_p}(R_p - R_{30}) + e_i.$$

This model has little to commend it. However, it is a standard model used in the immunization literature. We will use it only in the section on immunization.

IV Empirical Analysis

In this section of the paper we use three types of performance measures to differentiate among the six alternative models of bond returns and our naive models. First, we examine which of the models appears to best describe the return generating process. Second, we perform a type of test which is closely associated with immunization as the term is used in the bond literature. If we have successfully defined the return generating process, then two portfolios that have the same parameters (sensitivities) to the indexes in that return generating process should have a very similar pattern of returns over time. Finally, we examine each model as a description of differential returns.

All of the tests in this paper are done on a relative, rather than an absolute, basis. It is impossible to prove that a particular model is the 'appropriate' model for describing reality. All that can ever be shown is that one model performs consistently better than an alternative model. In addition, all of the tests are evaluated in a forecast mode. Parameters are fitted in one period and performance evaluated in a subsequent period.

The most widely used model in the bond area is the simple duration model which we have labeled Dur-1. Throughout our paper, this model will serve as a benchmark for all other models. Despite the simplicity of this model, it has performed about as well as more sophisticated models in previous empirical work.

4.1 *The Return Generating Process*

The first set of tests performed in this paper are designed to differentiate between the six models discussed earlier as estimates of the return generating process. The empirical work in this section differs from previous tests of the return generating process in that all tests will be done in a forecast mode. Past empirical work (in the context of stocks) has, almost without exception, fit and tested the return generating process over the same period.

We employ two types of tests. The first type concerns the ability of each model to forecast returns with small errors. The second concerns the ability of each model to explain and predict the covariance between returns.

Before examining these tests, we will discuss the parameterization of the models and examine the characteristics of these parameters.

4.1.1 *The Parameterization of the Return Generating Process*

We can represent the general return generating process as

$$R_i = a_i + b_{i1}F_1 + b_{i2}F_2 + e_i.$$

We parameterize our models (select values of b_{i1} and b_{i2}) from one period of time and use these parameters to estimate returns over the subsequent period using the values of the indexes which arose in that period (F_1 and F_2). The values of b_{i1} and b_{i2} were selected as follows:

For Dur-1 and Dur-2 the duration measures described earlier are calculated at the end of each month and used as estimates for the next month.

For Reg-1 and Reg-2 the parameters are estimated by running the appropriate regression over the previous 60 monthly observations and the b_{i1} and b_{i2} obtained are used as an estimate of the appropriate value for the next month.

For Fact-1 and Fact-2, both F_1 and F_2 are estimated by performing a 1 and 2 factor maximum likelihood factor analysis on the previous 60 months of data. The b_{i1} and b_{i2} are estimated from a least square regression over the same 60 months using portfolios that are perfectly correlated with the unstandardized values of F_1 and F_2 as the independent variables. The weightings of the eight bond portfolios that are found to constitute F_1 and F_2 are used to obtain values of F_1 and F_2 in the next month. The b_{i1} and b_{i2} obtained from the regression are used as the estimates for the next month.

(a) The Indexes (F_1 and F_2)

The indexes used in the one and two index duration models are the same as those used in the one and two index regression models. These indexes were specified before the empirical work was begun. For the single index models Dur-1 and Reg-1 an equally weighted index of all CMP's was selected to accomplish this. For the Fact models factor analysis is used to determine the weighting on each CMP for the index. The average portfolio weights that accomplish this are shown in table 2. Note that these portfolio weights are not uniform. They tend to be symmetrical around CMP's 4 and 5 with smaller weights being placed in the extremely short and long portfolios. Despite the heavier weights placed on the intermediate CMP's because of the symmetry of the weighting, the correlation between the index produced by Fact-1 and the equally weighted index used by the other single index models is 0.990.

In specifying the indexes for the two index models Dur-2 and Reg-2 the goal was to have one portfolio which represented the short end of the maturity spectrum, and one which represented the long end, while preserving some diversification. To accomplish this, the first index was defined as the average of the three CMP's in our study with the shortest maturity, and the second index was defined as the average of the two largest maturity CMP's. When we estimated the two indexes which best explain returns via factor analysis, we employed the additional constraint that the indexes be orthogonal. This resulted in a complex set of weights with the first index broadly representing the market (all portfolios enter with positive weights) and the second portfolio representing differences between short and long rates (short term CMP's have weights with the opposite sign of long term CMP's). In addition it is worth noting that the weights for the second factor are very unstable over time.

(b) The Sensitivities (b_{ij}'s)

Recall that if the single period duration measure is a perfect description of the return generating process and if the duration on each portfolio is stable over time, then the estimate of a b_i obtained from Reg-1 should be identical to the estimate of the sensitivity used in Dur-1. Table 17.2 shows the value of b_i from Dur-1 for each of the CMP's over the 15 year period as well as the relative size of other estimates obtained from each of our models. Note that the estimates of sensitivity from Dur-1 are very stable over time. Reg-1 produces sensitivity estimates which are, on the average, larger than those produced by Dur-1. Furthermore, there is a clear pattern in the average value across the eight portfolios. The regression coefficient is larger than the sensitivity of Dur-1 for the first seven portfolios. The ratio starts out at 1.294, gets larger for the second portfolio and then gets closer to one moving down continuously from CMP 2 through 7. For the eighth CMP, the sensitivity from Reg-1 is smaller than the sensitivity from Dur-1. While we do not present the results, we should point out that this pattern was found in each of the three five-year samples as well as over the full 15 years. When we examine column 6 of table 17.2, we see that the b_i's estimated from Fact-1 are very close to the estimates obtained from the regression analysis. This is not too surprising since the correlation between the indexes used in this model is 0.990.

When we turn to the two index models, the analysis becomes much more complex. The sensitivities of the Reg-2 model and the Dur-2 model are not very close to each other. A pattern does arise and is closely linked to the fact that for Dur-2 the sensitivity of CMP 2 to the long index must be zero by design while the sensitivity of CMP 7 to the short index must also be zero. When we turn to the two factor model we find that the ratios of the sensitivities take on extreme values. What isn't shown in table 2 is

Table 17.2
Value and relative values of b_i.

CMP	Dur-1		Reg-1/	Fact-1/	Reg-1/	Average	Dur-2		Dur-2/Reg-2		Dur-2/Fact-2	
	Mean	Standard deviation	Dur-1	Dur-1	Fact-1	weights for Fact-1	b_{1i}	b_{2i}	b_{1i}	b_{2i}	b_{1i}	b_{2i}
1	0.103	0.007	1.294	1.256	1.003	0.024	0.475	−0.008	1.10	3.53	1.06	0.55
2	0.227	0.014	1.439	1.005	1.002	0.051	0.962	−0.008	1.06	2.41	1.04	0.49
3	0.431	0.021	1.393	1.405	1.003	0.151	1.563	0.016	0.93	2.96	0.76	0.84
4	0.723	0.028	1.237	1.255	0.996	0.259	2.002	0.099	0.79	1.81	0.58	0.38
5	1.000	0.027	1.123	1.128	1.004	0.253	1.928	0.238	0.72	1.44	0.46	0.25
6	1.226	0.027	1.028	1.021	1.017	0.146	1.485	0.393	0.95	1.03	0.60	0.15
7	1.534	0.039	1.028	1.004	1.038	0.081	0.338	0.672	2.59	1.04	2.38	0.12
8	2.765	0.134	0.755	0.701	1.089	0.034	−0.338	1.328	2.59	0.98	−0.93	0.08
Average			1.161	1.156	1.019				1.34	1.90	0.74	0.36

that the ratios are also very unstable over time. This occurs because, as discussed earlier, the composition of the second index in Fact-2 changes by large amounts over time.

4.1.2 Forecasting Returns

Each of our models is used to forecast returns for each CMP, for each month over the three five-year sample periods as well as the overall 15-year period. The model which produces the smallest error in forecasting returns is the preferred forecast model and should be a candidate as the best description of the return generating process.[14] To be more exact, we have a forecast for each of the eight CMP's in each month prepared by each of the different forecasting techniques. For each model we calculate the absolute value of the difference between forecasted return and actual return. We have a matched sample in that each technique is used to forecast the return for each of the eight CMP's in each month.

Two techniques can be compared by calculating the difference in absolute error between the two techniques and examining the mean of the difference and the standard deviation of the mean. Since we have a sample size of 1440 (15 years of monthly data for eight CMP's), the mean should be normally distributed.[15]

Before examining the results, one more point should be mentioned. Our results are based on pairwise comparison of forecasted returns. Before one looks at pairwise comparisons, one really should examine all techniques simultaneously to see if one can show that forecasts as a group differ from each other. Strictly speaking, it is only after ascertaining that the forecasts are statistically different that it is appropriate to make pairwise comparison. To test for differences in forecast accuracy, the Friedman two-way analysis of variance was used.[16] When the Friedman test was applied to all data, the chi-square value was 38.58. The Friedman test indicates that the performance of the alternative models is statistically different and it is appropriate to proceed with pairwise comparisons of the techniques.

The *t*-values associated with the pairwise comparison of techniques are reported in table 17.3. The entries are ranked from smallest forecast error to largest. The *t*-values indicate whether the technique in the first column dominates the lower ranking techniques. The superscript indicates the number of subperiods where the ranking is significant at the 5% level. There in only one reversal in ordering in one subperiod for the two index models. Thus, the findings seem robust.

Table 17.3
Absolute errors and *t*-values of differences in absolute errors.

	Mean absolute error in percent	Error as percent of Naive	Fact-2	Dur-2	*t*-Values[a] Reg-1	Fact-1	Dur-1	Naive
Reg-2	0.242	43.1%	0.22	3.861	5.722	4.792	9.093	17.843
Fact-2	0.244	43.5%		1.481	6.352	8.043	9.573	18.763
Dur-2	0.259	46.2%			3.23	2.941	7.983	16.973
Reg-1	0.285	50.8%				0.88	6.912	16.703
Fact-1	0.289	51.5%					5.642	16.613
Dur-1	0.347	61.9%						12.35
Naive	0.561							

a. A positive value indicates that the techniques at the left had smaller absolute errors than the technique noted across the top of the table.

A definite pattern is present in this table.[17] First, all six models have lower forecast error than the Naive model. This is not as obvious a result as might at first be assumed. The parallel test in the common stock area is to assume that the betas on all stocks are one. This has proved to be a very difficult model to beat.

Second, all two index models have lower forecast errors than the one index models.[18] There seem to be at least two distinct influences present in the return generating process and the presence of two influences is so strong that it shows up no matter which of the models we use.

Dur-1 and Dur-2 are models where we have prespecified the sensitivities on the basis of theory. For Reg-1 and Reg-2 we have prespecified the index but used past data to estimate the sensitivities. Finally, for Fact-1 and Fact-2 both the sensitivities and indexes are determined on the basis of past data. Dur-1, the generally accepted standard, did the poorest of all the models. The other prespecified model, Dur-2 did the poorest of the two-factor models. Since we derived Dur-2 it may simply mean we used an incorrect specification. However, Dur-2 did have a lower forecast error than did Dur-1.

The fact that Reg-1 and Reg-2 as well as Fact-1 and Fact-2 performed better than the duration models using the same number of influences indicates that estimating the sensitivities statistically is more accurate than the theoretical values of the sensitivities used in the duration measures. Furthermore, the fact that the factor analysis models did not outperform the regression models (the results are virtually indistinguishable) indicates that the ad hoc specification of the indices used in the regression model was no worse than the historically fit indices determined by factor analysis.

To examine the potential for three factors, we attempt to extract a third factor when we performed our maximum likelihood factor analysis. The correlation matrix became singular, and we were unable to extract the third factor. While three factors might be present if we allowed callability or examined corporate bonds, a maximum of two factors is all that we can find in non-callable government bonds.

4.1.3 *Correlation Tests*

One of the desirable characteristics of a return generating process is that the residuals be uncorrelated. This is of course a normal assumption when return generating processes are used for portfolio purposes. It is also useful in determining if a sufficient number of indexes are present in the return generating process. Significant correlation in the residuals is indicative that too many or too few indexes are present.

If indexes are left out, then the correlation between residuals is the product of the sensitivity on the omitted index for the pair of CMP's times the variance of the index assuming all indexes are orthogonal. A similar result holds if a spurious index is introduced. Once again our analysis is done in the forecast mode.[19] Thus, if a spurious index is introduced, in will remove from the residuals a correlation where none existed. This will cause correlation in the residuals of the opposite sign as that removed by the spurious index. Since we are looking at correlations in a forecast mode, looking at the correlation matrix as a way of comparing return generating models does not bias our results in favor of two index models relative to one index models.

Our results are shown in table 17.4. The first column shows the average absolute correlation for all pairwise combinations of our eight CMP's. These correlations are calculated over the 180 months of our forecast period. Note that to give some perspective on our results we have also included the average absolute correlation for the raw data. The other entries in the table are t-values.

First note that all models explain a significant amount of correlation. Once again this is not a foregone conclusion, because we are in a forecast mode. Each of the six models explain more than half the correlation between returns. In addition, for all the models, the correlation has been reduced by a statistically significant amount.

Table 17.4
Average correlation of residuals and *t*-values of paired differences.

	Average correlation in residuals	Fact-1	Reg-2	Reg-1	Dur-2	Dur-1	Naive	Returns
Fact-2	0.20	2.58	2.66	2.96	3.02	3.87	7.39	33.83
Fact-1	0.30		0.45	1.03	0.91	2.33	7.17	15.11
Reg-2	0.32			0.15	1.94	1.25	3.86	13.18
Reg-1	0.33				0.27	2.98	5.91	12.16
Dur-2	0.35					0.85	3.46	11.79
Dur-1	0.41						3.09	8.37
Naive	0.60							
Unadjusted returns	0.89							

For all pairs of models, the two index version dominated the one index counterpart. Thus Fact-2 dominated Fact-1, etcetera. The only dominance of a two index model to its one index counterpart *at a statistically significant* level was Fact-2 dominating Fact-1. The ordering of the models corresponds to the amount of model specification done empirically. For the Fact models, both the indexes and sensitivities are specified empirically. These models performed best. For the Reg models, the sensitivities are empirically estimated. This is the next best pair. Finally, the Dur models, which are completely prespecified, performed poorest on this test. Over the fit period these results are guaranteed. However, there is no structural reason for these results to hold over the forecast period.

Although the results are not shown there is a monotonic pattern for the one index models. The short maturity bonds have high positive correlation in the residuals while the long maturity bonds have negative correlation. There is not a distinct pattern for the two index models. Thus these tests would suggest at least two indexes are present in bond returns.

4.2 *Immunization Tests*

One of the most important reasons for modeling the return generating process it that one can immunize or protect against unanticipated changes in interest rates. The idea behind immunization is to reduce risk by forming a portfolio of assets which will have the same change in value (return) over all periods of time as a set of liabilities.

The portfolio of assets is constructed by finding a combination of assets that has the same sensitivity to each factor as the liabilities. These factors may be priced or unpriced. This is a stronger condition than is required in forming an arbitrage portfolio in the APT sense. For APT all that is required is that the asset and liability have the same expected return, and hence that the combined or arbitrage portfolio have zero expected return. Thus all that is required is that the assets and liabilities have the same sensitivity to *priced* factors.

In this section we shall test the ability of all of the models to aid in constructing immunized portfolios. Once again we will conduct all tests on a relative rather than an absolute basis. All tests will be conducted in a forecasting mode.

Our results are very different from prior immunization tests. Maturity matching and Macaulay's duration measures are statistically dominated by several other models. We believe these results come about in part because of a radical departure in the test procedure.[20] Prior immunization tests followed the test procedure developed by Fisher and Weil (1971). They utilized the result that a pure discount bond would yield the spot rate and have a duration equal to its maturity. They argued that an immunized portfolio of the same duration should have the same return over the full 20 years. Thus, their test involved estimating a 20-year spot rate and then testing if an immunized portfolio of the same duration had the same return over the 20 years.

The return over 20 years on the immunized portfolio was compared to the spot rate and also to the return on a portfolio with a maturity equal to the horizon. The latter was used as a straw man although it has no theoretical support. This methodology, which is the standard methodology in the area, is sufficiently weak that the authors have found it difficult to distinguish between a constant maturity portfolio, Macaulay's duration and whatever measure they were putting forth.

Our methodology is totally different. We take an arbitrary portfolio of bonds as our liability. The liability structure we are simulating is the cash flows on the bond portfolio. By using the cash flows on the bonds as our liability structure we can obtain a market value of that liability structure at any point in time. Our immunizing or matching portfolio is a portfolio with the same sensitivity to factors as the arbitrary liability. Since the liability we are using is publicly traded, we have a monthly value on the liability. With a monthly value on both the liability and assets, we can compare the change in the value of assets and liabilities on a monthly basis. If we have an immunized portfolio, the change in the value of the assets and liabilities should correspond over time. Our tests in this section are all based on examining the difference in return between the assets and liabilities. In this paper we compare the difference in returns between assets and liabilities over several different holding periods. A brief description of the appropriate time period to use is in order. Textbook presentations of immunization describe it as finding a set of assets to protect against changes in the value of a known set of liabilities. This has suggested to a number of authors that the appropriate horizon for examining differences in market values or returns is the maturity of the liabilities. There are two reasons why this is often a poor choice. First, when the market values of assets and liabilities react differently to a change in interest rates this has a direct effect on net worth. Financial intermediaries frequently use an immunization strategy. Since they are highly levered, small differences in the change in the value of the assets and liabilities are reflected in their surplus and can affect their ability to do business. In so far as the immunizer is a pension fund, differential changes in the value of the assets and liabilities can affect contributions and under recent accounting rules can flow through to the income statement of the company. Thus financial intermediaries and pension funds are concerned with differential market values over periods of time shorter than the original maturity of the liabilities.

Second, the maturity originally specified for the liabilities is almost never the actual maturity of the liabilities. Financial intermediaries, e.g. insurance companies, create new business and hence hopefully, increase the life and maturity of liabilities. In fact for some intermediaries the maturity of the liabilities may approach infinity. Even if we examine pension liability of retired employees, the actual maturity schedule of the liabilities may be different from the forecast for these liabilities. Mortality rates are never as predicted and COLA (cost of living adjustment) provisions cause liabilities to shift. The fact that liabilities used in immunization strategy are usually at best expected liabilities rather than actual liabilities means that a financial intermediary needs to ensure that the assets will cover the liabilities at more than one date.

Because of these reasons we have measured the difference in returns on assets and liabilities over several different holding periods. The correct holding period to use is uncertain. It probably is longer than one month but may be even longer than the duration of the liabilities. What we desire are techniques which perform well over ranges of potential holding periods.

As discussed earlier, we get distinct rankings. We believe it's due to this change in methodology. In addition, this methodology focuses on exactly what a manager constructing an immunized portfolio cares about: will the assets and liabilities move together. In the next section we discuss our tests in more detail.

4.2.1 *Test Design*

To test immunization we first had to select a target portfolio to represent the liability against which we wish to immunize. All of the tests were performed on each of three different target portfolios: groups 2, 4, and 7. These three portfolios approximate a short, intermediate and long-term liability.

For each target portfolio we constructed an immunized or matching portfolio for each of our eight models. Let's explain this in more detail. Take as an example Reg-1 with target portfolio 4. Each month we measure the value of b_i as of the end of the previous month for portfolio 4 from model Reg-1. We form a portfolio from groups 1, 2, 3, 5, 6, 7, and 8 which for that month has the same sensitivity (b_i) as group 4 and has the smallest sum of squared weights obtainable. This latter step was necessary since there are an infinite set of weights that will produce the same b_i (sensitivity value) and we wish to select the set of weights which gives maximum diversification. When we examine two factor models such as Reg-2, both sensitivities (b_{i1} and b_{i2}) of the matching portfolio must be matched to the target portfolio.

Thus, for any target portfolio we have a matching portfolio with the same sensitivities for each of our models for each month over our 180-month sample. If the liability is truly immunized, and there is no random error, then the return on the matching and target portfolios should be the same. No model is likely to be perfect nor is there likely to be zero random error so that we need to examine the properties of the errors that are necessary for one model to be preferred for immunization. There are three properties that are desirable.

First, we would like the mean difference to be zero. A mean difference close to zero is a necessary but not sufficient condition for immunization. Clearly if the matching portfolio persistently offered a higher or lower return over time than the target portfolio, it could not be said to be effective in immunization. In fact, if the differences were so perverse as to affect expectations it could not even be thought of as an arbitrage portfolio in the sense of APT. In addition, examining the mean difference provides an indication of how accurate our return generating process is. If we have misspecified the return generating process by leaving out factors or misspecifying factors and these factors are priced, then the mean difference should not be zero. Thus, the mean error provides information on how accurately we have specified those elements of the return generating structure that are priced.

A second desirable property, is that the absolute value of the monthly errors is small. Small absolute errors also provide evidence that we have correctly captured the return generating process. If we have misspecified the return generating process by leaving out unpriced factors or have misspecified included factors, we should observe high differences in the absolute size of the difference in returns between the target and matching portfolios. Thus our second test is the average size of the absolute difference in returns.

A third desirable property of the errors is that they are uncorrelated over time. If the errors are uncorrelated over time, then the return on the target and matching portfolio should converge. This is our third test.

Our final test is a combination of the prior tests and is our most important test. We test for small average absolute differences over alternative horizons. If a matching portfolio successfully immunizes against a target portfolio, then the absolute value of the difference in returns between the two portfolios should be small no matter what the horizon of the investor. Furthermore, this difference should get smaller as the horizon lengthens. It is to be noted here that we considered non-overlapping periods.

To recapitulate, our tests examine:

(1) The mean difference in return between the target and matching portfolio.

(2) The average size of the absolute difference in returns.

(3) The autocorrelation of the error terms.

(4) The mean absolute error of the difference in return over alternative time horizons.

4.2.2 *Mean Tests*

Our first set of tests involved examining the mean difference in returns. For all eight models including the Naive and maturity matching model and for each of the three target portfolios (2, 4 and 7), the differences in average returns between the target and matching portfolios were very small and insignificantly different from zero.[21] Furthermore, for the six models we specified and usually the two others as well, the average difference in mean returns was close to one month's difference divided by the number of months.

To elaborate, we had 180 months. As we accumulated more and more months, the ranking between models fluctuated dramatically. This fluctuation occurred because the sum of the prior months' errors was of the same order of magnitude as one month's error. Thus the ranking was dramatically affected by whether this month's error had the same sign as the sum of the prior months' error. To be specific, one month's error could be 5×10^{-3}, which divided by 180 yields 2×10^{-5}. After we accumulated a large number of months, the cumulative error we observed for the eight models was on the order of 10^{-5}. All models had mean errors insignificantly different from zero, and this test could be used to differentiate between models.

4.2.3 *Average Deviation*

Row 1 of table 17.5 shows the average of the absolute value of the difference in return between the matching and target portfolio for a one month horizon. The numbers are in percent per month. Column 1 of table 17.6 shows whether the differences are statistically significant at the 5% level. There are some distinct differences. The constant maturity portfolio and the portfolio assuming constant sensitivity perform the worst at a statistically significant level. This is in contrast to prior research where maturity matching could not be rejected. Within the six specified models some dis-

Table 17.5
Average absolute difference in returns (percent per month).

N	Dur-1	Dur-2	Reg-1	Reg-2	Fact-1	Fact-2	Naive	Mat
1	0.3122	0.3130	0.2928	0.2676	0.2935	0.3224	0.5605	0.3604
2	0.2095	0.2016	0.1872	0.1617	0.1860	0.2061	0.4131	0.2513
3	0.1828	0.1740	0.1687	0.1440	0.1665	0.1771	0.3733	0.2254
6	0.1266	0.1285	0.1078	0.0913	0.1059	0.1118	0.2278	0.1496
9	0.0964	0.0964	0.0739	0.0701	0.0728	0.0845	0.1960	0.1208
12	0.0701	0.0596	0.0514	0.0464	0.0521	0.0699	0.1724	0.0942
18	0.0762	0.0672	0.0514	0.0474	0.0505	0.0652	0.1448	0.0946
30	0.0514	0.0494	0.0369	0.0318	0.0322	0.0457	0.1086	0.0613

Table 17.6
Mean average ranking for specified periods.[a]

$N=1$	$N=2$	$N=3$	$N=6$	$N=9$	$N=12$	$N=18$	$N=30$
Reg-2	Reg-2	Reg-2	Reg-2	Reg-2	Reg-2	Reg-2	Reg-2
Reg-1	Fact-1	Fact-1	Fact-1	Fact-1	Reg-1	Fact-1	Fact-1
Fact-1	Reg-1	Reg-1	Reg-1	Reg-1	Fact-1	Reg-1	Reg-1
Dur-1	Dur-2	Dur-2	Fact-2	Fact-2	Dur-2	Fact-2	Fact-2
Dur-2	Fact-2	Fact-2	Dur-1	Dur-2	Fact-2	Dur-2	Dur-2
Fact-2	Dur-1	Dur-1	Dur-2	Dur-1	Dur-1	Dur-1	Dur-1
Mat	Mat	Mat	Mat	Mat	Mat	Mat	Mat
Naive	Naive	Naive	Naive	Naive	Naive	Naive	Naive

a. [indicates not statistically different at 5% level.

tinct rankings also exist. Reg-2 had the smallest errors at a statistically significant level. Reg-1 and Fact-1 are next and statistically better than the remaining prespecified models in order Dur-1, Dur-2 and Fact-2. These latter three models are insignificantly different from one other.

Unlike the mean test the average absolute deviation test results in some differences. While the ultimate test will be the ranking of techniques for different length time horizons the difference in absolute deviations over one period are important and suggestive of what we will find in the latter test.

4.2.4 *Autocorrelation Tests*

Our third set of tests was to examine autocorrelation in the errors (i.e., the difference in the return between the matched and target portfolio). We regressed the error at time t against the error at time $t-1$ and used the Durbin–Watson statistic to test significance. For the three errors combined (combined groups 2, 4, 7), the null hypothesis of no autocorrelation would be accepted at the 5% level except for Fact-2 which was inconclusive. When we examined the three subgroups separately we found significant negative autocorrelation for Reg-2 and Fact-2 when we matched groups 4 and 7. In addition we found significant negative autocorrelation for the one factor models when matching group 7 and for Dur-2 when matching group 4. Negative autocorrelation is useful in reducing cumulative errors. Thus autocorrelation tests would suggest Reg-2 and Fact-2 might be more promising.

Mean error, variability and autocorrelation are all useful and suggestive of which techniques might lead to lower errors over time. However the real test is to examine these techniques directly. It is to this analysis that we now turn.

4.2.5 *Performance with Varying Horizon*

The preferred immunization technique is the one where the return on the assets and liabilities converge over time. Table 17.5 shows that for each of our techniques the average absolute difference in return between the matching and target portfolios gets smaller as the time horizon lengthens.[22] For example, the average absolute difference in return between the matching and target portfolios for Dur-1 is 0.3122% with a one month horizon and 0.0514% per month with a 30 month horizon. Managers who utilize immunization are most concerned with differences in return over multiple periods so that this is a test that not only helps to differentiate between models but also is of economic significance. The easiest way to see the ranking is to examine table 17.6. All of our models dominate maturity matching at a statistically significant level.[23] Although maturity has nothing to commend it on a theoretical basis, it is employed in this study because it has been used as a standard of comparison in previous empirical work. Rarely has it been shown to be inferior to a duration model.

The second striking feature of table 17.6 is that Macaulay's duration is for almost all time horizons dominated by the other models usually at a statistically significant level. This is again in contrast to prior studies.

Of the remaining models, Reg-2 dominates in all periods, often at a statistically significant level. Fact-1 and Reg-1 are the next best performing models, normally in this order but the differences between them are not statistically significant. Finally Dur-2 and Fact-2 are the fourth and fifth best performing measures but the difference between them is not statistically significant.

There are some differences in our immunization tests compared to the tests of return generating models for forecasting. For Reg and Dur the two factor models perform better in immunization than their one factor counterparts. This is consistent with our earlier section. However, Fact-2 is worse than Fact-1. This is a surprising result. The weights of CMP's for constructing the factors in Fact-2 exhibit substantial fluctuation over time. This results in matching portfolios with very large variation in composition. Furthermore, the sensitivities seem to be very unstable

Table 17.7
Differential returns, $R_i = R_{30} + a_0 + a_1 b_{1i} + a_2 b_{2i}$.

Model[a]	Adjusted R^2	a_0	Number of times significant[b]	a_1	Number of times significant[b]	a_2	Number of times significant[b]
Reg-2	73.28	0.95	18	2.39	81	5.35	132
Dur-2	69.45	0.86	18	2.37	73	5.75	133
Fact-2	65.89	0.82	6	1.96	57	5.16	128
Reg-1	62.23	1.41	54	5.25	137		
Dur-1	61.94	2.04	92	5.28	134		
Fact-1	61.48	1.33	46	5.11	134		

a. Models are ranked from biggest to lowest by adjusted R^2.
b. Significance is measured by a two-tailed test at the 5% level.

intertemporally. Thus Factor analysis is not the preferred way to get multiple indexes for immunization purposes.

4.3 *Differential Returns*

The final topic we will examine in this paper is the ability of each of the models to explain differential return between our eight portfolios at each point in time (each month). This is not a standard cross sectional APT test in that we are not measuring the ability of each model to explain average return over our 15 year sample period. Rather we are examining the ability of any model to explain why returns on our CMP portfolios differ at an instant in time. The tests involve returns at $t+1$ regressed against parameters estimated at t. Thus once again these tests are in a forecast mode. Table 17.7 presents the average adjusted coefficient of determination (R^2) for each model, the average absolute value of the t statistic for each sensitivity, and the number of times each sensitivity was statistically significantly different from zero at the 5% level.

It is easy to see that the two parameter models outperform the single parameter measures in every case. The adjusted R^2 for the two parameter models are always higher. The intercept term, which according to theory should be zero, has a lower average absolute t in each case and is significant far fewer times. Once one decides the two parameter models are superior it is then clear which of the two parameter models worked best. On the basis of the coefficient of determination, Reg-2 would seem to perform best, followed by Dur-2 with Fact-2 performing the poorest.

However Fact-2 does produce an intercept which is less significant on average and is significant in fewer cases.

V Conclusion

The length and complexity of this paper has resulted from an attempt to accomplish several purposes.

First, we hope we have clarified the relationship between return generating processes, immunization and differential returns. Second, we have constructed type of test that are appropriate for each of these theories. Many of these tests differ from those which have been employed in previous studies. In particular we believe our alternative test of immunization is both more powerful than prior methodology and has a more natural and economically more important interpretation.

Finally we have tested the ability of a wide range of our models to explain the time series of returns, immunization and differential returns. These results showed clear differences in techniques with:

(a) two index models outperforming single index models in almost all tests,

(b) prespecifying the indexes outperformed allowing the data to determine the appropriate indexes (factor analysis),

(c) empirically estimating the sensitivity of bonds to indexes outperformed the theoretical sensitivity used in duration measures.

Appendix A

In this appendix, we derive a duration measure where the sensitivity depends on changes in both the long and short term rate. The derivation is the discrete version of the measure derived by Ingersoll (1983) except Ingersoll used changes in forward rates rather than spot rates. Assume that changes in spot rates are linked to changes in short and long spot rates in the following way:

$$\frac{d(1+r_t)}{(1+r_t)} = \begin{cases} \left[1-\frac{t-1}{T-1}\right]\frac{d(1+r_1)}{(1+r_1)}+\left[\frac{t-1}{T-1}\right]\frac{d(1+r_T)}{(1+r_T)} & \text{for } t \leqslant T \\ \frac{d(1+r_T)}{(1+r_T)} & \text{for } t > T \end{cases} \tag{A.1}$$

where $[d(1+r_1)]/(1+r_1)$ is the proportional change in the short rate and $[d(r+r_T)]/(1+r_T)$ is the proportional change in the long rate.

Thus the change in intermediate term spot rates is a linear function of changes in short term and long term rates. Changes in rates with term greater than T are only a function of the change in T. The price of a bond is

$$P = \sum_{t=1}^{H} \frac{cf_t}{(1+r_t)^t}, \tag{A.2}$$

where

cf_t is the cash flow in period t, principle plus interest,
H is the time of the last cash flow (e.g., the bond's horizon),
T is the maturity of the long rate,
t is the period indicator.

Calculating dP and substituting in (A-1) to represent the impact of an unexpected change in interest rates,

$$dP = -\frac{d(1+r_1)}{(1+r_1)}\left[\sum_{t=1}^{T} \frac{tcf_t\left(1-\frac{t-1}{T-1}\right)}{(1+r_t)^t}\right]$$

$$-\frac{d(1+r_T)}{(1+r_T)}\left[\sum_{t=1}^{T} tcf_t\left(\frac{t-1}{T-1}\right)(1+r_t)^t + \sum_{t=T+1}^{H} \frac{tcf_t}{(1+r_t)^t}\right].$$

If T is more than H the last summation is, of course, not included. This results in

$$\frac{dP}{P} = -D_1\frac{d(1+r_1)}{(1+r_1)} - D_T\frac{d(1+r_T)}{(1+r_T)},$$

where D_1 and D_T are the terms in the prior brackets divided by price.

Appendix B

Consider a bond index of short term bonds. For this index designated by S, the return generating process is

$$R_S = \bar{R}_S - D_{1S}\frac{d(1+r_1)}{(1+r_1)} - D_{TS}\frac{d(1+r_T)}{(1+r_T)} + e_S. \tag{B.1}$$

Now consider a bond index of long-term bonds. For this index, designated by L, we have

$$R_L = \bar{R}_L - D_{1L}\frac{d(1+r_1)}{(1+r_1)} - D_{TL}\frac{d(1+r_T)}{(1+r_T)} + e_L. \tag{B.2}$$

For a well diversified portfolio e_S and e_L should be approximately zero. Substituting eq. (B.2) and eq. (B.1) into eq. (5),

$$R_i = \bar{R}_i + \frac{D_{Ti}D_{1L} - D_{1i}D_{TL}}{D_{1L}D_{TS} - D_{1S}D_{TL}}(R_S - \bar{R}_S) + \frac{D_{1i}D_{TS} - D_{Ti}D_{1S}}{D_{1L}D_{TS} - D_{1S}D_{TL}}(R_L - \bar{R}_L) + e_i. \tag{B.3}$$

Then, following an analogous procedure to derive expected returns to that followed in the case of the single duration measure, and substituting in (B.3) we find

$$R_i = R_{30} + \frac{D_{Ti}D_{1L} - D_{1i}D_{TL}}{D_{1L}D_{TS} - D_{1S}D_{TL}}(R_S - R_{30})$$

$$+ \frac{D_{1i}D_{TS} - D_{Ti}D_{1S}}{D_{1L}D_{TS} - D_{1S}D_{TL}}(R_L - R_{30}) + e_i.$$

Notes

1. Examples of attempts to determine the return generating process include Roll and Ross (1980) and Gibbons (1983).

2. Examples of research to explain differential returns at a point in time are typified by Sharpe (1964), and attempts to explain long-run differentials in return are typified by Roll and Ross (1980) and Chen, Roll and Ross (1983).

3. Exceptions to this are Gibbons (1983) and Gultekin and Rogalski (1985).

4. Ingersoll (1983) and Lau (1983).

5. Nelson and Schaefer (1983) are an exception and have a test procedure similar to ours.

6. The exception is that using CMP's biases the results in favor of one of our Naive models: using maturity in place of duration. This makes subsequent results even more interesting.

7. The maturity, duration, and other sensitivity measures of a bond change as the remaining life of the bond changes.

8. See Ingersoll (1983), Lau (1983) and Brennan and Schwartz (1983).

9. A model identical to (Dur-1) would follow from an assumption of the expectation theory. Both $\bar{R}_i$ and $\bar{R}_p$ would be the 30-day T-bill rate. However, Dur-1 as we derived it is more general since R_p and R_i need not be equal to the 30-day rate in Dur-1. Thus, Dur-1 is consistent with the expectations theory but does not require that it holds.

10. We used the 60-day rate as our short rate and the interest rate for CMP 7 as our long rate in this study.

11. Analytical expressions for D_{1_i} and D_{T_i} are derived in appendix A.

12. See Ingersoll et al. (1978) for a discussion of the assumptions behind Macaulay's duration measure.

13. The natural matrix to factor analyze is the variance–covariance matrix. Gibbons (1983) presents evidence that the correlation matrix is more stable and therefore preferred as an input to a factor analysis.

14. All of the tests use forecasted values of the b_{ij}'s and actual values of the F_j's in forecasting returns. By doing this we are actually conducting a joint test of the stability of the parameters of each model and the ability of each model to explain returns.

15. A question arises about using the difference in absolute forecast error rather than the difference in squared forecast error or some other function of error. In fact, the results were repeated with squared forecast error and, except where noted, the results were identical. In addition, stochastic dominance tests were used as a separate test. The ranking of techniques reported here was preserved with second order stochastic dominance when either absolute or squared error was examined.

16. See Siegel (1956).

17. A similar table was constructed in terms of squared errors with essentially identical results obtained. The ranking of methods is preserved.

18. There is a potential bias in favor of the two factor models over the one factor models in that we use two known pieces of information, the index values, rather than one. If this bias is present we should be able to observe it in the pattern of errors across the eight CMPs. We did not observe a pattern which suggests that any bias is important. The correlation tests do not have this bias.

19. Returns are forecast from each model using historic data. Then errors (realization minus forecasts) are computed and the correlation of errors is calculated.

20. Nelson and Schaefer (1983) have a procedure somewhat similar to ours.

21. The significance of the mean difference between models was tested using the mean differences and the standard deviation of the difference. The values of all t's were below 0.6. The differences were never even close to statistically significant and the order of techniques showed no consistency between samples.

22. The time horizon refers to the time interval over which we compute returns. We first examine average absolute differences in returns computed over a monthly interval, then those computed over all consecutive two month intervals, three month intervals etcetera.

23. Statistical significance was tested using both a t-test assuming the mean difference is normally distributed and the Wilcoxan matched pairs test. The results were virtually the same.

References

Brennan, M. and E. Schwartz, 1983, Duration, bond pricing, and portfolio diversification, in: G. O. Bierwag, G. G. Kaufman and A. L. Toevs, eds., *Innovations in bond portfolio management: Duration analysis and immunization* (JAI Press, Greenwich, CT).

Chen, Ni Fu, R. Roll and Steve Ross, 1983, Economic forces and the stock market: Testing the APT and alternative asset pricing theories. Working paper (Yale School of Management, Yale University, New Haven, CT).

Fisher, L. and R. Weil, 1971, Coping with the risk of interest rate fluctuations: Returns of bondholders from naive and optimal strategies, *Journal of Business* XLIV, Oct.

Gibbons, M., 1983, An empirical examination of the return generating process of the APT, Working paper (Stanford University, Stanford, CA).

Gultekin, B. and R. Rogalski, 1985, Government bond returns, measurement of interest rate risk, and the arbitrage pricing theory, *Journal of Finance*, 40, no. 1, March, 43–61.

Ingersoll, J. E., Jr. 1983, Is immunization feasible? Evidence from the CRSP data, in: G. O. Bierwag, G. G. Kaufman and A. L. Toevs, eds., *Innovations in bond portfolio management: Duration analysis and immunization* (JAI Press, Greenwich, CT).

Ingersoll, J. E., Jr., J. Skelton and R. Weil, 1978, Duration forty years later, *Journal of Financial and Quantitative Analysis* 13, Nov.

Lau, P. W. P., 1983, An empirical examination of alternative interest rate risk immunization strategies, Ph.D. dissertation, University of Wisconsin, Madison, WI.

Lawley, D. N. and A. E. Maxwell, 1963, *Factor analysis as a statistical method* (Butterworth, London).

Nelson, J. and S. Schaefer, 1983, The dynamics of the term structure and alternative portfolio immunization strategies, in: G. O. Bierwag, G. G. Kaufman and A. L. Toevs, eds., *Innovations in bond portfolio management: Duration analysis and immunization* (JAI Press, Greenwich, CT).

Roll, R. and S. Ross, 1980, An empirical investigation of the arbitrage pricing theory, *Journal of Finance* 35, Dec., 1073–1103.

Sharpe, W., 1964, Capital asset prices: A theory of market equilibrium under conditions of risk, *Journal of Finance* 19 Sept, 425–442.

Siegel, S., 1956, *Non parametric statistics for the behavioral sciences* (McGraw-Hill, New York).

18

The Structure of Spot Rates and Immunization

Edwin J. Elton, Martin J. Gruber, and Roni Michaely

Modern theories of bond pricing hypothesize that the value of a default-free bond is a function of a small number of state variables that follow a diffusion process. These include the one-state models of Cox, Ingersoll, and Ross (1985), Brennan and Schwartz (1977), and Vasicek (1977) and the two-state models of Cox, Ingersoll, and Ross (1985), Richard (1978), Brennan and Schwartz (1979, 1980), and Nelson and Schaefer (1983).

When these models are approximated empirically, a change in one or more spot rates is almost always used as a proxy for the state variables. The one-month rate is sometimes chosen. (See Brennan and Schwartz (1977), Babbel (1983), and Nelson and Schaefer (1983).) The one-year rate is often a choice, and, finally, some researchers use a short and long rate (Brennan and Schwartz (1980) or Nelson and Schaefer (1983)).

The assumption behind the use of a small set of rates to describe bond prices or changes in bond prices (rate of return) is that all spot rates can be modeled as functions of this set. This is true for most bond pricing models and for all of the immunization literature from the simplest model of Macaulay (1938) to the more complex two-index models which have appeared in recent literature. Empirical tests of these sophisticated theoretical models have not demonstrated a superiority to much simpler models (see Ingersoll (1983), Nelson and Schaefer (1983), and Brennan and Schwartz (1983)).

One possible explanation is that no research has been done on the structure of spot rates. Rather, in almost all empirical research, the structure that was utilized and the proxy for the state variable (key rate) were specified on an ad hoc basis. The purpose of this paper is to analyze empirically the structure of spot rates. The structure is of interest in its own right. In addition, it is our hope that understanding this structure will allow more accurate models of bond pricing, immunization, and bond portfolio management to be developed.

The remainder of the paper is organized as follows: Two alternative models describing the expected shift in the yield curve are presented in Section I. Section II describes the sample. In Section III we determine the optimal proxy for the state variable when the one-state-variables model is assumed. The analysis necessary for the two-state-variables model directly parallels that employed for the one-state-variable model and is presented in Section IV. In Section V we evaluate whether the proxies for the state variables outperform the commonly used proxies. It is shown that using the method developed here to select the optimal proxies to the state variables outperforms the proxies utilized elsewhere. Section VI concludes the paper.

I Anticipated and Unanticipated Bond Returns

Bond returns can be divided into expected (anticipated) and unexpected (unanticipated) returns. A world with only anticipated returns implies that all bonds have the same rate of return over any time period but does not imply a world with a stationary yield curve. For example, if the expectations theory held and spot rates were different from each other, the yield curve would change over time in a deterministic manner. In such a world, pricing models would be irrelevant since all bonds and portfolios of bonds would have the same rate of return.

Of course, actual bond returns also include unanticipated components. These unanticipated components can be systematic (affect multiple bonds) or unsystematic (unique to a bond). For noncallable government bonds, the unanticipated systematic components arise from an unanticipated change in the shape or position of the yield curve. In this paper we will be concerned with unanticipated systematic returns. For equilibrium modeling and immunization, this is the element of return that is important. For active bond management models, this is the element of return that influences risk estimation. Finally, the systematic unanticipated return is an important component of models for generalized bond pricing.

To measure unanticipated shifts, we need to model what the expected yield curve should be one period hence. We employ two alternative models in this paper. In the first we assume that the yield curve is expected to remain unchanged. All changes in spot rates are assumed to be unanticipated. This model is the simplest model of expectations we can utilize and is the one which has been employed in most previous empirical work (see Nelson and Schaefer (1983) and Babbel (1983)). It is also consistent with some recent empirical work of Mankiw and Miron (1986) demonstrating that short-term interest rates follow a random walk. Finally, it is consistent with a liquidity preference or a preferred habitat theory of the term structure of interest rates.

As a second model of the anticipated term structure, we assume the expectation theory holds exactly. (Babbel (1983) also assumes this.) Thus, in each period t, we derived from the yield curve in t the forward rates for period $t + 1$.[1] These forward rates were assumed to be the expected spot rates in $t + 1$. In all future sections, we use these two different models of unanticipated returns: the change in spot rates and the difference between the spot rate and the forward rate calculated in the prior period.

II Sample

Our sample consists of McCulloch's estimates of spot rates for a series of maturities over the 30-year period, 1957–1986. McCulloch's estimates are derived in a consistent manner from yield curves over a long time span and have become an accepted standard for empirical work. For each month in the sample period, the data consist of spot rates for maturities of 1 to 18 months on a monthly interval, for maturities of 18 to 24 months on a quarterly basis, and on a yearly basis from 2 to 13 years.[2] We divided our data into six five-year subsamples for two reasons. This enables us to test the models in a forecast mode (have holdout sample periods) and to replicate the results over several periods in order to study the robustness of our results.

III Single-Factor Models

Empirical tests of one-state-variable models of bond pricing employ the unexpected change in a single spot rate as the systematic factor affecting the unexpected change in all spot rates. In some models, the unexpected change in the interest rate is used as a proxy for an unobserved factor affecting innovations in the term structure; in others, it is used as a proxy for the unobserved state variable.

The implications of such a model can easily be seen. Define the price of a bond as the discounted value of a series of cash flows C_i's at the appropriate spot rates r_{0i}'s. Assume that the unexpected change in all spot rates depends on the change in one factor F. Taking the derivative of the bond price with respect to the change in F, dividing by P, and rearranging yield an expression for the unanticipated rate of price change:

$$dP/P = -1/P \sum_{1}^{N} \frac{iC_i}{(1+r_{oi})^i} \frac{dF}{(1+r_{oi})} \frac{\partial r_{oi}}{\partial F}, \tag{1}$$

where dP/P is the return due to an unanticipated change in the yield curve.

Consistent with the literature, e.g., Babbel (1983) and Brennan and Schwartz (1983), we assume that the change in the factor can be proxied by the unanticipated change in a spot rate. However, in contrast to prior literature, we present and utilize a methodology for determining the best single-factor proxy.

A Best One-Factor Proxy

In this section we first set forth the methodology for determining the best proxy. Then we present some empirical evidence on how well the proxy performs.

A.1 Determining the Best Factor Proxy

Assume that the unanticipated change in spot rates is linearly related to some unknown factor; then,

$$dr_{it} = a_i + b_i dF_t + \varepsilon_{it}, \tag{2}$$

where dr_{it} is the unanticipated change in the ith spot rate at time t, and dF_t is the unanticipated change in the unknown factor at time t.

The derivation of the optimal proxy for any maturity is contained in Appendix A. The derivation assumes stationarity of the factor structure and minimum squared forecast error as the criteria of choice between models. In Appendix A we show that under these assumptions the factors's proxies can be ranked by the variance of the spot times the R^2 (square of the correlation coefficient).

While this technique allows us to rank the proxies for each maturity, the problem of combining or weighting the performance across maturities still remains. We examined two alternative weighting schemes. The first weighting technique simply assumes that it is equally important to forecast unexpected changes at each yearly interval. The second weighting scheme employs a set of weights that might typically be used to reproduce the rate of price change on a portfolio of bonds. The effect of this weighting scheme (called cash flow weights) is to place more importance on forecasting accurately the unanticipated change in spot rates of intermediate maturities.[3]

Table 18.1
Determination of the optimal factor's proxy for the one-state-variable model

	Model 1				Model 2			
	Largest period value	Maturity employed (4 yrs)	1 yr	13 yrs	Largest period value	Maturity employed (4 yrs)	1 yr	13 yrs
Panel A: 1957–1961								
Equal weights	0.612 (4)[a]	0.612	0.512	0.531	0.550 (3)	0.549	0.462	0.491
Cash-flow weights	0.503 (4)	0.503	0.405	0.432	0.449 (4)	0.449	0.361	0.398
Panel B: 1972–1976								
Equal weights	1.029 (2)	0.994	0.926	0.613	0.932 (1.75)	0.910	0.867	0.518
Cash-flow weights	0.827 (5)	0.823	0.712	0.478	0.746 (5)	0.744	0.657	0.398

a. The number in parentheses is the maturity with the maximum value.
Entries in the table are values of the modeling objective function which we define as the product of R^2 and the dependent spot rate's variance, averaged across all maturities, $\Sigma w_i R^2_{i,x}\,\mathrm{var}(dr_i)$. Two models are examined. Model 1 assumes that the innovation in the spot rate follows a random walk. (All changes are perceived as unexpected.) Model 2 derives the innovation in the spot rate under the pure expectation theory. (The unexpected change is the difference between the actual spot rate and the forward rate from the previous period.) Two weighting schemes are employed. In the first, equal weights are given to each yearly interval. For example, since for the first yearly interval there is information about 12 different spot rates, each of these spot rates receives a weight of $(1/12) * (1/13)$. In the cash-flow-weighting method, weights are given according to the relative importance of the spot rate in a portfolio of 13 bonds, each maturing in a different year. Results are reported for four factor proxies: the one with the largest value for each period and model, the 4-year spot rate which is the overall optimal proxy, and the 1-year and 13-year spot rates which have been employed in previous studies.

While it is impossible to test the forecasting ability of every technique for all possible uses, if one technique performs well both for individual rates and for the rates on a portfolio of bonds, one can have some faith in the robustness of the technique.

A.2 Empirical Evidence

Two time periods (1957–1961 and 1972–1976) were employed to select the best key rate. The entries in the body of Table 18.1 are the product of R^2 and the variance of the dependent spot rate averaged across all maturities using the models of unexpected change described earlier. Initial investigation showed that a key rate equal to the 4-year spot rate was the optimum if one rate was selected over both time periods and both weighting schemes. In Table 18.1 we compare the 4-year choice (which is used throughout the paper) with three other rates: the rate that works best for the period, model, and weighting scheme under investigation; a 1-year rate; and a 13-year rate. The latter two benchmarks were chosen because they were the key rates employed by Nelson and Schaefer (1983) and Babbel (1983) in the case of the one-year rate. Notice in Table 18.1 that in every case the key rate of four years significantly outperforms the 1- and 13-year benchmarks and that the differences in performance between this rate and the best are quite small even when the differences in maturity are large. This leads us to use the four-year-rate as the key rate in all further sections.

B Pattern of Sensitivities

In Table 18.2 we present the average intercept (a_i) and slope (b_i) of the regression of the unexpected change in different spot rates against the unexpected change in the 4-year spot rate. This is done for both models of unexpected change, and their results are quite similar. Note first that the b's not only differ from one (the assumption in the Macaulay measure of duration), but they have a distinct pattern. They start below one, rise above one, and fall to well below one for long rates. While we report in this table only the average results over all six of our 5-year data periods, examination of each 5-year period shows a very similar pattern.

In most previous empirical work where the independent variable was selected to be the shortest rate in the sample, the sensitivities decline uniformly with the maturity of the spot rate. While it is more convenient to have such a pattern for developing duration measures, the cost, as seen in the previous section, is to have less explanatory power. Using the four-year spot as the independent variable increases explanatory power but creates a more complex pattern for sensitivities.[4]

There also appears to be a discernible but less distinct pattern in the intercepts which implies a nonzero mean in unexpected changes in spot rates. If either of our two models of estimating the unexpected change in spots were perfectly correct, all intercepts should be equal to zero. We can think of four reasons that can account for finding nonzero intercepts. The first is the error in variables problems. To the extent that the four-year rate is an imperfect proxy for the factor driving interest rates and that deviations of the four-year rate from the factor are random, the errors in the independent variable will cause the intercept to be positive and the

Table 18.2
Estimated sensitivities for the one-factor model: $d(r_{it}) = a_i + b_i d(r_{4t}) + e_{it}$

Time to maturity (in yrs)	Model 1		Model 2	
	a_i	b_i	a_i	b_i
0.16	−0.0043	0.798	−0.2193	0.886
0.5	−0.0064	0.878	−0.1137	1.071
1	−0.0081	1.084	−0.0637	1.134
1.5	−0.0074	1.117	−0.0366	1.161
2	−0.0059	1.125	−0.0211	1.138
3	−0.0023	1.072	−0.0590	1.055
4	0.0000	1.000	0.0000	1.000
5	0.0023	0.930	0.0046	0.942
6	0.0042	0.863	0.0081	0.886
7	0.0058	0.803	0.0180	0.836
8	0.0072	0.753	0.0128	0.790
9	0.0084	0.710	0.0142	0.748
10	0.0093	0.671	0.0151	0.707
11	0.0100	0.636	0.0157	0.669
12	0.0105	0.604	0.0164	0.619
13	0.0109	0.573	0.0181	0.571

The factor proxy is the 4 year spot rate. The time period is 1957–1986, using monthly observations. Model 1 assumes that the innovation in the spot rate follows a random walk. (All changes are perceived as unexpected.) Model 2 derives the innovation in the spot rate under the pure expectation theory. (The unexpected change is the difference between the actual spot rate and the forward rate from the previous period.)

slope to be lower. The second is the problem of omitted variables. If the process driving interest rates is really a two-factor model (and we present evidence later in the paper that it is), one would expect a pattern on the intercept similar to that found. The third reason is the presence of liquidity premiums. While this could impact both models, its impact is easiest to see (and should be larger) for model 2. The presence of the liquidity premium would mean that the changes in the expected spot rates we derived are overestimates of the true expectations. Liquidity premiums change more rapidly for shorter maturities than for long maturities and would result in the pattern of intercepts we found. The fourth reason applies to model 2. It is easy to show that an underestimate of the true thirty-day spot rate would cause the intercept to be negative when the dependent variable is a short-term spot rate and positive when it is a long-term spot rate.

We have not tested the statistical significance of the intercepts and slopes, for we believe that the importance of the presence of an intercept different from zero and of a slope different from one relates not to whether these differences are statistically significant but to recognize whether these differences lead to better estimation (conditional forecasts).

IV Parameterization of Two-Variable Models

The analysis necessary for the two-variable model directly parallels that employed for the one-variable model. Table 18.3 is directly analogous to Table 18.1. The best pair of rates over the two time periods, weighting schemes, and models of unexpected return is the six-year rate and the difference between the six-year rate and the eight-month rate (referred to as the selected key rates).[5] This model was compared against the two rates that work best for each individual time period weighting scheme and expectational model and against the two-rate model of Nelson and Schaefer (thirteen years and the difference between the thirteen-year and five-year rates). The selected key rates outperformed the Nelson and Schaefer two-rate model in all time periods and under the two weighting schemes employed. Like the case of the one-index model, the two-parameter model using the selected key rates works almost as well as the two-parameter model which is optimal for each time period, expectational model, and weighting scheme. We use the selected key rates as the basis for further analysis of the two-index model.

When different maturity spots were regressed on the selected key rates, there was a clear pattern to the regression coefficients. While these are modeled later in the paper, we should note now that the slope coefficients on both rates are not monotonic with respect to the maturity of the dependent spot rate.

V Selecting the Best Forecasting Model

In this section we evaluate whether the methods developed in the paper lead to better conditional forecasts of the unexpected change in spot rates than do commonly used benchmarks.

A Alternative Forecast Methods

The analysis to this point has been concerned with determining the best one-and two-index methods to use in forecasting unexpected changes in

Table 18.3
Determination of the optimal factor's proxies for the two-state-variables model

	Model 1			Model 2		
	Largest period value	Maturities employed[a] (6y, 8m)	Nelson & Schaefer maturities	Largest period value	Maturities employed (6y, 8m)	Nelson & Schaefer maturities
Panel A: 1957–1961						
Equal weights	0.653 (7y, 8m)[b]	0.652	0.597	0.600 (6y, 6m)	0.598	0.539
Cash-flow weights	0.529 (11y, 7y)	0.509	0.487	0.465 (12y, 8m)	0.464	0.439
Panel B: 1972–1976						
Equal weights	1.141 (6y, 6m)	1.137	0.722	1.056 (7y, 14m)	1.055	0.656
Cash-flow weights	0.880 (6y, 6m)	0.879	0.580	0.811 (7y, 16m)	0.806	0.516
Panel C: The two periods combined						
Cash-flow weights	1.389 (6y, 8m)	1.389	1.067	1.271 (7y, 14m)	1.270	0 995

a. The maturity employed is the innovation in the 6-year spot rate and the difference between the 6-year and the 8-month rates. Nelson and Schaefer maturities are the 13-year spot rate and the difference between the 13-year and the 5-year rates.
b. The number in parentheses is the maturity with the maximum value. For example, (6y, 8m) is the 6-year innovation in the spot rate and the 6-year innovation in the spot rate minus the innovation in the 8-month rate.

Entries in the table are values of the modeling objective function which we define as the product of R^2 and the dependent spot rate's variance, averaged across all maturities, $\Sigma w_i R^2_{i,x}\,\mathrm{var}(dr_i)$. Two models are examined. Model 1 assumes that the innovation in the spot rate follows a random walk. (All changes are perceived as unexpected.) Model 2 derives the innovation in the spot rate under the pure expectation theory. (The unexpected change is the difference between the actual spot rate and the forward rate from the previous period.) Two weighting schemes are employed. In the first, equal weights are given to each yearly interval. For example, since for the first yearly interval there is information about 12 different spot rates, each of these spot rates receives a weight of $(1/12) * (1/13)$. In the cash-flow-weighting method, weights are given according to the relative importance of the spot rate in a portfolio of 13 bonds, each maturing in a different year. Results are reported for three factor proxies: the one with the largest value for each period and model, the 6-year spot rate and the difference between the 6-year spot rate and the 8-month spot rate which are the overall optimal proxies, and the 13-year spot rate and the difference between the 13-year and the 5-year rates which have been frequently employed in previous studies.

spot rates. The one-index model (denoted by opt 1 in Table 18.4) bases forecasts on a univariate regression where the independent variable is the unexpected change in the four-year spot rate. The two-index model (denoted by opt 2) bases forecasts on a bivariate regression where the independent variables are the unexpected change in the six-year rate and the difference between the unexpected change in the six-year rate and the eight-month rate. For each of the models, sensitivities were estimated using data for the five years prior to the forecast period.

This way of estimating sensitivities is perfectly feasible as a way of getting estimates for bond pricing. However, it does not result in a closed-form specification. For many purposes, a closed-form model is desired. Hence, we constructed and tested two such models. The data analysis from previous sections suggests a form for sensitivities that is quadratic in the natural logarithm of time. Thus, we construct regressions of the following form:

$$b_i = c_0 + c_1 \ln(i) + c_2(\ln(i))^2 + \varepsilon_i, \tag{3}$$

where, b_i is the sensitivity of a spot rate of maturity i to an unexpected change in the factor.

This model performed well in fitting the cross-sectional pattern of sensitivities (b's). The average R^2 is higher than .97 for the regression of sensitivities on time in the one-index method and higher than .93 and .99 for the first and second sensitivities in the two-index model. Forecasts from these models are labeled opt 1 s for the one factor smoothed and opt 2 s for the two factors smoothed. While the motivation for this specification is to allow the derivation of a closed-form bond pricing model, its smoothing properties might result in better forecasts than using the historical sensitivities directly.

We have a number of benchmarks with which to compare our forecasts. The natural benchmark is the assumption inherent in Macaulay's duration measure. This measure simply assumes that the sensitivity of all rates to a change in any rate (including the four-year rate) is one. In Table 18.4 these forecasts are labeled as naive. Our other benchmarks were the models used in Nelson and Schaefer (1983) and Babbel (1983). Both Babbel and Nelson and Schaefer use the one-year rate in their single-index models, and Nelson and Schaefer use the thirteen-year rate and the difference between the thirteen-year and five-year rates in their two-index models. We adopt these rates additional benchmarks in Table 18.4 calling them 1 yr, 13 yr, and 13, 5 yr. We use them only for tests of expectational model 1, for this is the framework in which they were proposed by Nelson and Schaefer.

Table 18.4
The out-of-sample performance of competing models

	1 Overall	2 Period 1	3 Period 2	4 Period 3	5 Period 4
Panel A: Model 1	opt 2	opt 2]	opt 2	opt 2	opt 2
	13, 5 yr	opt 2 s]	opt 2 s	13, 5 yr	13, 5 yr
	opt 1	13, 5yr	13, 5 yr	opt 1	naive
	opt 1 s	opt 1 s]	opt 1]	opt 1 s	opt 1 s
	naive	opt 1]	opt 1 s]	1 yr	opt 1
	opt 2 s	13 yrs]	naive]	opt 2 s*	opt 2 s
	1 yr	naive]	1 yr]	naive*	1 yr
	13 yrs	1 yr	13 yrs	13 yrs	13 yrs
Panel B: Model 2	opt 2	opt 2]	opt 2	opt 2	opt 2
	opt 1	opt 2 s]	opt 2 s	opt 1	native
	opt 2 s*	naive	opt 1	opt 1 s	opt 2 s
	opt 1 s*	opt 1 s	opt 1 s	opt 2 s*	opt 1
	naive	opt 1	naive	naive*	opt 1 s

* Indicates that the order of these two models is reversed for the cash flow weighting.
] Indicates a difference that is insignificant at the 5% level.
† The subperiods are 1962–1966, 1967–1971, 1977–1981, and 1982–1982. The two subperiods (1957–1961 and 1972–1976) that were used to determine the optimal factors' proxies are excluded since they do not represent true out-of-sample periods.

Model 1 assumes that the innovation in the spot rate follows a random walk. (All changes are perceived as unexpected.) Model 2 derives the innovation in the spot rate under the pure expectation theory. (The unexpected change is the difference between the actual spot rate and the forward rate from the previous period.) For each model the coefficients are estimated in the prior period. The Mean Square Error is then calculated as a basis of comparison. The models are ranked from best to worst for each subperiod (columns 2–5), and for the overall sample as well (first column).† "Opt 1" is the optimal one-factor proxy, the 4-year rate. "Opt 2" is the optimal two-factor proxies, the 6-year rate, and the difference between the 6-year and the 8-month rates. "Opt 1 s" is the smoothed one-factor proxy, estimated by equation (3). "Opt 2 s" is the smoothed two-factor proxies, estimated by equation (3). "Naive" assumes that the sensitivities of all rates to a change in any rate are one. "1 yr" is the model in which the 1-year spot rate is used as the factor proxy. "13 yrs" is the model in which the 13-year spot rate is used as the factor proxy. "13, 5 yr" is a two-state-variables model in which the 13-year spot rate and the difference between the 13-year and the 5-year rates are used as the factor proxies.

B Tests

Each of the techniques discussed above is used to prepare forecasts for spot rates in each of four five-year periods. Parameters of all models are estimated over the previous five-year period. The two five-year periods 1957–1961 and 1972–1977 were excluded from the forecasting sample period because they would not constitute a true hold-out sample since they were used to select the indexes that worked best.[6]

The methodology used to compare and rank forecast techniques involves tests of differences in mean square forecast errors. More specifically, for each forecasting technique, squared forecast errors were computed for each maturity. This was repeated each month in the sample period, resulting in a matrix of 60 (months) by 31 (maturities) for each forecasting technique. For forecasting methods taken two at a time, differences between all pairwise entries were calculated along with a mean standard deviation. In computing the mean and standard deviation, we used the same two weighting schemes discussed earlier. From the central limit theorem, the differences in forecasts from any two techniques should be normally distributed, and we tested the significance of the differences.

We compare four sample periods as well as combining the four sample periods into one, using 240 months. Table 18.4 shows the results when each maturity is weighted equally. The results when they are weighted by their importance in impacting the change in the bonds portfolio price are identical, except for those cases that are shown by an asterisk. All differences are significant at the 5% level except where there are brackets indicating insignificance.

C Empirical Results

From Table 18.4 we can see some definite differences in performance of the methods. The first striking result from Table 18.4 is that, for the overall sample and in each subperiod, the optimum single-and two-factor proxies we developed outperformed the proxies utilized by others, including Macaulay's duration model. This would clearly hold in the period where we search for the optimum. However, the results shown in Table 18.4 are for different periods. This consistent outperformance is evidence that the ranking of preferred proxies for the unknown factor is sufficiently stable from period to period, so that the procedure discussed in earlier sections leads to better results. The second striking characteristic of Table

18.4 is the dominance of the two-factor models over their one-factor counterparts. This dominance holds in each period and for both definitions of unexpected change in spot rates. Elton, Gruber, and Nabar (1988) also found strong evidence of two factors affecting returns.

The third result shown in Table 18.4 is that the smoothed sensitivities underperformed the sensitivities from the prior period. However, the smoothed sensitivities outperformed the naive or Macaulay model. Thus, for those who insist on a closed-form solution, there seems to be one that dominates Macaulay's. However, for most purposes, calculating duration and storing a vector of sensitivities are not inconvenient.

The last result that needs to be highlighted is the overall performance of the naive or Macaulay measure. Previous literature has shown that this measure has not been easy to beat. However, in our tests, both the one-variable and two-variable optimum models always outperform Macaulay's measure. Moreover, for expectational model 2, it was the poorest performer, and, for expectational model 1, it outperformed the smoothed two-variable method and two benchmark one-variable models.[7]

In summary, our technique for choosing the optimal proxy worked well with both one- and two-variables models. Overall, the two-variables model outperforms the one-variable model, and all outperform benchmark models.

VI Conclusion

Empirical work on bond pricing needs to assume something about the relationship between unexpected spot rate changes of different maturities. In the most common approach, unexpected changes in all spot rates are described by changes in one or more key spot rates. While previous studies have chosen these factors in an ad hoc manner, this paper shows how to select the factors and structure which best describe the correlations across unexpected changes in spot rate.

In fact, our findings indicate that the four-year rate serves as the best proxy in the one-state-variable model, while the eight-month and six-year rates do best in the two-state-variables model. Also, we find that the two-factor model outperforms the one-factor model. Our model produces out-of-sample predictions superior to those using Macaulay's duration model and those using other state variable proxies. These results may explain why models used in the area of immunization, which assume complex relationships between changes in spot rates, have not, in general, outperformed the simplest immunization model put forth by Macaulay: the inferior results may be due to an inappropriate choice of factors describing the unexpected changes in spot rates.

A deeper understanding of the structure of unexpected changes in spot rates is of fundamental importance as an aid to understanding risk in the bond markets. Thus, our results may be used in the pricing of debt instruments, the pricing of options on debt instruments, the construction of bond portfolios, and performance evaluation of bond portfolios.

Appendix A

Assume that the model determining the unanticipated change in a spot rate is a linear model with an unknown factor. Let the subscript x represent the optimal spot rate to choose as a proxy for the unknown factor, and let subscript i represent any factor. Thus,

$$dr_{i,t} = a_i\, dr_{x,t} + \varepsilon_{i,t}, \tag{A1}$$

where $\varepsilon_{i,t}$ is a normally distributed random variable with mean zero and variance σ^2, and

$$R^2_{i,x} = 1 - \frac{\text{var}(\varepsilon_{i,t})}{\text{var}(dr_{i,t})} \tag{A2}$$

or

$$R^2\, \text{var}(dr_{i,t}) = \text{var}(dr_{i,t}) - \text{var}(\varepsilon_{i,t}). \tag{A3}$$

Minimizing the residuals' variance is equivalent to maximizing the right-hand side of equation (A3). Hence, in order to find the best proxy for the state variable, we maximize the weighted average of $R^2_{i,x}\, \text{var}(dr_{i,t})$ over the choice of the appropriate proxy, x:

$$\max \sum w_i R^2_{i,x}(\text{var}(dr_i)). \tag{A4}$$

Notes

We would like to thank Chris Blake, Ernest Bloch, Linda Canina, William Greene, and Bruce Tuckman for their helpful comments.

1. When we did not have monthly intervals, we interpolated.

2. For some years there are estimates of spot rates for maturities beyond those we used.

3. Computing the weight on the forecast error for the portfolio of bonds involved estimating the coefficient of the term involving $(\partial r_{oi}/\partial F)$ from equation (1). This is obviously a func-

tion of coupons and spot rates. Simulations were run assuming constant yearly coupons and spot rates varying between 8% and 12%. The relative importance of any $(\partial r_{oi}/\partial F)$ was relatively stable over the different scenarios, and we utilized the average weights. These weights were 0.58, 0.79, 0.92, 0.98, 0.98, 1.0, 0.96, 0.89, 0.79, 0.71, 0.61, 0.51, and 0.40 for years 1 through 13, respectively. When we had multiple forecasts within a year, we divided the weight equally among them.

4. The reason for the more complex pattern is the following. The b_i for any maturity spot is the product of the correlation between that spot and the four-year rate and the standard deviation of the spot divided by the standard deviation of the four-year rate. As we move to higher maturities, the standard deviation of the spot rate uniformly decreases. On the other hand, as we move from very low maturities to longer maturities, the correlation with the four-year rate increases (reaching a maximum when the maturity is four years) and then decreases. It is this pattern for the two elements affecting b_i which accounts for sensitivities at first increasing and then decreasing as we increase maturities.

5. We chose the difference between the long and short rates, rather than the short rate, as the second key rate in order to minimize the problem of multicollinearity.

6. For the periods 1962–1966 and 1972–1981, we tried alternative variations of *opt 1* and *opt 2*. We explored the forecasting ability when an intercept was used or left out. We also tested forecasting ability when sensitivities and intercepts were calculated for the three 5-year periods and then averaged for forecasting purposes. These variations were not statistically different from one another, and their ranking varied considerably when we went across the two periods. Using an intercept and just one prior 5-year period to calculate values performed no worse than any other and was simpler.

7. We performed one other set of tests. We added the errors at each point in time across the maturities, weighting each maturity equally or weighting according to their importance in price sensitivity. This allows cancellation of errors. If errors are random, then allowing overestimates for the maturity to cancel with underestimates for second maturity will produce a better measure of the sensitivity of price to an unexpected change in interest rates. However, there is a second pattern. In this pattern the sign is very much a function of maturity: short maturities having positive residuals and long maturities having negative residuals, or vice versa. Hence, this technique is very sensitive to the choice of the longest maturity. A bond with a maturity different from 13 years would perform very poorly because the errors would not tend to cancel out. Thus, the results of Table 18.4 are more reflective of true relative performance.

References

Babbel, D., 1983, Duration and the term structure of interest rate volatility, in G. Bierwag, G. Kaufman, and A. Toevs, eds.: *Innovations in Bond Portfolio Management: Duration Analysis and Immunization* (JAI Press, Greenwich, CT).

Brennan, M. and E. Schwartz, 1977. Savings bonds, retractable bonds, and callable bonds, *Journal of Financial Economics* 5, 67–88.

——— and E. Schwartz, 1979, Continuous time approach to the pricing of bonds, *Journal of Banking and Finance* 3, 133–155.

——— and E. Schwartz, 1980, Conditional predictions of bond prices and returns, *Journal of Finance* 35, 405–419.

——— and E. Schwartz, 1983, Duration, bond pricing, and portfolio management, in G. Bierwag, G. Kaufman, and A. Toevs, eds.: *Innovations in Bond Portfolio Management: Duration Analysis and Immunization* (JAI Press, Greenwich, CT).

Cox, J., J. Ingersoll, and S. Ross, 1985, A theory of the term structure of interest rates, *Econometrica* 53, 385–408.

Elton, E., M. Gruber, and P. Nabar, 1988, Bond returns, immunization and the return generating process, *Studies in Banking and Finance* 5, 125–154.

Ingersoll, J., 1983, Is immunization feasible, in G. Bierwag, G. Kaufman, and A. Toevs, eds.: *Innovations in Bond Portfolio Management: Duration Analysis and Immunization* (JAI Press, Greenwich, CT).

Macaulay, F. R., 1938, *Some Theoretical Problems Suggested by the Movements of Interest Rates, Bond Yields and Stock Prices in the United States Since 1856* (Columbia University Press, New York).

Mankiw, N. G. and J. A. Miron, 1986, The changing behavior of the term structure of interest rates, *Quarterly Journal of Economics*, 211–228.

McCulloch, J. H., 1971, Measuring the term structure of interest rates, *Journal of Business* 44, 19–31.

———, 1975, The tax adjusted yield curve, *Journal of Finance* 30, 811–830.

Nelson, J. and S. Schaefer, 1983, The dynamics of the term structure and alternative portfolio immunization strategies, in G. Bierwag, G. Kaufman, and A. Toevs, eds.: *Innovations in Bond Portfolio Management: Duration Analysis and Immunization* (JAI Press, Greenwich, CT).

Richard, S., 1978, An arbitrage model of the term structure of interest rates, *Journal of Financial Economics* 6, 33–37.

Vasicek, O., 1977, An equilibrium characterization of the term structure, *Journal of Financial Economics* 5, 177–188.

Index

Made in the USA
Monee, IL
08 November 2026

67812148R00254